something like rain

Jay Bell Books
www.jaybellbooks.com

Did you buy this book? If so, thank you for putting food on our table! Making money as an independent artist isn't easy, so your support is greatly appreciated. Come give me a hug!

Did you pirate this book? If so, there are a couple of ways you can still help out. If you like the story, please take the time to leave a nice review somewhere, such as an online retail store (my preference), or on any blog or forum. Word of mouth is important for every book, so if you can recommend this book to friends with more cash to spare, that would be awesome too!

Something Like Rain

by Jay Bell

Part One:
Austin, 2007

Chapter One

I need you. It's as simple as that really. Before you answer, just listen, because I've got a lot to offer. I'm strong. These muscles aren't just for show! I'm sure they could be of use. I'm young, but I'm not without talent. I can swim. I've been training every day, and I can handle taking orders. I'm definitely loyal. I'm willing to do just about anything because I need the Coast Guard to fix me. I'm sorry if that sounds dramatic or vague, but if I told you the truth, you would never accept me. Please give me a chance. Please please please please…

William forced himself to stop so he could reread what he had written. About halfway through he flipped the pencil over, eraser poised to scrub out any words too damning. Not that it mattered much. Filling out this application was just an exercise. In reality he would apply online, and if all went well, meet with a Coast Guard recruiting agent, but a test run had seemed like a good idea. Now he was glad he had done so. The item he had gone overboard on simply read *Additional Interests*. Heck, it wasn't even a question, but William had made it one by using the neighboring blank space to plead his case, writing on the back of the paper when he ran out of room.

The scribbled words looked like they belonged to an emotional mess—exactly the impression he was trying to avoid. If he lost control of his tongue during the actual interview and started saying such things, he would never get a chance to fix himself. William nearly crumpled the application until he realized he still needed to study it, so instead he snapped the pencil in half and tossed it aside, the pieces clattering on the kitchen's linoleum floor. Then he felt bad, because the pencil was part of a set his grandmother had bought for him, his name embossed on each. What if she found it during her next visit and her feelings were hurt, thinking he didn't appreciate her gift? William scrambled to collect the two pencil halves, returning to his chair and lining up the jagged edges so he could put it back together. A little tape and it would be like new.

He sighed, letting the two pencil pieces fall to the kitchen table. This is exactly the sort of behavior he needed to correct. Why couldn't he be like the other guys at school? Strutting around, burping and farting, making lewd comments about any girl in the vicinity. They were masters at not caring, each one a monarch in his own mind. Kings without kingdoms. And William? He was a queen. He was pretty sure that was the right term, but then again, history was full of queens who were tough and strong. William was more like a damsel of the court, always blushing when the handsome knights rode by. Or maybe the stable boy, skin dark from working outside in the sun, clothing mere rags, taut muscles visible through holes in the fabric.

William felt a stirring in his shorts and fought against it. Hopeless! Absolutely hopeless. He worked hard to discipline himself, both academically and athletically, but this one area seemed beyond his control. He wouldn't give up though. He truly believed that the Coast Guard could make him into a man. In the meantime…

William grabbed a cookie from the plate his mother always kept full on the table, an ever-changing centerpiece of baked goods. Currently oatmeal raisin cookies were on offer. He shoved one into his mouth, chewed, and swallowed. But of course it did nothing to satiate his true appetite. He went still, listening to make sure the house was empty. His parents had gone shopping for a new car, and his older brothers were unlikely to stop by their former home this early in the day.

The upstairs bathroom would be safest. William pushed away from the table, trying not to overthink. He wanted this. Sure, he'd feel bad afterwards, but the urge was too strong now, the blood rushing through his veins and to one area in particular. William took the stairs two at a time. Once in the bathroom, he flipped the light switch and locked the door. Then he approached the mirror, hips pressing against the counter. As always, he avoided looking at his own face. That would ruin the illusion. Instead he focused lower on his body, deluding himself into thinking he was seeing someone other than himself. The muscles were bigger than he preferred, the skin too pale, but he couldn't afford to be picky. This was the only naked guy he was ever likely to see. In real life anyway. He might have ample opportunity in the shower room at school or at the YMCA, but he wasn't dumb enough to look. None of those guys would allow him to stare as long as he wanted, or do the things he yearned to do.

Already his white canvas shorts were bulging outward, but William started with his polo shirt, hooking a hand beneath the mint green fabric and lifting slowly. Teasingly. He saw one hip and took a step back to examine the angled line diving into his underwear. Partially revealed too was his six-pack, which was only lightly defined instead of carved into the stomach like the guys he saw online. Maybe he should be looking at such images now, but somehow this felt more real. He lifted his shirt higher, still trying to pretend he was watching someone else strip. Plenty of girls at school commented on his chest, implying it was impressive. If only guys would notice instead. His arms were big too, his vision momentarily obscured as he pulled the shirt over his head. He tossed it aside, still keeping his gaze focused downward on his narrow waist.

As he worked on the button of his shorts, the rush of hormones made it easier to get lost in fantasy. He was standing behind a guy, arms wrapped around him, hands undressing him completely. The button popped open, the zipper came down. William slipped a thumb beneath the band of the underwear and slowly lowered them, gasping when his cock flopped out. He didn't know how he stacked up to other guys, especially since everyone appeared so huge in porn videos, but if a guy in real life presented him with this one, he wouldn't mind. He would do so many things with it. More than he could now.

William grabbed hold of himself and started pumping, thinking about how he would drop to his knees, or even roll over onto his stomach, offering himself, if he really were with another person. His thoughts became more abstract as he continued and the pressure built. He focused intently on the way each muscle twitched, his arm like the piston rod of a locomotive, cranking in perfect rhythm, his pecs bouncing in response. He stood on his toes and leaned forward over the sink as he got closer, biting his lower lip and hissing like a steam engine. All aboard, because this train was about to depart! Right before it did, William raised his gaze, locking eyes with himself in the mirror, staring into the green irises and dilated pupils and seeing absolute certainty there. This is who he was. So what!

If only he could hold on to that state of mind, make this his new identity. He already knew how quickly it would slip away. Right now, in fact. His body tensed, pleasure coursing through him like a tidal wave, the fleeting strength washed away after crashing against the shore.

Heavy breaths followed, each a little slower than the previous. He splayed his hands out on the cool marble counter, supporting himself. William risked one last look in the mirror, no longer liking what he saw there. This wasn't who he was meant to be. This had to be the last time. Right. How often had he said that already, only to break his own promise? No, he definitely needed help. After cleaning up his mess, he'd return downstairs to finish the application. The online version. Then he would submit it, taking his first step toward recovery.

William was stuffing swimming gear into his backpack when he heard a car honk. He ignored the noise at first, feeling frustrated. He had filled out the online application with great care, triple-checking each answer. When he'd finally found the nerve to click submit, he was rewarded with a vague error message. Naturally when he hit the back button, all his answers were lost. Didn't the world want him to get better? When pleading with the laptop didn't work, he decided not to try again just yet, opting instead to continue his training at the YMCA.

The honking continued as the garage door rumbled open. Curious, he went to investigate. When he opened the front door, his attention was forcibly drawn to a cherry red sports car. Polished lacquer reflected the autumn sun, intensifying the light and making it feel more like summer. The convertible top—which was currently down—added to this illusion. William felt pulled forward as he pictured himself behind the wheel. That wasn't hard to do, considering how much he had in common with the man in the driver's seat. His father, Lewis, had a similar build, albeit with twenty-two more years of wear. This meant a slightly pronounced belly and skin that was perpetually baked from years of working on roofs. His hair was considerably darker than William's and currently windswept. The grin he wore was soon matched by his son.

The passenger-side door opened as William hurried forward. A slight woman stumbled out and tried to get her blonde hair back in order. His mother's cheeks were flushed. Probably from excitement. Or perhaps not, considering the way Kate looked back at the car and shook her head.

"This is too cool!" William said, walking around the vehicle to inspect it. "Is this a test drive or... Don't tell me! It's a late birthday present!"

"Absolutely not," his father said, stepping out of the vehicle. "Considering how many dents and dings your car has, it'll be a cold day in Hell before I ever let you drive this baby."

"So it's ours?" William asked, still overcome with disbelief. He couldn't remember his parents ever buying a car that wasn't used. They normally made such boring choices, like minivans or fuel-efficient sedans.

"She's all ours," Lewis confirmed.

"That's still up for debate!" Kate said sharply. "We really need to discuss—"

"The papers are already signed," his father said dismissively.

William turned to his mother and saw that her mouth was a hard flat line. Never a good sign. "You don't like it?" he asked.

"No!" she replied emphatically. "Maybe as a weekend rental, but the higher insurance rate, not to mention how much gas it will guzzle… Don't you think your parents are a little old to be seen in such a vehicle?"

"Yes," William said. "Better give it to me. You guys can have my old car."

His parents didn't laugh. Instead they stared each other down.

"It's pathetic," Kate snapped.

"It's what I want," Lewis shot back. "God forbid I do anything for myself!"

"We can't afford—"

"Why not! William isn't going to college. He'll graduate next year and—"

"He doesn't graduate until the year after. So nice to see that you're paying attention to your children's lives!"

"Guys!" William pleaded. "It's just a car! It's not worth fighting over."

His parents had been bickering nonstop lately. He wasn't used to seeing them argue, and they certainly weren't used to their son telling them to stop. The atmosphere grew thick. Then Kate shook her head and walked toward the front door. William looked to his father.

"It'll be fine," Lewis said.

"Maybe you should get something you both like," William suggested.

His father appeared wounded, as if he had been betrayed. Then he got back in the car and started the engine.

William approached the driver's side. "Are you returning it to the dealership?"

His father glowered. "No. I'm taking it out on the highway to see how fast this sucker can go." Without another word, he pulled out and drove away.

William stood there, looking down the street at a neighborhood that—while not poor—rarely had brand-new cars in any of the driveways, and never any so frivolous. As cool as the convertible was, he found himself agreeing with his mother. The car didn't match their family at all. Then again, maybe that's why his father liked it so much.

Girlfriends. William had a few. Not of the romantic variety, although he never corrected anyone for misinterpreting what they saw. His oldest brother, Spencer, had once been sent to pick him up from school. When he pulled up to the curb, he found William surrounded by female friends, just as he always was. His brother had grinned and shook his head ruefully once William was in the passenger seat, shooting a few reappraising glances his way during the drive. "You've got it all figured out," Spencer had said. "When I was a freshman, all I did was hang out with my buddies, acting stupid and getting into trouble. What I should have done is spend more time with the ladies." Then he had punched William playfully on the arm, which hurt like hell because Spencer was a Marine.

Little had changed over the past few years. William had the same group of friends, and people kept making assumptions. This had helped him get through high school without ever having an intimate relationship, although pressure was mounting. Something about junior year had changed the dynamics of his friendships. Not that he hadn't experienced missteps previously, like when he had agreed to be Holly's boyfriend during their freshman year. That had resulted in hand-holding, late night phone calls, and one teary conversation when William had to explain that he didn't want to risk ruining their friendship. Holly did the crying while he did some fast talking, and in the end, he had successfully scared her off.

Temporarily, it would seem. Holly was currently holding on to his arm as they walked down the hall. On his other side were Lily and Abby, who were either shooting daggers at Holly or finding little excuses to touch his back, as if he needed guidance on the way to class. He tensed and wondered if he should follow in his brother's footsteps and find a group of guys to hang out with instead. That would be easier than pretending to have the flu to avoid the homecoming dance, a tactic that definitely hadn't been forgotten.

"Prom isn't until next semester," Abby was saying. "Why would you worry about a dress now?"

Holly gripped his arm tighter. "You've gotta plan ahead for such things. This is our last chance!"

"You don't even have a date," Lily said, always the practical one. "And there's still senior prom."

"Fine," Holly said, "I'm still planning ahead. I won't let *junior* prom be a disaster like Homecoming was. I want this dance to be magical!"

"Is this about losing your virginity?" Lily asked with a snort.

"No!" Holly insisted. Then she amended, "Maybe."

"You're ridiculous. Why wait for some stupid dance? Am I right?"

She jostled William, which made him tense up further. Oh yes, Lily was extremely practical, which is why she posed the greatest threat. Any other guy would be thrilled, but lately William ensured he was never alone with her. He really was hopeless. Holly was funny and energetic, Lily was athletic and clever, and Abby was thoughtful and artistic. Each was attractive, the variety of skin tones and hair colors leaving him spoiled for choice. Holly was just as blonde and pale as himself, Lily tan and tough despite her delicate name, and Abby's stylish clothes and Asian features were enchanting. He tried to imagine them as guys instead and quickly had to shove the thought aside.

They reached his next class, stopping outside the room. None of the girls shared this period with him, and yet Holly still held on to his arm. Lily and Abby weren't going anywhere either.

"Better get going before the bell rings," he prompted.

His friends seemed to size each other up. Then they grudgingly continued on their way. He breathed out in relief and turned to enter the classroom. Before he could, a familiar voice said his name. Lily was loping her way back toward him.

"Hey," she said, wearing a smile.

"Fancy seeing you here," he responded, trying to make light

of the situation. Or did the banter come across as flirtatious?

Maybe so, because Lily's smile widened. "I need to tell you something."

"What?" William said, resisting the urge to swallow.

"I think Holly has a crush on you."

"Oh."

"Isn't that messed up? Or do you like her back?"

William struggled to find the right answer. He failed. "Uh…"

"I know that you two have a history," Lily continued. "Or at least, she already made her move and you shot her down. That was years ago though, so maybe your feelings have changed. Maybe you like her back now."

William wished that was true. "I don't want her to get hurt," he blurted out.

"So you don't?" Lily's smile was bright, her head bobbing optimistically. "Okay. Cool!"

"Cool?" he repeated, understanding but pretending not to.

"Yeah," she said with an easy shrug. "I like you. So I'm glad you don't like her. In that way."

"Oh." He clutched a textbook to his chest. "Um."

"Relax," Lily said with a laugh. "I'm not worried about prom or anything complicated like that. I just want to hang out and see what happens." She took in his expression, amusement fading. "Would that be such a bad thing?"

He looked her over, noticing again the athletic build and tan skin that came from playing baseball, her auburn hair stopping just short of shoulder length. She really was fun to be around, more easy-going than the other two. Her brown eyes often twinkled, like life was one big joke, and she never made a big deal of anything. She probably wouldn't even mind if he needed a little extra coaxing to get things going.

William found himself nodding. It was worth a shot, right?

"Yeah?" Lily said, the smile returning.

"Okay. Sure. Class is about to start." He inched toward the door, hoping a parting kiss wasn't expected. Lily seemed to have more to say. Her mouth even opened, but the voice that rang out definitely wasn't hers.

"William!"

He nearly snapped to attention, bewildered as someone nudged Lily out of the way and stepped into his personal space.

Not that he minded much. He smelled the musky cologne at the same time he noticed dark skin and brown eyes that made him react in a way that Lily's didn't. He was less fond of the clenching jaw and thick lips that were tight with indignation. Still, there was something attractive about the anger radiating off this person, since it was exactly the masculine sort of trait he found himself lacking. He even admired the scowl and angry words that followed.

"Do you know who I am?"

William searched his memory. The face was familiar, although it had been a little chubbier, the short-cropped hair in cornrows back then. He definitely knew this person, even though they had never really spoken or shared a class since junior high. "Kelly, right? Yeah. Kelly Phillips."

"Wrong! I'm the fastest guy in school. No one can outrun me. No one's ever come close!"

Okay. William looked around for some clue of what was going on and saw many leering faces. Lily appeared concerned, probably because of the excited whispering about a fight. William had never been in one, and he had no desire to change that. Then again, why was Kelly talking about being the fastest? That didn't sound like he wanted to fight. "Are you saying you want to race?"

"I'm saying there's no point!" Kelly raised himself up to be the same height as William, which didn't take much effort since he was only an inch or so shorter. "You'd never keep up with me. I thought no one could, but yesterday, Jared Holt beat me."

"Jared Holt," William repeated. Then it all fell into place. On the way to class, some guy had sauntered up to him and snidely implied that William would lose the upcoming triathlon. He hadn't understood the point of that or thought much about it since. "The guy from yesterday?"

"That's right. So when he came up to you and said you'd never win, you should have listened. Don't even bother showing up next week, because—"

Kelly lunged forward. Or someone had pushed him. Either way, the situation was clearly escalating. William pressed his back to the wall, wishing the classroom door wasn't blocked by rows of curious onlookers. He eyed Kelly warily. The guy had a runner's build, which meant he was a good deal lankier than William, but the muscles he did have were ropey and tight. He might be stronger than he looked, but that didn't really matter, because surely he was tougher. William assumed all black guys were. They had to be. The world wasn't as fair to people like Kelly, or as generous, which made William feel even weaker. This fight was lost even before it began.

Kelly was facing him again, teeth bared. "You might be good at swimming," he said, "but most of this race is on foot."

"I'll keep that in mind." William decided to bluff, to pretend he was anything but intimidated. He made himself stand up straight. "See you at the finish line."

"I won't be there, but Jared will. He'll be waiting for you."

Brown eyes remained fixed on his, intense with anger. Then Kelly spun around and shoved his way through the crowd. William watched him go, heart pounding. The crowd surged forward, buzzing with questions.

Lily was the first to reach him. She placed a hand on his arm. "What was that all about?"

"I don't know," William said.

"Do you know him?" she pressed.

He shook his head. "Not really."

"Where's the fight going to be?" someone asked.

"And when?" someone else shouted.

"There's not going to be a fight!" William said, the panic evident in his voice.

Someone near him laughed. "Of course there will be! After school. In the east parking lot. That's where they always are."

"Fight!" someone else yelled in excitement.

This started chanting, the word repeated over and over again until a new voice cut through the air with practiced authority.

"There won't be a fight." Mr. Miller, his physics teacher, had come to investigate. "Not unless someone wants to be suspended and repeat the school year. Mr. Townson? Do you want to be suspended?"

"He didn't do anything wrong," Lily said. "Some guy was picking on him."

William felt a surge of gratitude toward her, but he just wanted this all to be over. "You better get going," he whispered.

"Sage advice," Mr. Miller said, addressing the remaining spectators. "Everyone report to class. *Now.*"

William kept his head down as he slunk into the room. When

he took his seat, his stomach churned with nerves. His car was currently in the east parking lot. He'd have to go there at the end of the day—the same location where the promised fight was to take place. Not that Kelly had challenged him directly, but maybe that's how these things worked. Maybe he was expected to know where to be and when. William sat perfectly still during the remainder of the class, trying to find a solution. What he really wanted was to call in the Marines, or at least his brother, to give him a ride home. Mostly he just struggled with the injustice of it all. A mere half an hour ago, he had felt safe. Now, despite not having done anything wrong, he was in danger. He could either fight or run. As the bell rang and he rose from his desk, William already knew which option he would choose.

Sweaty palms gripped the steering wheel of a blue Ford Taurus, the driver tense as it slowly and silently coasted free of the school parking lot. William expected alarms to sound as he pulled into the street. Instead he heard an engine roar as a car zipped around him impatiently. William exhaled and eased his foot down on the gas pedal. He had made it. So far. Leaving school an hour early—skipping sixth period—would have serious repercussions. He glanced over at the phone resting in the center console, waiting for the call that demanded to know where he had gone. He reached home without this happening, and as he parked in the driveway, decided that he had made the right decision.

Angry school administrators? Disappointed parents? Piece of cake compared to slugging it out in the parking lot after school. William would park in the north lot tomorrow, or maybe he'd start taking the bus. Safety in numbers. For now he just wanted to get inside, stress-eat some cookies, and maybe watch an episode of—

He opened the front door and froze, one foot already inside. Directly ahead of him, in the space where the living room blended into the kitchen, was an older version of himself with darker features and freshly mussed hair. His father appeared to have just awakened from a nap.

"You're home early," Lewis said accusingly.

"So are you," William responded.

"When did you get here?"

"Just now," he said, puzzled by the question. Wasn't that obvious? He considered his father's hair again. "Ugh. You and Mom aren't…"

"No, she's still at work." Lewis was the first to relax, gesturing for him to enter. "Shut the door."

William did as he was told, hoping that his father wouldn't ask any more questions. After all, it was his mother who paid attention to things like grades, or made sure he went to the dentist twice a year. His father was only called upon when William or his brothers got too out of control.

"Shouldn't you be in school?"

William winced as he made his way to the kitchen cabinets for a drinking glass. He didn't respond until his back was to his father. "There was a situation."

"Bomb threat?" Lewis asked. "Because it sure as hell isn't a snow day!"

"Not exactly."

Lewis sighed. "You skipped school."

"I have a good reason!" William turned around, hoping to plead his case. "This guy came up to me in the hall and tried to pick a fight. We were supposed to meet after school—or at least everyone acted like… Basically it was either get in trouble for skipping sixth period or get in trouble for fighting. Which would you prefer?"

Lewis leaned against the counter and crossed his arms over his chest. "Someone is giving you a hard time?"

"Yes!"

"Is he bigger than you?"

"Not really," William said, squirming a little. "He looks pretty tough though."

"But you stood a chance."

William nodded grudgingly. "I guess."

"Then you should have held your ground."

"What?"

"People are bastards," Lewis said with a shrug. "You can't let them walk all over you. This other guy is probably feeling pretty good about himself right now. He's got someone bigger than him scared and on the run. You really think it's going to end there? Whatever his issue is, he's going to keep coming back, keep pushing you until you stand up for yourself."

William shook his head. "This isn't a stupid TV show. He's not going to back down just because I stand up to him. He'll just end up hitting me."

"And you'll hit him back. It'll hurt him just as much as it hurts you. No matter if you win or lose, I promise you he'll find an easier target next time. Or you can keep being that easy target. Either way, this won't end until you man up."

Man up. If only it were that easy. He watched his father grab an apple and noticed how small it looked in his gnarled hands, how his strong jaw flexed as he took a bite and chewed. Guys like him, Spencer, even Kelly—they had it easy. They understood how to play this game.

"You know what your brother would do," Lewis said as if reading his mind.

No need to ask which one he meant. Spencer the Marine. "He'd get the guy in a headlock," William answered, "hold him there, and tell him he didn't want to fight."

Lewis barked laughter. "Exactly! How'd you know?"

"Because he did the same thing to me whenever I talked back to him." William smiled at the memory. His brother had been gentle most of the time.

"We saved so much money on babysitters, you have no idea. Spencer is a born leader." Lewis gestured at him with the apple. "You are too. You just have to believe in yourself."

And get punched around by some angry guy at school. William still didn't like the idea, so he tried changing the subject. "Why are you home already?"

"Don't concern yourself with my business."

"I'm just surprised. You always work late these days."

Lewis studied him. "I won't tell Mom if you don't."

William perked up. "Really?"

"Sure. If the school calls, I'll tell them I picked you up for—I don't know—a doctor's appointment. But you need to take care of this bully situation. Understood?"

William swallowed, and although it was a promise he didn't want to make, he nodded. "Okay."

William paced his bedroom, unable to enjoy his free time. Instead he thought of Kelly, trying to work up the courage to drive back to school. If he went now, *right now*, he would get there in time to fight. But would Kelly be waiting for him, or that Jared guy, or maybe even both? That made him stop in his tracks. What his father had said made sense. William needed to prove he wasn't an easy target, but if that meant getting beat up by two guys at once…

He clenched his jaw, wondering what he had done to deserve this. Entered a triathlon? Fun had been his only motivation. And to keep busy. His lawn-mowing business didn't occupy as much of his time as it used to, which wasn't good for his mental well-being. The busier he kept himself, the less he worried about other issues, such as girls who wanted more from him or what he wanted from guys. Not having time for either was a good excuse and a helpful distraction. Except now, entering into a simple race had made him a target. Why? Were all the other entrants facing similar scare tactics? Perhaps that's all this was, a couple of guys trying to frighten away the competition.

William blinked. Maybe there was another way to prove he wasn't a pushover. He went to the dresser, stripped off his clothes and put on an old T-shirt and athletic shorts. They wanted to keep him from competing? Both Kelly and Jared had bragged about how fast they could run. A triathlon wasn't about speed. Endurance was key, and William had been training tirelessly to make sure he had plenty of that. He flung open a drawer full of letters and knickknacks he had kept over the years. This included a number of medals and ribbons. William might not swagger around the school picking fights, but he was still an accomplished athlete. He gathered these up, spreading them on the dresser's top. Then he grabbed his phone and texted Holly, who prided herself on knowing everything about everyone. Being friends with a hopeless gossip could be useful at times.

Kelly and Jared, he texted. *I think they might be on the cross country team. Ever heard of them?*

He had to wait longer than usual, picturing Holly covertly poking at her phone while in class.

Yup! You fight Kelly after school, right? In the parking lot?

William grimaced. News sure traveled fast.

I won't be in the parking lot. I'll be on the track. Can you give one of them the message?

Okay. I'm scared!

Don't be.

That sure made him appear confident! If only he could face

this conflict using text messages instead of fists. Still, his plan wasn't bad. It might even work. William left his room, grabbing a towel and a bottle of water before he went to his car. He cranked up the music on his car stereo to maintain the illusion of confidence during the drive back to school. Parking in the east lot as he always did, he marched across the campus, ignoring the bell and the students who poured out of the buildings. When he reached his destination, he put the towel and bottle on the bleachers, then did the minimum stretching exercises before heading to the track. He wanted to be in motion before the first people showed up. William managed to run a full lap before anyone did. Holly, Lily, and Abby. Other students were with them, no doubt having heard the news. Jared and Kelly didn't arrive until his second lap. Kelly sat in the bleachers. Jared remained standing. William ignored them and focused on running. Another lap. And another.

Already he was feeling the pain. As intensely as he exercised when he swam, he knew the water provided a softer environment and minimal impact. Here William's feet collided with a hard surface every step, the vibrations jarring the muscles and bones in his legs. He focused on maintaining a steady rhythm as long as he could. Already many of his peers had gotten bored and wandered away. Kelly and Jared remained stationary. They didn't rush out to meet him, or try to tackle him to stop him from running. In fact, when he risked a few sly glances in their direction, he saw Jared looking distraught. Kelly, on the other hand, remained disarmingly cool, his narrowed eyes tracking William's progress. He didn't seem braced for action. There wouldn't be a fight today. The spectators had decided as much too, everyone except William's friends having left.

Time to prove he wasn't an easy target. William slowed to a walk, then headed directly to the bleachers where he had left his things. Kelly was standing now. Despite how nervous this made William, he did his best not to acknowledge either guy, pretending they were of no consequence. He drank from his bottle, looking their way only once to make sure they wouldn't attack. Jared was frowning, Kelly glaring, but they hadn't moved. William threw the towel over his shoulder, then walked away, joining his friends.

Lily was the first to speak. "What exactly just happened?"

William shrugged. "I guess they weren't in the mood to fight."

"Who can blame them?" Holly said, taking his arm. She pulled away as if burned. "Ew! You're soaking wet!"

"Gosh, I wonder why," Abby murmured. Then she added, "I'm glad there wasn't a fight."

"I wouldn't have minded seeing them get their asses kicked," Lily said, "but that was an impressive display."

"Super cool!" Holly agreed.

Abby nodded. "I don't think they'll mess with you again."

William would have sighed in relief if he hadn't been panting. Hopefully his friend was right and this whole mess was finally over.

William reclined in his bed, watching the television across the room. Currently he was tuned to Cartoon Network. After his demonstration at the track, he had taken a shower, which was pointless since a client needed her yard raked and bagged. He hurried to finish the job in the dwindling sunlight, and by the time he made it home for dinner, he was seriously exhausted. Now sleep was calling to him as he stared almost unseeing at the bizarre programs of *Adult Swim*. He was too tired to think, the events of the day forgotten. At least until his mother knocked on the door, entered the room, and brought it all up again.

"Your father told me what happened," Kate said, sitting on the edge of the bed.

William felt betrayed. His father had promised to keep it a secret! Kind of. William lifted the remote to mute the television and didn't say anything.

"I'm so sorry you were bullied," his mother continued.

Okay. So far she didn't seem angry that he had skipped class. Maybe his father had kept that part quiet. "It wasn't so bad," he said. "It's not like I got hurt."

Kate pursed her lips together. "Your father also shared the advice he gave you. If you believe fighting with this boy will help matters, think again!" She shook her head. "I don't know what's gotten into him lately. First that stupid car—"

"It *is* kind of cool," William said. "I'd love to have one like it. Dad probably felt the same way when he was my age. Now he can actually afford it."

"That's debatable, and what you're describing is called a midlife crisis, which is nothing to be proud of. Or act upon. You let us worry about that. Tell me what happened at school."

"Nothing," William said. "Just an argument, really. It's not a big deal."

His mother didn't seem convinced. She always saw right through him. "Have you tried making friends with this boy?"

Was she serious? Probably. Kate was a kind person and had tried to instill that virtue in him too. The older he got, the harder this became, because the world wasn't always nice in return. Still, she managed somehow. He liked the idea of making friends with his enemies more than punching and getting hit in return. "How?"

"Try talking to him once things have calmed down. It sounds to me like you two had a misunderstanding."

"I don't think there's any reasoning with him. Believe me, this guy is disturbed."

His mother patted his hand. "More often than not, people like him have their own issues. He could probably use a friend. Show him what a good person you are, and I'm sure everything will be okay."

William adored her optimism. Not that it mattered. The situation had mostly blown over, but his mother still appeared concerned, so he said, "I'll try."

"That's my boy. Man! You aren't a boy anymore." This didn't stop her from leaning over to kiss his forehead. She looked back when leaving the room, eyes shining with affection before she shut the door, William already determined not to disappoint her.

William woke up with a severe case of leg pain and couldn't have felt happier. For the past year, he had been pushing himself physically, and while that had been grueling at first, his muscles had eventually adjusted. Occasionally he got a little sore, but this was more like the first week of swimming every morning. Running had targeted muscles that he hadn't worked as hard. After his standard four-egg omelet for breakfast, he headed to the YMCA. Swimming laps helped work loose the kinks in his muscles and chased away most of the pain. He still felt a mild burn when rising from his desk at the end of every class, but he took this as an invitation—a challenge—to return to the track after school and push himself further.

That's exactly what he did. Part of him worried that Kelly and Jared would be looking for him there, perhaps with a strategy in mind this time. Then again, nobody at school was talking about yesterday. Not only did news travel fast, but it also grew stale quickly. William's little confrontation was no longer of interest. After sixth period, he found himself trapped in a conversation with Holly when all he wanted was to focus on moving his body. Eventually he made a polite excuse, went to the locker room, and changed into running clothes. William was walking to the track when he noticed Kelly approaching from the opposite direction.

Even from a distance, William could see he was bristling with anger. His posture was wide, fists balled. Kelly stomped across the grass like he was heading for a duel. William started to tense. Then he noticed Kelly's eyes. They were watery. Red. Had he been crying? Hard to imagine, considering how twisted up his expression was. He definitely looked pissed. Even odder was how soaked his clothes were. Kelly's burgundy dress shirt was wet and clung to his body. Sweat dripped down the side of his face and sparkled in his hair. The tan pants weren't ideal for running either, nor were the fashionable shoes. Maybe he wasn't on the track team after all. Otherwise he would have worn more appropriate clothing before running, and William was sure that's what he'd been doing, because his chest was still heaving.

As they passed each other, Kelly eyed him briefly, continuing his march forward. William turned around to watch him, puzzled but also relieved. Kelly clearly had his own problems, and they no longer seemed to involve William.

Not needing to prove a point today, William took his time stretching and allowed himself a slower pace. His sore legs protested, but once they had warmed up, the pain wasn't so bad. On his third lap he was surprised to see that Kelly had returned. He was seated in the bleachers, watching him run, but he was no longer glaring. William might not enjoy conflict or fighting, but that didn't mean he wasn't competitive. With an audience present, he picked up the pace, trying to show that he could run just as well as he could swim. Except that wasn't true. Once again his body felt too heavy, bogged down by gravity. His feet were really starting to hurt! He stopped before he injured himself and tried to catch his breath. When he glanced over at the bleachers, Kelly was in the same place, except no longer watching. Instead he was leaning forward, elbows on his knees as he stared at his feet. Okay, so he wasn't impressed. Or maybe Kelly was just *de*pressed. He thought of his mother's words and wondered if she was right. Maybe he just needed someone to talk to. Only one way to find out.

William walked over to the bleachers, choosing a question he hoped would lead to conversation. "Any pointers?"

Kelly looked up in surprise. Then those brown eyes traveled over him briefly. "Go home and watch YouTube."

So much for his mother's theory. "Funny," William said. He clenched his jaw and pivoted, intending to walk away, but the earnest tone in Kelly's voice stopped him.

"I mean it! Search for videos of sprinters running in slow motion. They look like they're leaping over and over again. It's practically ballet. Do the same with distance runners. Notice how they move their arms and hold their bodies. Running isn't just practice. It's form."

William stared, not having expected to get such useful advice. Or for running to be described as if it were art. "Okay," he managed. "Thanks."

"No problem." Kelly's eyes darted over him again, reassessing. "Shouldn't you be focusing on your strength? You don't want to fall behind."

"Swimming?" William smiled. "I do that every morning. I'm not going to forget how."

One corner of Kelly's mouth tugged upward. "Where do you practice? The school doesn't have a pool. Do you fill up one of those plastic kiddie pools to flail around in?"

"Something like that." Guy banter! This was progress, but also unfamiliar territory, so he started rambling. "There's a public pool down the road. They set aside certain hours for the school. Not in the morning though, which is when I like to swim, but the YMCA not far from here opens nice and early. Um… Thanks for the pointers. I gotta get to work now."

"Wow," Kelly said, cocking his head. "When do you find time to sleep?"

"That's what class is for." William winked, surprising even himself. "See you around."

He turned and strolled back toward the school, feeling a bounce in his step. The encounter had felt good. Worryingly good? No, of course not. He simply felt proud of himself for making peace. That's all. Nothing more to it. Still, as he headed toward the locker room, he couldn't help whistling a happy tune.

Chapter Two

The world was still soft and gentle in the early hours of the day, untouched by the chaos of activity that would follow. William loved mornings, preferring to be up by five and out the door half an hour later. His parents and his brothers thought he was crazy, all of them preferring to sleep as late as possible. Most people seemed to agree with his family, which was just as well since it kept the mornings private. The world was a different place then—quieter, slower, and somehow fresher. The cool air hadn't been filled by the daily dose of exhaust fumes, the grass still wet from bathing in dew. William often left the house early enough that he could walk to school and enjoy it all.

Or ride his bike, which was what he decided to do today. With the triathlon coming up, he figured he might as well start training for all three legs of the race. As for his own legs, they weren't happy with the additional exercise, so he pedaled slowly and coasted where possible. William cycled first to the YMCA. He no longer needed to show his annual pass to the woman behind the counter. Or wait his turn for a lane once he had changed into his Speedos, because as usual, he had the indoor pool all to himself. He didn't bother with a swim cap or goggles today, unconcerned with speed and preferring to reach a steady rhythm. Usually he counted each lap, making sure he reached his goal. Today he listened to his body, letting it tell him when it was finished. He reached that point and pushed himself beyond it, unwilling to leave the cool comfort of the water. Eventually he slowed to a wade. The sound of water churning continued, echoing off the walls and ceiling of the pool area. William turned and saw that the lane next to his was occupied.

The body moving through liquid was slender, dark, and vaguely familiar. Or maybe William was getting paranoid, because Kelly couldn't be here. Right? He glanced over as he climbed out, spotting an older woman idly swimming in the main pool, but she looked unrelated to the guy in the lane. William turned a critical eye to the newcomer. His lower body was too high and his hand entry inefficient, but he had an acceptable grasp of the front crawl stroke. That he didn't know what to do with himself when ending each lane, stopping and turning around, confirmed his suspicions: This was an amateur. Either Kelly had a twin, or he was here.

William thought he saw a sly smile just before it disappeared into the water. Then Kelly was kicking toward him, quickly reaching the side of the pool where he waited. William made sure to focus on the face as Kelly pulled himself free, the amusement there transparent.

"Got any tips?" Kelly asked.

Now it made perfect sense. William had shown up in his territory, and Kelly had responded by doing the same. He didn't seem hostile, so William addressed the question, which allowed him to examine Kelly for anything that could be improved. His eyes traveled over a light frame, tight muscles, and flawless dark skin. The red swimsuit was still wet enough to cup a bulge, and it was this William focused on. Briefly. "Lose the swim trunks," he said.

"Skinny dipping?" Kelly's eyes flicked to where the old lady was still wading around. "Think she'll mind?"

William snorted. "I mean you should get a pair of these," he said, tugging at the waistband of his own swimsuit. "Those trunks you're wearing are like a parachute behind you, dragging you back. Did you feel the water pulling on them when you climbed out?"

Kelly nodded, eyes still sparkling. "So I need to buy some underwear from the little boys' department instead."

"Joke all you want. My scuba panties will give me the edge in the triathlon. If your friend shares your fashion sense, he'll never keep up with me in the water."

And speaking of water, William was purposely testing it by mentioning the triathlon. Kelly's reaction was difficult to read as he turned to fetch his towel and dried himself. William finished doing the same, wrapping the towel around his waist and feeling more exposed than usual. He had been around plenty of other guys while wearing so little, but with Kelly, he somehow felt more naked. Maybe because of the way he was openly looking him over.

"Maybe I should do some heavy lifting too," Kelly said, draping his towel over one shoulder. "Is that how you move through the water so fast?"

William shook his head. "You have a better build for

swimming than I do. Once I hit puberty, the weight started piling on. Because of that, I'm not so fast. Normally I don't care. Endurance is more important to me."

Kelly's brow came together in confusion. "Not big on racing?"

"Not usually. I'm training to be in the Coast Guard."

Kelly looked amused again. "You know they've got boats these days, right? You don't have to swim everywhere."

William smiled, still unsure about the purpose of this visit, but an idea had occurred to him. Kelly was here to learn William's techniques so he could pass them on to his friend. That would explain why he was being so personable. "We'd better get going," he suggested. "School starts in fifteen minutes."

They walked to the locker room in silence, ending up in separate rows. William continued to mull over his theory as he pulled on his jeans, wanting to discover if he was right. "How come you're here instead of your friend? I got the impression you aren't entering the triathlon."

A pause preceded the answer. "I changed my mind."

"Oh." So *he* was entering now and was here for his own benefit, not Jared's.

"Does that scare you?" Kelly asked, but his tones were teasing. "Is that the sound of your knees knocking together?"

William pulled his polo shirt over his head and smiled. "After what I saw today, I've got nothing to worry about."

"Harsh! But probably true."

William slipped into his sandals. "Of course I haven't seen you running yet. I've heard there's no one faster. Then again, you were the one who told me that, so…"

"I'll be on the track this afternoon." Kelly replied. "After school. Come and see."

He sounded serious. William shut his locker, then headed for the exit. He hesitated at the door. Was this a trap? The fight the other students had longed to see? He honestly didn't know, but the Coast Guard demanded more than just skill and endurance. William would regularly be faced with frightening situations and still be expected to perform his duties. He didn't care about the drama surrounding the triathlon, but this could end up being practical training regardless. "Yeah, okay. See you there."

* * * * *

"They're totally gay."

William was walking down the hall after sixth period, girls on either side of him. For the first time, he wondered if this made him seem gay. It wasn't a word he allowed himself to think often. He tried to keep it far from his mind so he wouldn't spiral down another cycle of questioning who he really was. It didn't matter either way because the Coast Guard was going to set him right. Regardless, he still found Holly's words jarring. He had been telling them about his encounter in the morning and his plans after school when the subject took an unexpected—and uncomfortable—turn.

"Extremely gay," Lily agreed. "Totally explains everything."

"What?" William managed a chuckle. "Who?"

"Jared and Kelly," Holly said.

"It's just gossip," Abby murmured. "Jared is dating Martha Huffman."

"Really?" Lily replied. "I knew she had a thing for him but—"

"Then how do you explain it?" Holly interrupted.

"Explain what?" William said, not hiding his confusion. "I have no idea what you're talking about."

Lily looked over at him. "The reason Kelly got all up in your face."

"He's gay," Holly clarified. "For Jared. Although I still think they both are."

William stared. "Kelly is gay? You're sure?"

"He admitted it to his entire team," Holly said matter-of-factly, but William turned to the others for confirmation.

Lily nodded.

Abby was less certain. "Kelly didn't deny it. That's what I was told."

William stopped walking, trying to make sense of it all. "Then why was Kelly at the YMCA this morning? And why is he now in the triathlon if he was so set on Jared winning?"

"No idea about the race," Holly said, "but Kelly was probably at the YMCA so he could see you naked. Did you take a shower together?"

"Together?" William spluttered. "No!"

"Just ignore her," Lily said. "She's full of depraved fantasies."

Holly didn't appear ashamed. In fact, her smile got bigger.

"Okay," William said. "Have fun gossiping. I'm going to train."

Three girls groaned in unison. "You're no fun!" Holly said.

"That's right," William replied. "So unless any of you want to run a few laps…"

This was enough to scare them away. Once they rounded a corner and were out of sight, William leaned against a row of lockers, mind racing. His friends loved to gossip. He had learned all sorts of sultry details about other people, thanks to their tales. They had a good instinct for what was true and what was bullshit. Very little they shared with him turned out to be false. Kelly was probably gay. William searched himself, trying to decide how this made him feel. Apprehensive? Excited?

Both? Yeah. That about summed it up. He found himself wanting to be around Kelly to confirm it and see if anything would happen, like a litmus test for his own sexuality. *If you turn blue when another gay person is around, then you're gay too!* The halls were empty now, which made it easy for him to move quickly. William left the building and entered into a gray day, clouds covering the sky, trees swaying in the wind.

He hurried toward the track and spotted someone running there. Jared was in the middle of a lap. On the bleachers, a girl with blonde hair and pink glasses clapped in appreciation. Martha Huffman. No freaking way! If his friends had been right about that detail, and clearly they were, then…

Where was Kelly? Still getting changed? The thought of being in the locker room with him again took on new meaning, almost seemed risqué. Part of him was scared and wanted to deny his curiosity. The rest just wanted. William made a beeline for the athletic building, entering a side door and walking down the hall. He reached the doorway to the locker rooms at the same time Kelly did from the other side. The angry expression had returned.

"Hey!" William tried. "Sorry I'm late. Why do girls like to talk so much?"

Kelly broke eye contact and pressed forward, forcing William to move aside. He was dressed in normal clothes, and unless he was planning a repeat of the other day, it meant he wouldn't be running.

"Aren't you training today?" William asked. Then, in an attempt to lighten the mood, he added. "Wait, don't tell me you're done already! You're not *that* fast, are you?"

Kelly kept walking. "Not quite."

"Then where are you going?"

"I'm going to get in my car, find a really tall bridge, and drive off of it."

"Awesome," William said. "Mind if I tag along?"

This worked. Kelly slowed. "You have a death wish?"

"Not really, but I was hoping you could give me a ride home on your way. I've been biking to school every day, and honestly, my legs are still sore from running and everything else."

"You need to take a break," Kelly said. "Give your muscles time to heal and build up. Not that you need to get any bigger. You really want a ride?"

"If you don't mind. There aren't any bridges on the way to my house, so we should be okay."

Kelly raised an eyebrow. "I thought you had an after-school job."

"I started a lawn mowing business when I was twelve. Most of my clients have moved away or now have kids old enough to do it themselves, but some still depend on me. I'm not busy every day, leaving my afternoons free to beg strangers for rides."

Kelly remained silent, but gestured with his head that William should follow. As they left the school and strolled across the parking lot, William fell behind a few paces, trying to determine if Kelly was gay. He didn't walk different, and he wasn't really feminine. All Kelly seemed was miserable. They reached a silver car much nicer than his own. Kelly went to the driver's side, William the other. So far he had seen Kelly angry and confrontational, then disarmingly friendly, and now completely despondent as he just stood there, not even unlocking the door. Maybe he was bipolar and hadn't been joking about wanting to end his life.

"You all right?"

"Yeah." Kelly shook his head, as if to clear it. "I thought I forgot something, that's all. Hop in." He squeezed a keychain and the doors unlocked.

Once William was inside and buckled up, he looked for further clues. A rainbow air freshener hanging from the rearview mirror, or a gay magazine in the backseat. All he found was a clean and neutral interior. Except for the container of gum in one of the cup holders, which only implied an aversion to bad breath.

"Where do you live?" Kelly asked, starting the car.

"Not far from here. I'll be your GPS." In a more mechanical voice, he intoned, "Please turn right and proceed to the next stop light."

Kelly's expression remained impassive. William wasn't even sure he had been heard until his instructions were followed.

"Stay on this road for a few blocks. Then it's another right."

Still no response.

He leaned forward in his seat to gaze out the windshield. "Now I'm glad we bailed on training. Looks like a bad storm blowing in."

Kelly snorted, reacting at last. "Anyone still out on the track is going to get soaked."

"For sure. I actually swung by there looking for you. Saw your friend Jared running like a mad man."

"He's not my friend," Kelly snapped. "Not anymore."

"Oh."

The first drops of rain splattered against the windshield, building into a steady rhythm. William didn't try to make further conversation. He just provided the remaining directions until they pulled into the driveway of his house, Kelly still not speaking. The anger had fled his features again, replaced by misery.

William shook his head. "I don't get it."

"Get what?"

"You and Jared. At the beginning of the week, you're ambushing me in the hall, trying to get me to drop out of the race. Then you show up at the pool this morning, acting friendly. I figured maybe you were doing a little reconnaissance for Jared, but then it turns out that you're also in the triathlon and you guys aren't even friends any more. Is that why? Did he get pissed because you entered too?"

Kelly narrowed his eyes. "I don't think he knows yet. But when he does find out, he's going to freak. And when I win..." His grin was vicious.

William shook his head in exasperation. "You guys are intense. It's just a race. You know that, right?"

Kelly turned to face him. "Then why did you enter?"

"For fun! Now I feel like I'm caught up in some sort of sports vendetta or something."

Kelly frowned. "I just really wanted him to win."

"And now?"

The rain drummed against the windshield, the wipers swiping at it mercilessly. Kelly's attention remained focused ahead as he spoke. "He doesn't like who I am. And I like him a little too much."

"Oh." There it was. Confirmation.

"Yeah."

William felt dizzy. He had never imagined another guy confessing these feelings, or daring to share such information, especially with someone he barely knew. He felt like doing the same, but he wasn't even sure it was true. If anyone could tell him, Kelly seemed the most qualified. He opened his mouth only to discover that he needed more time. "Do you want to come inside?"

Kelly glanced over in surprise. Then he shook his head. "It's okay. I should probably—"

"Really," William said, not wanting him to get away. "We can hang out. It'll be fun."

Kelly's eyes searched his. Then he put the car in park and shut off the engine. William gave him an encouraging smile and led the way inside. Once they were in his room, maybe he could get Kelly talking about the situation with Jared and—

"Willy! I didn't expect you home so soon." Ugh! How could he forget? He loved his mother, but her timing wasn't ideal. She brightened when noticing they had company. "And who's this?"

"Kelly," William said. "He's a new friend of mine."

"Oh, nice to meet you!" She offered Kelly her hand, appearing pleased. Kate was a sharp woman. She had asked her son to make friends with a bully, and here was someone new in their home. That wouldn't be lost on her. "Cookies and milk?"

"I would," William replied, still longing for privacy, "but we're going to hang out upstairs."

"You're a big boy now." His mother winked at Kelly. "I think you can handle eating in your room. I'll bring some up. Just try not to get crumbs all over the place."

"No promises," William said.

He climbed the stairs in a hurry, eager to get away. He reached the top and turned to find that Kelly was still at the halfway point. He had stopped to look at the family photos hanging on the wall. If William's mother saw, she'd probably start bragging about her other sons or who knew what else.

"Coming?" William prompted.

"Yeah, sorry." Kelly took the remaining stairs two at a time.

Once in his room, William found himself at a loss. With his mother returning soon with milk and cookies (so embarrassing!) he could hardly broach the subject he wanted to discuss. The *only* subject, leaving him unsure of what to say.

Kelly slowly walked around the room to take it all in. William hadn't expected to have anyone over today, but he always kept his room tidy. Still, he felt exposed having a virtual stranger in his most private of spaces. Kelly wasn't shy about inspecting everything. He took off his jacket while doing so, tossing it on the bed. Then he moved to the dresser where William still had all of his ribbons and medals on display.

Rather than try to explain this, William picked up Kelly's jacket so he could fold it neatly. Touching the fabric felt personal, a whiff of alluring cologne coming from it when he shook the folds loose.

"Now I see why you invited me up here," Kelly said, running a finger over one of medals. "You're trying to intimidate me."

"You're not far off. Those are usually in a drawer, but when you came up to me in the hall…"

Kelly turned around. "Seriously? I actually got to you?"

William shrugged and draped the jacket over the bed's footboard. "A little. I put those out to remind me that you don't stand a chance."

"We'll see." Kelly returned his attention to the medals. "Would you say you're the best on your team?"

"Sometimes I win, sometimes I lose. I don't worry about it much. What about you?"

"I worry about it all the time. I have a very competitive nature."

William snorted. "I hadn't noticed."

"Staying competitive is important," Kelly said. "Nobody coasts their way into the Olympics. Drive is essential!"

"The Olympics? Is that your dream?"

"No." Kelly turned, a smirk on his face. "It's my future."

Kate showed up then with the promised snacks and managed to embarrass him despite being present only a minute or two. William was grateful regardless because his stomach was growling and her cookies were phenomenal. After taking one,

Kelly resumed his inspection. William was proud of his medals, but the shelf Kelly turned to next caused the opposite reaction, especially when he picked up an action figure—Airazor, to be precise—and held it aloft. William *loved* his Beast Wars toys. Sure, he might have outgrown them years ago, but for the past decade they had been a part of his life, and he wasn't ready to say goodbye.

"I've had those since forever," he explained. "They're actually robots."

Kelly appeared puzzled. "You mean like Transformers?"

"Yeah," William said, moving closer to survey his collection. "But not like the crazy movie that came out earlier this year. These are from when we were little. Do you remember *Beast Wars*?"

Kelly shook his head. "I was into *Power Rangers*."

"I could never get into that show. *Beast Wars* was so much better. It was all CGI, which was new at the time, and the plots were amazing." And his collection was awesome, the action figures representing all the important characters from the show, except for X-9 Ravage, which had only been released in Japan and commanded high prices on eBay. Maybe if he saved his money, he could splurge and finally complete the—

"Wait, do you collect these?" Kelly asked, sounding amused.

"Nah," William said, playing it cool. "They're just sort of around. I've had them since I was a kid. Don't know what to do with them now."

Kelly looked at the figures appraisingly. "You know, my kid brother is still young enough to appreciate these. I'd be happy to take them off your hands for you."

William blanched… and stumbled right into a very obvious trap by doing so. He laughed at himself. "Don't tell anyone," he whispered theatrically. "It's my deepest darkest secret."

"I can only imagine the scandal this would cause at school," Kelly teased. "So show me how this one transforms."

William was happy to comply, talking about the character as he did so, how Airazor and Tigatron had a really romantic story arc in the show. He considered mentioning that in the Japanese dub, they had decided to make Airazor a boy, changing the dynamic of their relationship to be homosexual. That might be a good segue. Then again, talking about toys was way more fun.

In the course of his lecture, he discovered that Kelly had never even seen *Beast Wars*. Easily corrected. Soon they were both seated cross-legged on his bed, snacking on cookies while watching the two-episode premier. It didn't hold his attention the way it usually did. He kept looking to Kelly, at the way he took small careful bites, as if determined not to allow a cookie crumb to fall.

"If you want," William said once the episodes were over, "we could watch a few together now and again. It doesn't take long to get through the series. And just wait until you get to a certain episode in the next season! You'll cry. Not that I did or anything. Um."

Kelly considered him, features tensing. "Did you get what I said earlier? When I told you that I like Jared too much, did you get what I meant?"

William's smile faded. "What did you mean?"

"I'm gay," Kelly said matter-of-factly.

How the hell did he do that? William couldn't even say those words to himself. He didn't dare! Doing so might make it permanent. Incurable. He wasn't sure if he admired Kelly for being strong, or pitied him for admitting defeat. The bed shifted as Kelly stood. He snatched his coat, body stiff as he moved toward the door.

"Wait!" William stood in panic and placed a hand on Kelly's shoulder, noticing how strong and warm it felt. "You don't have to go."

Kelly turned, tone accusing. "Don't I?"

"Uh." He didn't want his mother overhearing any of this, so he led by example and lowered his voice. "It's okay. What you said. I'm okay with it."

"That I'm gay?" Kelly asked, still just as loud.

William winced and responded in a whisper. "Yes."

"Then why are you—" Kelly finally lowered his voice. "Are your parents homophobic or something?"

"I don't know."

Kelly faced him fully now, eyes searching his. "Look, there's one more thing I'd like to get out of the way, because it'll make things easier on me. And don't get all offended, because this doesn't mean I'm hoping that you are, or that I'm even interested. But I've told you what I am. So now it's your turn."

Jesus, what a question! He looked to the bedroom door,

worried it would open or maybe hoping it would, so he didn't have to answer. He thought about saying yes, then decided to say no, but he couldn't quite manage either. "I don't know."

Kelly's brow knitted up. "You don't know?"

William's mouth went dry. He looked at the door again, deciding it could be an excuse after all. "This probably isn't the best time."

"Okay. I get it. I think." Kelly's hand rubbed at his chin and mouth as he searched for a solution. "Do you want to go for a drive?"

"Dinner will be ready soon."

Kelly peered at him, clearly unsure of what to think. "Yeah, it is getting late. Maybe we can get together tomorrow?"

William nodded, then he tried to dispel some of the tension. "When do I get to see you run? I'm starting to think you're all talk."

"I'll prove I'm not. After school. Tomorrow." Kelly seemed to reconsider. "Let's go somewhere else. I'm sick of the track. I know a good park with jogging paths. Meet me by my car?"

"Yeah," William said. "Okay."

They stared at each other, conversation having dried up. Not for the first time, William wished he was normal, that this was just a guy friend who had come over to watch cartoons and pig out. That part had been so carefree and fun. Why couldn't the rest of his life be too?

"Walk me to my car?" Kelly said with a hint of mischief.

"Oh!" William said. "Uh…"

Kelly rolled his eyes. "It was a joke. I know the way. See you tomorrow."

"No, I'll walk you out!"

"You really don't need to."

"It's polite," William said. He slipped around Kelly to the bedroom door, bowing as he opened it, as if he were royalty.

Kelly chuckled appreciatively, and when they reached the front door, waited for William to open it too.

"My liege," William declared dramatically.

They were both smiling as they stood at the spot where walkway met driveway, the storm having blown away. Before they could say goodbye, they heard the sound of bass thumping. William recognized it instantly. It was the song his father had cranked up when taking him for a ride in the new car. The same song he was always playing, and one Holly and Abby both loved too: *The Sweet Escape* by Gwen Stefani. Admittedly, it was a fun tune, but a burly construction worker in his forties listening to it? At least the windows were up and the roof closed. The car roared into the driveway. His father sprang out a second after the engine shut off.

"Hey guys!" Lewis said. "How's it hanging?"

William braced for even worse—his father offering a high-five or a fist bump. Thank goodness then that Kelly initiated a formal handshake.

"Dad, this is Kelly." William said, making the introductions. "Kelly, this is my dad."

"Hey man, how's it going?" Lewis said, grinning proudly. "What do you think of the car?"

"Very sexy," Kelly replied generously. "Is it new?"

"Just got it last week! Not sure what the point is, because now I'm working overtime every night."

"Then you should let me have it," William tried.

"Not a chance." His father hopped from foot to foot, pretending to box with him. Maybe this wasn't a midlife crisis but a new habit. William squinted, looking for signs of white powder around the nostrils as his father continued speaking. "You staying for dinner, Kelly?"

William felt a surge of panic. What if Kelly was just as unabashedly gay around his parents? The offer was declined, and William found himself being pulled toward the house, his father having wrapped an arm around his shoulders.

"What's gotten into you lately?" William laughed, sparing one glance back to see Kelly pulling out of the driveway.

"I'm happy," Lewis responded.

"Because of the new car?"

"Because of everything." His father released him to open the door. "Life begins at forty. Just you wait and see!"

His upbeat mood was contagious, although Kate didn't seem as pleased when her husband kissed her. In fact, she appeared hurt.

William didn't understand this or anything about their relationship lately. "Do you need help?" he asked, crouching to peer through the oven window at sizzling cheese and noodles that were browning around the edges. "Lasagna!" he cried happily. "You're the best!"

This seemed to cheer his mother up. He made it his goal to keep the vibes positive during dinner. He asked his parents questions, stoking conversation, and soon they were both telling a story about how William had gotten lost at a shopping mall when he was young and had been found an hour later, sleeping in one of the racks of clothes. Everything felt fine again.

Externally.

Later in the evening, when the house grew quiet, William found himself unable to sleep. He had stripped down to his underwear and kicked off the sheets, but he still felt hot, like he was coming down with a fever. His mind kept returning to Kelly and the different guises he wore. Aggressive athlete, rejected friend, lonely outsider, and rarest of all, happy homosexual. William wondered if that's what being gay was like. Conflict with very little payoff. There had to be other benefits. He wondered if Kelly had ever been with another man, or was sleeping next to one now. William grabbed his extra pillow and clutched it to his chest. As he drifted off, he pretended it was another person. Man or woman. Kelly or Lily. Temptation or salvation.

Chapter Three

School the next day was frustrating. William couldn't concentrate on his classes as each hour crawled by. Conversation with his friends in the hallways and at lunch revolved around topics that didn't matter to him. Who had broken up with whom, or who had been kicked off of various reality television programs last night. He wanted to ask questions about Kelly to see what else his friends knew—if anything—but it seemed prudent to hold his tongue. As far as they were concerned, he and Kelly were still enemies.

Was this the beginning of a crush? Or what being in love felt like? William had experienced neither, but surely being able to think of only one person was a symptom. Did he love Kelly? If so, that left little room for doubt about his own sexuality. This concern was still on his mind when William headed out to the parking lot after school. Funny that he had worked so hard to avoid meeting Kelly in this place. Now he could hardly wait, but he was equally apprehensive. Kelly didn't appear happy either. From the outside, anyone would assume they were meeting so they could attend a funeral.

Then Kelly smiled, and William found himself doing the same, remembering how much fun it had been yesterday when they had hung out in his room. That's all the afternoon had to be. They were going to run together. Kelly was dressed for the occasion, wearing a charcoal tank top and purple basketball shorts.

"We're really going to do this," William said. "No more excuses, right?"

Kelly smirked and unlocked the car. "Only one way to find out. I might drive you to the middle of nowhere and leave you there, eliminating the competition."

William opened the passenger-side door. "Anything to win that race, huh?"

"You know it!"

Once they were on the road, William found one of his legs bouncing up and down, but not out of nervousness. "I skipped my usual swimming routine this morning," he said. "I didn't even bike to school."

"Saving your strength?" Kelly asked.

"I slept late, that's all."

"And you forgot to set your alarm?"

William chuckled. "On purpose. Do you ever do that? Pretend you don't know what you're actually doing?"

"Sounds like you've mastered self-denial," Kelly murmured.

William coughed, not wanting to travel down that path. "I figured I deserved a break. I always rewarded myself in little ways when I was first starting out. I'd keep a candy bar in my backpack and only let myself have it if I did enough laps. Or for the bigger goals, I'd uh… order things off eBay."

"More Transformers?" Kelly asked.

"They aren't all from my childhood," William said with an embarrassed chuckle. "What about you? Do you collect anything?"

"Photographs," Kelly said, still focused on his driving.

"Oh. Like old photos you find places, or ones by professionals?"

"Both."

"Do you ever take your own?"

"Yes."

"Cool." William shifted uncomfortably. Kelly's responses were short. Maybe he was annoyed by people who talked too much. William tried being quiet to see if Kelly had something else he would rather discuss, but evidently he didn't, because they traveled to their destination in silence. The park was secluded. No other cars filled the parking spaces. Kelly didn't seem in a hurry either. He turned off the engine but didn't move to leave the car.

"Nice." William leaned forward to get a better view of the green outside. When Kelly didn't respond, he added, "Very nice."

"It is," Kelly said, his voice a little husky. "Secluded too. It's just you and me out here."

William felt a jolt of panic. *That's* why they had driven so far?

"Easy now. That wasn't a pickup line. I only mean we have privacy to talk."

Oh. Kelly was suggesting they pick up the conversation where it had left off yesterday. William laughed at his own presumptions, then grew serious, because he still wasn't ready to have that conversation. He'd rather run.

"I knew you were all talk. About being so fast, I mean."

Kelly smirked. "Okay. If that's how it's going to be, let's go."

William was first out of the car, hopping from foot to foot in anticipation. "So how do you want to do this?" he asked. "Should we race or take turns or—"

"Just run," Kelly said. Then he took off toward the nearest path.

William laughed happily and raced to catch up, which was easy because Kelly wasn't so fast. A mowed field dotted with park benches gave way to woods when the path narrowed, forcing them together. William tried to match Kelly's rhythm, the sound of their feet beating along the pavement in perfect unison. His body warmed up, his muscles loosened, and while he still found the pavement jarring as his feet made contact, this wasn't so different from swimming. Heck, it was almost relaxing!

"Ready to start running?" Kelly asked.

"Huh?" William replied. "I thought we already were."

Kelly laughed. Then he nodded toward the distance. "See the light ahead? That's a clearing. I'll race you there. Give it everything you've got. Ready?"

"Ready."

"Go!"

William drew on all of his strength, letting muscle drive him forward. This didn't result in a satisfying burst of speed the way it would have in the water, but he already had a lead on Kelly. So much for all his bragging and boasting! Kelly wasn't any faster than—

A burst of air ruffled his clothes. William's eyes and mouth widened in surprise. Kelly was ahead of him, not by just a few steps or feet, but yards. William tried to run faster but was already maxed out. Kelly continued to pull ahead and disappeared around the trees ahead.

William kept chugging along, feeling like a semi-truck that had challenged a Porsche to a race. When he reached the clearing, Kelly was sitting on a picnic table, casually inspecting his nails. What a show off!

"Holy shit," William said, leaning on the table for support as he tried to catch his breath. "You're like the Flash!"

"And you're like Aquaman," Kelly replied. "Out of your element."

William looked up, shook his head, and grinned. "Tomorrow.

You and me at the YMCA. Then we'll see who's out of his element."

Kelly shrugged. "It's a deal, although not in the morning. I hate getting up early. After school?"

William nodded. "After school. Every day. We'll keep switching back and forth, teaching each other our tricks. You show me yours, I'll show you mine. That way we're on even footing for the triathlon."

"Agreed." A cloud passed over Kelly's features. "Frankly, I don't care who wins as long as it isn't Jared."

"Still pissed at him?"

"Yeah. Want to know why?"

William nodded.

Kelly scowled. "He said it was bad enough that I'm black without being gay too."

"He said that? What an asshole!"

"I know. As if I have a choice. I can't change my skin color *or* who I love."

"I wanted to talk to you about that."

Kelly raised an eyebrow. "You want to be a black man?"

William laughed. "No, but for the record, I think it's cool. That you're black, I mean. Wait, is that racist?"

"Probably, but I'm flattered and willing to forgive you. So it's the other thing you're worried about?"

William looked away. "Yeah."

He heard leaves being brushed off the table, and when he looked, Kelly was patting the cleared spot in invitation. "Come tell me about it."

William climbed onto the table, his feet on the bench. He hunched over to stare at them so he wouldn't have to make eye contact. "So you're gay."

"Yup."

"How did you know?"

For a moment, the only sound was bird song. "Around the time other guys were noticing girls, I starting noticing them noticing girls." Kelly said this as if it were a joke. How could he be so nonchalant? "It's all down to attraction. Put me in a room full of supermodels with guys on one side and girls on the other, and I know which direction I'll be looking."

"But have you ever looked at girls too?" William asked.

"Sure. I've done more than just look, because all of this is confusing. If you like vanilla ice cream but everyone else eats chocolate, eventually you're going to give chocolate a try. So, uh, which flavor do you like?"

"Strawberry," William said distractedly, because he was feeling hopeful. He turned to Kelly. "So if you've looked at girls before, do you think it's normal that guys sometimes check out other guys?"

Kelly nodded. "Absolutely. Even if it's just to compare size in the locker room, or figure out how they stack up in other ways. But that's not the same as attraction."

"But it's normal," William pressed.

Kelly's tones were patient. "All of this is normal. Yes."

"Good." William breathed out in relief. "I scope out a lot of guys in the hall. I don't during swim practice because that would be creepy, but I'm always looking around. I make myself look at girls too, and I know everything works in that regard."

"Wait, what?"

"You know." He made sure they were still alone. "Have you ever jacked off?"

"Once or twice," Kelly deadpanned. "Are you kidding me? I'm a pro! I'm probably nearing a world record by now."

"Oh." He filed that image away for later. "Well, I can jack off while looking at nude women. Everything works down there, if you know what I mean."

"A demonstration might help," Kelly said, nudging William playfully. "And for the record, the gay youth group I go to has plenty of guys who lost their virginity to a girl but still identify as gay."

That wasn't welcome news. "But how can they sleep with a girl if they're really gay? How can they even get it up?"

Kelly shrugged. "Hormones are hormones. Tell anyone this and I'll kill you, but I once jacked off to Aladdin."

"The cartoon?"

Kelly appeared defensive. "Yeah. I was thirteen and clueless, okay? Besides, Aladdin is kind of hot. But that doesn't mean I'm Disneysexual or whatever."

William laughed. "Yeah, but at least Aladdin is a guy."

"He's a two-dimensional drawing of a guy wearing parachute pants, a dopey vest, and a fez. My point is that when we're horny, all sorts of crazy things can turn us on."

He had hoped Kelly would provide him with answers, but now William felt more confused than ever. If a wide variety of things turned people on, then how could he figure out if he had a problem or not?

"Returning to my original scenario," Kelly continued, "say you're in a room with the hottest guy in the world on your left, and the hottest woman in the world on your right. Which direction are you going to be looking?"

"Is anyone watching me?"

"No. Better yet, you're invisible. No one can see you no matter what, and the guy and girl are both slowly getting undressed. Which one do you want to see get naked?"

He started to visualize this scenario, imagining a room without windows or doors. Perfect privacy. Then he pictured both models, but it was the guy who was more aggressive, lifting his shirt to reveal a muscled stomach, unbuttoning his jeans to show off the bulge. The poor female model was so ignored that she tossed herself in front of the competition, but it didn't matter. There was only one person William wanted to watch, and frankly, he wished he and the guy could be alone together. "Fuck."

"Which one?" Kelly asked.

"The guy," William spat. "I'd want to watch the guy."

"Is that so bad?"

Once again Kelly sounded amused. William rounded on him, but it wasn't fair to remain angry. Kelly didn't understand the implications. This was more than him worrying about what his parents would think. "I want to join the Coast Guard." His desire to do so wasn't just in the hopes of being cured. The Coast Guard had long since been his dream, one that he eventually decided could save him.

"So?" Kelly said. "It's not like the idea of a gay sailor is anything new."

"That's the Navy. I'd be a coastie, and it's the idea of an openly gay sailor, coastie, soldier, or anything else that's the problem."

"Oh. Right." Kelly breathed out and considered this. "What about Don't Ask, Don't Tell? Doesn't that protect you?"

"Yeah, but only if I live a lie." William took to his feet, pacing back and forth, old worries finally being spoken aloud. "If I fall in love with some guy, or if someone catches us kissing, or if I even talk about it, I could get kicked out. I can't exactly go four years without dating anyone. That would raise suspicion too, so I'll have to get a girlfriend. That's why I've tried a couple times to… you know. I need to figure out if I can do that, if my body will go along with me."

"Or you could not enlist."

William looked to Kelly disbelievingly. "What about you? What if gay people weren't allowed in the Olympics?"

"Okay, that would suck. But I'm in a similar situation. How many openly gay athletes can you name? There aren't a lot, and I worry about not finding a coach or a sponsor just because of who I am."

"So what are you going to do?"

Kelly scowled at the ground, then looked up. "Fall in love with the most wonderful guy possible. If I'm going to risk my entire athletic career, he better be worth it."

"Seriously."

"I am serious!" Kelly said, sounding more determined than ever. "I refuse to change who I am to please people who are bigoted and small-minded. Why let them win? I've had to put up with this crap my entire life. I wish I could make you black, even just for one day, because that's not something you can hide. I can't mosey down the street and pretend to be white—everyone can see that I'm not. In fact, it's the first thing most people notice. So I'm used to it. All I can do is wait for the world to get over it and start noticing the rest of me."

William gawped. "Would it be cheesy if I started applauding?"

Kelly's smile was subtle. "Normally, but considering that we're alone out here, go for it."

William clapped.

Kelly fanned himself as if flattered. Then he cocked his head. "So let's hear you say it. The big scary 'G' word. You're still tiptoeing around it."

"Okay," William said, feeling silly. "I'm gangsta!"

"No, you're definitely not." Kelly grew somber. "Come on. For real this time."

William looked away, his eyes landing on the path they had arrived on. Then an idea occurred to him. "Okay, but only if you can beat me in another race. First one to the car!"

He took off, knowing he needed every advantage he could

get, unfair or otherwise. He had a huge lead on Kelly. Enough that William worried he might not be playing along. Then, like last time, he felt the wind blow past him, Kelly seemingly carried along with it. William watched him pull ahead. The way his body moved was beautiful. He admired how shameless Kelly was, how he could be so emotional and yet somehow remain strong. If Kelly represented what it was like to be gay—well, William wouldn't mind being more like him. Or being with him. He let his eyes move over Kelly's body again, for once not trying to censor himself or quarantine his feelings. The tight ass, the sheen of sweat on his dark skin, the strong line of his jaw when Kelly looked back, eyes half-lidded in amusement… He was fucking hot, and fucking around with him would *be* hot. William would have laughed at the idea if he had any breath left. And if his blood wasn't pounding to his heart, he was pretty sure where it would choose to flow. He still didn't know what it meant to be in love, but it wasn't difficult to imagine falling for someone like Kelly. Much easier than any girl he had met, so that settled it. William was gay, and for once, he felt pretty damn good about it.

Remaining resolute wasn't as easy away from Kelly's confident presence, but William tried. After dinner with his mother (his father was working late again), William went up to his room, walking around and straightening things while coming to grips with how his life was going to change. He'd need to be prepared for hateful comments at school, but the tradeoff was that he could finally do what everyone else did. Find someone, fall in love, and have sex. He wanted that, badly, and not just because he was always horny these days. He felt like there was an entire world he had never been initiated into. Being intimate with someone, sharing private thoughts in a dimly lit room, exchanging declarations of love, bodies close beneath the sheets—he hungered for that, and until now, it had never seemed possible.

There was a price to pay. He turned his attention to the vintage Coast Guard poster in his room, a sailor grinning and asking if William—or whomever—cared to join him. And he still wanted to. He didn't feel passionate about college or any other course of action. He wanted to get out there, fly in helicopters, and put his swimming skills to good use by helping others.

William swallowed, tasting guilt. Was he really going to turn his back on people who needed him, just because he wanted to hook up with another guy?

"Jesus, you're obsessed!" an unexpected voice declared.

William leapt into the air. When he landed on his feet again, he spun around, placing a hand on his chest when he saw it was just his brother. Not Spencer, with his chiseled chin and huge muscles. The comparatively scrawny guy in front of him had a permanent slouch and almost always wore a crooked smile and a day's worth of stubble.

"Did you drool on the carpet?" Errol asked. He was named after some old movie star. William had been luckier than his brothers when it came to his name, although his family always called him— "Willy, if I didn't know better, I'd say you're in love with that sailor."

"Shut up," William responded. "I was just—"

"Dreaming of the Coast Guard, I know." Errol's grin widened. "Has your boner subsided yet?"

William shook his head and sighed. His middle brother lacked any sort of filter, which more often than not, ended up embarrassing those around him. Not Errol though. He seemed comfortable with any topic.

"You've got to broaden your horizons," his brother said, flopping down on William's bed and putting his hands behind his head. "There's nothing wrong with the Coast Guard, but you don't need to be such a conformist. Have a little fun before you ship out or whatever."

"I'm not a conformist," William said, eyeing the dirt on the bottom of his brother's shoes. Shoes that were currently wiggling over the comforter he had recently laundered, but complaining would only prove his point. "What about you? Still working hard to keep Austin weird?"

"You know it. Like the new shirt?"

The screen-printed illustration was of a pinup girl sucking on a lollipop while squirming against a giant eyeball, one of her long nude legs rubbing the violet iris. "It's freaky. And gross."

"Thanks!" his brother said, sitting up to look down at it proudly. "I've been going around to concert venues lately, asking to set up a booth. Everyone keeps shooting me down, but I'll find one eventually."

Determination ran in the family. Spencer had his career in

the Marines, something that required plenty of drive. Errol had barely managed to finish high school because he was so focused on his art. He did though, relocating downtown and sharing a ridiculously small apartment with some other artist types so he could chase his dream. William, of course, was still determined to make the Coast Guard work. Somehow.

"How old are you?" Errol asked appraisingly.

"Seventeen. And you forgot my birthday."

"I'll draw you something," Errol said dismissively. "Anyway, you're old enough that you're probably smoking now. Know what I mean?"

William knew *exactly* what he meant. "I don't smoke."

Errol appeared confused. "Drink?"

"No! When I meet with a recruiter, I want to be able to look them in the eye and answer truthfully. Besides, they test for that stuff."

Errol chuckled. "My baby brother, the last honest guy on the planet."

William averted his eyes, which didn't go unnoticed.

"Don't tell me you've got a dark side?" Errol said. "What did you do? Take a free sample at the grocery store without asking permission first?"

"I killed a man." William said this with grim seriousness. "It was late at night and I was driving… It was an accident! But I needed, I still need—" He choked in air. "I need help hiding the body."

The amusement fled from Errol's features. When William couldn't maintain it any longer and cracked a smile, Errol flopped back on the bed, clutched at his sides, and cackled. "It's always the quiet ones," he said. "Come smoke with me. Sorry, come keep me company."

"Fine."

He followed his brother downstairs. They stopped to grab a couple of sodas from the refrigerator. Then they stepped out on the back patio. The neighborhood was old, the lighting minimal compared to modern subdivisions. William liked it since they could enjoy the natural dark of the night without having to suffer orange artificial light. And it meant not being seen by the neighbors, which was especially good now, since his brother had lit a joint.

William sidled away from him so he wouldn't accidentally

inhale anything. "What are you doing home? You're not moving back in, are you?"

"Don't worry," Errol croaked before exhaling. "I don't want my old room back. The guy I live with has a girl over tonight, so I'm steering clear. It's his turn to use the bedroom."

"There's only one?"

"Yup!" Errol said. "You haven't seen the new place, huh? It's like Bert and Ernie in there, except platonic. Normally I would just hang out in the living room, but last time I made too much noise and my roommate kept thinking of me when he should have been trying harder to stay hard. Ha ha!"

William tried to remember if his brother's roommate was handsome or not. "Still, I figured you'd have something better to do on a Friday night."

"I could say the same to you. Where are all your ladies?"

William shrugged.

"Yeah, same here." The ember of Errol's joint glowed brighter. Then he exhaled. "The last one, she loved her cats more than me. Paige and her pussies. She was a good girl."

He said this longingly, once again making William feel like he was missing out.

"There's gotta be someone," Errol continued. "You and Spence both got Dad's muscles. Lucky bastards. That must turn heads at school."

"I did meet someone recently," William said carefully.

"Oh yeah?" Errol flicked the end of the joint, knocking the cherry loose to extinguish it. "So how come you're not hanging out with them now?"

William hesitated, noticing that his brother had kept the pronoun neutral. Did he know? If so, maybe he was capable of subtlety after all. "I'm not sure if the other person likes me that way."

"Then ask them out."

"I'm not sure if *I* like them that way."

Errol chuckled. "So? You won't know if you really like each other until you try. A date is like a job interview, except you'll both be in the hot seat. If it works out, awesome. You're hired. So is the other person. That's when the real work begins." His brother smirked. "You're going to love clocking in though. Trust me."

"So I just ask?"

"If you don't, it's called stalking. I remember being freaked out by dating when I was your age, but man, the worst that can happen is you'll get rejected. The idea of *that* freaked me out too. It's not a big deal though. Most people let you down easy."

The porch light switched on, and a second later, the glass door slid open. Their mother noticed Errol and became instantly joyful. "I thought I heard your voice! When did you get here?" Then she sniffed, eyes widening. "Errol!" she hissed. "The neighbors!"

"Relax. The old lady next door, Mrs. Higgins, she's on medicinal."

"She is not!" Kate chastised. "That's not even legal here! Although I do sometimes smell something strange from her yard."

"I'm tellin' ya!" Errol said, stepping forward. "Give me a hug."

"You stink," Kate said, but she was already hugging him tightly.

William rolled his eyes, long since used to seeing his brother get away with murder. If he tried the same thing—

"You aren't partaking, are you?" his mother said sternly, having similar thoughts.

"No," Errol answered for him. "He's hopelessly square, I swear."

"I'm not square!" William grumbled.

"It's okay, honey," his mother said. "How's that song go?"

"Mom," he said, hoping to stop her.

"It's cool to be square! I think that's it…"

William grimaced, hoping nobody at school would ever discover how lame his Friday nights were.

"Where's Dad?" Errol asked.

"Having drinks with coworkers."

"You should have gone," Errol said. "I could have babysat Willy."

"You suck," William replied.

"Does he still wet the bed?" his brother continued.

"I really hate you."

Their mother shook her head. "You're both silly. I'll let you have your fun. Oh, and honey—" She was addressing Errol. "—there's a batch of peanut butter raisin on the table. Just in case."

She silently mouthed the word munchies.

"You're a baking machine! You should stop licking stamps at the post office and open up a bakery."

"But darling, if I quit my job, who would pay your rent?"

"Burn!" William declared. "Nice one, Mom!"

"Thanks, honey. Have a good night. I love you boys."

"We love you too," they droned.

"She's all right," Errol said when they were alone again.

"She's a different person when you're around."

"Only because she doesn't want you to be messed up like I am."

They returned inside, grabbed the promised cookies, and went back to William's room. There they flipped through channels, settling on none for long and talking over most of the shows. When the hour grew late, Errol rose, stretched, and headed for the door.

"I'm gonna crash on the couch," he said. He surveyed the room before leaving, attention settling on the Coast Guard poster again. "You're not square," he said, "because you don't try to be anything other than who you are. That's really cool. Most people your age aren't like that. Good night, baby bro."

"Good night," he said, feeling a surge of affection for his sibling. When he was alone again, this feeling was replaced by guilt because as far as his family and friends were concerned, they didn't know the real William at all.

William stood in front of the bathroom mirror. Not to relieve sexual frustration, although amorous thoughts *were* on his mind. Sort of. He had brushed his teeth, gargled with mouth wash, and shaved with the utmost care, not wanting a stray hair or bloody cut to detract from his appearance. He had even swabbed out his ears to make sure no unsightly wax was visible. He couldn't remember the last time he had primped like this, but now it seemed advisable. He didn't know if Kelly was interested in him, and William didn't really feel ready for anything to happen, but he figured he should be prepared in case he changed his mind.

He grabbed the bottle of cologne Spencer had sent him for his birthday and sprayed it on his bare chest, even though it would get washed off again as soon as they were in the pool. Still, for that initial five minutes when he and Kelly were together, he intended to smell good. Worrying about his outfit seemed equally pointless, since they wouldn't be wearing much. That thought gave him pause. Maybe he should take care of business, just to prevent any embarrassing situations from popping up. Literally.

The doorbell rang, but he didn't react. The plan was for him to pick up Kelly at his place, so it was probably a Jehovah's Witness or a package delivery. He debated putting product in his hair, decided against it, and returned to his room to pick out a shirt. William found his bed occupied. Lily was reclined on it, her pose seductive. She laughed as if this was a joke and got to her feet.

"Surprise!" she said.

"Hey," he managed, tensing up as she hugged him. They often hugged in greeting, but normally he was wearing more than just a pair of jeans. "What are you doing here?"

"It's Saturday, I'm bored…" Lily pulled back, a hand sliding around to his chest. "We talked about hanging out alone. Remember?"

"Yeah!" William said. "It's just that I have plans."

"Oh." Lily frowned. "Starting when?"

"Three."

They both looked at the clock. He wished he had lied, because it was only half past one.

"I'll keep you company until then."

"Okay." He moved around her to the dresser, grabbing the first shirt he found and putting it on. It was pale blue and oversized, since his mother was convinced he was a giant, but at least he wasn't as naked now.

"It's been ages since I've been over," Lily said. "Your mom didn't recognize me at first."

"There's not much to do here. Maybe we should go somewhere else."

Lily shook her head. "I like it. My brother's room stinks. Yours is nice." She sat on the bed and patted the mattress next to her, reminding William of when Kelly had done the same with the picnic table, except he didn't feel as motivated to sit. Not wanting to be rude, he did so anyway. She started talking, first about the usual things, like what had been happening at school. Then the reminiscing began. Lily focused on memories they had made together. She brought up the time they had all gone to the airport, wandered around the corridors and pretended they had a flight to catch, even running at one point and shouting "Excuse me! Out of the way! My gate is about to close!" Or the time Lily had first gotten her license, and Holly begged her to drive them to San Antonio because she wanted to see the River Walk. The trip took longer than any of them expected, so they had all broken curfew that night and gotten in trouble. Except for Abby, who had managed to sneak back in undetected.

William relaxed, laughing along with these stories and adding his own details. But he noticed how many of Lily's memories focused on him. He had bought her a necklace at the River Walk. At the airport they had pretended they were a husband and wife catching a flight to Hawaii. That she was interested in him wasn't a complete surprise, but now he was starting to wonder if she felt more. Did she love him?

"That weird place with the go-karts," she said. "Remember? They had a few waterslides off to one side."

William groaned. "How can I forget? You guys dared me to go down one, but none of us had a swimsuit, so I—"

"Stripped down to your underwear." Lily was sitting upright, her legs crossed beneath her as she smiled.

"Hey, I had boxers on! I just didn't expect them to be so heavy when they got wet."

"The whole world saw your left ass cheek!"

William laughed but noticed he was alone.

Lily's teeth were hidden behind her lips now. "Do you think I'm pretty?"

"Yeah!" he said. And she was. Of his three female friends, she had the most boyfriends, although none seemed to last for long.

"It's crazy how handsome you've gotten," she said. "When I first met you…" She shook her head, as if it didn't matter. "You deserve to be with someone who cares about you."

She leaned forward, reaching out a hand. His first instinct was to pull away. Then he thought of drowning people, a capsized boat, and a helicopter hovering over it all, except no one leapt from it. No rescue swimmer was there to help them. Instead he was at a seedy gay bar, sitting on one of the stools and drinking, ignoring the hungry stares of guys in leather chaps. Is that really what he wanted?

He could at least try. If not for those drowning victims, then for Lily, because rejecting her would also mean hurting her. He cared too much to do that. Not in the way that she wanted but enough to try.

Just as their lips were about to meet, William turned his head. This didn't stop her. She began kissing his neck, rubbing her hands over his body. That felt good, although her fingers were more dainty than he preferred. His neck was getting awfully wet too, so he pulled away and laughed nervously.

Lily looked at him like he was being sweet. Then she stripped off her shirt. William stared. Part of him was curious. He had seen his mother in a bra, but this was different. Lily had a nice body, her muscles toned but feminine. He definitely found her more attractive than he did most girls. She didn't wear a lot of makeup. She didn't need to, her lips naturally pink against her dark skin, the light sprinkling of freckles across her nose making him long for lazy summer days. What guy wouldn't find her attractive?

"What's fair is fair," Lily prompted.

She nodded at his shirt. Okay. No big deal. He stripped it off, feeling a little thrilled. This was getting crazy! Then Lily scooted closer, one of her breasts pressing against him, the fabric of her bra itchy. She made another attempt to kiss him. Worried he would mess it up, he avoided her lips again and kissed her shoulder, then her neck. Her skin smelled like soap and sunshine. The breast pressed against his arm started rubbing back and forth. Then she grabbed his hand and moved it to the bra strap on her shoulder.

He pulled it down, wondering if the contents would cause him to catch fire, if he would become boob-obsessed like other guys. Part of him was mildly curious, but— He gasped as a hand slid up his thigh. His body reacted, hungry as ever. The caress of someone else's hand instead of his own… Wouldn't that feel good on his cock? Wouldn't her mouth feel even better? He was hard now and could practically see himself churning through the water to save those victims, a victorious grin plastered on his face. He could do this! Except one of the heads bobbing in the water sure looked familiar, as did the self-assured smirk.

Kelly.

William jerked away, Lily's hand sliding off his bulge. "I don't want to rush things," he stammered. "I really should get going."

Lily appeared confused. Then she looked at the clock. William did the same. Time had flown by because it was nearly three.

"You can't cancel your plans?" she asked.

"They're important. Sorry."

Lily nibbled her lip. "Can we meet afterwards?"

"I'm not sure how late I'll be."

"Tomorrow?"

"Uhhh."

Lily stared at him. Then she gave a barely perceptible shake of the head, which continued as she grabbed her shirt to put it on.

"Sorry!" he said. "It's just..." He faltered, unable to find a good excuse.

"It's fine," she said tersely. "Give me a call if you ever have time for me. Or don't. Whatever."

"Lily!" he said, standing to follow her out of the room. He ended up chasing her all the way to the driveway. "I'm sorry! I'm going through some weird stuff right now and it's not you. I know how that sounds, but it's true."

Lily spun around, car keys in hand. "Then tell me what's going on! Explain it to me!"

"I..." William choked. "I will. Just not right now."

She exhaled. "Fine. You know where to find me."

William watched her get in her car, pull out, and drive away. Then he sighed and trudged back inside. His father was in the entryway, wearing a knowing expression. He clapped William on the shoulder and chuckled, like his son had finally grown up and become a man, when in truth, he felt more like a lost little boy than ever.

Chapter Four

William was freaking out. After Lily had left, he returned upstairs and washed his face, just in case there was lipstick on it, which made him feel silly when he remembered Lily didn't wear any. He also washed off his cologne because romance was now the furthest thing from his mind. Then he noticed the time and rushed over to Kelly's house, getting lost repeatedly in his addled state. He was nearly an hour late when he finally arrived. Kelly's jaw was clenching when he opened the door, but he had gotten over it by the time they arrived at the YMCA.

Exercise was usually just what the doctor ordered, but the Y was a different place in the afternoon, especially on a Saturday. Families filled the main pool, splashing around and having a good time. That was fine. The problem was how many of them kept spilling over into the swimming lanes, especially when those lanes were already occupied by other swimmers. He and Kelly were forced to wait their turn, and even then William felt pressured not to remain in the water too long. Soon he gave up entirely, leading the way back to the locker room and getting dressed.

"Isn't there a hot tub?" Kelly asked. "We could try swimming in circles."

"They would have to be tight," William said. "Besides, the hot tub is probably stuffed too."

"A sauna?"

"I've never understood the appeal of sitting in a hot room and getting sweaty."

"We could hit the track."

William grimaced. "My feet are still sore. I think I'd rather go home and forget this day ever happened."

"Something wrong? Besides me making you miss out on your early morning routine. If I had known it would ruin your day…"

"It's not you," William said with a sigh. A couple of guys entered the locker room, making him yearn for privacy. He grabbed his duffel bag. "Let's go."

"Okay. You're the boss."

He couldn't shake the bad mood, maybe because he wasn't sure why exactly he was upset. Yesterday had felt so good—finally coming to terms with himself and having a nice evening with his brother. So he had thought. Now everything had returned to being complicated.

When they reached his car, William set his duffel bag on the trunk and spun around to face Kelly. "I did things. With a girl. That's why I was late."

Kelly's mouth dropped open. "But yesterday…" He raised his eyebrows and shook his head. "I thought we covered this already."

"I know."

"What did you do exactly?"

"I kissed a friend of mine. Sort of. Not on the lips. Um."

Kelly's eyebrows managed to climb even higher. "Then where?"

"Not *there*. Just on the neck. She kissed me a little too. And we took off our shirts."

Kelly exhaled and looked across the parking lot to the horizon. "Did you like it?"

"I don't know. I, uh, reacted."

"You got hard," Kelly said, eyes intense as they met his again. "Yeah."

"I had a similar experience once, and as I already told you, I know plenty of other gay guys who have too. I don't know what you want from me. There isn't a test to prove one way or another what you are, but if you're more interested in men than—"

"Maybe I'm bisexual," William blurted out.

"Fine," Kelly said with a shrug. "Maybe you are. If so, what stopped you from going further with her?"

William was looking at the reason right now, but he wasn't about to admit that. "I started thinking of guys instead." There. That was close enough to the truth.

"Sounds to me like we've reached the same conclusion."

"I guess so," William mumbled.

"Are we going to do this again tomorrow?" Kelly's tone made clear that he was joking, but William answered seriously anyway.

"No. I'm gay."

"Congratulations. I'll buy you an ice cream."

"Should I tell everyone?" William asked. "I don't really want to."

"No ice cream then," Kelly said with a sigh. He leaned against the rear of the car. "Who you tell depends on a number of factors.

How do you think your family will react?"

William thought of Errol and how upset their mother had been the first time she had caught him smoking pot. They had argued, and she even staged an intervention, but in the end she had accepted who he was and adjusted accordingly. Her love for him mattered more than a drug habit. Being gay wasn't the same thing as being a stoner, and his family wasn't religious. He couldn't imagine her having any real objections. His father's reaction was harder to predict, since William didn't feel as close to him, but he did know he was loved.

"They'll be okay. I think."

"All right. And your friends?"

William's cheeks began to burn. This didn't go unnoticed. "I don't know. Two of them are interested in me. Maybe more."

Kelly smirked. "Wow. Most guys would love to have that problem."

"Not me!"

"Keep that in mind the next time you start having doubts. Anyway, if they like you enough to want to be with you, I'm sure they'll be willing to accept you for who you are."

William walked a few paces from the car. Then he spun around. "I don't want to hurt anyone's feelings."

"I'm sure they'll forgive you."

William wasn't so certain. "If you liked someone and then found out you could never be with him, how would that make you feel? Maybe they'll start hating me instead."

Kelly was quiet. Then his expression became defiant. "People like that aren't worth your time."

William continued to stare at him, his own problems forgotten. "You and Jared stopped being friends because he's a racist homophobe. Right? That was the only reason?"

Kelly tensed. "I had feelings for him. Don't ask me why. I'm just glad I wasn't stupid enough to let him know. And don't you dare tell him! Or anyone else!"

"I won't. I promise."

"Listen," Kelly said, his posture relaxing, "it's nice that you don't want to hurt anyone, but sometimes it can't be helped. I think your friends learning the truth now would be kindest in the long run. Besides, you're not choosing some other girl over them. You're not choosing anything. You're attracted to guys, and there's nothing anyone can do about it. If your friends possess any intelligence, they won't blame you for what you can't change."

William thought about it and nodded. He couldn't let things continue the way they were. "So I just tell everyone that I'm gay?"

"Up to you. It's not how I introduce myself. I let people get to know me, and when such subjects come up naturally, that's when it makes sense to be truthful. For me, anyway."

"But if Jared is homophobic and racist, then how did you end up being best friends?"

"He said something racist, but that doesn't *make* him racist exactly. He realized he was wrong and apologized. As for the gay thing, you've got me there. I purposely didn't tell him. I'm out to my family and friends, I've gone to a gay youth group for years, and I've had more boyfriends and lovers than most people my age, but when it came to him…" Kelly shook his head. "I was deluding myself. I wanted to be with him, even though in my heart I knew he was straight and that I didn't have a chance, so I avoided the subject completely. I let myself dream we were both too scared to confess our feelings to each other. Basically I was stupid. Learn from my mistake. Tell your friends."

"But you telling Jared ended your friendship."

"Him being a douche is what ended our friendship. Girls are cooler about these things. Usually. I don't think you have anything to worry about. It's either that or you can keep making out with them. And more."

"She rubbed her boobs against me," William said with a frown.

For some reason this sent Kelly into a fit of laughter. His smile was nice. And contagious. No wonder he had so much experience in love. The thought made William feel intimidated, and as he watched Kelly try to get himself under control, he felt even more certain about what he wanted. Kelly was an amazing guy, and anyone—himself in particular—would be lucky to have him as their boyfriend.

"Do you still like him?" William asked. "Jared, I mean. Do you still have—"

"Of course not," Kelly spat, sobering up. "I don't feel anything for him at all."

William knew that wasn't true. Kelly still got angry when

Jared's name was mentioned and was still dead set on him not winning the triathlon. Feelings definitely remained, but if they weren't romantic in nature, then maybe he stood a chance.

William circled the dining room table, searching for any imperfection. The utensils were spotless and straight, the napkins carefully folded. Even the handle of each teacup was aligned horizontally with the edge of the cloth placemats. Small plates awaited each guest, a platter in the center stocked with cupcakes and petite sandwiches. Everything appeared flawless until he looked up and saw one big problem standing in the doorway.

"Mom!"

"I know you wanted the house to yourself," she said, moving forward to inspect the table.

He blocked her path. "I thought you and Dad were supposed to be out shopping today."

"That's what I thought too. Apparently he was called in to work this morning."

William briefly shared her irritation before he resumed being selfish. "You promised me—"

"I know, I know," Kate said, raising a hand. "I'll be taking a nap. I have a headache. You just enjoy yourself." She turned to leave but then hesitated. "I thought you were only having Lily over."

He shook his head. "Abby and Holly too."

"All three girls?" his mother said, sounding scandalized.

Did she think he was planning on having an orgy? "Mom!"

"I'll be in my room," she said, shaking her head.

She left, giving William just enough time to put a few more things on the table—including the kettle of water he had brought to a boil—before the doorbell rang. His friends' expressions were just as puzzled when he answered it, even more so once they were all seated at the table. "Thank you for coming," he said. Then he walked around the table, placing a tea bag in each cup before pouring steaming water over it. He smiled at his friends as he did this, greeting each of them one by one. Holly appeared giddy, Abby kept looking from him to the spread, and Lily refused to meet his eye.

"Okay," he said once he had sat. "Everyone help yourself. Enjoy."

Nobody moved. Only Holly reached for food, but Lily grabbed her wrist to stop her. "What's this about?" she demanded.

From her tone, she was still hurt.

William hoped today would put an end to such feelings. Yesterday he and Kelly had stood in the YMCA parking lot, talking for almost an hour about how the coming out process had gone for him and other people he knew. Kelly compared the process to an adhesive bandage—best ripped off swiftly and without hesitation. William felt more tact was called for. "Aren't you hungry?" he asked. "Please, have a—" Lily's expression stopped him short. She had looked away, her features darkening. "Okay. Well. I asked you all here because there's something I need to say."

Holly perked up. "What?"

William shifted nervously. "It's about me," he said. "Who I really am. Um. Geez."

"I told you so," Abby murmured.

"Shut up!" Holly shot back.

"He's gay," Abby insisted, rolling her eyes at Holly, who shook her head adamantly in response.

"No, he isn't! We're here so he can tell us who he's chosen." Holly looked to him with transparent hope. "Right?"

William stared at her, any response caught in his throat. Then he looked to Lily, whose cheeks remained flushed, arms crossed as she glared at the table. This wasn't going as smoothly as he had hoped.

"Abby is right," he managed. "I'm gay."

Holly scrunched up her nose. "Are you sure?"

Lily lifted her head, waiting for his answer.

"Yes," William said. "Trust me, I've thought long and hard about this."

"Could have fooled me," Lily muttered.

Holly turned to her slowly. "What's that supposed to mean? Did you guys—"

"No!" William said. Then he frowned. "Not exactly."

"You knew I had a crush on him!" Holly shouted.

"It doesn't matter," Lily said, staring her down. "He's not interested in any of us, so get over it!"

"I'm fine with this," Abby interjected. "William, you're very brave for telling us. I'm proud of you and accept you for who you are."

"She read that online," Lily said.

"So what?" Abby shot back. "At least I'm not clinging to false hope."

"I still am," Holly said. "Are you really *really* sure?"

"Yes!" William said, starting to lose his temper. "I know it's an adjustment, but I thought part of you would be happy for me. If you really like me, then—"

"We do," Lily said, voice strained. "And we are."

The table was quiet.

"Thanks," William said. He felt terrible. Holly had put on a smile but still seemed deflated, Lily's expression was tight, and Abby... Well, she at least seemed okay with it all. "How did you know?" he asked her.

"You're not like other guys," she replied.

"That's what I like most about him," Holly said.

Abby ignored her. "At first we thought maybe you were just shy, but you're the only guy in school not interested in our boobs, and if that wasn't enough, you invited us over for a tea party."

Holly giggled, covering her mouth. "With cupcakes. *Pink* cupcakes."

"You're girls," William said defensively. "I thought you'd like them."

"Great," Abby said, "he's gay, but he still manages to be a sexist pig."

William stared. Maybe the stress had gotten to him, but he started laughing. To his relief, the girls joined in, even though Lily's laughter seemed a little forced. They continued to tease him, finally enjoying the food and making it feel more like a celebration. Holly generously made fun of herself too. "I can't believe I thought you invited us over to say who you chose."

"To date?" William said. "Abby, of course." He thought it was the safest answer, since she never really expressed much interest in him.

"No thanks," she replied.

"You don't want my body?"

"Nope. You're hot, don't get me wrong, but you're too nice."

"She likes the bad boys," Holly explained.

"I have a leather jacket," William teased. "I can slick back my hair, roll a pack of cigarettes in my shirt sleeve."

"That's not her type," Holly said. "Tell him."

Abby covered her face with both hands, but through them she murmured. "Is your brother single?"

"Spencer?" He asked, but then he understood. "*Errol*? Yeah! I'll give you his phone number."

They spent the rest of the afternoon talking. He fielded the same questions he had asked Kelly so recently. When did you first realize? How can you be sure? There were a lot of mixed signals he needed to explain away too. Eventually the topic became more lighthearted; Holly quizzed him about what sort of guys he liked, and even more embarrassing, all three girls gave him advice about boys.

"Don't wait for them to make a move," Lily said. "Guys take forever to work up their courage."

"Just be sweet," Holly said. "And pretty. Or handsome, in your case."

"Try reading a freaking book," Abby said, shaking her head at her friend. "I hate a guy who doesn't have anything interesting to say."

William stopped blushing and started taking notes. Mentally, at least. By the time his friends left, he felt closer to them than ever. He was only worried about Lily, who didn't smile as much as she usually did. He was glad when she lagged behind, giving them privacy to talk without the others overhearing.

"I still don't understand what happened the other day," she said.

They stood in the driveway, her bicycle creating a barrier between them. It was the racing kind, which only made him like her more. They had ridden together many times. It wasn't hard to imagine why she thought they might be compatible.

"I'm sorry," he said. "It's been confusing for me too."

"Okay." She squeezed the brakes absentmindedly, attention on the bike as she spoke. "I want you to know that I'm not like Holly. She likes you, but then she also falls in love with celebrities who don't know she exists. The feelings I have for you, they aren't superficial."

William felt terrible. All he could do was keep apologizing. "I'm sorry I can't be what you—"

"I know," Lily said, raising her head. "I just needed to tell you that. For me. We're not meant to be together. I can accept that. You being gay doesn't change anything, and neither do my dumb feelings. We'll always be friends. I promise."

"Thanks," he said. He wanted to hug her but was worried that would only confuse matters more.

Lily nodded at him, swung a leg over her bicycle, a dejected smile tugging at one cheek. "I'll see you in school on Monday."

"Yeah," he said, throat tight. "See you then."

William still felt overwhelmed by the experience when he sat down at the dinner table that night. On one hand, a weight had been lifted from his shoulders. He just wished that he hadn't shifted that weight to his friends. He kept thinking of the brave face Lily had put on just before they parted. She would bounce back. Plenty of guys vied for her attention. He just hoped they would be good to her.

A sigh pulled him from these thoughts. He looked up to see that his mother hadn't touched her food either. Maybe she was waiting for him to start. He lifted his fork and jabbed at the salad, but she still didn't move.

"What's the point?" she said. "We might as well eat in front of the television."

He looked at the empty chair where his father should be. Lately he was never around. Maybe William should say something to him, because surely once he knew how unhappy his wife was, Lewis would make more of an effort.

"I like sitting here," William said. "It gives us a chance to talk."

"Is there something you would like to tell me?" The question felt loaded. It didn't take him long to guess why.

William's mouth went dry. "You spied on us."

"I overheard! It's hard not to when you and your friends get so loud."

"Sorry," he said, breaking eye contact. Then he raised his head high. "But not for being gay."

"Of course not!" His mother looked anguished. "Honey, all I want is for you to be happy!"

"Then you're okay with it?"

"No!" she placed a hand on her forehead, as if the headache from earlier still persisted. "I don't know. I'm worried about you.

That boy… What was his name? Matthew Shepard?"

"Oh."

Her lips trembled. "I don't want anyone to hurt you!"

Then came the tears. William hadn't been prepared for them, but he rose and walked around the table. He made his mother stand so that he could hug her. This only seemed to make her more emotional. He fought back tears of his own, not understanding them at first. Then he realized what she was feeling because he shared the same sentiment. The last thing he had ever wanted was for his mother to get hurt. Now he felt like he'd been the one to do so.

"Totally normal," Kelly said, doing stretches beside the track after school the next day. "Mothers—the good ones anyway—care most about your wellbeing. My mom was worried I wouldn't be able to get married, or that I'd be lonely without children in my life. I just had to explain that gay people can have those same things. There might be more legal hoops to jump through, but that's not going to stop me. Your mom loves you, so she's scared you're going to get gay bashed or whatever."

"That would explain why she gave me this," William said. He reached into his backpack and pulled out his keychain, which normally fit in his pocket, except now it had a large tube attached to it. If that weren't enough, the tube was inside a purple leather condom. That's how he thought of it, anyway.

"Is that pepper spray?" Kelly asked.

"Yup. It used to be hers. It might have fit okay in her purse, but now I'm forced to carry my backpack around. I feel ridiculous."

Kelly grinned and shook his head. "She loves you. And come to think of it, that might save me some trouble. Think you can spray Jared with that stuff during the triathlon?"

"No way." William put it back. "My dad tried giving me a knife."

"Wow. I had no idea your family was so violent." Kelly started jogging in place, either to warm up or because he was eager to get moving. "How did he react besides that?"

"Kind of distant, but that's how he's been lately anyway. What about you? Do you worry about self-defense?"

"You think I'm going to let anyone punch this pretty face?"

William took the opportunity to stare. Kelly's face had been showing up in his life a lot lately. In his dreams, his fantasies, or on his computer screen when he'd done a search to find a photo of him.

"You're better off running," Kelly continued. "We had a guy talk to us about it in the gay youth group. He said that the best way to avoid getting hurt is to not stick around. I've got pride, but I don't want to end up in the hospital because of it. Why give some asshole the satisfaction? I say run and live to plot your revenge. Speaking of which, your parents might feel better if their son learned how to run."

"I can run!" William said in mock offense. "I'll prove it. Let's go!"

Kelly took off, zipping down the track. William was all too happy to chase after him.

"What's the point of being gay if you're not getting any?"

This was the second question Errol asked after William had confided in him. His brother had shown up on Sunday night, kicked out by his roommate again. He was standing in the kitchen and cramming cookies into his mouth when William decided to tell him the truth. At this rate he would forever associate baked goods with coming out. Errol hadn't been surprised in the slightest. The first question he had asked was, "Got a boyfriend?"

William had shaken his head, leading to the next line of inquiry, to which William responded. "Getting any what?"

"Trouser snake. Meat popsicle. Bone cigar. Pudding torpedo."

The list had gone on and on, William increasingly horrified until he broke down and started laughing. Then he had tried coming up with some of his own. "Party stick, beef thermometer, trouser trunk, baby bazooka." It only got worse when they started dredging up colorful terms for anal sex. All that really mattered was that his brother was cool and accepted him fully. Errol wasn't exactly wrong either. William had faced the most difficult part and told those nearest to him. Now he should reap the rewards, which meant actually *doing* something gay. Like going on a date. With a guy.

He spent most of the school day obsessing over how he could make this happen. Obviously he had to ask someone. He already knew who. Even if he had other options, William couldn't imagine doing any better than Kelly. That's what made it so intimidating. He was pretty sure Kelly was out of his league. Better looking, more experienced, and quicker. Not just in terms of running speed. Kelly was smart! He still wanted to try though. They met after school, as they had done for two weeks now, alternating between the high school track and the YMCA pool. Today's session was particularly good. Kelly finally got the hang of flip turns, which he had asked William to teach him. After this breakthrough, Kelly couldn't stop doing them, and William couldn't stop watching his lithe body twist and turn gracefully beneath the water. Kelly was grinning by the end of their session. They sat on the edge of the pool, letting their muscles relax after the long workout.

"He's done for," Kelly said, still appearing elated. "Jared can't do flip turns. I don't care how fast he swims. I've finally got him beat!"

William furrowed his brow, not liking how worked up Kelly got over Jared. He was determined though to focus on the positive and show what he had to offer. He stretched out, feet in the water and towel off to one side, meaning his full body was on display. To his delight, he caught Kelly looking.

"Tomorrow's the last day to train," William said.

Kelly finished patting his head dry and let the towel settle over his shoulders. He was sitting cross-legged, but enough of his body remained in plain view too. "We should take tomorrow off. Make sure we're well-rested for Saturday."

The last thing he wanted was to spend time apart! "I'm still nowhere near as fast as you. In fact, I'm pretty sure you've learned more from me than I have from you."

"Blame the student, not the teacher." A smile played about Kelly's lips. "One more day won't make much difference. Save your strength and load up on carbs."

Then again, maybe this was the perfect opportunity. "Wow, free time after school. What will I do with myself?" Then, as casually as possible, he added, "Maybe we should celebrate."

"We haven't won yet."

"No, but we've been working hard. I figure we deserve some fun." William tore his eyes away from Kelly's body, not wanting to accidentally launch a pudding torpedo. "You know how to play pool?"

"You mean the non-swimming variety? No."

"Me neither. We'd be on equal standing for once. Maybe afterwards we can get some of those carbs you mentioned."

Kelly nodded. "Yeah, okay."

Simple as that? Kelly had pulled one foot close to examine a toenail. William had just asked him on a date, and Kelly had accepted without even thinking about it. Or reacting much. William supposed he already had lots of experience with such things and probably got asked out all the time. He tried to play it cool by not verbalizing all the questions he had. What should he wear? What would Kelly wear? Who was the top in this scenario? Please let it be Kelly! Were they going to kiss? Should they now?

"Do you know a place?" Kelly asked.

"No," William said. "I'll look one up and text you the info."

"Cool," Kelly said.

"Cool," William repeated, even though he felt anything but. This was way too exciting. He was going on a date!

As soon as William was home from school the next day, he took a shower, scrubbing every inch of his body and laughing, because he was pretty sure Kelly wouldn't be performing an inspection. No way would they hook up on the first date. Right? Would they? He started scrubbing twice as hard. Once finished showering and drying off, he put on the only suit he owned, which he had worn once before. To his aunt's funeral. With that cheerful thought in mind, he decided he was being an idiot and opted instead for a more casual approach. A pair of jeans, a light blue dress shirt, and some of that cologne that had driven Lily wild. He chuckled over the memory and was still smiling as he went downstairs.

He was digging around in his parents' bathroom for dental floss when he heard a car pull into the garage. His mother probably, since she often got off work around now. He walked to the dining room to see that he was right. Kate entered and set her purse on the table, hair a little unruly like it had been a particularly hard day.

"Do you know where the floss is?" he asked.

"The drawer closest to the medicine cabinet," she replied.

He went to fetch it and intended to take it upstairs to his own bathroom so he could brush his teeth afterwards. Then he saw his mother sitting in the dining room, elbows on the table, a hand pressed to either side of her face.

"Are you okay?" he asked.

"I'm fine, honey." No smile, just exhaustion.

"Should I get you something to drink? Coffee? Or something sweet? My mom makes the best cookies."

His attempt at humor didn't cheer her up. Instead she said, "We need to talk."

"Okay." He moved closer to the table.

His mother looked him over. "Very sharp. Do you have plans?"

"I'm going out," he said, unable to suppress a goofy smile.

"Oh. Okay. You go have fun. We can talk some other time."

William's smile faded. He sat down at the table, attention not leaving her face. "What's going on?" he said. "Tell me. Please."

Kate grabbed her purse and dug inside it with a trembling hand. He didn't know what she was searching for. Tissues maybe, because she started crying, shoving the purse away in frustration. William was on his feet in an instant, rushing to her side. He tried to hug her, which was awkward because she was still sitting down. Then he hurried to the kitchen and grabbed a few paper towels. Not ideal, but he didn't want to go farther into the house where he couldn't keep an eye on her.

"Thank you," she said when he offered them. She blew her nose, head shaking back and forth. "I hope you won't be angry at me."

"Why would I be?"

"Please. Sit down."

William did as she asked, apprehension making his skin prickle. "What's going on?"

"As I'm sure you're aware, your father and I haven't been getting along lately. We've tried to keep as much from you as possible, and I'm sorry if you've overheard anything or if we've made you feel uncomfortable by—"

"Mom!" he pleaded, wanting her to get to the point.

"Your father and I might be taking a break."

"Like a divorce?" he said, sounding panicked even to his own ears.

"I don't know. We have a lot of issues to figure out and—"

"Because he bought that stupid car? Is it really worth ruining everything just because you hate it?"

Kate's mouth became tight. "There are more issues than just the car. I only want you to be prepared in case he and I can't find a way to resolve our problems."

"I'll talk to him," William promised. "I'll make him sell it."

"Thank you, honey, but this is between me and your father. He and I need to work on this."

"What about a marriage counselor?"

His mother nodded. "That's what we'll do. I didn't mean to upset you, but I feel you're old enough to handle the truth. I didn't like how my own parents' divorce came as a surprise. That made it harder for me."

"But you're just talking about separation."

"Yes."

"Does that mean he won't live with us anymore?"

Kate clenched the paper towel in her hand. "Yes, and if that happens, I need you to think about who you want to live with. We won't decide for you."

William felt lost. He had assumed his parents would always be together, that he would never be faced with a choice like this. In his heart, he knew he wanted to stay with his mother, but the idea of his father being alone and incapable of taking care of himself… Kate did everything. The cooking, the cleaning, and keeping everyone on schedule. She wasn't only a housewife. She had worked full time at the post office for as long as William could remember. Maybe that was why she was sick of his father, because he wasn't pulling his weight.

"I'll help out around the house," William said. "Just tell me what to do. Don't give up on Dad yet. Okay?"

His mother managed a smile. "What I want you to do is to go out and have fun. I'm sorry I burdened you with all of this."

"You need to have fun too," he said. "When's the last time you and Dad went on vacation? I'm old enough now to be on my own. You guys could take a trip together, figure everything out and—"

"Nothing has been decided yet," Kate said patiently. "You're very sweet to care so much. I love you."

He reached across the table to place a hand over hers. "I love you too."

Normally this was enough to make her smile, but as William rose and left the room, she didn't seem to notice him go. Regardless, he still felt bad for doing so.

* * * * *

Trying not to think about something usually leads to thinking about trying to not think of that thing. Errol had gone through a Buddhist phase when he first entered high school and had sung the praises of meditation to William, instructing him on how to achieve a higher state of consciousness. "Clear your mind. Think about nothing. Like… don't think at all." William had tried his best, but his thoughts never went completely silent. The closest he could get was thinking really hard about not wanting to think. "Your mind is too young, too undisciplined," Errol had said back then. The most insubordinate guy in the world accusing him of being undisciplined!

Age had nothing to do with it. William still couldn't clear his mind like that. He had gotten pretty good at denial, but his thoughts and emotions still came unbidden. He tried anyway as his date with Kelly began. They met at the pool hall, and even though Kelly looked handsome and smelled good and felt warm when standing next to him at the billiards table, William's mind kept returning to his mother. For a short period, he did manage to have fun and put on a good show for Kelly, but then it all came rushing back: his mother sitting at the table, hands trembling, face crumpled in anguish as she tried to hold back tears. How could he enjoy himself when she was in so much pain?

"You okay?" Kelly asked. He had left to use the restroom. William, guard still down and turmoil in plain sight, hadn't noticed his return. He pushed away his sad feelings when he saw the concern on Kelly's face. He cared! That was a thrill of its own, and it certainly didn't hurt that he looked so fine. They had spent hours together nearly naked at the YMCA, but for some reason, seeing him in a purple dress shirt, the sleeves rolled up over his dark skin—well, it sure made forgetting his problems easier!

William smiled and suggested they grab a bite to eat. He focused on being on his first date. With a guy! If things continued to go well tonight he might even have a boyfriend! Such a simple word, but it sounded magical. He couldn't help wondering if it held as much significance for Kelly. He did seem to be enjoying himself, even though a booth at Burger King was far from luxurious. No doubt he had been on better dates.

"How many boyfriends have you had?" William asked, dragging french fries through ketchup.

"Oh." Kelly lifted the bun of his fish sandwich and peered at it critically. "I'm not sure. Do you want me to count?"

"Yes."

Kelly laughed. "It's hard to say. Some guys you date for a few days before you figure out it was a bad idea. Do they count?"

"I want a complete list," William said. "Names, ages, and photos. Everything."

Kelly smirked. Then he bit into his sandwich, face thoughtful as he chewed. "Seventy-three," he said after he had swallowed. "Not counting one-night stands."

William didn't hide his abhorrence. "Seventy-three?"

"It was a joke! Wow, you must really think I'm a slut!"

"I do now!"

They laughed and consumed a few more bites.

"More like seven," Kelly said. "And only one of them felt serious. Maybe because he was my first."

"First boyfriend?"

"Yes, and just about everything else."

"Tell me about him," William said, cramming more fries in his mouth.

"His name was José, but his parents were Italian. I guess they just liked the name. He had dark hair and skin, so everyone assumed he was Mexican. I used to tease him about it." Kelly's smile was soft. "He was a year older than me, but also inexperienced. I'm not sure what else to say. Our time together was fun. And sweet. I liked him a lot."

"Were you in love?" William asked, jealousy making a stab at him.

Kelly exhaled. "I was fourteen years old, he was fifteen. It felt like love at the time, but we didn't have anything in common. I'm pretty sure I was more in love with the idea of being in love."

"Huh?"

Kelly considered him. "Unlike you, I didn't struggle with my sexuality. I figured out early on who I was and what I wanted. Waiting until I was old enough to *get* what I wanted—that was my challenge. I had plenty of years to dream about being with another guy. Not just sexually. A lot of romantic fairytales played through my mind. When I finally found someone who wanted me back, that's all I needed. I didn't worry about what else we might have in common."

"So what happened?"

"José got a driver's license, and with it a lot more freedom. He met someone online he liked better. A new guy at the gay youth group had caught my eye, so José and I agreed to explore our options. I remember feeling like that was a very mature decision, when in retrospect, we were both just horny and looking to sleep around. What about you?"

William blinked. "I want more than just that!"

Kelly laughed. "No, I mean have you been in any relationships?"

"Remember my friend who rubbed her boobs on me? That's as far as I've gotten."

"Seriously? Wow!"

Kelly's smile was difficult to interpret. Was this a good thing? Did being a virgin make him somehow more appealing? William had heard other guys treat a girl's virginity like it was a prize, preferring that anyone they date begin as one. For guys, being a virgin was considered shameful. Funny how that worked.

As for being in love with the idea of love, he felt they had enough in common for it not to be that. He and Kelly were both athletic and driven. Kelly cared about competing more, but William enjoyed it too. As they were finishing their meals, they talked about the triathlon again, but for once Jared's name wasn't mentioned. This made William happier than it probably should have.

"So what happens once it's all over?" Kelly asked. "Are you going to keep running with me every other day?"

"I'd rather go back to swimming in the mornings. I have the most energy then." Concerned about pushing him away, William added, "Unless you want to keep practicing. Then I guess I could wait until the afternoon."

"No," Kelly said. "The Olympics aren't looking for swimmers. Well, they are, but that's not how I'm hoping to get there. So I guess we're done training together."

"Everything ends eventually." He swallowed, the words having more significance than he intended, the conversation with his mother haunting him once more.

Kelly leaned forward. "Of course, there are plenty more episodes of *Battle Beasts* for you to show me."

"*Beast Wars*," William murmured automatically. Then he

looked up. "I still want to hang out with you. A lot. Every day."

Kelly studied his face. "Is something wrong?"

Busted. William exhaled. "Sorry. I promised myself I wouldn't let it ruin our night."

"It won't. Tell me."

"My mom," William began, shaking his head at the memory. "After school she sat me down at the kitchen table. She said she needed to talk, but then she just started crying."

"What? Why?"

"She's been arguing with my dad a lot. I don't know why. They always bickered, but lately it's gotten really bad. Bad enough that she's thinking of leaving him."

Kelly's mouth fell open. "She said that?"

"Kind of. She said they might take a break. Then she asked who I'd want to live with. I couldn't answer. How am I supposed to? I love them both." William struggled to collect his scattered thoughts. "They just need a break from everything else, not each other. I told them to take a trip together. I don't remember the last time we had a family vacation, and now I'm old enough to stay home. They just need to reconnect."

Kelly nodded. "Probably. All couples argue."

"Exactly." He frowned, scowling at the empty wrappers on their table. "I'm having a talk with my dad this weekend. No stupid car is worth ruining a marriage over." He wasn't going to let his father's mid-life crisis destroy their family. William's mother was probably too nice to say what needed to be said, but he wouldn't hesitate. Not anymore. She needed him. "I should get home. To be honest with you, I feel a little guilty having fun when I know my mom is so upset."

"Okay," Kelly said. "I understand completely."

They left the smell of fried grease behind, returning to the billiard hall where William's car was parked. As they drove, he alternated between troubled thoughts and longing glances at Kelly. Their date was ruined, but he couldn't feel sorry for himself when a marriage had been too.

"You'll be okay," Kelly said. They were standing in front of the car, about to say goodbye. "No matter what happens, your parents love you. That won't change. Even if they split up—and they might not—you'll still be the bridge that connects them. You'll still be a family."

He was right. Family wasn't defined by everyone living under the same roof. His brothers had moved out, but they were still family. If his parents couldn't live together—that would hurt, but he would still love them both, and he was certain they would keep loving him. As for the guy who had given him hope… William threw his arms around Kelly, pulling him close. He touched his nose to Kelly's neck, smelling his skin, before pressing his lips there. Then he squeezed tighter, emotion rising in his chest.

"Thanks," William rasped, taking a step back to look him in the eye. "For everything."

"Yeah." Kelly seemed a little taken aback. Was he moving too fast?

"Okay." William wanted a real kiss, but maybe that was best saved for a happier occasion. "See you at the race tomorrow."

Kelly nodded. "See you there."

William walked to his car, opened the door, and glanced back at Kelly, heart thudding in his chest. One story might be coming to an end, but another had just begun.

Chapter Five

Butterflies! William was used to them in his stomach, but never had the metaphorical creatures spread to the rest of his body. From the tips of his fingers down to his toes, he felt tingly, excited, and lightweight. Only his head didn't allow room because it was too filled with memories of his date yesterday and dreams of what might be. Kelly. That's all he could think about. Kelly, Kelly, Kelly. He even found himself whispering the name out loud, laughing gleefully afterwards.

He was braced for this bliss to dissipate when he went downstairs for breakfast, but instead he found his parents sitting calmly at the table together. He couldn't remember the last time that had happened. When he tentatively mentioned the triathlon, they both implied they would both be there. Deciding the day would be full of sunshine and rainbows after all, he focused on feeding himself. When it was time to go, they drove him to where the race was set to begin. They took his mother's minivan instead of the convertible, but at least his parents didn't bicker on the way.

They dropped him off at the public pool, then continued to the high school to wait at the finish line with the other friends and families of entrants. William sought out Kelly, who seemed jittery about the race, and did his best to reassure him. Then it began. First each participant swam a practice lap to qualify for their starting position. Everyone was silent as the results were called out. William didn't have long to wait. He would be second to enter the pool. He moved to the nearby bike stations to get set up before that part of the race began. While arranging his items around the bike as efficiently as possible, he heard Kelly's name called. Fifth place! Not bad! He felt warm inside while fussing over some final details, his thoughts drifting back to their training sessions at the pool. Then he went to see how Kelly was doing.

"Congratulations," William said, placing a hand on his shoulder as an excuse to touch him.

"Thanks," Kelly said, half-turning to shoot him a smile. "So what exactly am I doing here? Should I douse the bike in holy water or something? Can I get a priest to bless it for me?"

William chuckled. "Just make sure your stuff is ready to go. I put my shoes next to the rear wheel, since I'll need them first. I'm not bothering with socks, are you? I'm also leaving my pack open so I can pull on my bike shorts. The girl next to me is swimming in hers. That's either clever or stupid. I can't decide."

Kelly shrugged. "I wouldn't bother at all if no one was around, but I don't want people to see me running around in scuba panties."

"The pros use special suits for the entire race. Anyway, be sure to check your bike helmet too. Mine had the strap buckled, which would have slowed me down."

"I think I've got the wrong size." Kelly stooped to pick up the helmet. "Like they gave me one intended for a child."

He put it on his head, and sure enough, it mostly sat on top of his skull, looking more like a mushroom cap than headgear. William smiled and took the helmet from him but stayed near while examining it. He liked their bodies being so close. A little too much. They were in their swimsuits, skin drying out in the sun after the brief swim. He could feel their combined heat growing in the space between them.

William cleared his throat, trying to focus on the task at hand. "This is adjustable," he said, reaching inside the helmet. "You just turn this wheel here aaaand…" He put the helmet back on Kelly, and this time it slid over his head, but only just. "That's the maximum size. You have a big head."

"I have a big brain," Kelly corrected.

"Or maybe it's your ego taking up all that room."

Kelly smiled, eyes half-lidded. He snatched the helmet from his head and hung it on one handlebar. Then he placed shorts and shirt on the seat.

"Maybe I should start doing this every morning," William said. "I'll just hop out of bed and race out the front door where the day's outfit will be waiting on my bicycle."

"Does that mean you sleep naked?" Kelly asked.

"Oh," William said, cheeks starting to burn. "Uh…"

"What are you doing here?" a new voice demanded.

Kelly tensed. Then his expression became controlled. Together they turned to face Jared. William recognized him from their brief confrontation in the hall, but now he scrutinized Jared with renewed interest. For a guy Kelly used to have a crush on, he was surprisingly average. Jared had a runner's build, light acne dotting his shoulders and face. His brown hair was a little poofy and not styled in any specific way. His eyes might have been nice if not so hard and joyless as he scowled at his former friend.

Kelly's voice was equally cold when he responded. "I took another look at that trophy and decided it would look good in my room. You didn't have any plans for it, did you?"

Blood flowed to Jared's face, turning it crimson. "You're not going to ruin this for me. Either of you." He glared briefly in William's direction. Then he turned and stomped away.

Kelly watched him go. Scratch that, he *stared* after him, gaze unwavering, arms crossed over his chest. Even as Jared worked to get his own bike prepared, Kelly maintained his vigil.

William's stomach sank. "Geez, you must really like him."

"Seriously?" Kelly said, finally tearing his eyes away. "That's the vibe you're getting?"

"If you didn't care about him, you wouldn't get so upset. It signifies an emotional investment or whatever."

"*Whatever* is right." Kelly turned around and searched his bike, seeking some other advantage. They were both in the triathlon, but for very different reasons. To William it was the culmination of their time training together, moving side by side toward a common goal. For Kelly it was about hurting the guy he still had a crush on. William felt certain that was correct. If Kelly didn't still have feelings for Jared, there wouldn't be so much emotion there. Where did that leave William? Was he just a rebound? An option Kelly was exploring but didn't take seriously? William waited for Kelly to say more, or to even acknowledge that he existed. He didn't. William had served his purpose and was no longer needed.

Feeling both hurt and slighted, he quietly returned to the pool, taking his place in line behind Anna Herbert, a heavy-set girl who had slid through the water with impressive agility.

"Looking forward to the race?" William asked her.

"Mm-hm," Anna replied.

"If you don't mind me asking, what's your motivation?"

Anna shrugged. "I thought it would be fun."

William nodded. "In that case, I hope you win."

He studied his feet as the other contenders took their places. Part of him hoped Kelly would come apologize, but he probably wasn't even looking this way. Chances were he was facing in the wrong direction, just so he could glare at Jared.

Coach Watson gave them a lecture about good sportsmanship. Then the starting whistle blew. Anna Herbert dove in. William watched her, eager for his turn, wanting to exercise and burn off some of his frustration. When the whistle blew again, he plunged into the water. Each contender would swim up and down every lane of the pool before moving on to the next portion of the race. William didn't usually focus on speed, but he did now, because he found he wanted to get away. Kelly was somewhere behind him—the first guy he had developed feelings for, the first guy to hurt him and choose someone else. William wanted nothing more than to escape those emotions.

He passed Anna two lanes before climbing out of the pool. When accepting a towel, he glanced over in time to spot Jared diving in. Once again he wondered what Kelly saw in him. They were both runners. Was that what made Kelly love him? William had been running lately, despite not being very good. Didn't that count for anything?

He made it to his bike, pulling on his shirt and his shoes—which wasn't easy with damp skin. He was getting ready to pedal when Anna dropped her helmet and it wobbled over to bump against his wheel, so he got off to fetch it and hand it back. She smiled her appreciation, which made him feel a little better. Not everyone in this race was crazy! As he began biking, he wished people could just be nice to each other—the whole world, not just to those in the triathlon. If everyone agreed to be kind, most problems would be solved. No more war or violence, rape or murder, or anything else horrible. Just people being decent. That's how his mother had raised him. Too bad she couldn't be a mother to everyone.

Not that his brothers were perfect. Errol could be selfish, and Spencer... He was pretty great, except when he had decided to enlist in the Marines. Then he had become a monster, lifting weights constantly, consuming protein shakes, snapping at William or anyone else who dared interrupt the endless military-related videos he watched. One time, when William refused to relinquish the laptop to him, Spencer had shoved him aside, taken it by force, and then slammed the door in his face. William ran straight into that door, hurting his nose bad enough that it wouldn't stop bleeding. Once Spencer finally got accepted into the Marines, all that bad energy had disappeared. Spencer went back to being a bossy and overbearing but generally cool older brother who always looked out for him.

Maybe this was a similar obsession for Kelly. A white whale that needed to be harpooned before he could return to calmer seas. William abandoned his bike, accepting a paper cup of sports drink from a volunteer. He thanked the man, then started jogging. So far he hadn't seen anyone pass him on the bikes. Anna hadn't been far behind, taking her drink shortly after him. That meant he was in the lead. Kelly only wanted Jared to lose. William was in a position to make that happen. If he did, maybe Kelly would be free to love him. Hell, maybe it would *make* Kelly love him. Who else could give him such a present? William picked up speed, feeling motivated. All the training had paid off. Sure, his body was hurting and starting to fight against him, but he was used to that. He wasn't out of resources yet. That's what counted. He kept his pace steady, remembering to breathe, trying to think of any other advice Kelly had given him.

He was nearing the school when he heard footsteps from behind. William tried to outrun them, but it was no use. He simply wasn't fast enough. The beat behind him drummed nearer, then caught up. He glanced over and saw Kelly, who had slowed now to run by his side. William knew Kelly could go faster, but he chose to match his pace. If this kept up, they would cross the finish line together. Romantic, but why risk losing the race? William smiled his appreciation, then said, "Win this."

Kelly's grin was wild. Then he nodded.

From the other side of William, another form blew past. Jared! Kelly had noticed, determination hardening his features. Then his beautiful legs stretched out, becoming impossible arcs that propelled him forward. William, amazed, enjoyed a perspective no cameraman would be fast enough to capture. Kelly had already reached Jared. Now they ran side by side, but not in harmonious union. William could see them both straining to take the lead as he continued to fall behind. If either one of them ran out of energy, or found more, then—

The tip of his foot hit something, just the very end of his toes, but at this speed it sent him flying. The sensation was almost enjoyable until his body hit the ground. He rolled, feeling his least padded bones take the brunt of the fall: his shins, elbows, and forearms. He had the sense to cover his head and ended up on his side, eyes winced shut against the pain. He mentally checked himself before moving. Nothing felt broken. Just sore. Rolling over onto his back, he groaned and lifted the arm that hurt most.

"What happened?" Kelly asked.

William's eyes shot open. "What are you doing? Run!"

"What happened?" Kelly repeated with concern. "Are you all right?"

"I tripped. It's just a scratch. Go!"

Kelly looked toward the finish line, muscles tensing, ready to launch toward it. Then he looked back at William, the urgency draining from his face. His lips twitched, as if fighting down a smile. William forced himself to sit up, hoping it would convince Kelly that he didn't need help.

"You know," Kelly said, crouching next to him, "they say dogs have antiseptic saliva. I saw one not far back. If you want, I can fetch it for you so it can lick your wounds."

William gawped. "The race—"

"Doesn't matter," Kelly said with a shake of his head.

William felt emotion rushing to his chest. "What about Jared?"

"Doesn't matter," Kelly repeated.

Okay, now he felt like crying. Or laughing. "What about me?"

Kelly's white teeth flashed. He stood and held out his hand. "That's a very big question. One I'm not ready to answer just yet."

William accepted the hand and was pulled to his feet. Then he waved Kelly away. "Come on. Let's finish the race."

Kelly shook his head. "You go ahead if you want. I never should have entered. You're here for the right reason. So is Jared. I'm not."

"You sure?"

"Yeah." Kelly looked to the crowds. "I'm going to join my family. Once it's all over, come find us. Okay?"

William nodded. His body had gone stiff, but he forced himself to keep moving, hoping to loosen up again. A guy he didn't recognize zipped past him. William felt momentarily proud that he had managed such a huge lead. He was still in third place, now that Kelly had walked to the sidelines, but he didn't expect that to last. He lurched along, seeing his parents cheering him on. That got him the rest of the way to the finish line, but Anna Herbert huffed past him just before he could cross it. William didn't focus on her though, because his parents were both there, hugging him, fussing over his injuries, smiling at each other in mutual pride. He hadn't expected this as a prize! Or the feelings Kelly had all but confessed. Even though he hadn't come in first, William still felt like he had won the race.

Gay paradise. That's where Kelly had brought him. William was in a church, but instead of pews and Bibles, he was surrounded by people his own age, all of them gay. Or perhaps it was more accurate to say that none of them were straight. Even that seemed inadequate. At least one person there was transitioning to a different gender, and he overheard a brief argument about pansexuality—whatever that meant. William had a lot to learn, but one fact was now clear to him: He wasn't alone. No matter how understanding his friends and family had been, this was a place where he didn't have to explain himself. Here he would be safe and understood. No wonder Kelly had come out sooner and had so many relationships. William felt like he was at a boy buffet!

"My name's Mike."

"Hey, I'm Julian. Welcome!"

"Are you new here? I'm Richard."

William couldn't keep track of all the guys who introduced themselves, one after the other. He felt giddy, but that had more to do with Kelly than anyone else here. The triathlon had cemented their relationship. No more Jared. He didn't come up in conversation anymore. William had even met the family, Kelly's mother and father just as wonderful as their son. Same with his little brother, Royal, who despite attempting to act aloof, clearly admired his older sibling. As for William's own family, they had celebrated his completion of the race by going out to eat, his parents getting along just like they used to. Crisis averted. Now he could focus on more important matters. Speaking of which… He tried to locate Kelly, but yet another guy had blocked his vision, this one thin, blond, and cute.

"Hello!" the newcomer said. "I'm Layne, and yes, you will fall in love with me. Have you eaten? You look famished. Come along!"

Before he knew what was happening, William found an arm wrapped around his, dragging him toward a folding table covered with snacks and drinks. For such a skinny guy, Layne sure had an iron grip!

"I'm actually here with someone," he said.

"I noticed," Layne replied. "All good things must come to an end so that better things can begin. I already feel a connection, like we know each other intimately. By the way, what's your name?"

"William."

Layne appeared delighted. "I *love* that name. Can I call you Will instead? Or how about Billy. Bill? No, Billy is best. Like my doll. He's anatomically correct, you know."

William's mouth moved, trying to keep up with the conversation. "I have action figures," he managed.

"See!" Layne slapped his arm playfully, leaving it there so he could rub William's bicep. "We have so much in common. You know what we should do? Set up a play date so Billy can meet your… What are they?"

"*Beast Wars* figures."

Layne scrunched up his nose. "Okay. That might work. Do you have a bear?"

William finally spotted Kelly. He was in one corner and talking to his friend Bonnie, who they had picked up on the drive over. "Um, I don't have a bear, but I do have a cheetah."

"That's not even remotely witty," Layne said in chastising tones. "Are you new at being gay? Maybe your blood sugar is low. Have something to eat."

William reached for a brownie, but Layne slapped his hand. "Are you trying to ruin your figure? This is better." He grabbed a whole-wheat cracker and held it up, like he wanted to feed it to William.

"Uhhh…"

"It *is* a little dry," Layne said. "I suppose we can let our hair down just this once. Here." He thrust an aerosol can at William. "Squeeze my cheese."

William took the can, pointed the nozzle at the cracker Layne still held, and squirted out a dollop of orange goo. "Why does this make me feel dirty?" he murmured.

"We're just getting started," Layne said, holding up the cracker again.

He opened his mouth unwillingly, but thankfully Kelly

appeared, snatching the cracker away. "I saved you a seat, William. Let's go."

Layne opened his mouth, but before he could speak, Kelly popped the cracker inside to silence him. As they walked away, William heard a garbled "Call me!" from behind.

"Are you okay?" Kelly asked, leading them to a circle of seats.

"I think you just saved my life."

Kelly laughed. "Layne is harmless. Mostly. He can get a little handsy at times."

"Oh." They sat down on two folding chairs. "Did you guys used to date?"

"Layne?" Kelly said incredulously. "No! I have standards."

William looked back at Layne, whose tongue was sticking out one corner of his mouth as he decorated more crackers with the squeeze cheese. He was definitely cute. If Layne was beneath Kelly's notice, then just how picky was he? And who had he been with? William spotted a guy with dark hair and a number of tattoos. "What about him?"

Kelly followed his gaze but didn't answer the question. "Do you really want to know my history with each of these people?"

William thought about it. "Yes."

"Why?" Kelly asked, as if genuinely confused.

Before William could answer, an older man clapped his hands to get their attention. The remainder of the seats filled as the lecture began, the group leader speaking about the pioneers of gay rights. The history went back further than William had realized. He wished he could take notes because he discovered so many heroes that—until now—he didn't realize he had. Audre Lorde, Harvey Milk, Barbara Gittings, Ruth Ellis—he promised himself to research these names and to learn more about them. He might have been nervous about coming out, but they had fought for change!

The only time his attention wavered was when he noticed Layne staring. His leg was crossed over one knee, foot bobbing in the air or occasionally waving back and forth to get his attention. When this succeeded, Layne's eyebrows waggled, or his lips puckered. During one such display, Layne's eyes moved to Kelly. Then they widened and quickly averted. William glanced over to find Kelly glaring in Layne's direction. He liked that, the idea of being protected, of belonging to someone.

Once the lecture was over, Kelly seemed determined to make sure he wasn't hit on again. He led them away from the other guys and toward his female friends. Lisa was one of them, a quiet mousey girl who kept looking between them and blushing. "Are you two dating?" she asked.

William joined her in the red cheeks club. Yes, they were dating, but they hadn't put an official title on it yet. Presumably he was Kelly's boyfriend. God that sounded good! He wanted to hear this said out loud, but instead, Kelly's mouth clamped shut. Maybe he was private about such things.

"Who drew penises on all of the crackers?" Bonnie demanded, walking over to show them one. Sure enough, the orange outline of a crude phallus had been created with squeeze cheese. She narrowed her eyes at William with faux accusation. "It was you, wasn't it?"

"No," William said. He noticed Layne watching from a distance, having overheard the conversation. He held a finger to his lip and winked. William took the cracker from Bonnie, tossed it in his mouth, and winked back. Why not give the guy a thrill? Layne pretended to swoon. Then he lost his balance and fell for real.

"So what do you think of our little group?" Lisa asked.

William chuckled. "I love it here."

When to kiss someone? When to hold their hand? When to touch them in any way more intimate than friendship? William wished such things were taught at school, because he truly didn't know. Kelly must though. He had relationship experience, so William patiently waited for guidance. When it was time for the next step, Kelly would let him know.

After a week, William decided he was sick of waiting. He wanted more. If he was accused of rushing things, he could play it off as a beginner's mistake. All he needed was an opportunity, and one just happened to present itself. Kelly's birthday. A first kiss would make the perfect present, assuming he didn't mess it up. Kelly had invited him to the festivities after school. William had the time and the place. He just needed the knowhow, so he called Errol, who was always happy to discuss such things.

"Just watch some lesbian porn," his brother advised. "That's always full of kissing. Study what you see and then tone it down by seventy percent."

"Okay," William said, "but do you think it's somehow different when a guy kisses a guy?"

"Not really," Errol said. "I remember there being more stubble. That's about it."

William checked the name on the phone's display to make sure he was speaking to his brother. "Wait, you've kissed a—"

"It was a dare, and not a big deal. As far as I can tell, lips are lips, no matter who they belong to."

That had made him feel little better. Technically he did have some experience, but he followed Errol's advice anyway, searching online for lesbian porn. He watched it with disinterest, beginning to question if kissing was worth pursuing. Then he stumbled upon an animated gif of two guys kissing, their lips mashing together in an infinite loop, and his interest revitalized.

On the big day, his anticipation doubled when Kelly didn't show up for school. His mother always let him take birthdays off, which was a great idea, and one William hoped to convince his mom about next year. He went through his daily routine, feeling like his life was about to change. Most guys would probably laugh at him, having already lost their virginity, but for William this was still a big deal.

After school he went home to get freshened up. Then he drove to Kelly's house for the first time. The neighborhood was more upscale than his own, the architecture newer, many of the houses having three-car garages. He rang the bell, taking note of the etched glass on either side of the door. Then he turned to consider the manicured lawns, wondering if he should advertise his mowing services here. When the door opened, he spun around to find someone even more beautiful than the surroundings. Kelly always looked good, no matter the clothing. Right now he wore a dress shirt and slacks. He was practically glowing, meaning his special day must be going well. William promised himself not to mess it up.

"I heard rumors there's a birthday boy somewhere around here," he said. "Is it you?"

Kelly continued grinning at him.

"I had no idea you lived in such a nice neighborhood. I didn't know you were rich."

Kelly put on a cool expression. "I try to keep a low profile. I get a lot of gold diggers after me. Come on in."

William followed, noticing the nice furnishings and the

spotless house. His own home was rarely dirty, but everything here seemed more organized, which appealed to him. Kelly led him to the kitchen. Bonnie was seated on one of the bar stools. Mrs. Phillips stood at the counter and conversed with her. Laisha was a large woman who didn't seem to share her son's athleticism, but had definitely passed on her sharp wit to him. When Kelly had first told him about his mother being a lawyer, William had pictured someone severe, but she was delightfully warm.

"We're just waiting for the ice cream to soften a bit," Laisha said. "Then we'll have cake."

"Great," Kelly said, seeming restless. "I'm going to show William my room."

Together they walked up the stairs, the carpet fluffy and white, like it had just been vacuumed. The stairwell in William's home was dim, but this one was light and airy, overlooking the front room. Pristine furniture, clean surfaces, and not a hint of dust. Was it too late to be adopted? He loved it here!

"It's cool to finally see where you live," he said. "Makes me embarrassed about my place."

"I like your house," Kelly responded. "Besides, I'm just as broke as you are. At least until I open my presents. My grandparents always send cash."

"Nice," William said, the subject of gifts making him nervous. "I'll give you my present later, okay?"

"You don't have to give me anything," Kelly said.

He didn't believe that for a second. "It's in the car," William lied. Then again, maybe they *would* kiss in his car. He had a few locations in mind, but nothing concrete.

They entered Kelly's room and he felt like kissing him right then and there, because it wasn't so different than his own. Orderly. Controlled. Not quite as tidy, but from his experience, few people their age ran such a tight ship. Kelly's room had an extra touch of class. The vaulted ceilings were nice, and the computer in one corner sported a monitor so huge that he mistook it for a television. He eyed the bed next to the desk, a fleeting fantasy racing through his mind that he banished by focusing on the loaded bookshelf on the opposite wall.

"Sorry to disappoint you," Kelly said, "but I don't have any Transformers."

William grinned, noticing the framed photos on the wall. He

moved to examine them. "Are these yours?"

"Some of them," Kelly said, joining him. "Most of the black and whites are, although the smoking-hot guy pouring water over himself is by Will McBride. And this one is by Nan Goldin. The sailor boy and captain obviously isn't mine. You're familiar with Pierre et Gilles, right?"

William shook his head.

"Oh. Well my photos aren't next to theirs because I think they deserve to be. I'm not that vain. I only hung them up recently to help me compare what I'm doing. And to see what I need to learn or which direction I should go."

"My action figures seem even lamer now," William said. "I don't have anything artistic like this."

"Sure you do! Someone had to sculpt that rhino figure, decide how it would be painted, and design the parts to move correctly. That's art too. Maybe even of a higher caliber, since all I have to do is point a camera and push a button."

"It's not that easy," William said, examining the photos that Kelly had identified as his own. A photo of the high school track taken from ground level made it appear more like the barren landscape of an alien planet. In another, Royal flexed nonexistent muscles, tears of laughter in his eyes. "Remind me to show you the photos on my phone," he murmured. "They're terrible. Oh." Another photo had caught his eye. Jared. He might have been running on a cold winter day because his breath was visible, hanging on the air. Jared's hair was mussed, his brow low in concentration, which made him look tough. And sexy. Worst of all he was featured on the wall as part of a collection of things that Kelly loved. His brother, competitive running, and guys. He wondered if he'd ever end up there too.

"I've been meaning to take that down," Kelly said. "Unfortunately it's one of my best."

"Yeah, in more than one way."

"Meaning?"

William looked over at him. "I never found Jared attractive before. Now I know what you saw in him. This photograph reveals it."

Kelly looked to the photo and stared.

"Honey!" shouted a loud voice that sounded like it was in the same room. "We're ready!"

William flinched.

Kelly laughed. "She should have been an opera singer instead of a lawyer. Let's go before she really gets loud."

They went downstairs to a cake alight with tiny flames. As Kelly blew out the candles, William attempted to set aside his jealous feelings. Maybe it took time to get over a crush. That could be the reason they hadn't kissed yet. William wouldn't let that discourage him. He liked Kelly and was willing to fight. Someday he *would* be included on that wall!

Presents followed, as did a trip to a camera store, where Kelly traipsed around gleefully like a little kid who had won a Toys "R" Us shopping spree. He chose a new lens for his camera, a ridiculously long one that would let him take photos from far away. Then they went to a nearby restaurant for Italian food. Kelly's father, Doug, told one funny story after another, most of them embarrassing work-related anecdotes. When his wife chastised him for this, he said, "Hey, if you don't like toilet humor, you shouldn't have married a plumber!"

William smiled throughout most of the meal. What a great family! He wondered if they knew he was dating their son, but he wasn't too concerned. He hadn't told his own parents yet, wanting to give them more time to adjust to him being gay. When the festivities wound down and everyone left the restaurant, Kelly's family returned home and Bonnie hitched a ride with them. Before they left, William saw more than one pair of eyes filled with a knowing twinkle. He supposed that answered his question. He felt elated once they were alone again, Kelly pointing his new camera at the restaurant.

Then he turned, aiming it at William. He remained still as Kelly took a few steps back. William summoned the affection he felt to the surface, hoping it would be captured on film. The shutter clicked.

Kelly lowered the device. "Have you been in front of a camera before?"

"No more than anyone else."

"Go on, admit it," Kelly said, raising the camera again. "You're a supermodel, aren't you?" He took a series of photos, William grinning in elation. Take that, Jared! Kelly kept backing up, now standing in a lane where he could get hit by a car.

"Shouldn't we find somewhere more scenic?" William suggested.

Kelly stopped playing around. "You're right. I need a view. This thing is made for distance."

"I think I know a place." One of the locations he had singled out. The kind ideal for giving someone a present.

He drove them downtown, Kelly playing with his camera on the way. That was fine. He wanted their destination to be a surprise. Maybe he should have used a blindfold. They parked next to the Pfluger Bridge, which stretched over the Colorado River. William led them to it, heart pounding in anticipation. Or fear. He really didn't want to mess this up. The evening had grown dark enough that Austin's skyline was lit, Kelly gasping in appreciation. Once they reached the middle of the bridge, Kelly leaned against the rail, taking more photos, checking the display, making adjustments, and snapping even *more* photos. This seemed to stretch on forever, and while William was glad the location was a hit, the wait wasn't helping his nerves.

"So…" He cleared his throat, hoping to attract attention. "Is that thing digital, or do you have real film inside?"

"Digital." Kelly lowered the camera. "I used to have a film camera, but I blew through way too much cash on refills and development."

"Oh." William thought of the Italian food, in particular the garlic bread, and worried about his breath. He searched his pockets, finding the gum he had brought. After shoving a stick in his mouth, he extended the pack to Kelly. "Want a piece?"

"Sure," Kelly said, his expression difficult to read.

This was it, he supposed. The scene was set, the backdrop romantic. Almost. He kept waiting for solitude, since they weren't the only ones on the bridge. Finally, the area was clear of pedestrians. All they had to do was kiss, except now they both had gum in their mouths, which would surely get in the way. William spit his out in the wrapper. "I'm done," he said. "Are you?"

"I guess so." Kelly mimicked his actions. This was so inconvenient! Why did people need to mash their mouths together? There had to be a better way of expressing feelings. Kelly started messing with his camera again, switching back to the normal lens and snapping a picture of him, probably looking all stupid and indecisive.

"I thought you were done taking photos."

"I can be," Kelly said. "If you can think of something better to do."

William glanced around again. They were still alone. He licked his lips, not wanting them to be dry. Then he worried they were too wet. God this was ridiculous! He just needed to do it! "I wanted to give you your birthday present."

Kelly smiled, leaning back against the rail. "I'm ready."

"Yeah. Good." William moved closer and accidentally kicked Kelly's shoe. "Oh sorry."

"It's okay."

Kelly appeared patient and maybe a little amused, like he already knew the game. William would soon wipe that smirk from his lips! He moved forward with new determination, only to look down at a camera lens pressing against his chest, holding him at bay.

"Sorry," Kelly said. He lifted the strap from his neck and bent down to place the camera in its case. When he was upright again, he said, "So. About that present."

Ugh. Everything was ruined. William had wanted this moment to be spontaneous, to surprise Kelly and sweep him off his feet. Instead he had bungled it multiple times now and—

Kelly moved closer, expression serious, eyes inviting. Little space remained between them. William's entire world became that handsome face. He reached out, running a thumb along brown skin, the mouth parting slightly. Then their lips touched, so gently at first that he worried he had missed the mark, but no, they brushed together again and suddenly kissing made sense, because William wanted nothing more. He pressed his lips against Kelly's, reveling in the sensation. His hand remained cupped against Kelly's cheek as they kissed, fingers stroking his ear. Then he took a step back.

Kelly was wide-eyed, as if William had managed to surprise him after all. "That was incredible!"

William grinned, feeling proud.

"And here I was thinking it was your first time," Kelly said.

"It was."

"Then you're either a fast learner," Kelly chuckled, "or one of your pillows at home is covered in slobber."

"A little of both," William said. "So what do you think? Is that a good birthday present, or should I have actually spent money?"

"It's perfect," Kelly said, looking dreamy-eyed. "Although

I'm more interested in the implications. No, that can wait. What I really want is a rerun."

No problem! With the first time out of the way, and having seen how much Kelly appreciated his efforts, William felt more confident. They locked lips, and this time it was closer to what William had seen on the Internet. Feeling extra brave, he even tried a little tongue, which felt super weird. He broke off the kiss again, the tingling sensation making him laugh.

Kelly bent down to pick up his camera bag and slung it over one shoulder. Then he cocked his head, as if reappraising him.

"What did you mean by implications?" William asked.

"Ah. I wasn't sure if you were interested in me or not."

That didn't make sense. "We're dating, aren't we? Of course I'm interested!"

"We're dating," Kelly repeated, like it was news to him. Apparently it was, because he added, "Since when, exactly?"

"Since our first date," William said. "When we played pool together. Right?"

"Sure!" Kelly nodded eagerly. "Yeah! Of course!"

In other words, *whatever you say!* It all became clear then. The reason they hadn't discussed titles, or made much progress, is because they hadn't actually been a couple. "Oh my god."

Kelly, sharp as ever, had also put the pieces together. "It would help if we had actually talked about it. Or if you had made a move sooner."

"I didn't want you to think that I thought you were easy!"

"Sounds like you were thinking a little too much. Maybe we both were. So are we just dating, or are we boyfriends?"

"What's the difference?"

"Boyfriends means being in a relationship," Kelly said with a playful smile. "Dating means you're playing the field, trying to find the right person. There is no commitment."

"Boyfriends," William said firmly. "If that's okay with you. I know what I want."

"I know too," Kelly said. "So, boyfriend, how do you feel about holding hands in public?"

"I've never tried it before," William said, taking Kelly's hand. "But don't worry, I've been told that I'm a fast learner."

They strolled down the bridge, heading for the city proper and toward an older couple. William felt self-conscious and wondered what they thought. Then he decided he didn't care, because to him it felt right. His resolve was tested when he spotted a group of guys further along, so he tried to focus on Kelly instead.

"I can't believe I've been dating myself this whole time," he moaned.

Kelly laughed. "I was just reviewing events and trying to see them from your perspective. Why did you think I took you to the gay youth group?"

"To broaden my horizons?"

"Hardly," Kelly said, shaking his head. "I wanted you to see that you have options."

"Like Layne?"

"Like pretty much any guy there." Kelly peered at him. "You realize that, right? You could have any of them."

"I don't want them," William said, making their arms swing back and forth. "And besides, you were totally trying to scare them all away."

"I might have regretted my decision to bring you there."

"Meaning you liked me too. Even then."

"Yes," Kelly said, gently squeezing his hand.

"So why didn't you make a move?"

"No reason."

William tried to read his face. "I don't believe you."

"Okay," Kelly said, shaking his head at his own foolishness. "Maybe, just *maybe*, I wasn't sure if you were into me or not."

William started laughing. "So basically, one of us was arrogant enough to assume we were already dating, and the other was insecure enough to assume we never would. We make quite the pair, don't we?"

"That remains to be seen," Kelly said. "There's so much we haven't done yet."

"Like what?"

"Like finding a quiet place by the river where we can make out. One kiss does not a birthday present make."

William grinned. "How many will it take?"

Kelly picked up the pace, yanking on William's arm and dragging him along. "I'll keep count and let you know when we get there. Be warned, I'm not a cheap date. You'll need lip balm by the time I'm through!"

William guffawed as he stumbled along, feeling like it was his birthday instead.

Chapter Six

"So what's it like being with another guy?"

William and Lily were walking to class when she asked him this question. Their dynamic had definitely changed. No longer did she flirt with him, although he occasionally caught her checking him out. He took that as a compliment. He felt closer to her now, their conversations less superficial. That hadn't happened with the other two girls.

"It's awesome," William enthused. "Kelly is so amazing! I look at him sometimes and can't believe he's mine, you know? Or that he wants me. I love watching him run after school, or how serious he gets when he's taking photos."

Lily's expression was patient. "That's nice, but I meant sex."

"Oh!" William felt himself blushing and wondered if there was medicine he could take to prevent it. "We haven't done it. Kelly has. With other guys. But not since we became a couple! Ha ha!"

"You've been together two weeks now, right?"

"Yup!"

"And you haven't— Nothing at all?"

"Just kissing."

"I'm surprised. Most guys I've been with rush right into sex. Usually. With one or two, I did the rushing."

"You're not a virgin?" William said a little too loudly. Quieter, he added. "I didn't know."

Lily hugged her books to her stomach. "Remember my boyfriend sophomore year?"

"Patrick. He was your first?"

"And not the last. I love sex."

"Wow," William said, seeing her in a new light. "Why didn't you ever tell me? Do the others know?"

"The way those two gossip?" Lily shook her head. "If a guy has lots of sexual partners, he's considered a stud. If a girl does, she's branded a slut."

"I hate that," William said with a scowl. "It's not fair."

"No, it isn't, but that's why I make sure no one brags about sleeping with me."

"How?"

"By threatening to tell everyone that he has a small dick.

Doesn't matter if it's true or not. No guy wants that said about him."

William laughed, even though he didn't like that she was forced to resort to such tactics. "How many times have you had to do that?"

"Just once," Lily said with a playful smile. "In his case it was true. Not that it really matters. I've been with a guy so big that it hurt. Not fun at all. Another was small, but he had all the right moves."

She laughed. William did too, but he also looked around the hall at all the straight guys he would never have a chance with. "I'm going to need details."

"No problem. I'd like to hear some too, eventually. So what are you waiting for? Playing hard to get?"

"I want it to be special," William said.

"Oh." Lily walked a few paces in silence. Then she said, "Was that first kiss the best one? Or the most special?"

He thought about it. "Not really. The more Kelly and I kiss, the better it gets. This one time Kelly showed up at the Y when I was getting dressed, and he pressed me up against a locker. Maybe it was the environment, but I swear I nearly blew a load." He was about to apologize for getting graphic, but Lily seemed cool with it.

"There will be more like that. You can't plan these things. Sometimes you're both on fire. Other times, no matter how special you want it to be, it just isn't. There's no controlling that kind of chemistry."

"So you're saying I shouldn't wait?"

Lily tilted her head. "More like don't put so much pressure on the first time. You'll have enough to worry about without it having to also be perfection. Once you're more comfortable with each other, chances are *that's* when it'll really be special."

William thought about it. He was tempted to move things further along, but he still had reservations. "I want to be sure that I love him, and that he loves me. Then we can take the next step."

They stopped outside his classroom. Lily shook her head at him, but she sighed. "You're really nice. That's so rare."

"Lots of people are nice," William said. "You are, Holly is, Abby—"

"Relationships are different. Believe me. They change people, and no matter how they begin, people rarely remain nice for long. Don't let this one change you."

"My relationship with Kelly *is* changing me," William said. "For the better."

"If anyone else told me that, I'd think they were being naïve." Lily smiled gently. "When you say it, I can almost believe it's true. Is everything else okay? The whole school is talking about you guys. Everyone knows."

"Good," William said. "We aren't hiding it. I've been called a few names, but so what? I'm more worried about you. Don't let anyone be mean. Or take advantage of you."

"Oh trust me," Lily said. "The reverse is much more likely to happen." She poked him in the chest. "Your friend is a stone-cold player. You're lucky you escaped unscathed."

William chuckled. "Anyone would be lucky to be with you. The fact is, I missed out on a good thing, but at least I've got you as a friend. Right?"

Lily leaned against him and sighed theatrically. "I'll take what I can get!"

"You're not listening to me!"

"I *am* listening! I'm just not giving you the answer you want!"

William wasn't eavesdropping. The shouting was too loud to ignore. His hair was still wet from the shower, his muscles relaxed from an early morning swim. His routine had changed. Every other day he started with a bike ride to the YMCA at dawn and his usual workout before he rode home again and got cleaned up. Then he would wait for Kelly to pick him up for school. On alternate days he drove his car to the YMCA and then picked up Kelly on the way to school. Afternoons were always spent together. Occasionally William would sit on the track bleachers and watch Kelly run, or they would return home to watch more episodes of *Beast Wars*. He was pretty sure he had his boyfriend hooked on the series. A month of viewing had brought them to the second season where the plot took a few interesting turns. Lately they found it more comfortable to watch these at Kelly's house, where peace and quiet was more common.

"Maybe you should listen to yourself," William's mother shouted. Even though his parents were on a different floor, their muffled voices were loud enough to be understood. "You can't even look me in the eye! You're ashamed because *this is wrong.*"

"I'm doing what's best for everyone!" his father yelled.

"You're only thinking of yourself!"

William grabbed his backpack, deciding to stomp down the stairs on the way out. Hopefully they would remember he was in the house and stop arguing. He was halfway down the hall when his mother's words halted him in his tracks.

"William deserves a choice!"

He understood what that meant. Who did he want to live with? He had agonized over the question, sometimes late at night, even during the brief reprieve when his parents seemed to be doing okay. That hadn't lasted long. The bickering had started up again, but the current argument sounded really bad. He crept down the hall and took the stairs one at a time, his steps soft and cautious.

"He doesn't need to decide," his father shouted. "He's a child! We make decisions for him! That's called being a parent. All I want is what's best for him."

William was torn. His father was fighting to keep him, which made him feel loved, but his mother wasn't backing down. William didn't want to be separated from either of them.

"He's almost an adult," Kate said. "This is going to be hard enough on him if he doesn't have the support of us both. Like it or not, we're in this together. Our relationship falling apart is one thing, but our relationship with our children—"

"What am I supposed to do with him?" Lewis demanded.

"Take care of him!" Kate cried. "Feed him, clothe him, make sure he's safe and educated, because *that's* what being a parent is all about! Not... I can't even say it."

"You'll need a man in the house," Lewis said, voice lower. "You won't want to be alone. There's no point in asking him if he wants to live with me. It's not going to happen."

William's stomach sank. His father wasn't fighting to keep him. The opposite was true. Abandoning caution, he thudded his way down the stairs, wanting to escape the house. His mother heard, catching him at the door.

"Honey!"

He turned to her, cheeks burning, showing with his expression that he had overheard it all. Lewis appeared behind her, looking as though his misgivings had been proven right.

"We need to talk," Kate said.

"No." He didn't want to have this conversation. Ever. "I'm going to be late for school."

"After school then," she said, her voice soft. "We'll all sit down and we'll talk this out. Okay?"

He looked again at his father, who had crossed his arms over his chest and was shaking his head. William felt his chin tremble. Not wanting to cry, he fled the house, eyes on the concrete walkway. The cold winter air nipped at his skin, but no way was he returning inside for his jacket. Kelly was waiting in his usual spot, perched on the hood of his car in the driveway. He stood and stumbled forward, as if sensing William's pain.

"You okay?"

William nodded and hustled to the car, wanting to escape from the house more than the cold. He was inside and seated before Kelly opened the driver-side door. Once his boyfriend was inside, he sat there and stared with concern.

"Just drive," William said. "Please."

Kelly complied. As they pulled out, William refused to look at his home, fearing he'd find his parents watching him leave, hurt on his mother's face and disdain on his father's. Halfway to school, Kelly parked in a strip mall parking lot and asked for an explanation. William started talking. He let it all spill out, Kelly taking his hand to comfort him. William gripped it tightly, as if he'd found something solid when the rest of his world was falling apart.

"Maybe they're only taking a break," Kelly said when William had finished. "Separating so they can work through things, but not splitting up completely."

"Maybe."

"Let's skip school. We can go back to my place. We'll have the house to ourselves, and we can talk about everything. Or we'll just watch TV. Whatever you need!"

"I don't want to get in trouble."

Kelly was silent. "It's the last day before winter break. No one will care. Tons of people don't show up. In situations like these, you need to take care of yourself. Give yourself time to think."

Why not? Who cared if he followed the rules anymore? His parents were breaking their promise to stay together. He would break his to attend school and everything else that was expected of him. Then he pictured his mother in the principal's office, already at wit's end. Putting her through even more would be cruel. "Things are already bad enough. Let's go. We're going to be late."

Kelly looked out the window on his side of the car, then released his hand so he could turn the key in the ignition. They rode the rest of the way to school in silence, William certain he had done something wrong.

"Are you sure?" Kelly pressed as they neared the school. "We could hit the mall. I'll buy you lunch."

William shook his head, worried that talking about it more would start an argument. That's the last thing he wanted. If it was up to him, he'd never be in—or witness—another argument again. Kelly hugged him before they parted in the hallway, reassuring him that things between them were okay. As the day went on, he began to regret turning down Kelly's offer. He couldn't concentrate on any of his classes. His mind wandered, imagining every possibility and accepting only one: This was just another fight. One more bump in the road. His mother had asked him before who he wanted to live with, and nothing had come of it. Obviously they still had issues to work out, so they would take time off, realize they missed and needed each other, and patch things up. His father needed a break to pretend he was a teenager again. His mother needed some downtime to rest and focus on herself. William would help by making sure he wasn't underfoot, and soon all of this would be resolved.

He felt better as the school day came to an end, even joking around with Holly in their sixth period class. Then he went outside and met Kelly in their usual place, but their conversation was cut short when William's mother drove up. That never happened. He tried to ignore the dread stirring inside.

"Text me," Kelly said. "As soon as you know something, text me."

William nodded and went to her car. She rolled down the window, but he didn't need to ask for an explanation. He simply went to the passenger-side door and got in.

"How was your day?" she asked.

"Mom," William pleaded.

Kate rolled up the window and pulled the car forward. "If you're hungry, we can stop somewhere on the way home."

"I'm fine," he said. "Besides, we don't want to keep Dad waiting."

William wasn't looking forward to sitting down and talking with his parents, but he was prepared. He would state from the beginning that he wanted to stay with his mom, cutting off any potential arguments. He would also support the idea of them taking a break, proving his maturity and relieving them of extra burden. They didn't need to worry about him. Not when it would only add strain to their relationship.

When they reached the house, he went to the kitchen table where family meetings always took place. He wished, not for the first time, that his brothers still lived at home so he wouldn't have to face this alone. His mother fetched his usual after-school snack—a glass of milk and whatever she had baked. Brownies this time. The gesture seemed pointless, because it didn't make him feel better about the situation. On the other hand, it did reassure him of her love. The situation couldn't be easy on her, and yet she was still thinking of him.

Kate sat on the opposite side of the table, hands flat on the surface, fingers trembling regardless. "We have some difficult things to discuss," she began.

"Where's Dad? Shouldn't we wait for him?"

"No. You're not quite an adult, but you're old enough to understand the complexities of relationships. You even have your own now, and I'm sure you and Kelly sometimes don't get along."

"Yeah," he said with a shrug. "I understand. Don't worry. You don't need to explain anything to me. Really."

This didn't seem to comfort his mother much. "I'm sure you've noticed your father behaving differently lately and—"

"Mid-life crisis," William said, almost feeling upbeat. This was easier than he had expected! "I agree it's weird, and it's obviously driving you nuts. You guys are going to take a break, and he'll get it all out of his system. Then things will go back to normal."

"I'm afraid this goes beyond your father wanting to feel young again. Or maybe it doesn't. I don't know." Kate sighed, one of her hands sliding over to cover the other. "Your father has been seeing someone."

"What do you mean?"

"He has a girlfriend."

The idea was ridiculous. His father, going on dates and doing romantic things with someone other than his mother? Impossible! "Are you sure?"

"Yes."

"An affair?"

She didn't answer. Her eyes were red in an effort to hold back tears but a few broke free. "I'm sorry that you have to hear any of this, but it's important you understand that this wasn't about that silly car or your father not wanting to get old. I could have handled that, but another woman… She's nineteen years old!" Kate shook her head. "I don't know what he's thinking."

William felt repulsed. And angry. "When does he get home?"

"He's not coming home."

"Good!" William stood up from the table, jaw clenching. "I don't want him here anymore."

"Honey," his mother said gently, "he's still your father. I want you to have a relationship with him."

"No! I don't ever want to see him again!"

"You will," Kate said, tone firm. "It's okay that you're angry now. I am too. But our marriage failing doesn't change the fact that you're his son. He loves you."

"If he loved me, he wouldn't have—" William's voice cracked. Without a target for his anger, the emotion had shifted to sorrow. "I'm sorry, Mom."

"It's not your fault, baby." She stood and walked around the table to give him a hug. "We both love you. I'm sorry this upsets you. I wish I could protect you from it all. I really do."

William hugged her back, knowing that she had gotten it wrong. She needed protecting, not him. He would do everything in his power to make certain she wouldn't be hurt. Not after today. How? He wasn't sure, but he already knew that his father would never be welcomed into their lives again.

I thought I knew you.

William paced his room, phone in one hand. He had tried calling his father, intending to demand an explanation, wanting to give him a chance before William shut him out of his life forever. Lewis hadn't answered his phone, or responded to the voicemail messages, which William had kept short. "We need to talk," or

"Call me back. It's important." While he waited for a response, his feverish mind went over every detail he had pried out of his mother. She had been unwilling to tell him much, but she was hurt and needed someone to confide in. She spoke of how she had followed her husband after work, how he had picked up a waitress from Hooters, a restaurant chain famous for its busty and flirtatious employees. She had watched her husband stand next to his convertible and—top down—lift a woman to swing her around, placing her carefully in the passenger seat. Then he had trotted proudly around the front of the car, leaping into the driver seat and leaning over for a kiss. That's when Kate had pressed the horn of her own car, holding it down even after shock had separated them and the two passengers had turned to look at her—one appearing puzzled, the other guilty.

William struggled to reconcile the image of his father with this high-energy Romeo. The exercise wasn't impossible. William had seen his parents being romantic with each other: little kisses, embraces, and weekend dates. None of these demonstrations were quite so passionate though. He also struggled to imagine anyone but his mother being attracted to Lewis. Not that William didn't like him. His father had carved a pumpkin with him every Halloween or snuck off with him to a parking lot to set off fireworks on the Fourth of July. He was always there Christmas morning. His father would yawn and watch the proceedings, smiling occasionally and guessing what his presents were before he opened them. William still didn't understand how. Most of his memories of his father centered around special occasions. Lewis cut the ham during Easter dinner or served slices of turkey on Thanksgiving. His father's presence and participation helped make those holidays special.

During the rest of the year William's mother took care of everything, kissing cuts, taking him shopping for clothes, lecturing him when his grades slipped at school, doing his laundry, telling him to sit up straight, and making sure he went outside for sun and exercise when he'd rather stay home and watch TV. His father's role was more glamorous: the guy who made special guest appearances every holiday, or played tour guide on family vacations. Lewis had always seemed so cool, but when William considered it all, his father had the easiest role. Kate had taught William to read and count. Learning to ride a bike? Not nearly as important. His mother had raised him. His father had merely supported him.

Despite this conclusion, William couldn't hate him. He tried his best anyway, drawing a line between the authority figure of his childhood and the stranger who had appeared in recent years. Two different people. One he had loved. That man was dead. The other William never wanted to see again, and so he returned to the text message he had started.

I thought I knew you.

Goodbye. I hate you. Fuck off and die! So many ways he could finish it, but he kept thinking of thrusting his hand into a pumpkin to pull out a fistful of slimy seeds, his father chuckling and appearing proud. William deleted the text message, arm falling limp at his side.

The worst part is that she stayed. Despite the betrayal, his mother had tried to make it work. Lewis had been caught with another woman—this girl—more than a month ago. Around the time William's mother had sat him down and warned him that he might face a difficult choice. Nothing had happened then because Kate chose to stay. He couldn't help wondering if that was his fault, if she had attempted to reconcile things because of William's feelings. She should have left Lewis right then and there, but instead she had quietly suffered, and from what he understood, his father had only pretended to call off his affair.

He was reminded of when Lily's mother had a short affair with one of her clients and had confided in her daughter, for some inconceivable reason. As for Holly, her parents had gotten divorced some years back, keeping the reason from their child. He didn't have to think hard to find other examples of broken families. Few of his classmates made their relationships last longer than a month or two. Maybe having kids and the benefits of a dual-income household kept some couples together for longer, but relationships never seemed to last. He thought of Abby declaring herself an atheist and insisting that people should believe only in things that could be proven. What proof was there of love? Mutual attraction and social bonds, yes, but love itself? Maybe it was just a lie.

He raised the phone in his hand, needing to know the truth and hating the idea of being right. He sent a text, this time to a different recipient, too upset to bother with proper grammar.

i need to see you

Seconds later, Kelly replied. *Okay. Where?*

can I come over?

He knew it was late. Past midnight. It would be even later once he made the drive, but only if he was invited. He held his breath, realizing this might be the answer he sought. If Kelly said no, turned him away now, then William was done believing in love.

Okay. Drive safe.

William exhaled. Then he put on his shoes and slipped out into the night.

Cool air, heavy shadows, and a long lawn—tidy and maintained all the way to the stone patio. William stared at the back of the house, no longer trusting appearances. What he saw was a stately home with everything in order. Mr. and Mrs. Phillips were no doubt asleep in the same bed, but how many secrets did they keep from each other? From their children? William was seated on a swing, part of a jungle gym for children, but he remained stationary, hands gripping the chains despite the biting cold of the metal. Kelly had escorted him here where they could talk without disturbing anyone. He eyed William before taking a seat in the swing next to his, silent and awaiting an explanation. William was unable to look at his boyfriend for long, not trusting his own treacherous feelings.

"They're getting a divorce." William said, jaw wanting to snap shut around the words. "My dad's been cheating."

"Oh shit," Kelly whispered. "I'm sorry."

"It's not your fault," William snarled. "He's the one who needed some woman—some *girl* nearly my age—to make him feel young again. It's fucking pathetic! He didn't even have the guts to face me. He and my mom were supposed to talk it over with me after school. Remember what I heard this morning? How I should have a choice? I don't think my dad wants to be reminded that he has kids. I wouldn't want to live with him anyway. I hate him!"

This booming declaration sounded powerful, despite being false. His eyes burned as he looked at the house again, expecting lights to flick on. Then he turned his head away, willing himself not to cry.

Kelly's response was gentle. "All you can do is be there for your mom."

"Yeah. I won't abandon her. And if my father thinks we're selling the house, he can forget it! He's not a part of this family anymore."

"Has there been talk about any of that?"

William's breath was visible when he exhaled. "I don't know. My mom kept saying I shouldn't worry about it. She put on a brave face, which only made me more pissed at him. How could he do this to us?"

"I don't know," Kelly said. "I really don't."

William felt a hand touch his own, warm and reassuring, but he pulled away, not wanting to be deceived. He stood, needing to put distance between himself and Kelly.

He heard footsteps on the grass, trailing behind. "What's going on?"

William stopped but didn't turn around. "Don't you get it? My parents used to love each other. You never got to see it, but they were always kissing and saying romantic stuff, even though my brothers and I acted like it was gross. But it wasn't. My dad made my mom laugh when she was in a bad mood, and she always took care of him. Just look at them now! Hell, look at your own parents because mine weren't so different once. And look at us, because even though everything is new, this is our future too. No one thinks of that when first starting out, but it happens. More often than not, relationships fall apart."

When the response came, Kelly's voice was just behind him. "I won't let that happen to us. No matter what."

William turned around, hating the idea that their story would be the same. No matter how much they loved each other, someday they would fall apart, their once-invincible feelings faded and broken. "I don't want to be like them!"

He grabbed Kelly, clutching him close, needing the fleeting comfort. He held on as tight as he could, hoping to stave off the inevitable.

"Stay the night," Kelly murmured.

William released him and took a step back. He wanted to. William had thought about sharing a bed with Kelly more times than he could count, but he had held out, wanting to be certain of love. Now, more than ever, he was *uncertain*. Love was either real, or they were deluding themselves. Either way, he wouldn't deny himself the benefits any longer.

Kelly took his hand, leading him toward the house. "We have to be quiet. Even once we're in my room."

They tiptoed through a dim dining area, the only light coming from kitchen appliances on the other side of the breakfast bar. Kelly still held his hand, even as they navigated the living room and made their way upstairs. Only once in his room did Kelly let go to quietly shut the door behind them. Then he turned, his expression concerned instead of lustful.

"Are you hungry?" Kelly asked. "Or thirsty? We have—"

William silenced him with a kiss. His lips took over, long since familiar with this game, while the rest of him focused on Kelly's body. He pressed his own against it, finished with mysteries. Let Kelly feel how hard he was. William intended to take just as much in return, his hands groping the thin muscles beneath Kelly's shirt. He was tired of clothing separating them. He reached over to turn out the light, then backed up, taking Kelly with him until his legs hit the bed. William sat, nearly eye level with Kelly's crotch. He ripped at the belt, eager to claim his prize.

"Hold on," Kelly said. "Is this what I think it is?"

What else could it be? William nodded.

"Okay." Kelly bit his lip and looked around. "Uh, just give me a second."

William crawled farther into the bed. He wasn't leaving the room until they saw this through. Kelly fetched a lighter and walked around, lighting candles. Then he shut off the computer monitor, the remaining light warm. Still he stood there, as if seeking further improvements.

"Kelly. Please."

His boyfriend looked over, assessing him. "Shoes," he said.

"Oh." William noticed they were on the comforter, a shriveled wet leaf stuck to the side of one. "Sorry."

"Let me." Kelly patiently loosened the laces enough to pull off the shoes, then did the same for himself. William hoped he would remove the rest of his clothes too, but Kelly climbed into bed on his knees, still fully dressed. William rose up to meet him, determined to correct this oversight. He reached for the hem of Kelly's flannel shirt and lifted it up and over his head instead of messing with the buttons. Kelly helped by yanking his arms out of the long sleeves. Then he returned the favor, pulling off the swim-team sweatshirt William wore. They stopped to look each other over, a familiar sensation nudging William, except this time the man in the mirror didn't look like him. Dark skin, a slim body, tapered waist, and trained muscles that were different in shape and size from his own. He was eager to see where else they contrasted.

He began with touch, placing a palm over one of Kelly's pecs, which felt tighter than his, and let his hand slide down to one of the boney hips. Kelly started exploring too, touching William's nipples. This tickled and made him laugh. Then both hands massaged William's chest, which brought more pleasure than he had ever expected. Now he understood why Lily had been so eager for him to touch her breasts. She vanished from his thoughts when Kelly moved closer, pressing their torsos together. William kissed a neck still chilly from being outside. Then he grabbed Kelly's ass, yanking him closer, their cocks rubbing together through their jeans.

"Lie on your back," Kelly said.

Not a chance. William flexed in effort and flung Kelly over so he was on the mattress instead. Then he looked down at a bulge larger than the one he had stolen many glances at while swimming. He reached for the belt, Kelly not resisting. After impatiently struggling with the leather strap and the button of the jeans, he yanked the rest down unceremoniously. This definitely wasn't like looking in the mirror. Kelly's cock was long, not nearly as thick as his own, and of course brown. His pubes were tight curls against his skin, his balls like two dark walnuts, completing a perfect package. He loved it. Kelly should never be allowed to wear clothes again. He'd forbid it!

"You can do more than just look at it," Kelly suggested, seeming amused.

"Naw, I'm done. This is as far as I want to go." He laughed at Kelly's reaction, then made up for his cruel joke. "Want to see mine?"

Kelly nodded. "Show me what you've got, white boy."

William grinned, unbuttoning his jeans and tugging on the zipper, taking his time. He did likewise when sliding the denim downward bit by bit. Kelly was transfixed by his underwear, or more accurately, what William was intentionally flexing inside of them. He put his thumbs in the waistband, lowering the cotton slowly. Then he was free, his cock bobbing in the air and getting bigger now that it had room to swell.

Kelly stared, then looked up at him. "Bring that thing here."

William walked on his knees, moving toward the top of the bed and bracing his hands against the wall. Kelly's tongue reached out to meet him. There were many things William had managed to do in front of the mirror, but this wasn't one of them. He scooted closer, Kelly opening his mouth to accommodate him. Wet, warm, and welcoming. The sensation was too good. He thrust a few times, but didn't need to because Kelly's head was moving back and forth. Soon all William could do was brace himself against the wall as pleasure filled him in the way air could fill balloon, causing it to pop.

"Uh," he said, pulling away.

"Close already?" Kelly asked.

He felt his cheeks flush, which probably matched the rest of him. "That's usually not a problem."

"I'll take it as a compliment," Kelly said, licking his lips. "Get back here."

"No. I want this to last."

William flopped onto his side, kicking off his jeans the rest of the way. Then he scooted down so he was on eye level with Kelly's dick, cheek resting on his stomach. He stroked it with the tip of one finger. Kelly made sounds of appreciation, especially when he took it and started pumping. Then William scooted further down, determined not to mess up. He had researched tips and advice on the Internet, which had been informative. And hot. He knew Kelly had a lot of experience and William wanted to impress him, so he went through just about every trick he could remember. And it worked!

"If you keep that up," Kelly said in a husky voice, "I'm going to come in your mouth."

William redoubled his efforts, and a few minutes later, felt hot salty liquid splash against the inside of his cheek. That was kind of weird. An acquired taste maybe, because revulsion competed with a desire for more. William had barely been touching himself, but remained close. He was back on his knees, thrusting in Kelly's mouth, groaning and on the verge of a heart attack. Then came release, the sensation ten times more pleasurable than anything he had done on his own. What he hadn't expected—and never experienced with the man in the mirror—was the rush of affection that followed. He looked down at Kelly, who must have felt the same, because he stretched out his arms. William tumbled into them gratefully, rolling to one side and pulling Kelly close. Words weren't needed. Not at first, the emotions between them almost tactile, but like everything, they began to fade.

He released Kelly, who rolled over onto his back, candlelight dancing over his naked body.

"We won't fall apart," William whispered. He intended it as an oath, but he also needed to hear it in return. "Promise me."

"We won't," Kelly said. "I know we won't."

William felt a pang of sorrow. "You sound so certain."

"Because I love you." Kelly's eyes locked onto his. "I love you and I'll never stop. That's all it takes."

William studied Kelly's face before he nodded. Then he settled down, rolling his boyfriend onto his side to snuggle near. The world was brimming with evidence that told him he shouldn't dare to hope, or expect this to last forever, but what he had felt tonight made him wonder if they could beat the odds. He nestled his nose against Kelly's ear, finally uttering his heart's response.

"I love you too."

A tree decorated with ornaments, twinkling lights, and soft angelic music, all flanked by three angry men. William and his brothers sat in the living room, the smell of lunch still in the air, and forced themselves to appear jovial. Spencer reclined on the couch, stuffed into an intentionally ugly Christmas sweater. Errol sat on the floor, dressed more appropriately for Halloween, his clothing various shades of black. William wore what he always did, a polo shirt and jeans, as he stood next to his mother. She was digging around under the tree, searching for more presents.

"Here we go," she said, handing William what was unmistakably a book. "And here's one for Errol." The box was tall and narrow. Hopefully she hadn't bought him a bong. The last thing he needed was encouragement.

William delivered the present to him, then turned to Spencer. "Looks like you were on the naughty list this year."

His oldest brother shrugged, brow creased with anger.

William understood. The ill feelings weren't directed at him but their father, who Spencer resembled most. Dark hair, brown eyes, and the impressive build of a Marine. His chiseled jaw stopped clenching when their mother turned around, and he feigned a happier disposition. "Being around my family is present enough," he said.

"Oh stop!" Kate beamed at him. "I didn't forget you. Here." She handed him a medium-sized box, then appeared amused. "Well, open them! I never needed to tell you when you were children!"

As they ripped open their presents, William struggled to concentrate. His book had something to do with lifeguards, which normally would have piqued his interest, but all he could think about was his father. Conflict raged within him. He missed the man, especially on a holiday like today when he would be more involved than usual, but William also resented him for putting them through this. And for what? Sex with a younger woman?

"What do you think?" his mother asked, placing a hand on his arm.

"It's great, Mom. I love it." His brothers murmured similar responses. Then Kate started digging under the tree again. "I'm certain there's more where that came from."

While she was distracted, they exchanged glances. None of them were happy. But what could they do? A sniffing noise pulled his attention away. William glanced over and saw his mother wiping away a tear. "Hey!" he said, stooping to put an arm around her. "Are you okay?"

"I'm fine," she said, shoving away a present. The half-open gift tag revealed a familiar name: Lewis. "I'm just being silly."

"You're not," William said, helping her stand. "You don't have to put on a brave face. We're here for you."

He embraced his mother, then felt a larger pair of arms wrapping around them both. "He's right," Spencer said with a squeeze. "We'll be strong for you."

"We'll protect you," Errol said, joining the group hug, "and keep all the bad vibes away. We love you, Mom."

"We love you," William echoed. Then Spencer did the same. This made their mother really start crying, but he hoped it was because she was happy or relieved. He hated the idea of her being sad, especially today.

"Hold up, you guys," Errol said. "I've got just the thing!"

He rushed to the kitchen where he turned up the Christmas music. When he returned with eggnog, he handed a glass mug to each of them. William took a sip and grimaced. It was definitely spiked with something. His mother seemed to like it, chugging half and laughing at the milk mustache this left. Or "nog stash," as Errol called it.

Afterwards the holiday spirit felt a little closer. They tore through the remaining presents, ignoring those intended for the man who wasn't there. Kate looked happier, her cheeks rosy with warmth. Or rum. She sat on the couch with them, talking about her favorite holiday memories from their childhoods, being careful to never mention their father. Then she started yawning.

"I woke up early out of habit. You boys never could wait. This year I was the only one up!"

"You didn't go for a morning swim, Willy?" Spencer asked, elbowing him playfully. "Just wait until the Coast Guard hears about this. Aren't you trying to convince them that you're a fish?"

"Even I take the holidays off," he said, "although we could drive north until we find a frozen lake. You'll use that big hard head of yours to crack the ice, and we'll all go for a dip!"

"He's probably not kidding," Errol said.

"I think I'll take a nap instead," their mother replied. She yawned again, patted the legs of her two nearest sons, and stood. They watched her leave the living room, silent until the bedroom door shut.

"This sucks," Errol said. "What an asshole."

William didn't need to ask who he was referring to. "What do you think he's doing right now?"

"Dad?" Errol shook his head. "I don't even want to know."

"He's with his girlfriend," Spencer grumbled, standing up and stretching. Then he noticed their stares. "What?"

"How do you know?" Errol said.

"He called me a couple days ago," Spencer said. "I asked him what his plans were."

William felt hurt. His father hadn't tried making contact with him, but then he always had been closest to Spencer. One look at Errol showed that he hadn't heard from him either.

"He's living with her now," Spencer continued, starting to pace. "In a one-bedroom apartment."

"Do you know the address?" William asked.

"Yeah."

"Then let's go over there."

Spencer turned to face him. "Why?"

William thought of Kelly, who was never afraid to speak his mind. "To tell him to stay away. From Mom and from us."

"I don't know," Errol said. "Maybe she's hoping they'll patch things up."

"No." William shook his head. "I asked her. Sort of. I was trying to cheer her up the other day, and I said that maybe Dad would come around. If this *is* a mid-life crisis, he'll come out of it again and stop being such a jerk. She looked at me like I was crazy and said she never wanted to see him again. So let's make sure he stays away."

"We've been drinking," Spencer said. "We can't drive."

"I only had a sip," William said. "Sorry, Errol, but yuck."

"More for me," his brother replied easily. "Are you sure about this?"

"Yes," William answered.

"Maybe we should." Spencer glowered at the unopened presents. "Yeah. Let's go."

William acted on inspiration and gathered up the gifts. His mother didn't have to see them again. They filed outside to his car, the sky gray, a chill in the air that the setting sun hadn't chased away. The day was dark by the time they reached an apartment complex next to railroad tracks. William had hoped the building would be in disrepair, but it appeared respectable enough.

As they parked and left the car, a family of parents and children were getting into their vehicle a few spots down. William envied how picture-perfect that family seemed and wondered if it would remain that way. Then he and his brothers plodded up the stairs to the third floor, located the right apartment number, and knocked on the door.

"What are we supposed to say?" Errol whispered.

The door opened before anyone could answer. The girl standing there looked like someone Spencer would bring home, pretty and young, wearing a generous amount of makeup and perfume. She seemed confused until she spotted Spencer. Then she made the connection.

"Oh hi! You must be… I'm Gina."

"Are we supposed to call you Mom?" Spencer grunted.

"We're here to talk to our father," William said, "not you."

"Okay." Gina appeared wounded. "Come in."

"No thanks," Spencer said. "We're fine right here."

"Hold on. I'll get him for you." Gina started to shut the door, then perhaps deciding that would be rude, left it cracked. After she had retreated, they were left with a partial view of a living room. Christmas music was playing, and they could feel heat leaking from the apartment. Then their father appeared, expression jovial, as if their visit was a happy surprise. "Boys!" he said, opening the door wider. "Come in!"

"Shut up!" Errol said, surprising them all. "You really hurt Mom, you know that?"

The grin slid off their father's face. "I know things haven't been easy, but that's between your mother and me. Nothing has changed between us though. I'm happy to see you three."

"These are for you," William said, thrusting out the presents. "They're from Mom. Your wife. Merry Christmas."

Lewis took them, looking ashamed. "Boys—"

"She's just a girl!" Spencer said. "You're dating someone our age!"

"That's no concern of yours!" their father said, mustering some anger.

"I think it is," Spencer growled, trying to push past them. "You're ruining this family!"

William did his best to block his brother, which wasn't easy, but he worried alcohol might throw the situation out of control. "Mom didn't ask us to bring these presents," William said. "She never wants to see you again. Stay away from her. If you need to talk to her, or give her something, you go through us. Understand?"

"Go through one of them," Errol said, his voice cracking. "I don't want to see you again either. I'm done." He turned away, the warm light of the apartment reflecting off tears as he went.

"I don't know if I want to see you anymore," Spencer said, "but I'd rather you talk to me than her."

His father locked eyes with William. "And what about you?"

William swallowed against his anger, trying to tame it. "If there's something you need from the house, let me know and I'll bring it to you. We're trying to stop her from getting more hurt than she already is. That's all."

"Okay," Lewis said. "I understand. Won't you come inside? Please?"

"No," Spencer said. "We need to go find Errol." Then he stomped away.

That left William alone with his father. "I should go."

"I love you boys," Lewis said. "Tell your brothers that for me. Okay?"

Gina reappeared, hanging back, expression worried.

William nodded at her. "Merry Christmas," he said. Then he turned and walked away.

Chapter Seven

Change arrived like a tidal wave, the waters washing away anything weakly rooted and providing life-giving nourishment to what remained. Such catalysts often came without warning, with the exception of when one calendar ended and another began, the traditional time for change. William's life no longer resembled that of the previous year: out of the closet, dating an awesome guy, and living in a broken home. The good came with the bad, he supposed. At the moment, he was looking forward to more of the good.

William stared at himself in the mirror, his old habit nearly forgotten. These days, when considering his reflection, he only thought of one person. Kelly. That's what the freshly pressed slacks were about, and the dress shirt with a little too much fabric around the waist. Larger shirts tended to be tailored for chubby guys, but those were the only ones that fit his shoulders right. He tried tucking in the baby blue fabric tighter, then considered the navy blue tie, which was an absolute mess.

"Moooooom!" he whined, heading down the hall to her bedroom. "I need help!"

His mother was unloading towels from a laundry basket, placing two on the counter of her private bathroom even though she only needed one these days. She was coping better with that fact. Kate turned around and saw him, hands on her hips as she cocked her head and sighed. "Aren't you handsome!" she declared.

"Thanks," William said, moving closer. "I can't get my tie straight."

"Just like your father," she said without bitterness. "Here."

He studied her face as she loosened the knot and redid it. Her expression remained warm until he spoke. "Do you think Kelly will like it?" Then he saw a flicker of irritation.

"If he doesn't, that's his problem." She frowned slightly. "There are other fish in the sea."

"Mom! It's Valentine's Day!"

"That doesn't make it any less true," she said. Then she patted his shoulder, her work finished. "There you go. I'm sure he'll be thrilled."

She only said that for his benefit. For whatever reason, since his father moved out, Kate and Kelly hadn't seen eye to eye. His boyfriend insisted they had a misunderstanding, but his mother assured him otherwise. William decided they both were telling the truth as they understood it, which made the issue difficult to resolve.

"Put on some cologne," Kate said. "Not too much, okay? And don't be out late. You have school tomorrow."

"Okay."

He hurried back to his bathroom, finally satisfied with his appearance. After a few sprays of cologne, he went to his bedroom and gently picked up the bouquet of red roses resting on the bed. They had cost a fortune, convincing him they were a good gift, but now he wasn't so sure. Kelly had never shown any interest in flowers. Maybe he wouldn't like them. Too late now. He checked the time, then went downstairs and stood before the front door, trying to think of poetic words he could say when Kelly arrived. "Welcome to a night of romance, my love," or "These flowers aren't nearly as beautiful as you, but I bought them anyway." Yeah. Real smooth. He heard a car pull in the driveway followed by Kelly's footsteps on the walkway.

William felt so jittery that his hand shook a little as he opened the door rather than waiting for a knock, breath catching when he saw the handsome man there. Kelly was decked out in dark colors: a black button-up shirt, charcoal gray pants, and shoes that glistened like polished onyx. "Uh…" William said, cheeks turning the same color as the flowers he thrust out.

Kelly acted appropriately impressed, taking the bouquet and holding it close, eyes sparkling as he inhaled. "Thank you," he breathed.

"You're welcome," William said. "Happy Valentine's Day."

Kelly responded with a kiss. "Ready to go?"

"Yeah!"

They used Kelly's car—or at least the one his parents let him borrow—because it was nicer than William's and tonight was special. Not just because of the holiday. They were treating themselves to a romantic dinner. The restaurant they had selected wasn't a steak house, or a Chinese place, or a seafood joint. The website promised in a cursive font that it served "fine cuisine." Alongside this claim were images of elegantly folded cloth napkins and petite cutlery. William's palms were already sweaty as he imagined knocking over a wine glass and making a mess. Not that they were old enough to drink.

"I'm so excited," Kelly said, not sharing his nerves. "I already know what I'm going to order."

"We agreed not to look at the online menu!"

"I couldn't help it. I'll still pretend to be indecisive. Sound fair?"

William shook his head. "You know I can never make up my mind, especially if the other person has already chosen. I'm just going to close my eyes and point."

"Or I can order for you." Kelly laughed, but the idea sounded good to William.

The dynamic of their relationship often felt a little odd to him. Kelly, despite his fierce drive and hot temper, tended to be softer in more intimate situations, treating William as the more masculine one. He didn't feel that way. He wasn't as aggressive as most guys, Kelly included. Of the two of them, he also had the least experience and was the most submissive. He thought back to the most recent time they had slept together. Kelly had a condom handy, and as things became heated, William told him to put it on. Words weren't always sufficient, because Kelly had then put the condom on William. That arrangement hadn't even occurred to him. William made a lame excuse not to go through with it, and when the topic came up later, he had said he needed more time and left it at that.

"Here we are," Kelly said. "Holy shit, look at that parking lot! We'll be lucky to find a spot."

"Are all those people waiting to be seated?" William asked, grimacing at the crowded curbside.

"Looks that way. I'm glad we made a reservation. Where's the valet parking? I expected better!"

William laughed at his joke, then pointed at an older couple walking away from the restaurant. "Follow them. We'll take their spot."

They slowly stalked the couple, cruising along behind and waiting for them to get into their car and drive away.

"Finally," William said, once they had parked. "I'm starving. Think there'll be chips and salsa on the table?"

Kelly raised his eyebrows. "Uh, no."

"I was being funny. Come on, give me a little credit."

Kelly smiled, reaching over to take his hand. "Only because you're cute." He led them through the waiting crowd.

William felt like a VIP for being allowed to move ahead of the line, and as Kelly gave his last name and the hostess ran her finger down a list, William took the chance to look around. This place was definitely nice, tablecloths and all, but it was also packed. He had imagined bored waiters and classical music, but the interior was loud with burbling voices, the staff too busy to turn up their noses at anyone using the wrong fork. That was good.

They were shown to their table, which was small and in the middle of the room. This made William squirm, feeling like he was on display.

Kelly didn't seem to mind. "This is so cool," he said, grinning at their surroundings. "Could you imagine if we could afford to eat here every day? On our lunch break? It sure beats the school cafeteria."

William would rather be seated on one of those cafeteria benches, poking at a tray of hot gloppy food, but he didn't say so. Instead he peered at the menu, annoyed by how many words were… French? Italian? He wasn't sure, so he chose a main course that was easy to pronounce and made his peace with that.

"Good evening!" a voice said. "My name is Stefan and I'm here to make your dining experience pleasurable. Can I start you off with a bottle of wine or an appetizer?"

William didn't know how to answer. He simply stared at the red vest, gaunt face, and slicked-back hair.

"What sort of wine do you recommend?" Kelly said smoothly.

Stefan looked back and forth between them. "We have a variety to choose from, but could I ask to see some identification?"

"Busted," Kelly said.

Stefan looked to William. "You're not twenty-one?"

"No," he answered, feeling flattered. "I'm seventeen."

The waiter seemed displeased by this news. "A selection of appetizers then?"

William's eyes darted back to the menu. The appetizers cost nearly the same as the main courses. He and Kelly had already agreed not to get one, since they didn't have that much money. "No, thanks. Could I get an orange juice?"

"I'd like a Coke," Kelly said.

"An orange juice," Stefan repeated in deadpan tones. "And a soda."

"That's right," Kelly said. "Thanks!"

Stefan walked away, then they eyed each other.

"Steff-on," Kelly said, imitating the way the man had said his name.

William snorted and tried his own imitation. "What vintage of wine will you be drinking tonight? You *are* twenty-one, aren't you?"

They laughed together, forcing themselves to be serious when the waiter returned with their drinks and took their food orders.

"This is nice," Kelly said, once he was gone. "We should go out more often."

"I wanted to talk to you about that," William said. "Have you ever been to Galveston?"

Kelly leaned forward. "Not since I was little. I wouldn't mind visiting there again."

"Good, because I thought we could go. Your brother too, since he's been interested in—"

"Royal worships the ground you walk on," Kelly interrupted. "You know that, right?"

"Oh." William grinned. "Thanks."

"As much as I love him, wouldn't he cramp our style?"

"Not really. The Coast Guard is having a family night next weekend, and I thought we could all go together and check it out."

Kelly leaned back, nostrils flaring. "The Coast Guard? I'm surprised you're still into that."

William blinked in surprise. "Why wouldn't I be?"

"I thought that was mostly about you not wanting to be gay."

"I've told you how much it means to me," William said. "Ever since I taught myself to swim. *How* I taught myself. I nearly drowned, and that's why I decided—"

"—to be a lifeguard, and later you learned about the rescue swimmers." Kelly shook his head. "The whole military thing though..."

"What's wrong with the military?"

"What's wrong with killing other people?" Kelly retorted.

"That's not why I'm joining the Coast Guard, and you know it. And besides, the military keeps this country safe. I support our troops."

"I've got nothing against the troops," Kelly said with a shrug. "I just don't like what politicians do with them. Protecting our borders is one thing—"

"Then you would like the Coast Guard. You should go with me. It'll be fun. They're giving tours of the different vessels."

"You mean the boats? Didn't you say this was a family night? You don't have any family in the Coast Guard."

"No, but it's an open house. I emailed them to make sure it would be all right. My mom said she would get me a motel room. It'll be fun."

Kelly's expression became devious. "Forget family night! Have your mom get us that room! We'll leave my brother at home and make it a weekend to remember."

"Seriously," William said. "This is important to me."

"I know." Kelly toyed with the corner of his napkin. "Maybe you should explore your options. Think about where else the future could take you."

"I've been training for this for most of my life," William said. "I swim. That's what I do."

"What about the Olympics instead?"

"Endurance is my strength. Not speed."

Kelly looked him over. "You could lose some weight."

"Gee, thanks!"

"Just so you could get faster. That would help, right? You could slim down and start focusing on competitive swimming."

"That's better than wanting to rescue people? To save lives?"

"Yes, because at least then we could—"

Stefan arrived with their food, setting down large plates with ridiculously small portions considering the price. "Is there anything else I can get for you? More juice?"

"No," Kelly said. "It looks great. Thank you."

"My pleasure," Stefan said without joy. Then he moved to check on a neighboring table.

William noticed the tension on Kelly's face and imagined it matched his own. He loved Kelly, but it wasn't unusual for them to butt heads like this. "Let's focus on the food," William said, trying to make peace.

Kelly examined the contents of their plates. "I thought yours would be bigger."

"Words no guy wants to hear," William joked.

They flashed each other smiles, then started in on the food. William had a tiny strip of steak, three stems of braised asparagus, and some sort of grain he didn't recognize. The portions might have been lacking, but the flavor was impressive. He just wished there was more of it. "How's yours?" he asked.

Kelly shook his head as he swallowed, but his response was positive. "Makes what I usually eat taste like dog food. Maybe I should apply for a job here. Do you think the waiters get a free meal every shift?"

"Probably. At the very least you could eat whatever people don't finish. I bet that's how they wash dishes here. Some guy in the back just licks them clean."

"Gross," Kelly said. "And tempting. I would totally do that."

William laughed, feeling more relaxed. That is until Stefan returned.

"Anything else I can get you?" he repeated.

"We're still fine," Kelly said.

"Very good. I'll leave the bill with you." Stefan placed a leather folder on the table. "If you could pay now that would be excellent."

Kelly raised an eyebrow. "We're still eating."

"Looks like you're nearly finished," Stefan replied. "I can box the rest. We have a lot of people waiting for a table so..."

"We've been waiting for this table since January," Kelly said. "That's when I made the reservation. I don't appreciate being rushed halfway through my meal, and frankly, I'm suddenly feeling hungry for dessert. So once we *slowly* finish this course, you can bring the menus back so we can order again. Understood?"

"As you wish," Stefan said, his mouth tight as he turned and stiffly walked away.

"Kelly," William said softly. "That wasn't nice."

"Are you kidding me? He's trying to kick us out before we've even had a chance to eat!"

"He's probably under pressure from the manager to get people in and out."

"I don't care." Kelly put down his fork and crossed his arms over his chest. "They should set up tables outside if they want to serve more customers. I plan on enjoying my meal."

"Then eat," William said, nodding at Kelly's plate. He

concentrated on finishing his own food. He soon had the plate cleared, not that it mattered because Kelly was still taking his sweet time.

"Let's just go," William pleaded. "I don't want dessert. It's too expensive and I'm already full."

"You are not," Kelly said. "I don't think I've ever heard you utter those words before."

"It's true," William said. "The steak was filling. So were those grain things."

"Quinoa," Kelly murmured, looking miserable. He took a couple more bites, then shoved away his plate and reached for the check. "Fine, we'll go, but I'm not leaving him a tip."

"It's probably not his fault," William said. "Like I said—"

"I know, I know." Kelly dug through his wallet. "The poor guy's manager is forcing him to be so rude. There. Let's go."

"Did you leave a tip?" William asked, not moving.

Kelly looked him dead in the eye. And lied. "Yes."

William didn't argue further. He just wanted to leave and go somewhere more comfortable for them both. Being out in the night air made him feel better. He took Kelly's hand and squeezed, relieved when it was squeezed back.

"What now?" William asked.

"I don't know," Kelly said. "I didn't expect that to go so quickly."

"Which means we still have plenty of time for other things," William said, trying to get him into a better mood. "More exciting things."

"Horndog," Kelly accused, but he smiled. "My place or yours?"

"Mine," William said. "But first, can we make a quick stop?" He nodded across the street to a supermarket.

"Okay."

Once they had parked there, William made Kelly wait in the car. He ran inside to the bakery section and picked up an entire cake. The store's management must have known customers would have a need for emergency Valentine pastries, because a large selection decorated with roses and hearts was still available. William paid for his purchase and carried it out to the car, presenting it to Kelly at the driver-side window.

"What is this?" Kelly asked, already laughing.

"Dessert," William said. "Twice as much at half the cost."

"More like ten times as much. Get in the car, you big lug."

The atmosphere was much nicer on the drive home. It got a little tense when his mother met them in the kitchen, but soon they were alone in his room.

"Do you want to watch something on TV?" William asked.

Kelly seemed confused. "I thought we were going to get freaky."

"We gotta have some cake first." They had brought two slices upstairs with them. "How about we watch an episode of *Beast Wars* while we eat? Then afterwards, you can show me what sort of animal you turn into."

Kelly grimaced. "Can we not?"

William was confused. "Not what?"

"It's a nice show," Kelly said, "but I've already gotten a feel for it."

"Yeah, but we're an episode away from one of the absolute best."

"I just thought it would be nice if we could watch something made for adults."

William shrugged like it didn't matter. But it did, because stupid or not, he loved the show, and realizing that Kelly didn't somehow felt personal. "I guess we could watch music videos or something."

"Good luck finding any," Kelly said, taking the remote. He switched on the television and clicked through a few channels. "Here we go. *Bones*. That's usually pretty good, although honestly, I mostly just watch it for David Boreanaz. He's crazy fine!"

"Who?" When he saw with his own eyes, it only made him feel more insecure, because the guy looked nothing like him. William sat next to Kelly and quietly ate his cake, intending to be open-minded, but the show just wasn't what he usually liked. In other words, it was a little too serious. Kelly seemed enamored, so he tried his best to follow along.

Once the show was over and the slices of cake consumed, William turned off the television, eager to find common ground again. He made sure the door was locked, smiling sheepishly when he turned around.

"What are you up to?" Kelly asked, batting his eyelashes

playfully. He rose and came close to William, reaching for his tie. Then he chuckled.

"What?" William asked.

"Nothing," Kelly said, working loose the knot his mother had so carefully tied. "It's cute."

"What is?"

"You dress like a Mormon."

The smile slid off his face the same time the tie slipped free from his collar.

Kelly held it up, grinning as he tossed it behind his back. Then he must have noticed how unhappy William looked because his expression became concerned. "What's wrong?"

"Nothing," William said, moving around him. With his back to Kelly, it was easier to express himself. "You don't like me very much, do you?"

"What? Why would you say that?"

He felt Kelly's hand on his shoulder, turning him around, but William couldn't make eye contact. "You think everything I like is stupid. *Beast Wars*—"

"It's a cartoon!"

"I know, but I like it. Or you act like I'm dumb for wanting to join the Coast Guard."

"I just want you to think about your options!"

"You want me to lose weight—"

"Stop it!" Kelly stooped to look him in the eye. "I *love* your body. Are you kidding? You're exactly my type. The bigger, the better. I was only trying to talk you into joining the Olympics so we could be together."

William swallowed. "Really?"

"Yes," Kelly said. "We both graduate next year, and I don't like the idea of us going separate ways. Have you thought about that?"

"Not really," William admitted.

"I like you," Kelly said. "But sometimes I don't understand you."

"Meaning?"

"The waiter."

"Not this again," William pleaded. "Can't we just drop it?"

"Can't you just admit that he was an asshole? I don't get why you're nice to people when they're mean to you."

"Because it only makes things worse," William said. "You're letting him ruin our night."

Kelly exhaled and looked away. "Maybe you're right. All I know is that other couples would bitch about him together. That can be fun. It helps blow off steam! I can't decide if you're genuinely nice or if you're just holding it all in. Maybe it doesn't matter. It's been a weird night. Should I go?"

"No," William said. "Let's give it one more chance."

"In that case," Kelly said, moving close and placing his hands on William's chest, "I suggest we don't let ourselves get tangled up in useless words."

William opened his mouth, but Kelly placed a finger over it. Then he understood, taking that hand and kissing it. The rest of the night would be expressions of the heart, not misunderstandings of the mind.

Patterns are defined by repetition. William found himself reliving the same scenario over and over again. He and Kelly would clash, then they would resolve any hurt feelings by having sex. Like when Kelly refused to join him on the trip to Galveston. Royal, his own brother, had gone with William, and they had a great time. Kelly stayed behind. Words between them were terse when William returned, but they hopped in the sack and worked out their frustrations that way. This pattern repeated when William was paired with Jared for a school assignment. He turned out to be not such a bad guy and actually shared more of his interests than Kelly did. They even hung out once, but when Kelly found out he was angry. And hurt. This time it took more than the usual to smooth things over. They had finally taken sex to the next level, William performing the way Kelly expected him to, and admittedly, it felt great. Not just physically but emotionally. This wasn't a permanent fix. They continued squabbling, hurt replaced by anger, anger diffused with sex, and over and over again it went.

He was reminded of those final months of his parents' marriage, the next argument never far away. For William and Kelly, they didn't have an affair testing their resolve, or a marriage and children to consider. Breaking up would be a lot less messy. At times William thought that might be for the best. Then he would picture it happening and his heart would ache.

Still, he wondered if they should at least talk about it. Maybe today.

He went to the closet and chose an outfit he knew Kelly would approve of, since he had picked it out for him during a shopping trip. He slid the navy blue shirt over each arm and turned back to the bedroom without buttoning up the front. That's when the door opened. Kelly was standing there, looking him over. William pulled the shirt shut to cover himself. "You're early."

Kelly walked in and shut the door behind him. "I'm not early. I said I'd pick you up before dinner."

"It's only five."

"Which is before dinner." Kelly unslung his backpack, setting it on the bed. "If I'm early, it's because I wanted to give you this."

He unzipped the pack and pulled out a wrapped present, tugging to get it free.

William quickly tried to remember if today was a birthday or any sort of important holiday, but couldn't think of much to celebrate in May except the school year coming to an end. "What's the occasion?"

"There doesn't need to be one," Kelly said, sitting on the mattress edge. "I like showering my men with gifts. I also like showering with my men. Ha ha. Um."

William sat beside him on the mattress, accepting the present and peeling back the tape and then the paper. This revealed a colorful box and a familiar logo—a Transformer, although different from the others he owned. This one was a helicopter with a very special livery.

"It's not an animal," Kelly said. "But I thought… Well, it's a Transformer and—"

"It's a Coast Guard helicopter!" William exclaimed. "This is a Eurocopter Dauphin! An AS365!"

"I'll take your word for it."

"Holy shit!" William said. "I didn't even know they made something like this!"

Kelly fought down a smile. "I figured it's two of your hobbies rolled up into one. I know it doesn't match the rest of your collection."

"I love it," William said. More than that, he appreciated what it symbolized, because on more than one occasion he worried

Kelly didn't like him as a person and looked down on his interests. This gift was an affirmation to the contrary. William leaned over, giving his boyfriend a kiss. "I love you!"

"I'm glad to hear it," Kelly said. "Now open it up. The helicopter mode has a little hook on a string that you can use to rescue drowning people."

William happily complied. He made a fool of himself, playing with the toy in front of Kelly and grinning like a little kid. He felt silly for questioning their relationship. Sure they had their ups and downs, but clearly they both cared deeply for each other. That was enough.

They headed out on a date, another restaurant, but this time everything was perfect. No pushy waiters or overpriced food. No Kelly making a scene. Just big portions and fun conversation. William felt as though the universe wanted to reassure him that everything was okay. This relationship was a good thing. After stuffing themselves, they agreed to go for a walk before returning to the car so they wouldn't feel so sluggish. Kelly seemed to have a destination in mind, and another surprise, because he fetched his backpack from the car. They rounded a corner, and William spotted a familiar landmark.

"The Pfluger Bridge!" he declared.

"Gesundheit," Kelly replied. His eyes were half-lidded, just as they always were when feeling amorous.

"That's where we had our first kiss."

"Is it?" Kelly said, feigning confusion. "I must have forgotten."

"Don't play coy." William took his hand, leading him forward. "You're just an old romantic. Admit it."

"You have no idea."

They strolled along the bridge, pausing to glance at the skyline, or watch a pair of ducks swim down the river. Then they reached the right spot. William would never forget it. A kiss had happened there, the first in a very long line. He pulled Kelly close, wanting to add another to his collection.

"Not so fast," Kelly said, dodging. "First you have to answer a trivia question."

"Seriously?"

"Yup. How long have we been together now?"

William did some mental arithmetic. "Six months?"

"To the day," Kelly said.

"Wait, I thought it was early November. We played pool together. Remember?"

Kelly rolled his eyes. "We weren't together then. I wasn't even sure it was a date."

"It was to me," William said.

Kelly shook his head in disbelief. "You can't date someone without their knowledge. I didn't know you liked me until we were standing right here. So it's six months ago today."

"Six and a half?" William bartered.

Kelly sighed. "It'll be a miracle if we make it to seven. Now be quiet and let me work my magic."

He opened his backpack again, which he must have reloaded on the sly. Either that or he was a magician, because like a rabbit from a hat, he pulled out a small bottle of champagne. It matched one they had shared on a previous special occasion.

"Now you're going to tell me we weren't official until New Year's Eve," William joked.

"Don't start," Kelly said. "Tonight is about celebrating our entire relationship. All the highlights that have made it special so far. Can you guess what we'll be reenacting later on?"

"You have a collapsible tent in that backpack?" William asked with a grin, thinking of the camping trip they had taken with the gay youth group. Not a perfect night, but it sure had ended well!

"Exactly. And no, I don't, but this time I remembered to bring glasses." Kelly produced two that were disposable.

"I can't believe your mom buys you this stuff," William said, taking the bottle and peeling the foil from the cork.

"Begging was involved." Kelly set down his backpack and held the glasses at the ready. "My parents don't mind me drinking, as long as I only do so at home and I don't leave after I've started. It's only on special occasions really. If I asked them to buy me a six-pack every week, there's no way they would."

"Might be worth a shot anyway," William joked. When the cork popped, they watched it soar into the air before it plopped into the river below. "I wonder where it'll end up?"

"Probably in our drinking water. Speaking of which, I'm parched."

"Coming right up." William carefully poured golden liquid into the plastic flutes, alternating between them until both were full. Then he set the bottle on the ground so he could take one of the drinks.

Kelly raised his glass, eyes shining. "May six months turn into six years, and six years into six decades. You've made me incredibly happy, and I can't wait until—"

"Gentlemen? I'm going to need to see some ID."

William's stomach sank as he turned to face a police officer. He could feel his entire future changing in that instant: Being charged with possession, a criminal record that prevented him from joining the Coast Guard, and a job as a public pool lifeguard because he didn't have other plans. They hadn't actually taken a sip yet, so if they were polite, and the officer was understanding, maybe the whole ordeal could all be avoided. William set down his glass and grabbed his wallet.

"Now!" the officer barked.

He was addressing Kelly, who hadn't budged. "We didn't actually drink any."

William felt like groaning. He recognized that tone of voice! He handed his driver's license to the officer, hoping to distract him.

The officer accepted it, attention still on Kelly. "I'm still going to need to see identification."

Kelly huffed, then set his glass on the ground and complied.

The police officer took his time examining their IDs. "Neither of you are old enough to drink."

"Busted," Kelly said. "So it's a good thing we didn't drink."

The officer's brow became more creased. "You're also not old enough to possess alcohol, especially an open container."

"My parents bought it for me," Kelly said. "That makes it legal. Texas law."

Now the officer glared. "The law says a parent can buy their child a drink so long as it's consumed in their presence. *That's* the law." The officer grabbed the radio on his shoulder and said a few codes. William had tried memorizing them all a few years ago. He was pretty sure the officer intended to take them to his patrol car to run a background check. "I'll need you both to come with me."

Kelly made a sound of frustration, his voice rising. "We didn't drink anything!"

"Kelly," William said warningly.

"What?" Kelly demanded, gesturing grandly. "My parents bought this for us." He turned to address the officer. "I'm supposed to drink it in their custody? Fine! I'll go home and do so. Or take it away from us, and I'll drink with my parents some other time. But we didn't do anything wrong, so there's no fucking way I'm going anywhere with you!"

The officer looked him over, clearly assessing whether or not Kelly posed a threat, when all he wanted to do was put them in the car while he made sure they hadn't been in trouble before.

William pinched the bridge of his nose. "You're only making it worse."

Kelly turned to face him, his expression pure disbelief, like William had betrayed him.

"I don't want to handcuff you," the officer said, "but I think it's for the best. Turn around."

"You're kidding me," Kelly said.

"Turn around!" the officer growled, stance becoming more aggressive.

William turned to face the river, arms behind his back, one wrist resting against the other. He felt relieved when out of the corner of his eye he saw Kelly do the same.

"It'll be okay," William said, trying to keep his boyfriend calm. "They'll call our parents, and it'll all get sorted out. Like you said, we didn't drink anything." Then louder, he added, "Can you give us breathalyzer tests, please? We want it on record that we haven't consumed any alcohol."

"I'll be glad to," the officer replied. "Thank you for cooperating."

Kelly was handcuffed first. No surprise there. Then William felt cold metal close around his wrists. The officer started talking into his radio again. Kelly turned around without permission, and when he wasn't reprimanded, William did the same.

The response came in that they had no prior convictions or outstanding warrants. The police officer took a photo of the champagne bottle. Then he picked it up and poured it into the river.

"Isn't that littering?" Kelly snapped.

"That's enough out of you," the officer grumbled.

"I know my rights," Kelly said, still pushing his luck. "I have freedom of speech."

The officer shook drops of spilled champagne from his hand. "I know your rights too. In fact, let me read them to you."

William groaned inwardly. They were being arrested.

Chapter Eight

As much as it irked Kelly, something about authority—be it military or law enforcement—fascinated William. The training process, the logistics of coordinating so many individuals, and especially the vehicles and gear, all captured his imagination. Squad cars, boats, bulletproof jackets, life vests—he couldn't get enough, probably because of the cool technological innovations. Then there was the thrill. Most people worked in an office, or stood behind a counter, but others fought crime and saved lives. Pretty badass! As they were taken to the police station, William focused on those aspects, even having a lively conversation with the officer during the drive. He had held his tongue since arriving though, sensing that he was only making Kelly angrier. Not that his silence seemed to help. Kelly paced the small concrete room they were placed in, repeatedly expressing his indignation. After some coaxing, William got him to sit down at the table.

"So what do you think will happen?" Kelly asked, sounding more concerned than angry at this point. "What's our punishment going to be?"

William cocked his head and considered the possibilities. "If we're lucky, they'll let our parents decide. We're too young to go to jail, and juvenile hall seems a little extreme."

"So we're grounded."

William sighed. "I know I will be." He thought back to the first time Errol had been caught smoking pot. Their mother had yelled, argued, and dished out every possible punishment until the day Errol moved out of the house. Now his brother had adult status, making her more tolerant, but William still had another year or two before he'd have such freedom. Kelly's parents seemed more liberal, since they had bought him the alcohol in the first place. "You said your mom will be understanding."

Kelly shook his head. "Wishful thinking. You have to admit it's pretty silly. It's like being caught raising a hammer in front of a jewelry store window. Why didn't the cop wait for something to actually happen?"

William smiled. "I definitely would have let us drink first. Hell, if I was an officer and saw two hot guys getting tipsy and romantic, I'd take a few steps back and enjoy the show."

Kelly chuckled, his shoulders relaxing. "Then again, it probably would have been worse if he'd let us."

"Probably."

Kelly considered him, a hint of a smile on his lips. Then he reached across the table. Any affectionate intent halted when the door opened. The officer was back, and with him was a true authority figure: William's mother. The door shut again, the officer leaving them alone. William was tempted to ask him to stay, just in case he needed protection.

"Tell me you have a reasonable explanation," Kate said. "You were walking across the bridge, you found an open bottle, and you picked it up at the absolute worst moment."

"I'm sorry," William said. "It was meant to be romantic."

His mother sighed, standing between them and setting her purse on the table. "Romance doesn't involve getting drunk. In public. In fact, I'd say that's the opposite of romance."

"We didn't," William said. "Did the officer tell you about the breathalyzer tests?"

"Yes, and frankly, it doesn't make me feel much better. He stopped you before you did something very stupid." She turned to Kelly. "How were you planning on getting home? Were you going to drink and drive?"

"No," Kelly said. "I was only going to have a few sips, maybe a glass at most. We weren't planning on getting wasted."

"It's champagne," she countered. "The sugar makes it go straight to your head."

"One drink is within the legal limit," Kelly retorted.

"For an adult! You're just a child!"

"I'm seventeen years old!" Kelly shot back.

Kate crossed her arms over her chest. "And hopefully in four more years, you'll have smartened up quite a bit, because most cities frown on stumbling around drunk in public. And when it comes to driving, you'll be lucky to keep your license."

"I wasn't planning on getting drunk," Kelly snarled. "We were only going to have one fucking drink together and—"

"Enough!" William's fists were clenching along with his jaw. This was all Kelly's fault! William was willing to forgive the champagne, because it had been a sweet gesture, but his smart mouth and bad temper were equally sour, making everything worse, and the last indignation he was willing to suffer—the absolute final straw—was someone back-talking his mom. "Don't argue with my mother! Don't argue with anyone else tonight either or you *will* regret it. Understand me?"

Kelly looked as though he'd been slapped. He remained wide-eyed as he nodded. Then he studied the table, lips firmly sealed. Kate sat down, appearing more disappointed than anything. William felt his anger drain away. He put a hand on his mother's shoulder, then reached across the table to take Kelly's hand. They would get through this. Everything seemed like a hopeless mess now, but they would find their way back to happier times.

"Heard you got into some trouble!"

Lewis said this in high spirits, like William had gotten reprimanded for kissing a girl at school or roughhousing with another guy. Boys will be boys! Then again, it beat another lecture from his mother, who reminded him every day of how big a mistake he had made. William passed a cardboard box to his father, then reached into his trunk for another. A number of trips like this had already occurred, Lewis's possessions leaving the house a few boxes at a time.

"So what happened?" his father pressed.

"I got caught drinking." William cradled the box under one arm so he could shut the trunk. "With my boyfriend," he stressed, hoping to upset his father. He wasn't sure why. Maybe because his brothers had completely turned their backs on the man, forcing William to remain in touch and face awkward situations like this alone. It was either that or leave it up to his mom, which he didn't want.

"Drinking, huh?" Lewis winked. "Spend any time in jail? Do you have to wear one of those ankle bracelets to track your whereabouts?"

This wasn't the reaction William had hoped to provoke, so he gave a less dramatic report of events. And the ramifications. "Just community service since we didn't actually drink anything. My court date was last week. I thought you'd be there."

Lewis led the way toward the apartment complex. "I didn't think your mother would be happy to see me."

"I guess not."

"So a slap on the wrist and a little community service? That's not so bad."

"No," William said. "Yesterday was my first day volunteering. I liked it. Mom probably knew I would, which is why I'm also grounded for a month. She's not exactly happy with me right now."

"I bet."

They walked up the usual stairwell, but his father turned left instead of right.

"Where are you going?"

"We moved out of Gina's apartment," Lewis said, "got a bigger place. Just two bedrooms, but there's more space now and—"

William dropped the box he was carrying. It hit the concrete walkway with a thud.

"What's wrong?" his father asked, turning around.

"You guys got a place together?"

"Well, yeah. We've been living together for months now. Why are you so surprised?"

"Because this makes it permanent!" William said, emotion rising. "I thought you would… Never mind."

"You thought I would come to my senses." His father set down the box in front of a door. His new home. "I love your mother—"

"No you don't!"

"Yes I do!" Lewis took a step closer and put a hand on William's shoulder. "And I love you. But you have to understand that your mother and I weren't getting along. I don't just mean we had a couple of bad days. This had been going on for a long time. Neither one of us was happy."

"And then you met Gina."

"Yes, and then I met Gina. I don't expect you to understand how that changed me inside, but I hope someday you'll see things from my—"

"No way!" William said adamantly. "I'll never understand, because even if you did have feelings for someone else, that doesn't justify what you did! If you had *any* respect for Mom, you would have left her before you started cheating."

"You're right," his father said, turning to the door and fishing keys from his pocket. "But things are never that simple."

William didn't respond. He picked up the box again and followed his father inside. He glowered at the interior, judging it harshly, when in truth it looked like most living rooms did: couch, television, coffee table, and shelves. At least Gina wasn't there.

"Something to drink?" his father asked. "I don't have champagne…"

"Ha ha."

"A soda?"

"No thanks."

Lewis sat on the couch. William remained standing. He had called a truce with his father, but he never stuck around very long.

"How's your mother?"

"Great." That's all William ever said about her to him.

"And your boyfriend? Did they let you share a cell?"

William thought of Kelly, the warm rush of feelings still absent. He hadn't felt it since that night. Something had broken inside, which made it even harder to be around his father, to be reminded of how feelings could falter and die. Not even sex seemed capable of repairing this crumbling bridge. Kelly had snuck over the other day when the house was empty. Sleeping together felt good, but afterwards they had argued about the kind of community service they would perform. Ultimately they had chosen different options. William couldn't help but wonder if they should follow that separation to its ultimate conclusion.

"Everything okay, son?"

William tried to hide his frown, but it was too late. Everything was definitely *not* okay, but he wouldn't let that change who he was. "I'm not going to end up like you. I'm not a quitter."

He turned away, wishing he'd done so before seeing the hurt on his father's face. Then he hurried to the door and left.

A fresh start. William promised himself he would make the effort. After storming out of his father's apartment, he had driven around until he was scheduled to volunteer again. Once he reported for community service and was busy packing canned food into boxes, he mentally reviewed each problem he and Kelly faced, trying to find a solution for each. He was done arguing. Kelly had a hot temper, but as long as one of them remained calm, they could avoid future fights. William's fading passion for their relationship wasn't a big deal either. They were both grounded, forbidden to see each other outside of school. Without privacy, they couldn't stoke the fire, but that would resolve itself once they were no longer in trouble. They were doing what they could regardless, William giving Kelly rides to school. That's where he was now, parked down the street so Mrs. Phillips wouldn't find out.

He spotted Kelly trotting down the sidewalk and rolling his eyes at the gray sky and drizzle. William impassively watched him approach the car, already not wanting to deal with a foul mood.

Stay positive. That was the key. When they were in motion and Kelly asked in venomous tones how volunteering at the Food Bank had gone, William made sure his response sounded upbeat. "Great! The people there are really cool. We worked our butts off, but everyone is so pumped that it's kind of fun. My voice was hoarse at the end of the shift from talking so much. How was yours?"

"My voice?" Kelly said. "Silky smooth. I didn't talk to anyone. I just kept thinking of you. We could have had our picnic. It would have been perfect."

That's what he got for volunteering to pick up highway litter. William had tried talking him out if it, but he never listened. "Kelly—"

"Of course Sunday the weather turned to piss, so it's just as well you weren't there. I had to wear a trash bag to stay dry."

William looked over, offering an amused smile. "Really?"

Kelly snorted, features relaxing somewhat. "Yes. I tore a hole in one of them for my face. And two little holes for my arms."

"I'm sorry I missed out."

"I bet."

What they needed, he decided, was to spend time together. Work toward a common goal. "You can still come to the Food Bank with me next weekend."

"And you can still join me for trash duty next weekend," Kelly huffed. "Why do I have to be the one to compromise?"

"You really want me to answer that?"

"Please do."

"Because none of this would have happened if—" William clenched his jaw. "Never mind."

"No, say it!"

Kelly had turned to face him in the seat, rearing for a fight.

William wouldn't play that game. He shook his head.

Kelly didn't relent. "You think this is all my fault? I was trying to make our anniversary special!"

"It's not that," William said, unable to hold his tongue. "It's your attitude. If you had been nicer to the police officer, admitted that we were about to make a mistake, he might have let us go with just a warning."

He kept his attention on the road, the drizzle turning to a steady downpour, but he could still see Kelly shaking his head and easily picture the narrowed eyes. "I doubt that."

"I don't," William retorted, "because you're right. He could have called your mom, verified that she bought you the alcohol, and that you had permission to drink it. At home. He probably would have taken away the champagne, slapped us on the wrist, and let us get on with our evening. Instead he ended up *handcuffing* you. You get why, right?"

"Gee, I wonder."

"This isn't because you're black!" William shot back, his voice louder than he intended. "It's because sometimes you let your anger control you. Instead of trying to reason with the other person, or charm your way out of rough situations, you fly off the handle. Of course the police officer handcuffed you! Hell, I felt like doing the same."

"Because I stood up for myself?" Kelly said. "Jesus Christ, I had no idea you were so subservient. I guess I shouldn't be surprised. You're desperate to join the Coast Guard where some jarhead will tell you what to do and how to think."

William gripped the steering wheel tighter and looked over at him. "You just love bringing that up, don't you? Enlisting means everything to me, and you never pass up a chance to make me feel shitty about it."

"Maybe you should!" Kelly said. "Especially if the Coast Guard is more important to you than spending the weekend with your boyfriend!"

"So what?" William focused on the road again, turning up the windshield wipers to combat the rain. "You think eating sandwiches together while picking up trash sounds appealing to me? And really, why should I reward you for getting us into this mess?"

"So it's all my fault?"

"Yes! How can you not see that?"

"Maybe because I'm not interested in placing blame." Kelly looked out the window, head shaking. "I didn't make you feel bad for costing me the race."

William felt a pang of guilt. "The triathlon?"

"Yes, the triathlon. I didn't give you shit just because you tripped and fell. You're not perfect either. You never will be, no matter how much you try, so come down off that high horse."

That hurt. The triathlon had been special to him, the event that had brought them together. Obviously Kelly didn't feel the same way. William exhaled and attempted to make peace again. "It's not about either of us making mistakes. It's about how you react to them. You were cool during the race. Why couldn't you have been that way with the police officer?"

"With the pig?" Kelly snapped. Peace was obviously the last thing on his mind. "Maybe because I don't love him!"

"And do you still love me? All we do these days is fight. I think you did love me back then. I believe you. But something has changed because it's obvious I don't make you happy anymore."

"You do," Kelly said, the anger in his voice turning to hurt. "But not when you put other things before our relationship. Not just other things. Everything! Your mom, the Coast Guard, and the needs of just about anyone who stumbles into your life. You're always thinking about them and not us. But despite all of that, no matter how much your chivalry makes me want to tear my hair out, you still make me happy."

William was tired. He wanted to turn the car around and go back to bed. He wanted to pull the blankets over his head and sleep until all of this blew over—the trouble with the police, his parents' divorce, and especially this relationship. Love is what he desired most, and yet it left him baffled and exhausted. He thought of Kelly's first relationship with an Italian guy named José and how they had both been in love with the idea of being in love. Now William understood because he was pretty sure he and Kelly didn't love each other. Lately they didn't even seem to like each other! All the good William had once seen in him—his single-minded focus, his refusal to compromise or care what others thought of him—now bothered him most. This wasn't working out.

"The thing is," William said, tongue feeling thick, "I'm not sure I'm happy anymore."

"What are you saying?"

"I don't know." William bit his lip, wanting to stop the words from pouring out, but he knew they were needed. He glanced over at Kelly, who looked as though he had been slapped, but even that wasn't enough to stop him. "Maybe just a break. We can try being friends again and—"

"Because I messed up?" Kelly yelled. "Because I'm human and actually let myself feel anger? What's wrong with that? Why do you have to be such a fucking robot?"

"I'm not a robot." William glared through the windshield, refusing to take the bait.

"Sure you are. Just like your toys. That must be why you admire them so much because you want to be the same way. Plastic and unfeeling."

"I get angry!" William snapped. Then the dam broke, and he was shouting just as loud as Kelly. "You *know* I do. But I also understand the concept of restraint! You flip out every five seconds like—"

"I do when I'm with you because you always—"

"That's why we shouldn't be together! Something's wrong!"

Kelly seethed. "You will never, *ever*, be in a relationship where you don't argue. Not that it matters. Where you're going, you'll never date again."

William glared at him, already knowing where this was headed. "And why's that?"

"You know why."

"Say it," William snarled. "Say it one more time. I fucking dare you, because if you do, it'll be the last time I listen to your crap."

For a second it looked as though Kelly was going to back down, but then those eyes became slivers, lips downturned in disgust. "Once you're in the Coast Guard—"

Shut up. William wanted nothing more than for Kelly to stop talking.

"—it's back in the closet or your superiors will disown you. You'll live your pathetic robot life—"

It's not that they didn't love each other, or didn't like each other. They *hated* each other. William had no doubt about it. He wanted to make a fist and swing at that mouth just so he would —

"—sleeping on a cold bunk every night—"

Shut.

"—sneaking off to a cruise park occasionally to suck—"

Up!

William jerked the wheel, cutting across a lane toward the side of the road. He felt a burst of satisfaction when Kelly sucked in air, too shocked to speak, voice faltering. He wanted to see anger? Fine! William would pull over, kick his sorry ass out into the rain, and be done with him forever. No more of his smart mouth and —

The wheels caught on the wet surface of the road, losing traction. The vehicle spun instead of pulling over. William hit the brakes, but that only made it worse. Headlights blinded him briefly as they faced oncoming traffic, so he tried jerking the wheel in the opposite direction. That did the trick! A symphony of screeching tires and honking horns filled the air as the car stopped sideways in the middle of the road, but he didn't care. He wanted Kelly out of his car and out of his life. He still felt like pummeling him, never wanting to hear that voice again. But he did, and it sounded like a mere squeak.

"William—"

He saw the beast just seconds before it hit them. Half of his attention was still on Kelly's face, surprised to see shame there, maybe even regret. The rest of him saw huge fat tires, a dirty metal grill, and headlights high and wide. Then came the explosion. They were in motion again, moving down the road even though the car remained sideways. William's head hit the steering wheel, the airbag exploding a second too late and knocking him back against the seat. The vehicle ground to a halt. William fought against the air bag, desperate to see what was going on around him. Even when cleared of obstacles, his vision remained a blur, heart convulsing so fast he thought it would burst, but at least the accident hadn't been fatal. For him.

Kelly! William managed to push the airbag to one side. He noticed first how cramped the interior had become, the metal frame now caved in and intruding on their space. Kelly had been pushed inward by the impact, one hip jutting toward him, like he sometimes did when feeling both silly and flirtatious. William swiped at the passenger airbag, trying to get a better look, comforted when he heard groaning because at least it meant Kelly wasn't… He focused on the task at hand, an idling engine falling silent outside. His progress was halted briefly when he felt warm liquid trickling down his face. William wiped at it, sparing only a glance to confirm the blood on his hand as he tried instead to fix blurry vision on his passenger. View unobscured now, he saw Kelly with his head hanging out the shattered window, like a dog wanting to revel in the breeze. He wasn't moving. "Are you okay?"

Kelly groaned in response and shifted, head raising to face the truck outside his window. William heard a door slam, feet hopping to the pavement. Then he looked down and saw red seeping into the material of the rapidly deflating airbag.

"Kelly!"

He pulled at the white fabric. The bag shifted enough that he saw metal and sinew, skin and fabric, all mashed together like a wretched stew. Panic blinded him briefly, his head throbbing, but he forced himself to focus, to face the ugly mess. Blood had pooled on the seat, trickled onto the floorboard, and he was pretty sure he saw the white of bone glistening within the same liquid.

"Stay still, stay still!" he said, fighting against the urge to scream. "Oh fuck! Where's my phone?"

Kelly grunted and shoved himself upright, looking at William with a quizzical expression, as if seeking an explanation. Didn't he feel the pain? Wasn't he aware of just how damaged his body was? William's gaze flicked downward, hoping he'd been mistaken, that it hadn't been so bad, but one glance confirmed that the nightmare persisted. This drew Kelly's attention downward. William wanted to stop him, knowing that his brain would finally register the pain when he saw the truth.

"Are you all right? What the hell were you thinking?"

William turned to his window and saw an older man who was unscathed but white as a sheet. He opened his mouth to say more but was cut off by a scream. It didn't sound human.

"Ambulance," William managed to grunt, but he didn't need to. The man outside his window was already backing away while pulling out his phone.

William turned his attention to Kelly, grabbing the hand that was clawing at the airbag to move it away. Kelly didn't need to see more. Neither of them did. Everything from his waist down was soaked in blood. It was a miracle that Kelly was alive at all!

"Stay with me," William said, clenching his hand tight. "Stay with me! Help is on the way. Stay with me."

Kelly's shrill screams stopped only when he sucked in air. Then he would resume. William ached in sympathy, blinking against his stinging eyes as blood fogged his vision and mixed with his tears. Kelly's screams ceased as suddenly as they began, his head lolling before his entire body went still. William released his hand to struggle with his seatbelt, wanting to move closer to Kelly so he could… what? Administer CPR? What little training William had came from summers spent as a lifeguard, or learning about rescue swimmers. Dragging someone out of the water, preventing hypothermia, forcing the water from their lungs—all of that was useless now.

Kelly was dead. William was pretty sure of that because he wasn't moving anymore, and the human body only contained so much blood. The cruelest part was how the absent affection finally awoke inside of William. He loved Kelly. Of course he did! Why else would they get so angry if they didn't have feelings for each other? And now he had ruined it all, had extinguished the life of the person he adored. "Take me, instead," William said, voice shuddering. He wasn't even sure who he was addressing. God? The Devil? Anyone with the power to undo this atrocity. He finally managed to get his seatbelt off, twisting in his seat, grasping Kelly's arm and not understanding what to do. "Please! I'm so sorry. Take me instead. I beg you. Please! Please…"

He touched Kelly's face and tried to make himself be silent so he could listen for another breath but was deafened by his own heartbeat thudding in his ears. William was trembling, his breath ragged, head aching and dizzy. Then he noticed that the distant sound of sirens had grown louder.

"They're almost here," William said. "Stay with me, Kelly. I love you, okay? I'm sorry about what I said. I love you."

He decided to get out of the car, to wave down the ambulances or maybe go around to the passenger side. CPR was better than nothing. At least Kelly would be breathing. Was he breathing now? Was he really dead? William found himself already outside the vehicle, his legs shaking until they buckled and he fell to his knees. He felt someone lifting him up. William shoved the man aside with barely a glance before he scrambled around the front of the car. The windshield on Kelly's side was opaque with cracks but still held together. Other cars had pulled over. He saw someone rushing forward with an umbrella, but none of them mattered. Only Kelly. He wanted to open the door, but the handle was lost somewhere in the folds of crumpled metal. From this angle Kelly appeared fine, his face serene. William reached for him through the remains of the window, but someone pulled him back.

"Son, I don't think you're supposed to move him!"

William glanced over at the man he had seen before, beard white and skin leathery. "Help me! We have to get him out of there. I can give him CPR."

The man released him, but only stood and stared as William yanked at the frame of the car door. His hand slid off wet metal so he grabbed the frame tighter and jerked. The door didn't open, but it shifted. Kelly's face knotted up in response. Then he moaned, eyes clenched shut. He was alive! Hope exploded in William's heart. He pulled twice as hard, the man behind him shouting. The sirens were so loud now he couldn't hear the words, but they didn't matter, because Kelly was alive! William would rip the car to pieces if need be.

Then more hands were on him, pulling him back. Firemen rushed forward, one carrying a heavy tool. The jaws of life? William resisted whoever was pulling him away, wanting to be of use. A police officer blocked his view.

"He's alive!" William shouted, straining to see past him. "You have to save him! Please!"

Then his stomach turned and his legs gave way again. He fell to his knees and retched, crimson drops joining the splash of bile that hit the street, both soon diluted by the rain. He tried pushing himself to his feet. One of his eyes was refusing to open now, the other nearly useless, but he had to see what was happening. He had to make sure Kelly was okay. His body convulsed again, dry heaves this time. He was aware of someone standing over him and holding an umbrella. Then a blanket was wrapped around his shoulders, as if it could prevent him from going into shock or provide any comfort. Hands helped him up and guided him toward the back of an ambulance. Once inside, a paramedic started asking him questions, touching his head with a gloved hand, shining a light in his eyes. William tried to ignore this, his attention focused on the wreck outside where a number of forms gathered around Kelly's side of the car. Then the ambulance doors closed, and panic hit William so hard he could barely breathe. He lurched for the rear of the vehicle, not wanting to leave without Kelly, but it was too late. They were taking William away from where he needed to be.

Chapter Nine

Pain and guilt. William couldn't decide which was worse, just that he deserved more of both. He had two stitches in his head, wore nothing but a hospital robe, and was propped up in bed. He ignored the television that the old man in the next bed over was watching, choosing instead to stare at the door, hoping for anyone in authority to appear. The nurse was avoiding him. At first she had been patient enough to find out for him that Kelly had reached the hospital too and was in critical care. Since then he had begged for an update every time she entered the room. Now he didn't see her at all. The doctor, during his brief visit, had only insisted Kelly was receiving the best possible care and refused to say more.

The hours ticked by. William grew increasingly agitated. The urge to do something—anything—was overwhelming. Turn back time, heal Kelly with a wish, start the day over and not make any of the same mistakes. But of course none of that was possible. He had ruined everything. Kelly was hurt, possibly fighting for his life, all because of him.

Then his mother showed up. She fussed over him, but he ignored her affection, launching into a description of what had happened. The old man turned off the television to listen, but William didn't care. He found himself describing the accident in morbid detail, obsessing over images that refused to be exorcised from his mind. Kelly half-conscious and bleeding to death. The gunpowder smell of air bags, one of them stained red. A scream like a wounded animal.

"Honey!" his mother said. "That's enough!" She placed a hand over his forehead, avoiding his stitches. "You feel hot. I'll talk to the nurse about giving you something. Maybe a sedative too."

"The doctor doesn't want to give me anything in case I have a concussion."

His mother looked even more concerned. "Are you in pain?"

"Yes," he said. His head still throbbed, but even if offered a painkiller, he would turn it down. He deserved this suffering, especially since it had to be a fraction of what Kelly was going through. "I need you to find out how he's doing. Last I heard he was in the ICU."

"I'm sure the doctor will tell us next time he—"

"Please."

His mother took in his pleading expression, then nodded and left the room. The old man turned the TV back on, having decided the live performance was over. After what felt like an eternity, Kate finally returned.

"I spoke to Kelly's parents," she said.

William sat up. "And?"

"I'm sure he'll be fine. You're both young. You'll heal quickly."

"But he's stable?"

Kate nodded, still looking pale.

"There's something you're not telling me."

His mother placed a hand over his, but he pulled it away, not wanting to be comforted. "The doctors have a tough decision to make," she said.

"What's that supposed to mean? I don't get it."

"They're not sure they can save one of his legs."

William stared at her. Then he almost threw up again, because it was impossible to imagine Kelly no longer speeding around the high school track, his expression cool and confident. He really was the fastest guy in school. William had no doubt those legs would have carried him all the way to the Olympics.

Not now. William had damaged him beyond repair and stolen away his dreams. His own too, because when the Coast Guard found out about this, there was no way in hell they would accept him. One turn of the wheel had ruined two lives. In truth, he only cared about one of them. The offer still stood, if God or whoever was willing. Let Kelly pull through this and let him remain whole. William would gladly give his own leg, his own life, to spare him.

"Willy!"

His mother's voice sounded distant. He didn't remember curling into a ball or covering his head with a pillow. The moan escaping from his lips sounded about right though, because it echoed the pain inside of him. When the doctor entered the room, nurse in tow and syringe in one hand, William fought them because he didn't want anything that would make him feel better. He was stronger than them both. Only his mother shouting his name made him relent. The needle slid into his skin, medicine rushing through his veins, numbing his heart, silencing his mind, and allowing him to escape the nightmare he had created by slipping into cold darkness.

William woke up slowly. The pillow beneath his cheek felt different than what he normally slept on. Thinner, the case scratchier. His body was stiff and his head was groggy. Both tensed at the sequence of images that came. Memories, or just a nightmare? He opened his eyes slowly, hoping none of it had been real, and nearly closed them again when he saw his surroundings. A hospital room. Only his concern for Kelly made him roll over and sit up.

Errol was seated not far away, tongue sticking out one corner of his mouth as he played his Nintendo DS. When he noticed that William had stirred, he looked up. "You're not going to make a run for it, are you?"

"What?" William replied, mouth dry.

"Mom thinks you've gone mental. She said I'm supposed to guard you, which is stupid, because you're twice my size. Hey, if you *are* going to break out of here, there's no need to punch me. I can pretend to be unconscious." Errol tried a smile.

William didn't return the gesture. "How's Kelly?"

"Don't freak out, promise?"

William nodded.

"He's doing better, but he lost the leg."

William swallowed and laid back down, staring at the ceiling. He was tempted to lash out so they would sedate him again, but he knew he needed to face this. Maybe he could find some sort of solution. Obviously Kelly's leg was beyond salvation, but maybe William could help rehabilitate him, encourage him to get one of those running blades and keep pursuing his dreams. Or maybe William could hang himself at the nearest opportunity, because that's what he deserved.

He covered his face with his hands, fighting against tears. How could he live with himself? This wasn't murder or rape, but it was just as despicable. He had ruined a life. His mind worked overtime to find a solution, only to come up empty. Nearly. He could apologize. It wouldn't really help, but it was better than nothing. He moved his hands away when he heard someone enter the room. His mother. "I want to see him."

"You're awake!" she said, hurrying to his side. "How are you?"

"I want to see Kelly," he repeated.

"I don't think that's possible right now. How's your head? I'll call the doctor."

"No. I'm fine"

She didn't listen. The nurse came first, a different one than before. Then the doctor showed up and looked him over. William remained on his best behavior, not wanting to be sedated again. He needed to stay awake. For Kelly. This didn't mean he ate his food when it was brought, or that he allowed himself to enjoy his brother's jokes, or even share in his roommate's television habits. He deprived himself of any pleasure. His mind raced to find a solution, his body wanting to rise and seek out Kelly, but he wasn't allowed to leave the room. He was trapped in his bed and useless. Maybe that was a fitting punishment.

"The police were here this morning," his mother said after his lunch had been cleared away. Errol had scarfed down most of it before leaving for his part-time job. "You'll need to talk to them soon so they can finish their report."

"Good," William said. "Maybe they'll throw me in jail."

"Stop it!" Kate looked at him incredulously. "Why would you say something like that?"

"Because it's what I deserve."

"It's not! Honey, it was an accident. Terrible as they may be, these things happen!"

"It wasn't an accident," William said. "I did it on purpose."

His mother's mouth opened. Then she looked over at the other patient, who was watching Wheel of Fortune, and lowered her voice. "What do you mean?"

"We were arguing and I wanted to scare him so—"

"Did you want to get into an accident?"

"No, but I—"

"Then you didn't do it on purpose. You understand me?" His mother glanced around the room again, her voice firm when she continued. "When you talk to the police, I don't want you spouting any of this nonsense. You were arguing and you tried to pull over. That's what you told me." She raised a hand to stop him from interjecting. "You were careless. That's all they need to know."

William sat upright, his jaw clenching. "I'm not scared to face my punishment. I don't care if I go to jail."

"That's fine," his mother said, mouth tight, "but I need you with me. Understand? You might not care what happens to you, but I do, and I can't handle my son going to jail on top of—" She shook her head. "Everything else."

The divorce. If William went away, she would be alone. No more mediator to act on her behalf. Just a broken marriage, an empty house, and a son behind bars.

"Your father was here this morning," she said, still searching his eyes. "He says he'll be back after work."

"Okay." William saw the strain on her features. "I'm sorry. For all of this."

Kate nodded. "Just promise me. When you speak to the police, tell them the truth: You pulled over without checking your blind spot. Simple as that. You're no good to anyone in jail. It won't make anything better."

Not for her, and not for Kelly. If there was anything he could do to make up for this, his best chance would be while he was still free. Physically at least. William didn't need anyone to place him behind bars. The guilt that lined his stomach was just the beginning of his punishment, and he didn't see it ending anytime soon.

The sky outside the window was dark. Even the activity of the hospital slowed during the late hours. William was finally alone. He had been on his best behavior, eating dinner when it came and not having another meltdown. He had stopped talking about Kelly or asking for updates. Hell, he even managed a pathetic smile for his mother when—on the verge of leaving—she had hesitated.

"It's going to be okay," she assured him.

"I know," he lied. "You're right."

The doctor cleared him of concussion. William insisted his head no longer hurt when offered painkillers. In truth a dull throb remained, but he didn't care. He had wanted his mind sharp for the evening. For now.

He slid out of bed and padded barefoot to the door. He looked back once to see his roommate, head back and mouth wide open as he snoozed, the TV still on. Then he stepped into the hallway. He had seen other patients walking around, so this wasn't exactly forbidden. He tried to appear casual and not like he was sneaking around, which he definitely was. He avoided the nurses' station and ducked into a different hall when he heard voices approaching. Once out of his ward, he went to the elevators and studied the floorplan on the wall. He assumed Kelly was still in the Intensive Care Unit, so he navigated his way there.

When William reached the correct door, his stomach sank. He had pictured this part of the hospital as being like his own—hallways and separate rooms, a patient in each. Instead the ICU was one large area and many beds, all within plain sight, separated only by curtained dividers. A monitoring station where two nurses sat was just beyond the door. He could see a third nurse checking on patients. He had made it this far, but he wouldn't get farther and remain undetected.

That left only one option. He pushed open the door, two sets of eyes on him before it had even closed again. William chose the pair that seemed the most sympathetic, addressing a young woman with long blonde hair.

"I'm here to see Kelly Phillips," he said.

She looked him over. "And you are…"

"We were in the accident together. I just want to see if he's okay. I mean, I know he's not, but—" William's voice croaked. He didn't need to pretend to be upset.

"You shouldn't have left your room," she replied, but her resolve was wavering. "Where are your slippers?"

"I just want to say goodnight to him. Please."

The nurse looked to her colleague. The man shrugged apathetically.

"I won't be long," William pressed.

That did the trick. She gestured with her arm, showing him where he should go. Then she walked alongside him. That wasn't ideal. William had imagined being alone with Kelly. He focused his attention on each bed they passed, hoping to see a familiar face. When he did, he almost cried out, because Kelly looked much the same. His face was gaunt and marred by a few small cuts, probably from the shattered window. Other than that, William could easily imagine him waking up and making a barbed comment.

"He's doing a lot better," the nurse said. "We're lucky he made it to the hospital in time. He lost a lot of blood, but he's okay now. He'll pull through."

William eyed the blanket covering his legs. Leg. Part of him was glad the missing limb was covered. The rest wanted to see, to confront what he had done. He felt tears rising again, his head dizzy. He grasped the bed's metal frame for support. To his surprise, Kelly stirred, eyes opening and struggling to focus. He braced himself for anger, but when Kelly saw him, he smiled.

"Hi, baby," he said. He lifted his arms, reaching out as if wanting a hug.

"Hey," William said, voice raw. He moved forward to take one of his hands. "How are you?"

Kelly smacked his lips a few times. "Thirsty."

"I'll get him some water." The nurse went to fetch it.

William didn't waste time. He kneeled next to Kelly's bedside, clutching his hand tighter. "I'm sorry," he whispered. "I'm so sorry!"

Kelly's expression grew somber. "Don't leave me."

"I won't," William said, wiping at the tears tumbling down his cheeks. "I'm right here." He grimaced when he heard footsteps approaching. "They might make me go back to my room, but I'm here, okay? I'm in the hospital too. I won't be far."

Kelly shook his head, as if not understanding.

"Here you go!" The nurse had returned with a paper cup. William stood again. When he realized he was in the way, he released Kelly's hand and backed off so she could raise the bed slightly and help him drink. He noticed the tubes snaking into Kelly's arms, and the machines and IV bags surrounding him, aware again of how all of this was his fault.

"All done?" The nurse took a step back.

Kelly sought him out again, reaching for William, trying to sit up further.

"No you don't!" the nurse said with a laugh. "You're fine where you are."

"Don't leave me," Kelly said, expression anguished, his attention fixed on William.

"I'm right here," he repeated.

"He needs his rest," the nurse said apologetically. "You should get back to your room."

William nodded grudgingly. He took Kelly's hand and squeezed it. "I'm sorry. I have to go."

"Don't leave me," Kelly repeated.

"He's on a lot of medication," the nurse explained. "He'll

settle down and sleep again, don't worry."

"Okay. I'm just one floor away, Kelly. I'm close."

"I don't want to break up."

The words hit William like a wall of frigid water. He finally understood what Kelly was saying. He wasn't worried about William leaving his bedside. He was worried about him leaving completely.

"I won't," William said, forgetting his surroundings. He was on his knees again, gripping Kelly's hand. "I don't want to break up either. I love you! I promise I'll never leave you. Do you hear me? Never! I belong to you."

Kelly smiled, facial movements sluggish. "I love you too."

"I'm so sorry. About all of this."

Kelly swatted at him with his free hand and laughed. Jesus, they sure had him doped up! William repeated himself, just to be sure he was getting through. "I love you."

Kelly closed his eyes as if content. "Okay."

After watching his chest rise and fall a few times, William slid his hand away. He got to his feet, wiped at his eyes again, and faced the nurse.

"I have a brother," she said. "He's gay too. I love him to pieces."

William forced a smile for her. As she escorted him out of the ICU, he thanked her once more, insisting he didn't need any help getting back to his room. When he was alone in the hall, facing elevator doors and waiting for them to open, he exhaled.

Kelly still loved him, maybe even forgave him, but what would happen when the medication wore off? How would he feel when sober? When he realized who was to blame.

William focused on folding his shirts into an organized stack on his bed. Next to this was a week's worth of underwear and socks. When finished, he considered the backpack he had planned to put them in, realizing they would get wrinkled no matter how careful he had been. He nearly shoved the clothing in anyway, but then wondered if his mom had a piece of luggage he could borrow. Not that he could get a suitcase onto his bicycle. He could ask his mother for a ride, but he didn't like being in cars anymore. Not if he had a choice.

A knock at his bedroom door made him jump. He had heard

the doorbell ring but ignored it, not expecting company. The police with more questions? Definitely not Kelly. He wouldn't be home quite yet. Rather than continue guessing, he opened the door a crack. A girl his own age was on the other side, biting her lower lip as if unsure she'd be welcome.

"Lily!" William said, opening the door wider. "What are you doing here?"

"Checking to see if you're still alive," she replied, coming close for a hug. "We never see you anymore."

"Sorry," William said. He squeezed her, then ushered her into his room. "Things have been…"

"I know." Lily walked in, paused to consider the clothes on the bed, then sat on the edge of it. He thought briefly of how she had tried her best to seduce him there and what a big deal that had seemed. What a problem to have! Grappling with his sexuality had been a cakewalk compared to the last few weeks. "Going on a trip?"

"No," William answered. "Not really."

"Oh. Well, I'm sorry it's just me. Holly can't deal with this kind of stuff. She loves you, but every time I mention the accident, she breaks down into tears. She'll get over it."

"And Abby?"

"Just started seeing a guy. And by seeing, I mean every part of him. It's her first serious relationship."

William smiled. "I'll try not to take it personally. After all, I practically ditched you guys after I started dating Kelly."

The name was like a phantom that floated into the room, turning the air cold. The happy expressions left their faces. That always happened now. The accident loomed over everything.

"How is he?" Lily asked.

"Fine," William said for the sake of simplicity. "He gets discharged from the hospital today. That's why I'm packing. He wants me to stay with him, be there to help if he needs it."

"Oh!" Lily considered the clothes anew. "That's so sweet of you."

Hardly, but William had learned to hold his tongue. If the accident made people uncomfortable, revealing how he felt about himself now sent them packing. They couldn't deal with it, and shouldn't have to. It had been his mistake, not theirs.

"Anyway," Lily said, "I'm here to drag you out for some

fun. It's summer. School's out!" She misinterpreted William's grimace. "You missed a lot of days. Please tell me that doesn't mean summer school."

He shook his head. "I showed up for the important tests. I passed." Everyone at school had heard about the accident. His teachers had been sympathetic. Not that it would have stopped him. He visited the hospital at every opportunity and had been at Kelly's side daily. If that meant repeating a school year, he would have done so gladly, but his mother had made arrangements. Kelly was taken care of too. The schoolboard had allowed him to pass his junior year, and rightly so, because Kelly had a lifetime of nearly perfect grades. At least that brain of his hadn't been harmed.

"You definitely need a break," Lily said.

"Huh?"

"We were in the middle of having a conversation. Then you went somewhere else."

William rubbed his forehead. "Sorry. Everything is still kind of weird, you know?"

"I don't, but if you need someone to talk to, I'm your girl."

He considered her, wishing he could turn back the clock and let her seduce him. Would it have been so bad? She wasn't exactly what he wanted, but she was still fantastic. They could have been together and history wouldn't have played out the way it had. Kelly would have won the triathlon and still be running every day. The fastest guy in school.

"Jesus," Lily whispered, looking shocked. "I don't know what's going on in there, but I'm sorry."

She stood and wiped away tears on his cheek that he hadn't noticed.

"I'm fine," he said, gently taking her hand to stop her. "Everything is still raw. That's all. I really need to keep packing. I want to be there when he gets home."

"Okay," Lily said. "I understand."

She couldn't, but it was nice of her to try.

"Sorry," he mumbled.

"It's fine." She hugged him again, then stepped back, her own eyes wet. "I miss you. You know that?"

William nodded. "I miss you too."

After she had gone, he shoved his clothes carelessly into his backpack. Then he went to the bathroom, grabbed everything he would need, and carried it all downstairs. He left the backpack by the door and went to the living room where his mother was reading.

"I'm taking off," he said.

Kate put down her magazine and gestured to the couch beside her. Resisting a sigh, William sat next to her.

"I could stop you," she said. "You're too young to live on your own."

"Do what you have to do, Mom, but I'm not living on my own. Kelly's parents will be there. I'm only staying over so I can help. We've been through this."

Kate patted his hand. "I know, but I'm your mother, and that means I have to try."

"This is still my home," he stressed. "I hope."

"Of course! How long do you think you'll—"

"I don't know." He stood again. "As long as he needs me. This is the only thing I can do to make it right." He shook his head, not liking his choice of words because nothing would make it right.

His mother stood, walking him to the door. "I'd feel a lot better if I still got to see you every day."

"I'll try."

"Okay. Don't be so hard on yourself."

She said that a lot recently. He didn't make any promises. He simply kissed her on the cheek and left the house. William biked down backroads to Kelly's house. Despite going to the same school, they lived in neighborhoods that weren't exactly close. He arrived later than he intended, sweaty when he knocked on the front door.

Mrs. Phillips opened the door. She didn't look pleased to see him, which came as no surprise. "If you're going to be staying here, there's no point in knocking," she said coldly.

"Sorry," William said. Lately he felt like he should be wearing a T-shirt with that phrase plastered across it. That way he could just point instead of having to say it over and over again.

Laisha wordlessly turned away, giving no indication if he should follow. William did so anyway, ending up in the living room where Kelly was seated on the couch. He looked more like himself than ever, free from hospital gowns and bandages. The basketball shorts he wore covered his legs and hid his stump.

The dress shirt with the sleeves rolled up didn't match. Maybe he was still trying to figure out his new style. Not for the first time, William realized how everything had changed. Speaking of which, Royal and Mr. Phillips were carrying a mattress through the room, heading for the stairs.

"What's going on?" he asked.

"I've been upgraded," Kelly explained. "The stairs are tricky, which means I get the master bedroom down here. Hey, Mom, does that make me master of the house?"

"It means I don't have to climb the stairs to swat your ass!" she replied, tone much warmer with her son.

Kelly shot William a smile. "Remind me to lock the door at night."

He was in high spirits, emphasis on the *high*. William had seen his moods rise and fall in direct correlation to when he was given his pain meds, but he didn't begrudge Kelly that relief. "I'll help carry things," William offered, setting down his backpack.

Laisha held up a hand to stop him. "You've already done enough."

The low blow barely fazed him. He already knew that Kelly's parents disliked him. Who wouldn't? He had crippled their son. At the hospital, rarely did a day go by that he didn't suffer some insult from them, but he tried not to care. He just wished they understood that they didn't need to bother. He already felt ashamed. He already hated himself. Why waste the energy when he couldn't feel worse?

"Is there anything you need, honey?" Laisha asked her son.

"Some privacy," Kelly said pointedly.

"It's too bad the doctors couldn't do something about your mouth," she said. Then she bent over to kiss him on the forehead. "It's good to have you home."

William remained tense, even when she was gone.

"They'll get over it," Kelly assured him. "It won't always be like this."

"It's fine," William said. "I think I'm going to help carry stuff anyway. It doesn't feel right to just stand here while they're working."

"Actually," Kelly said, lowering his voice. "I really *really* need to pee."

"Oh!" William hurried forward "Okay, should I carry you or—"

"I just need help getting up. I'm sinking into these cushions. They're a death trap!"

William bent over, wrapped an arm around Kelly's back, and lifted. Kelly had a grip on one of his crutches—the kind with a clamp near the forearm—which he balanced on. William grabbed the other crutch and handed it to him. "Need me to come with you?"

"No," Kelly said. Then he reconsidered. "Actually, that might be a good idea."

William followed him to the guest bathroom downstairs, which wasn't exactly spacious, but they both fit.

"I thought you'd never get here," Kelly said. "I don't want my mother knowing I need help getting to the restroom. Not only would she never stop asking if I need to pee, but she'd probably have me in diapers by the end of the week." Kelly looked at him when he didn't respond. "That was supposed to be a joke."

"Sorry," William said, thinking again of the T-shirt idea. "Uh, do you need any help?"

Kelly stood in front of the toilet, considering it. "Just take this one," he held out a crutch. "Thanks. Does this gross you out?"

"No!" William pressed his back against the wall. "It's nothing I haven't seen before. Shouldn't you sit?"

Kelly shook his head. "I may have lost a leg, but I'm still a man." He fumbled with the elastic band of his shorts.

William averted his eyes, wondering if this was going to be a new routine until Kelly adjusted to his situation. When the toilet flushed and his shorts were pulled back up, Kelly turned to face him. "Not the most romantic place for it, but at least we have privacy."

"Huh?"

"A kiss would be nice." Kelly swallowed. "Unless you don't want to. I totally understand. I'm a mutant now."

"You're not!" William said, moving forward, "And I do. It's just… I don't feel like I deserve to kiss you. Not anymore."

"Would you please stop with the guilt stuff?" Kelly said. "I'm tired of it."

"Sorry."

"And the apologies too."

William swallowed. "I know we've already talked about this, but I need to make sure. You know this is my fault, right? You remember me telling you about how I intentionally—"

"Sent us spiraling into traffic?" Kelly shook his head. "You didn't mean for us to be in an accident."

"No, but—"

"We were both arguing when we shouldn't have been," Kelly said. "It's not your fault."

William clenched his jaw. He was frustrated, unable to get the person he had most wronged to accept the truth.

"I want to get back to normal," Kelly said. "Please. I've got enough to deal with without us being broken too. Does that make sense?"

William nodded. "I guess so."

"Good, now unless you find me repulsive—"

William silenced him with a kiss. Whatever Kelly wanted—whatever he needed—that's who William would become. In many ways he had taken a life. Now he would give up his own.

Part Two
Austin, 2009

Chapter Ten

Don't turn the wheel. No matter what, don't turn the wheel. My eyes are on the road ahead, my palms drenched with sweat. I'm tempted to lift them one at a time and wipe them on my jeans, but that could mean losing control of the vehicle. From next to me, I hear a voice shouting endlessly. The words are nonsense but the underlying anger is unmistakable. I keep my attention forward, making sure the car remains between two lines, one solid, the other broken. Then the shouting becomes a scream, my passenger in pain, and I can't help it. I look over and see a zombie version of the person I love—arms and legs missing as blood pours from Kelly's eyes. My hands move instinctively. Turning. The car careens to the side and the screams become a high-pitched whine. I look up just in time to see a monstrous truck bearing down before it crushes us beneath impossibly huge tires.

William shot awake, the sheets around him hot and damp. He sucked in air, trying to fight against the adrenaline and fear. Just the dream again. How many times this week alone? Nearly a year later and it still haunted him. Like a ritual, he used the dim light of morning to make sure Kelly was sleeping safely beside him. Then he settled down again and tried to calm himself.

Eventually he rolled over to his side, staring at a room that wasn't his own. It wasn't even Kelly's. Despite mastering the use of his crutches and no longer struggling with stairs, Kelly still occupied the downstairs bedroom. William had all but moved in because Kelly didn't like to sleep alone. Considering how useless William felt these days, at least he could provide that service. His attention drifted to the nightstand, the rescue helicopter Transformer standing there in robot mode and reminding him of happier times. He toyed with the blades hanging off one arm. When he heard Kelly stir, he pushed up into a sitting position.

"Are you okay?"

Kelly raised an eyebrow, as if this was the stupidest question imaginable. William supposed it was. Things had only gotten worse. His theory about the painkillers had proven true. At first Kelly was okay without them, trying his best to make a full recovery. For a brief period, Kelly had been drug-free and wearing a prosthetic leg. Back on his own two feet, both literally and figuratively. That hadn't lasted long. Kelly despised the prosthetic, which was now gathering dust in the closet. He had also been caught with a prescription stolen from Bonnie's house. That had landed him in therapy, which he still went to regularly. Not that it seemed to help because—

"Stop staring at me," Kelly said, pulling the sheets over his head. "If you're horny, go jack off in the shower."

"Wanna watch?" William offered. He wasn't in the mood, but flirting tended to cheer Kelly up and might circumvent another bad mood.

"There's a mirror in there if you're looking for an audience," Kelly grumbled. "That's what you like to do, right?"

William didn't respond, amazed at what Kelly used against him these days, but then he supposed he had it coming. He rose and went to the shower, only touching himself to wash while visualizing the days to come. The weekend was here, meaning he would make himself scarce to avoid Kelly's family. Good thing he had to work. William had taken a part-time job at Juicy James, a Western-themed juice bar at the mall, to both earn money and get away from… everything.

When he returned to the bedroom, he found Kelly sitting on the edge of the mattress, naked except for the sheet draped over his waist. That meant his stump was in full view. William was used to seeing it these days. He didn't mind. He liked to think that if Kelly had only been born with one leg and they had met that way, William still would have found him attractive. The amputation's appearance was fine. The way it made guilt gnaw at his stomach wasn't.

"I think I'll head out for a swim," William tried.

Kelly shook his head. "Mom's making omelets. You don't want to miss out."

"Oh. Okay."

Kelly rose and went to get ready. William dressed, made the bed, and then waited, not wanting to leave the room. He tended to be treated worse when Kelly wasn't around. When he heard a light knock on the door, he didn't answer. Let whoever it was assume they were in the shower.

Only after Kelly was dressed did they leave the room together. Royal was already eating at the table. William did okay with him these days, having bribed Kelly's younger brother with enough presents to earn his forgiveness. Kelly's father, Doug, wasn't mean, but he wasn't warm either. It was his wife—

"Sit down. You're in the way."

Laisha pushed past him to deliver a plate to her husband. William made sure to be elsewhere on her return. He took a seat next to Kelly, not surprised when he was the last to be served, or that his omelet was not only smaller but the only one lacking tomatoes. He took such things in stride, thankful she didn't poison his food.

"This looks great," he said, the compliment falling on deaf ears. As did his next request. "Could you pass the salt, please?"

Royal was playing a handheld video game. Laisha and Doug didn't look up from their plates, so Kelly grabbed his crutches and stood. This got their attention.

"Did you need something, honey?" Laisha asked.

Kelly didn't answer. He went to the kitchen and opened a cupboard. When he returned, he had a small container under one arm. He placed this in front of William. Salt. "There you go," he said. "Sorry my family is so rude."

Kelly shot him a playful smile as he sat down. William struggled to hold back laughter. Little gestures like these kept him going, breaks in the clouds that made him hopeful the storm would blow over completely one day. The rest of the meal passed without incident. Conversation was minimal, and even though Doug insisted he didn't need it, William helped clear the table and load the dishwasher. Then he changed into his work clothes and went to find Kelly, who was on the living room couch.

"What do you want to do today?" William asked him. "I have to work—"

"I noticed," Kelly said, making a face at the red and white checkered shirt. "Where's the cowboy hat?"

"I forgot it at work."

"Thank goodness for that."

"Anyway, it's just a four-hour shift, so maybe afterwards—"

"I have therapy," Kelly replied.

"Okay. After that then. We could…"

Kelly raised an eyebrow. "What?"

Cruise around in the car? Neither of them drove anymore, meaning they had to bum a ride from someone else, usually Kelly's parents. William wasn't crazy about being a passenger, feeling nervous whenever in a car. Instead he rode his bike, but they couldn't share that. Athletic activities were out of the question. Kelly refused to try swimming or anything similar, even though the world was full of amputees who embraced every sport imaginable. Kelly let his missing limb ruin any potential joy. Once William had taken him to an animal shelter, hoping a pet would help bring a smile to Kelly's face.

"How am I supposed to walk a dog?" he had said. "A big one will drag me down the street, and a small one will get its leash tangled up in my crutches." And when they had moved on to the cats: "I'm not going to make my mom scoop the litter box just because I can't get down on my knees."

William had offered to do the scooping, but it didn't matter. Kelly always found an another excuse, another reason not to be happy.

"We could go shopping," he suggested finally. "Or catch a movie."

"Do you really want to spend more time at the mall? Besides, that place reminds me of Jared. That's all we ever did."

William stood there, helpless. "I don't have any other ideas. Sorry."

"It's not your fault," Kelly said easily.

William didn't agree, but he had learned not to argue. Instead he kissed Kelly goodbye, still feeling trapped even after escaping the house.

"Howdy, partner! Are you looking to wet your whistle?"

Customers visiting the Juicy James counter either smiled when William said this, or treated him like he was an idiot. The doofy greeting was required by the owners, who lived out of state and had a very skewed idea of what Texas was actually like. William didn't mind. He found the various reactions amusing. He had kept tally one day, adding a third category for the few customers who reacted with pity. His personal opinion was that people shouldn't take themselves so seriously. Sometimes he even mixed things up, just to keep himself entertained. "Welcome to the smoothie saloon, what can I getcha?" or "The sheriff has outlawed thirst in this here town!" This made his coworkers roll their eyes, but inventing ridiculous variations helped pass the time. He wasn't the only one fond of catch phrases.

"This job sucks."

William barely spared a glance for his coworker, Jade, whose bad attitude had only gotten worse during the three weeks of her employment. He had enough negativity to deal with at home, and her complaining seemed especially crass considering they had a customer standing there and waiting for an order. William had one hand on the blender, still needing the bananas he had asked for. Jade had retrieved them from the freezer, but not when he had originally pointed out that they were low. That meant the bananas hadn't had time to thaw and were much harder to peel. After watching Jade hammer one against the counter, he moved to take over.

Jade stepped aside, but only enough to watch him work. "Seriously," she said. "I don't know how you stand it. I get nauseous when I smell fruit now. My mom poured orange juice this morning and I nearly hurled."

"Coming right up!" William said to the customer, flashing his best smile.

"This job sucks so hard. I don't know how you stand it."

"It's better than standing in front of a greasy fry vat all day," William said. "At least we're providing people with healthy food."

Jade didn't hide how repugnant she found this optimism. She seemed to thrive on negativity. Jaded Jade. William wondered if the name was intentional, because it sure wasn't her real one. He had seen her paycheck, which was written out to Molly Dortch. A far cry from the image she tried to project with the tattoo sleeves and numerous piercings. And that fake name.

"I think I'm going to—"

William started the blender so he wouldn't have to hear more, thanking the customer for their patience when handing them their order. Then he braced himself, counting under his breath. He made it to four.

"I think I'm going to quit."

"Maybe you should," William said before he could help himself. "You don't seem very happy here."

Molly… *Jade*, wasn't fazed by his advice. "The shoe place downstairs is hiring. At least they play good music. I should probably apply there before quitting, huh?"

"Maybe," William said, desperately hoping they would hire her away. "Then again, if they see you already have a job, they might not think you're serious about needing one."

Jade squinted. "You think so?"

"Sure," William said, turning to clean up. "Better hurry though. Those shoe jobs go quick!"

"I could quit now," Jade said. When he turned around again, he saw her hands on her apron, ready to throw it off. "Still an hour left in our shift though."

"I'll be okay," William said. "Do what's best for you."

Jade's eyes caught fire. Then something really exceptional happened. She looked happy. "Okay! It's official. I quit! Tell our bitch of a manager that—"

"I'll even call her for you," William said.

His coworker took off her apron, grabbed her things from the backroom, and rode off into the sunset, never to be seen again. He hoped. Once she had disappeared down the mall corridor, he breathed out a sigh of relief. Then he considered the food court, which for a Saturday night, was mostly empty. This place was his sanctuary. He and Kelly shared most classes. They had arranged it that way at school so William could help him if need be. They lived together, which meant constantly having to suffer barbs from Kelly's mother or go out of his way to avoid her and everyone else when he needed privacy. He rarely got any. The only time he had alone was when he used the bathroom, and not always then. Here at least he could forget about it all, even if he was still at the beck and call of customers. Blending fruit into a smoothie was easy. Trying to figure out how to put a broken life back together was impossible, as far as he could tell.

A group of girls walked by, all of them his own age. One noticed him staring, nudged her friend, and then whispered something. This set off a chorus of giggling. William smiled back, not caring if the joke was at his expense. He envied them and what their days entailed. School work, unrequited crushes, and the occasional social drama that went no deeper than what someone had said about someone else behind their back. At times he could imagine running away and entering into some witness protection program just so he could have a normal life again. He saw two teenagers at a table, one showing the other something lewd on his phone. Not far from them, a group of sophomores from his school were pooling their cash and glancing around at the options, trying to figure out how to get the most for their money. Easy simple problems that he yearned to somehow find his way back to.

The Coast Guard. He had once hoped it could fix him. Now he did so again, albeit in a different way. He couldn't go. Not as things stood. Not without breaking his promise to Kelly. William had sworn to stay by his side, despite it not doing a lot of good. Maybe he was looking at the situation from the wrong angle. William no longer made Kelly happy, but what if someone else could? He pulled out his phone to check the calendar. The next gay youth meeting was the following weekend. That meant another chance for someone new to show up. A fiery guy who could keep up with Kelly and motivate him to stop feeling so sorry for himself. If such a person was out there, William prayed that he would speed his arrival.

"We need to talk."

William found Kelly sitting at the dining room table, cell phone in hand. The house was mostly dark, a few scented candles illuminating the neighboring living room, another on the table. When entering the house, William had noticed the low lighting and soft music, and worried he was interrupting romantic plans. Then he had found Kelly at the table and realized all of this was for them. They could use the extra romance. The previous week had been rough, Kelly's moods more often dark than upbeat. Jade having quit meant he was working extra shifts, which William secretly liked, but he knew Kelly didn't. His boyfriend finished texting, then set aside the phone.

"Talk about what?" William asked.

Kelly exhaled, flashing a tentative smile. "Everything. I don't really know where to begin. Please sit. Or do you need to use the restroom? Are you thirsty?"

"I'm fine," William said, surprised Kelly was so concerned for his wellbeing. "What's going on? Where is everyone?"

"It's Friday," Kelly said.

The night reserved for the Phillips family to go out for group activities. Participation was optional, but Kelly had a lot of happy memories revolving around these evenings. William had tagged along a few times, but of course his experience had been different.

"My therapy session last week gave me a lot to think about," Kelly said. "Allison made some good points that I can't argue with, and you know how I love to argue."

"I noticed that, yeah," William said, taking a seat. "I've

learned it's easier to just agree with you, so if you want, we can cut this short. You're right."

Kelly's eyes twinkled. "There's no getting out of this one. It's about the accident."

"Oh."

They both grew somber.

Kelly slid a hand across the table toward him, even though they were sitting too far away to touch. "I wanted to say that I'm sorry. I shouldn't have—" His voice became strained, but he forced himself to continue. "I was hurt. Things weren't going well between us, but I wanted them to. Remember the argument about community service? Picking up trash or packing boxes? When I look back, it seems ridiculous that I made such a big deal out of our choices. All I wanted was to be with you, but I was too proud to give up my own plans. Stupid me, because then we could have been together. So basically I was fighting against what I really wanted." Kelly shook his head. "No wonder you wanted our relationship to end! Still, you wanting to break up came as a shock, and I was hurt, so I wanted to hurt you back."

"Kelly—"

A raised hand cut him short. "Please let me finish, then I'll listen to whatever you have to say. I'm sorry for wanting to hurt you, and for putting our lives in danger by freaking out when you were trying to drive. I know it might not have seemed like it at the time, but I loved you. I still do."

William remained silent. He knew what he wanted to say, but he also knew that Kelly wouldn't agree, and that this heart-to-heart would turn into another shouting match. Then again, Kelly was sitting perfectly still, wearing an open expression.

"It's my fault you lost your leg," William tried.

To his surprise, Kelly nodded. "I don't think the blame is entirely yours. I did my part, but it wasn't the argument that caused the accident. Was it?"

"No," William said, his throat constricting. "It's not like I was distracted by what you were saying and didn't notice a car in my blind spot. I wanted to upset you because I'm not good at finding the right words. Not like you are. Especially when you want to hurt me. Jerking the wheel, that was my version of doing the same to you. I never thought it would cost you your leg. You could have died and—"

"It's okay," Kelly said.

"It's not!" William shot back, but he wasn't angry. Instead he felt like crying, which he did. Fighting against it while saying what he needed to was too difficult. "I robbed you of your dreams. Even worse, I took your happiness because you're not the same person anymore. Yeah, you always loved to argue, but there was more. You loved taking photos and running, and the old you never would have relied so much on me or your parents. He had too much pride. It's like the Kelly Phillips I fell in love with died in that accident, and what's left is…"

Kelly nodded encouragingly. "Say it."

"You're so bitter." William sniffed to stop his nose from leaking. "Every single day I try to find ways to bring you back, to make you happy even though everything has changed, and I always fail. You're miserable, and it's all my fault."

Kelly was quiet, his gaze to one side as he considered these words. "Do you still love me?"

"Yes!" William said. "Trust me, I wouldn't be here if I didn't."

Kelly looked to him, expression hurt. "Is it really that bad?"

William sighed. "It's more than just your moods. Your parents hate me."

"Your mom was never fond of me either, especially now that she thinks I've stolen you away."

"I know. I wish we could live on our own because then they wouldn't be involved."

Kelly nodded. "Maybe we can minimize that by no longer accepting rides from them. We're getting pretty good at using the bus."

"That would help," William said. "I'd also rather go swimming than have breakfast with them. Or any other meals, to be honest. I'd rather eat a sandwich in the bedroom than sit at that table again."

"If that's what you need," Kelly said.

"What about you?" William asked. "What can I do to make you happy?"

Kelly exhaled. "You don't realize how happy you make me. If you weren't around, I hate to think what my life would be like."

William held back. As good as being open with each other felt, he wasn't ready to talk about the Coast Guard. He hadn't given up that dream because it had returned to being his one chance at redemption. And yet he had made a promise. He had sworn to stay for as long as Kelly needed him, and that wouldn't change if things remained the same. "You have to find something else," he said. "Besides me. I want you to be happy, even if I'm not around."

"Like what?"

"I don't know. You're not as limited as you think."

Kelly shook his head. "I'm not going to be a one-legged snowboarder or anything ridiculous."

"Those people aren't ridiculous," William said. "They're brave. So are you. I know you hate hearing that from strangers, but it's true. Use it to your advantage. Please."

"I'll try."

William nodded. "Good. Is there anything I can do to help?"

Kelly smirked. "Take off that shirt."

William sighed. "I know you don't like my job, and I'll admit it isn't—"

"It's got nothing to do with you being a juice cowboy," Kelly teased. "I just want to see you with your shirt off."

"Oh!" William laughed. "You're supposed to find something that makes you happy that *doesn't* involve me."

"Sometimes it doesn't, and that also makes me happy, but sex is a lot more fun when you're around."

William grinned and stood. He still felt emotional from their talk, but getting into a different sort of mood wasn't difficult. He slowly unbuttoned his shirt and tossed it on the table. Then he swore and rushed to grab it when it landed on the candle. Kelly seemed amused rather than irritated, so William strutted over to where he was seated, putting on a terrible French accent.

"Welcome, monsieur, to Le Sausage House. May I take your order?"

"I already placed my order," Kelly said, having no trouble imitating an irritated customer. "I asked for a bratwurst surprise."

"Ah, of course! I have that right here." William unbuttoned his jeans, then unzipped them. He pulled them down along with his underwear, flopping out. He wasn't entirely hard, but Kelly wasted no time in correcting that. Soon William was thrusting in his mouth, trying to think of a good joke about tartar sauce or maybe mayonnaise, just in case they kept going like this. Instead Kelly pulled him free with a popping noise.

"I've got no patience for this," he said. "You want to know what I really want? Help me out of these pants and onto the table."

William had a good idea of where that would lead. His high spirits took a plunge as they got undressed. Then he tried pleasing Kelly with his hands and mouth instead.

"Get the lube," Kelly breathed after enough of this.

William hesitated. They had been so open with each other tonight. Maybe now was a good time to tell Kelly that he had needs of his own. He was tired of always being the top. It brought pleasure and he had no trouble performing, but when flying solo, his fantasies always took a different turn.

"It's okay," Kelly said, misinterpreting his uncertainty. "They won't be home until late."

Then again, why ruin what had been a very progressive evening? William hurried out of the room and back again, Kelly still on his back and appearing hungry. "Just go for it," he said. "No need to be gentle."

Those were the hormones talking. William was careful anyway, watching the strain on Kelly's face until it disappeared. Then, with one leg draped over his shoulder, he really started pounding, picturing as always how he would want to be treated. Maybe that made him a good lover because Kelly was all lolling eyes and moans of ecstasy, letting go of himself toward the end and coming a minute later despite not touching himself. William stopped holding back and raced to the finish line. Once he crossed it, he fell on top of Kelly, their sweaty bodies heaving together. Then William summoned up his terrible French accent again.

"Are you pleased, monsieur? Have I earned a tip?"

Kelly shook his head and laughed. "Correct me if I'm wrong, but that felt like way more than just the tip!"

A new guy! William didn't pray often, but he was starting to think he should. Even though they were getting along better, he hadn't abandoned his desire for Kelly to move on with someone else, even entertaining strange ideas, like creating a dating profile for him online. Which of course he hadn't. All of his hopes rested in the gay youth group. The usual faces had filed into the church classroom where they met, William's hope diminishing with each that he recognized. Then, at the last minute, two new people had shown up. One was easy to dismiss, disqualified due to her gender. She was a big girl and seemed thrilled to be there, like not only had she never been to a toy store before, but until now she hadn't even known they existed. He had seen similar reactions from a lot of people. It was either that, or like her companion, they slumped into themselves, awkward and bashful. This made William a little less hopeful, because Kelly needed someone who could keep up with him. Still, this guy was cute! Really really cute!

The newcomer's blue eyes were currently focused on the floor, occasionally darting around the room but without making contact with anyone. His messy brown hair stopped just above the dark eyebrows, a couple of curls visible behind each ear, and his skin was tan except for the bridge of his nose where he had gotten too much sun. William thought briefly of Jared, who shared the same attributes but wasn't all that attractive. William found this new person way hotter, but the best part was that he must be Kelly's type. He looked over to see if his boyfriend had made this same connection. Kelly seemed more interested in him than the new arrivals, placing a finger under William's chin to shut his mouth, which had been hanging open.

"Someone you know?" Kelly asked.

"No," William said hurriedly. "It's just been a while since anyone new showed up."

"I know," Kelly said. Then, in a Transylvanian accent he added, "Fresh meat!"

Okay, that was a good sign. Kelly had noticed the new guy too. But had the new guy noticed him? Keith, the group leader, took over then, suggesting they do a round of introductions. William waited until it was Kelly's turn before he looked across the room to where the newcomer sat. Jackpot! The guy's intense gaze was trained on Kelly and looking him over. Did he notice the missing leg? Would it turn him off? William felt sinking guilt, wondering if he had made it impossible for Kelly to ever find someone new. This person though was definitely interested. William forced himself to look away, listening to Kelly's short speech and giving one of his own. Then the new girl made a noise, like she was eager to go next. Keith allowed this. Her name was Emma, and her words were just as confident as her demeanor. She even managed to make the entire room laugh. Too bad she wasn't a guy, because she had the kind of personality Kelly needed to keep him in check. Confident and quick-witted. Maybe her friend would turn out to be the same way.

"And who did you bring with you?" Keith prompted.

"Jason," the newcomer said. "And I... uh..." His voice faltered, ending in a strained squeak.

Poor guy. Having over twenty strangers stare at you could be intimidating. William could understand, but he still felt disappointed, because this wasn't who he had been waiting for. He glanced over at Kelly and saw the way he struggled to hold back laughter, unable to take someone like that seriously. The worst part is the way Jason looked to Kelly for a reaction, his cheeks growing redder by the second. Jason was definitely interested, but it didn't matter. Kelly needed a fellow piranha, not a goldfish.

The introductions continued, William feeling guilty for playing matchmaker with his boyfriend, if only in his own mind. Who was he to decide what Kelly needed? Especially when they had talked about it so recently. William just wished they had found a solution instead of relying on sex to bring them closer together again. Maybe that's what Kelly had been trying to express. He needed William. Not just his presence, but his dedication.

Keith had begun the lecture, asking the group what they looked for in a relationship. William's hand shot up.

"Commitment," he said with new determination. "Loyalty is important."

Yeah! He needed to get back to how things were before the accident. Now that they had set that mistake behind them—

"Trust," Kelly declared. "You should be able to trust the person you're with."

Ouch. William had never considered it before, but the entire accident could be boiled down to one small transgression. He had broken Kelly's trust. He was supposed to ferry them safely to school and had instead nearly cost Kelly his life. He placed his hand over Kelly's, noticing how tense it was. No surprise. The anger was always there beneath the surface, lurking until needed, which was all too often.

"Humility," a voice declared.

William didn't recognize it at first, surprised by how clear it rang out. The entire room went silent, all heads turning to focus on one person. Jason.

"Humility?" Keith asked, standing in front of the marker board.

"Yeah," Jason said. "I don't want some guy I have to impress or one who feels like he needs to show off. I just want someone who loves me that I can love back. Simple as that. That's all it takes. I don't really care about honesty or being totally understood or any of the other stuff, because being human is all about messing up and breaking trust and telling lies. I wouldn't want to be with someone perfect. Just some humble, totally normal guy will do."

Being human is all about messing up and breaking trust. He felt like Jason had read his mind and granted him forgiveness, without even knowing his sins. William was human—fallible— and that was okay. God he needed to hear that! Jason seemed bolstered by his convictions, meeting each gaze with his own. Then it was their turn to lock eyes, William wanting to communicate his thanks or maybe fall to his knees and start crying, because there was something about this guy—shy and awkward until he rose up from the ashes like a phoenix, just like he had always wanted Kelly to do. The assessment from earlier had been wrong. Jason *was* good enough. He could hold his own with Kelly or anyone else, William was sure of it, because the light emanating from him was pure and bright. Strong.

"Humility," Keith said, sounding equally impressed.

William tore his attention away to look at the group leader, sneaking one glance back. Jason's attention was on the lecture again. William looked to the others, wondering if they were equally moved, but everyone seemed to have moved on, which was baffling and made William feel like he had been the only person to notice a heart-stopping explosion. Then everyone started talking, half of them standing. Keith had given them an assignment, but William had totally missed the details. He remained confused when Emma stood and walked across the room, attention on him. She smiled when close enough and said, "You seem nice. Let's be partners!"

"Sure!" William said with a chuckle. He had no idea what was going on, but it's not like he would be graded on his performance.

The room continued to split into pairs, all of them boy girl.

Emma plopped down in Kelly's seat after he wandered away. William had always found confidence attractive and Emma was no exception. Despite the fact that she was overweight, she carried herself with pride, even relying on her natural beauty rather than makeup, although her honey-brown hair was pulled back in an elaborate fashion, smooth and flat in the front and collecting into a playful bundle in the back.

"French twist," Emma said, noticing him staring. "I can do yours like this too, although you'll have to grow it out more. Or get a weave."

"This is the longest I've had it in years," William said. He actually needed a comb to brush it to one side! "I usually keep it short so I can get my cap on easier."

"You do have a big head," Emma said appraisingly. "Must be hard shopping for a hat that fits."

"My head isn't big!" William said with a chuckle. "I meant my swim cap."

"Swimmer eh?" Emma nodded approvingly. "I don't suppose you have a Facebook account with lots of photos? Or maybe a YouTube channel where you record yourself swimming."

"You know this is a *gay* youth group, right? Because I'm starting to think you're hitting on me."

"You mean you're not a lesbian?" Emma tsked and shook her head. "When will I learn? I always tell myself, 'Emma, make sure to notice their gender before you get so irresistibly charming!' So anyway, tell me more about you."

William grinned while shaking his head. "What's our assignment exactly? I don't know what we're supposed to be doing."

"This," Emma said. "Getting to know each other. I'll go first. My name is Emma, I'm from Houston, I plan on being a huge Broadway star before I'm twenty, and I'm determined to find a girlfriend by this time next week. Your turn!"

"Okay. Uh, I'm William, I live here in Austin, I work at the juice place at the mall, and I've been dating that guy over there for nearly two years." He jerked his thumb to where Kelly was deep in conversation with Lisa as they worked on the assignment. Whatever it was.

Emma peered in Kelly's direction critically. "Are you sure? You can do better than that!"

William laughed incredulously. "There's no one handsomer!"

"Well sure, but it's good to play the field, explore your options. Know what I mean?"

William made a face. "Are you sure you're not hitting on me?"

"Positive. So what do you look for in a guy?"

"Didn't we already play that game?"

"Right, right." Emma squinted thoughtfully. "You said that loyalty is important. Boy do I know the right guy for you! He's loyal to a fault."

William finally understood. "You're trying to hook Jason up. That's really sweet! None of my friends ever did that for me. Like I said though, I'm already spoken for."

"My mom says you should never let anyone speak for you."

"Why's that?"

Emma shrugged. "Something about being accountable for one's own opinions and actions, but me, I think it's bad for other reasons. If you let someone speak for you, pretty soon they'll be telling you what to think, how you should act, even what kinds of clothes to wear."

This made William shift uncomfortably. Kelly could be a little controlling at times, but it wasn't *that* bad. Although he did often try to get William to put a different shirt on. "My relationship is fine, and I'm sure it won't be long until someone sweeps your friend off his feet."

Emma perked up. "Oh? Why's that?"

William shook his head ruefully. "You're going to get me in trouble. What about you? What kind of girl are you looking for?"

"That depends," Emma said. "What can you tell me about her?" She nodded to where Jason was talking to a partner.

"Bonnie? She's my boyfriend's best friend!"

"Did I mention that I like him?" Emma said. "Whatever his name was. Kevin? He's a real great guy. You should introduce us!"

They kept talking, William laughing during much of their conversation. Emma was fun! He couldn't help but wonder if Jason was too. As the assignment came to an end and they were allowed to mingle freely, he kept thinking of the way she had tried to set them up, which felt oddly flattering. He found himself distracted by the idea, his eyes moving of their own accord to seek Jason out. William never saw him looking back. Emma had probably delivered the news by now. William was a dead end. Hell, that described his future as well. One big dead end going nowhere.

He tried to put the entire affair out of mind and nearly succeeded. They were leaving, Kelly done with the group earlier than usual. William was holding the exit door open for him when he heard voices in the hall behind him.

"Two more!" Emma said, hustling his way. "Coming through!"

William stretched out his arm and pressed himself against the far wall, creating a bridge that she had to duck under. Then it was Jason's turn. He kept his eyes averted as he ducked, allowing William to check him out from close up. Jason had a narrow build, his broad shoulders boney. William liked that, preferring a contrast to his own body. The jeans and hoodie were well-worn, a surprisingly comfortable choice when most people treated the meetings like a dating pool and dressed their sharpest. There was something honest about the way Jason conducted himself, like he wasn't trying to impress or be anything other than what he was. The butt filling out those jeans wasn't bad either, but William quickly raised his gaze when Jason spun around and spoke.

"Have we met before?"

Just when he thought he was safe! Getting hit on sure felt good though. "That's an old line," William said. Jason's brow came together slightly, like he was puzzled by this response. Maybe he wasn't flirting after all! "Wait, you're serious?"

Jason nodded. "Yeah. I feel like… okay, this is *really* going to sound like a line, but I feel like I know you."

William wondered if this was a joke after all. If so, Jason had a great poker face. He had a nice face in general, his features honest and humble, like he would imagine a farm boy having. The hint of a five o'clock shadow was masculine, a light scruff that William and Kelly never allowed themselves. Jason just seemed like the kind of guy that would throw an arm around you casually and pull you near for some cuddling, without saying a word. And speaking of words, theirs were silent now as they continued to stare at each other, caught up in a spell.

"Hey!" Kelly shouted from somewhere in the parking lot. "Are we going or what?"

Spell officially broken. William blinked, looked toward his boyfriend, and shook his head. "Sorry," he said. "I'm pretty sure we've never met." He made eye contact again. "But now we have. See you at the next meeting?"

"Yeah," Jason said, not laughing in embarrassment or attempting to lighten the mood. "See you then."

Then he turned and walked away. Talk about intense! With an act like that, it really wouldn't be long before Jason found a boyfriend. William couldn't imagine anyone not falling for him. Maybe even Kelly. He considered his original idea anew, how he hoped that Kelly would fall in love with someone else and move on. Jason might have what it took, but William found his stomach uneasy, not liking the thought of Jason being with anyone at all. That is, anyone other than himself.

A rumble in William's stomach signaled that it was nearly lunch. The variety of tantalizing scents filling the mall's food court only increased his appetite. He eyeballed the line of juice-thirsty customers, trying to decide how quickly he could clear the queue so he could get something to eat. Then he did a double-take, spotting a familiar face. They had spoken, not long ago.

"Have we met before?"

Jason. When someone new joined the group, they sometimes failed to pick up on his and Kelly's relationship right away and would get flirtatious. He usually found it flattering and moved on. This time was different. Jason had lingered in William's mind, popping up in his thoughts more than a few times since that brief encounter. William wasn't fantasizing about Kelly and Jason running away together either. Not even close.

A woman waiting in line made a face at the menu, shook her head, and left without ordering. That left no one between them. Jason shuffled forward, head still tilted upward as he searched for what he wanted to order.

"Hey!" William said. "Haven't we met before?"

This caught Jason's attention. He seemed genuinely surprised, and a little uncertain as to who William was. "Met before?" he asked. Then he flashed a smile, catching on. "No. Sorry. Don't think so."

William grinned back, recognizing the response he had given—what was it? Nearly two weeks ago? "Jason, right?"

"That is correct. And you are—" Jason peered at his chest. "Wild Wild Will?"

"Yeah." William scratched himself beneath the nametag,

feeling self-conscious. "They force us to choose ridiculous nicknames."

"I like it."

"Thanks. So, what can I get you?"

Jason seemed surprised again. "Uh, what do you recommend?"

"I always get the protein power smoothie," William said. This triggered a thought, which he indulged in before he could second-guess himself. "Actually, I'm about to go on lunch break. Want to keep me company?"

"Sure," Jason said, perking up a little.

"Great. Tell you what, your smoothie is on the house. Meet me over by the pizza place? That way I can grab something to eat."

"Okay." Jason grinned, then sauntered off into the food court.

William allowed himself a chuckle. He signaled to his coworker to take over his line. As he prepared the promised smoothies, he considered that he was about to sit down with a stranger. He knew very little about Jason. Next to nothing. Why were they about to eat together? His uncertainty dissipated when he saw Jason standing by the pizza counter. That line, asking if they had met before, made sense. He supposed they really had now, but even before then, he had felt *something*. An allure. Jason was holding a paper plate in each hand when he approached, a slab of greasy pizza on each, and yet William felt his pulse quicken. This was ridiculous!

"You got the drinks," Jason said. "I've got the food."

"Oh great! Thanks!"

Jason eyed their surroundings, not seeming impressed. "So should we…"

"I usually eat outside," William said. "Escape the chaos for a little bit."

"Okay."

The mall wanted people indoors and shopping, not out enjoying the weather. Still, as a courtesy to customers, a few benches, some potted shrubbery, and a trash can had been placed outside each exit. William chose the bench furthest away from the trash can, straddling it so they could also use it as a table. Jason mimicked his posture, a small feast laid out between them.

"I hope Canadian bacon is okay," Jason said.

"It's my favorite!" William replied, pretending to be stunned. "How'd you know?"

Jason's response was cool. "I've been stalking you for weeks."

Hunger poked at his stomach again, so William gratefully grabbed one of the over-sized slices and took a bite. "Good choice," he said while chewing. "I *love* Canadian bacon."

"It's delicious," Jason agreed. Then he looked puzzled. "I do wonder how they get the Canadian pigs all the way down here. Think there's a passenger train they all ride together?"

"Yeah." William resisted laughing lest he spit food out on his companion. "I bet the really fat pigs get to sit in the first-class wagon."

"And the poor skinny pigs have to ride with all the luggage."

William shook his head ruefully as he continued to eat. An eavesdropper might think they were old friends. That's how it felt. He was excited to hang out with Jason, more than he had any right to be. "So what are you up to today? Out doing some shopping?"

"Just stretching my legs," Jason said casually. "I actually work across the street at the pet store. I'm off today, but I always come here for lunch. I guess it's a habit."

William managed a few more bites before responding, searching his memory. "Then I'm surprised I've never seen you before."

Jason lifted the Styrofoam cup he'd been holding. "This is my first smoothie. I'll be honest with you. I'm terrified."

"Don't be. I made it myself. You're perfectly safe."

Jason pretended to work up his courage, as if facing a deadly viper. Then he took a sip. "So is this your secret?" he asked, nodding at William's torso.

"What do you mean?"

"Uh…" Jason's cheeks turned a little red. "You're in really good shape."

"Oh!" William's face became the same hue. "Thanks. I actually just like how the protein powder tastes. Is it gross?"

"No! I was just hoping I'd get great boobies like yours."

William laughed. "In that case, all you have to do is go swimming every day."

Jason seemed impressed. "Every day?"

William nodded. "Every morning, actually. Before school. And sometimes after work if I'm not too tired."

Jason sipped the smoothie, still considering him. "Don't take this the wrong way, but you don't look like a swimmer."

"Because I'm pale? Irish skin. Can't be helped. I'll get a little tanner in the summer, but not before burning a few times. Luckily, the YMCA has an indoor pool."

"That explains it." Jason's attention returned to an area above his shoulders, the intense gaze difficult to hold.

William grasped for a change of topic. "So what did you think of the youth group?"

Jason shrugged. "It was okay, I guess. I think I'd like it better if everyone just showed up to hang out."

William shook his head while he finished scarfing his pizza. "That's happened before when we were between group leaders. Everyone formed their little cliques and stopped talking to each other. The lesbians were on one side, the gay guys on another, and even those two camps split into smaller groups. Keith gets everyone interacting. I know his lectures can be tedious at times, but without him we're a mess. Are you coming to the next meeting?"

"I'll give it another try."

"Good."

He noticed that the other piece of pizza hadn't been touched yet. When Jason saw him looking, he offered it. William normally consumed two slices at a time, so he gratefully accepted. This seemed to make Jason happy. He watched as William ate, eyes twinkling as he sucked on his smoothie. William wasn't an idiot. The vibe here was more than just a little friendly. The attraction was mutual, which seemed silly because he knew next to nothing about the person before him. That was easily remedied.

"Are you still in school?" William asked.

"No." Jason said. "I'm done with high school, and I'm not sure about college. Right now I'm working full-time to save up some cash. What about you?"

"High school senior," William replied. "After I graduate—" He thought of the time and checked his watch. "Well, it's too complicated to explain now. I have to get back to work soon."

"Oh." Jason seemed crestfallen, which again was flattering.

A light breeze toyed with his messy hair, the sky behind him perfectly blue. The sort of weather that made anything seem possible. "Do you give swimming lessons?"

The question caught William off guard. He shook his head while drinking his smoothie.

"It's just that I never learned," Jason continued hurriedly. "I've been meaning to take a class for years, but the idea of being with a group of little kids is embarrassing."

"You really don't know how?"

"Just never got around to it."

"I guess I could try. You willing to get up early?"

"Yeah." Jason sounded thrilled by the idea, which isn't how most people reacted. "Let's trade numbers. That way we can talk and set up a date."

William grabbed his own phone, then decided to clear the air. "I hope I don't sound like a jerk for asking this, but you know I have a boyfriend, right?"

"Yeah," Jason said easily. "You and Kelly are together. That's totally cool. I have a boyfriend too."

"You do? What's his name?"

"Tim."

"Oh, okay." William laughed, feeling presumptuous. "I didn't want there to be any mixed signals. Well, not mixed signals… I just don't want Kelly to get hurt."

"Of course not." Jason focused on his phone, face growing red again.

Great, now William had made him feel awkward. No surprise considering what he had just implied. "Here's my number," he said, sliding his phone across the bench like an apology.

"Thanks." Jason ignored it to poke at his own phone, eyes darting up from the screen a few times. He looked insecure.

"Want me to read the number to you?" William offered.

"Actually, this is my first phone," Jason said. "I don't know how to add a new number."

That was a little strange, but okay. "Let me take a look. I think Kelly has a phone like yours."

William easily found his way to the list of contacts, and wow, was it minimal! Tim's name was there, to his mixed relief. Not an imaginary boyfriend then. Emma was also listed there. Just two more names remained, Ben and Michelle. That was all. Not that

William could judge. He had a bigger list of contacts, but he had all but lost touch with most of his friends. He still saw Lily and the others at school occasionally, but because of Kelly… William had a hard enough time handling Kelly's mood swings, and he loved the guy. His friends found it impossible.

"There you go," William said, handing back the phone.

"Townson," Jason said, reading from the display. "Too bad it's not Townshend."

"Huh?"

"Pete Townshend?" Jason tried. "Lead guitarist of The Who? I'm a big classic rock fan."

"Oh. What's your last name?"

"Grant."

"Like Amy Grant," William said.

"No! Definitely not! Please tell me you don't listen to that kind of music!"

William shrugged. "I'm okay with whatever's on the radio."

"You shouldn't be," Jason said. "There's so much good stuff that doesn't get played."

So his new friend was a music lover. Interesting. "What's your number?"

Jason needed help finding this too, not having it memorized. He acted a little awkward when William returned the phone to him, shooting to his feet.

"I should probably go."

"Okay." William stood, wiping his hands on his jeans, surprised to find his palms sweaty. "You'll call, right? To make plans?"

"Yup," Jason said, flashing him a smile. "I promise."

Then he waved, turned, and walked away into a day full of potential. For him, anyway. William's life was settled, but he allowed himself to wonder, briefly, where it might have led otherwise.

Chapter Eleven

William had once taught himself how to swim, so he figured teaching someone else shouldn't be that hard. Regardless, he threw himself into this new enterprise with enthusiasm, turning to the all-knowing Internet for tips and tricks. He grew more excited as the chosen day drew near. Jason called him, the short conversation focusing on when and where to show up and what to bring along. William was reminded of the summer after his freshman year when he'd offered to teach CPR at the YMCA. That had been fulfilling and was mentioned in his application to the Coast Guard. Maybe he could include this as well.

He was eager to get started as he biked to the YMCA, enjoying the cool calm of the morning as he always did. Jason didn't seem quite as chipper when he stumbled out of his car and into the building. After William showed his membership card to the woman at the front desk and got Jason set up with a free trial pass, they reported to the locker room. Jason opted for one in a different aisle than his. If he was feeling shy about his body, then he had chosen the wrong sport!

William finished changing into his Speedo and went to collect Jason, rounding the aisle and catching a glimpse of his butt just before it was covered by swim trunks. Nice ass, but bad choice in swimming gear. Not that Jason would be swimming laps today, so for now it was fine. Jason noticed him and straightened up. William quickly checked out the rest of his body. Purely for assessment purposes and to identify what sort of muscle training his new student might need.

Right.

Jason's shoulders were broad, his narrow hips boney. He didn't have much in the way of muscle or fat, both potentially useful in the water. A real swimmer would shave the light chest hair, but William liked how it looked. He found it masculine, especially since he and Kelly were both so smooth. Jason wasn't as hopelessly pale as he was, and that was nice too. Not that it mattered.

"Ready for your first lesson?"

"I think so," Jason replied.

"Let's go!"

William normally ignored the nearest end of the indoor pool, choosing instead to use the lanes farther down, but today's lesson would mostly be about getting Jason comfortable in the water.

William stood on the first step, ankles and feet submerged, and waited until his student did the same. "Let go of your fear," William said. "Any concerns you have, set them aside because I'm here for you. I'm a certified lifeguard—"

"Really?" Jason said, looking impressed.

"Yup! So if anything were to go wrong—and it won't—I'll be there for you. Put your trust in me."

"Do you know CPR?" Jason asked.

"Yes." William waited for an obvious joke or a lewd expression, almost disappointed when neither came. He walked down the rest of the steps, wading through water that was only waist high. Then he turned. "Okay. The first thing you should learn is how to tread water. Do you think you can handle that? We'll go a little deeper, but your head will still be above the surface. Once there, you'll kick both your legs, sort of like you're running in place."

"Yeah," Jason said. "I can handle that."

William led them toward the five-foot depth, the water lapping at his pits. Then he led by example, lifting his legs and moving his arms to tread water. Jason did the same without difficulty.

"That was easy," William said. "Uh, let's see. I guess next it would helpful if you learned to float. If you start to panic, try to remain calm. Allow yourself to go perfectly still, let your legs drift upward as you recline, and you'll end up on your back. You won't need to kick or anything. You'll be safe."

"Okay," Jason said with a nod. "Let's try it."

"I'll support you." William moved closer, placing an arm around Jason's shoulders. "Let your legs float to the surface. That's right. Just pretend you're settling into the most comfortable bed imaginable. A water bed! Ha."

Jason was horizontal now, but he still seemed tense and needed to relax. He turned to look at William as if seeking reassurance.

"You're doing great!" William said.

Jason's brow knotted up. "Listen, I have to confess something. I know how to swim."

William's stomach sank. "What?"

"I can swim. I'm not great, but—"

"You're serious?" William interrupted. "You can swim?"

"Yeah."

"In that case…" William pulled away and in a burst of irritation, pushed Jason under the water. Then he turned, wanting to get away. Luckily he was in his element. He took off, swimming toward the deep end. So much for his honest and humble guy! William felt foolish. All that effort he had spent coming up with a calendar of lessons! Time wasted, along with the stupid excitement he had felt. And for what? Just so some guy could get him alone and nearly naked in a swimming pool? Pathetic. He stopped and turned around to make sure Jason had recovered. He was fine. Refusing to waste more time and wanting to burn off some of the anger he felt, William fell into his usual routine, swimming laps. He was just finding his rhythm when he hit an obstacle. Jason. "What are you doing?" William demanded, wiping his eyes clear and wishing for his goggles.

Jason's hair was plastered to his forehead, expression pleading. "Just let me explain!"

"Fine."

"Uh." Jason seemed to struggle with himself. Then he rolled his eyes and spoke. "There's something about you. When I saw you at the meeting the other day, it's not like I was all 'Oh he's hot! I think I'll go after him!' I mean, you are, but that's not why I'm here exactly. It's hard to explain. When I saw you, something inside of me felt… drawn to you."

William had to give the guy credit for admitting the truth. And it wasn't like he didn't understand. They both might have boyfriends, but that hadn't stopped William from feeling the same or entertaining fantasies, not all of them sexual. He had imagined teaching Jason to swim, slowly growing closer in the process, both of them harboring secret feelings they could never act on. The notion had seemed romantic. And yes, as predictable as it was, he had fantasized about needing to teach Jason CPR, complete with many, *many* demonstrations. So what? William didn't blame himself for having wandering thoughts or Jason for wanting to get closer, but one indisputable fact still remained. "I have a boyfriend."

"I know," Jason said hurriedly. "You and Kelly make a

gorgeous couple, and I'm not deluded enough to see myself replacing him. I didn't come here to try to hook up with you, I swear. But I do want to get to know you. That's all. Nothing creepy. At least, nothing beyond what I've already done. Asking for swimming lessons seemed like a convenient excuse."

William snorted. "You should have just said you want to hang out."

"I know." Jason appeared sheepish. "I'm not very good at making friends. I never have been."

Hard to imagine, because aside from the deception, William had found him likeable. "So now what?"

"Well, I *can* swim, but I don't really know any techniques. I just sort of kick while underwater, but aside from that and dog-paddling, I'm not real good. I can't swim across the surface like you do."

"So you *do* want lessons?"

Jason smiled. "That's what we're here for."

Better than letting all his effort go to waste. William could salvage some of the plans he had made. "Okay. Time for the advanced course."

Most people knew how to move through the water, but that wasn't the same as swimming. Not in William's mind. He soon realized that Jason was being honest about not having learned basic techniques. Any fleeting interest they had for each other went out the window as he tried to teach the front crawl. Jason swallowed his fair share of water, but after struggling for an hour or so, he achieved something that at least resembled the stroke. All he needed from this point on was repetition, not guidance.

"One more lap," William kept saying, noticing small improvements the more he pushed Jason. Maybe he pushed a little too hard, because his student reached the edge of the pool, climbed out, and rolled onto his butt, mouth open and panting. William hid a smile, then decided to lead by example. He launched into his usual workout, hoping Jason would learn something from watching. And because he yearned for exercise.

"Hop back in," he said, swimming over to Jason during a break between laps. "Just one more."

Jason, wide-eyed, shook his head. "If you want to kill me, there are easier ways than this."

William climbed out of the pool, sitting next to Jason, who

had a towel wrapped around his shoulders. He let himself drip dry, still warm from exertion "I suppose I can take it easy today."

"You're kidding, right?"

"Nope. I push myself every single day." He watched the water's surface as it settled, deciding to pretend that all his training could still lead somewhere. "I need to if I'm going to become a rescue swimmer."

"Is that like a lifeguard?" Jason asked.

William laughed. "Yeah, except instead of sitting in a chair by the pool, you get dropped from a helicopter into massive waves. If a plane crashes into the ocean, or if a boat goes down, or if people need rescuing during inland floods, that's when a rescue swimmer is called in. It's not easy to become one, but I figure I've got a shot if I keep training every day."

"Where do you go to learn something like that?" Jason asked. "Superhero school?"

"The Coast Guard," William said, feeling a pang of guilt for not being more honest, but he was enjoying the dream too much. "Or the Navy, but I don't want to go international. It won't be easy either way. Most people don't make it through the AST program, but I've been planning this for years. I really think I've got what it takes."

Jason's eyes searched his. "Not that you need a reason to help people, but what's your motivation?"

Geez. That was a long story, but Jason seemed willing to listen. William thought back to when he was seven years old and staying with his cousins. He hadn't liked the water then, not even baths! He loved to play with his cousins though, and in the hot summer weather, they all gathered around the pool at his aunt and uncle's house. His cousins would hop in and out of the water with ease, unafraid. They splashed him when they realized he didn't want to get wet, called him a scaredy cat, and more than once tried to push him into the pool. William didn't have the muscle to defend himself back then, but he was fast, so in a way he did laps, but only by running around the pool rather than swimming through it. The teasing came to a head one day when he was trying to escape them. He had tripped and skinned his knee. His cousins got in trouble when the adults found out, which only made them taunt him more. Late that night while lying sleepless in bed, William had decided he'd had enough. He would learn how to swim. Without hesitating he threw off the sheets, put on swim trunks, and snuck through the silent house. Once at the pool he jumped right into the deep end.

Not the best idea because his lungs had burned as bad as his hurt knee as he struggled to find the surface. But he did. Panic nearly drowned him first, but William forced himself to calm down and float to the surface. Once on his back, he carefully waved his arms to reach the shallow end of the pool where he could stand and cough up water. He had done it! In his mind he had managed to swim, so he got out, went back to the deep end, and repeated what he had learned. When he showed off the next day, his cousins were more patient with him and willing to give him tips. That had been the beginning of his love for the water, his worst enemy becoming his greatest friend. He told Jason all of this, expecting him to yawn or roll his eyes like Kelly had done. Instead Jason leaned closer, their bare shoulders touching briefly, and said, "You're kind of awesome."

William felt himself flush and shook his head. "We'll see about that. AST school is going to kick my ass. If I make it through and become a rescue swimmer, then you can call me awesome. If you still want to."

"I'm pretty confident I will," Jason said.

Unlikely, because the Coast Guard wasn't happening. Still, he felt less depressed about it than usual, probably because he enjoyed Jason's company. Sadly, after talking a little longer, their time ran out. William had school and Jason had work, but they made plans to meet at the Y again on a different morning. Then they walked to the locker room in silence, a thought occurring to William as they reached it. "What are you doing this weekend?"

"Nothing besides work on Saturday."

"Day shift?"

Jason nodded. "Yeah."

Perfect. Bonnie, Kelly's closest friend, had a concert that evening. She wanted lots of people there. If Jason brought his boyfriend, not only would they get to spend more time together, but seeing each other as part of a functioning couple would cool any misguided fantasies. "A friend of mine is having a cello recital. She's nervous about it, so she wants a big support group there."

"Really?" Jason seemed skeptical. "I'd want as few people to show up as possible."

William laughed. "Yeah, me too. Anyway, maybe you could come along."

"I'd love to."

"Good. I'll be with Kelly. Maybe you could bring Tim."

"Tim?" Jason asked.

"Your boyfriend. That's his name, right?"

"Yeah! I'm just surprised you remembered."

William shrugged. "We can make a double date of it. Grab something to eat afterwards. Sound good?"

Jason shook his head, but his answer contradicted this. "Sounds perfect!"

They dressed in silence, William not having time for his usual shower if he wanted to get to school. They smiled sheepishly at each other when ready to go, not really talking as they left the building.

"Where's your car?" Jason asked.

"Right there," William said, pointing to his bike.

Jason stared. "Man, you're hardcore! See you at the recital thing. Text me the details. Or call! I don't mind."

"I will."

"I Jason," came the response, accompanied by a weird face that might have been meant to resemble a caveman.

William finally got the joke and laughed. "I think you swallowed too much chlorine."

"Maybe." Jason beamed at him.

"Don't you have to be at work?" William said helpfully.

"Oh. Right. See you around."

Jason hustled into the parking lot, not looking back. William watched him go, then started unlocking his bike. He had enjoyed talking about old dreams, even if he was only kidding himself. He couldn't enlist in the Coast Guard. Even if it wasn't too late to apply, he couldn't leave Kelly behind. William had made a promise, and no previous aspirations—and definitely no guy with an intense stare and messy hair—was going to make him break it.

The evening of Bonnie's recital had started well enough, if a little oddly. Jason had pulled up to the Bates Recital Hall in a freaking Bentley, like he was a millionaire. He wasn't the driver though. No, that was a ridiculously handsome guy named Tim.

William wasn't insecure. He understood that sometimes people got lucky. Kelly was exceedingly attractive. William was just okay. As hot as he found Jason, he wasn't part of the beautiful elite either. Tim definitely was and that, along with him being older and seemingly rich, set his teeth on edge. Then again, why did it matter? William had a hot boyfriend too, one who loved him, so what did he care if Jason had landed himself the perfect guy?

William tried to put any jealous feelings out of mind as they prepared to enjoy an evening of music. They had front row seats, due to Kelly's disability. He took his boyfriend's hand, enraptured when the first performance began. Most of these were short musical pieces, students demonstrating what they had learned. While few of the performances were perfect, he still admired them for having the dedication to learn such a skill and the guts to play in front of an audience. He wasn't sure if he'd be able to handle that.

Bonnie did great. Kelly's hand clenched his tighter while she was on stage, nervous for his friend, only letting go to applaud. He was the first to clap and the last to stop, which made William smile. Bonnie tended to bring out the best in Kelly. William envied this ability, wishing he could say the same. By the time the recital came to an end and they joined in a standing ovation, jealous thoughts were the furthest thing from his mind. Mostly.

"Not bad," Tim said as they slowly shuffled toward the lobby. "I know a guy who can out-sing them all though."

"They're students," William shot back, feeling defensive. "I thought they did a great job."

"So did I!" Jason said eagerly.

"There's nothing wrong with being honest," Kelly murmured. "If he's heard better, he's heard better."

"I didn't mean to offend," Tim said. When the crowd stopped moving, he turned to face William. He had a natural tan, or maybe Latino heritage. This, along with the jet black hair, made his silver eyes pop that much more. "I guess you had a lot of friends on stage tonight. You're still in high school, right?"

"Yeah," William said, not liking how this made him feel. Just one more department where he couldn't stack up. Tim was old enough that school probably seemed like an embarrassing part of childhood to him. He had the looks, the money, and the muscles.

But could he swim? William was tempted to ask how many laps he could do in an hour, but with his luck, the guy had probably set records swimming the English Channel. "I just don't think it's nice to criticize."

Tim looked him over, then ended the conversation by turning around again.

William grimaced. Why did he care exactly? He should be happy that he and Jason were both paired up, since it would prevent complications.

"That was fun," Tim said without much enthusiasm, eyeing the exit. "I guess dinner's next. Ready?"

"We're supposed to meet Bonnie here," William said.

"Actually, I could use some fresh air." Jason took hold of Tim's arm. "Coming?"

Tim was looking elsewhere and shrugged him off heartlessly. "I need a drink."

"You're the designated driver," Jason reminded him in hushed tones.

"Then I'll have a very small drink," Tim responded, not bothering to lower his voice before he shoved his way through the lobby crowd.

William watched him go. What a jerk! Jason deserved better than that! William would never... Yeah. That train of thought would run him over if he let it, so he turned his attention elsewhere, searching for Bonnie. When she appeared, she wasn't alone. Emma was trailing behind her. She might have chosen to go without makeup during the gay youth group meeting, but now she was gussied up and stunning, dress the same hue as her rosy cheeks. And she was holding hands with Bonnie! William grinned, remembering how good the beginning of a relationship could feel.

This made him look to Jason. William expected him to be excited to see his friend there. Jason hadn't noticed though, still staring in the direction Tim had disappeared, expression concerned. Maybe Tim had a drinking problem. William would bring it up during the next swimming lesson, just in case a sympathetic ear was needed. For now, he stepped forward to offer his congratulations. Bonnie was occupied by Kelly, so he began with Emma.

"You guys make a cute couple," he said.

"Aw shucks," Emma replied playfully, but her smile got a little bigger. "Did you see her up there on stage? She was amazing!"

"I agree," William replied. "I've seen Bonnie play before, but something was different tonight. Maybe she's found her muse."

Emma laughed. "Oh, I like you!"

The feeling was mutual. He didn't know her well, but similar to her friend Jason, she had an appealing vibe. Perhaps that's what they had in common. He was about to ask how they had met when someone said her name, attracting Emma's attention. Even odder is what she said in response.

"Uncle Tim?"

Uncle? They sure didn't look related!

"What are you doing here?" Emma and Tim said at the same time, like some sort of comedy routine, but their shocked expressions promised this was no joke.

Bonnie chimed in, addressing Tim. "Wait, you're Emma's uncle? The one who can sing?"

"No," Emma said. "You're thinking of Ben."

"And does Ben know you're here?" Tim asked, sounding stern. "Or your parents?"

"They think I'm staying at a friend's house."

"Which she is," Bonnie said. "She's staying with me tonight."

"No," Tim said. "She's staying with us. I'll call Ben and tell him to come pick you up. He'll decide what to do."

The conversation kept going, but William gave up trying to understand any of it. Instead he turned to Jason, and when he saw the shame on his face, and especially how he refused to meet his eye, that's when he knew. Jason Grant was a liar. The way Tim kept talking about Ben—the guy who could sing, the one he had bragged about at the end of the show—felt a little too intimate. Tim wasn't Jason's boyfriend. He was just a friend.

Kelly seemed to have a better grasp on the situation and insisted they reconvene at a restaurant so he could dissect the whole horrid affair. Most of the details were lost on William. He couldn't concentrate because he was too upset. At himself mostly, because he got it. Jason wanted to spend time with him. William wanted that too. How often had he looked at the line of customers while at work and hoped to see him there? What did that imply? Weren't his own feelings a betrayal too? Or what about the way he pretended the accident had never happened, telling lofty stories about his future in the Coast Guard? Weren't those lies too?

Self-deceptions maybe. Rebellious delusions in the face of cold hard facts that couldn't be changed. Jason had taken it a step too far, enlisting the help of a performer—Tim, the fake boyfriend. The show was supposed to be on the stage tonight, not in the audience.

At this point, he almost didn't care because Kelly absolutely reveled in exposing Jason's deception, putting on a show of his own during the meal, drawing out the truth and making it as painful as possible for everyone involved. Why did he have to be so mean? Being a sore loser was bad enough, but a tactless victor? William was done with the meal and everyone at the table. He crossed his arms over his chest and stayed silent. Only when they spilled out of the restaurant did he feel like he could breathe again.

Bonnie and Emma were still in high spirits, nestled close together and whispering. Jason was sticking close to Tim, his posture downtrodden. William stayed with Kelly, bringing up the rear. All he wanted to do was go home. Not to the Phillips household. He wanted to be shut in his old room, alone, so he could forget the entire evening.

Tim turned to face him, seeming more relaxed now that the ruse was over. "Need a lift to your car?"

"I don't drive," William replied. "Neither of us do."

"Then a ride home," Tim offered.

William instantly shook his head.

Kelly felt differently. "It's better than the bus!"

He could either argue or go along with him, and William didn't trust his self-control right now. Bonnie drove Emma in her car, leaving the four of them alone. Kelly took the front passenger seat since he needed more room for his crutches. Jason would drive. Good. That meant they didn't have to sit next to each other. What he didn't expect was for Tim to be so talkative.

"Jason tells me you like to swim," he said, sprawled comfortably in the backseat.

William caught Jason's eyes flicking away in the rearview mirror. No doubt he was tuning in. "I swim because it's important to my career goals. For some people, swimming is part of a game.

For me, it's serious." He hoped Jason was reading between the lines. Tim certainly didn't, but then he'd had a few beers.

"I know exactly what you mean. Pools aren't for splashing around in, and don't get me started on people who float on inflatable rafts. They're not even in the water, so get the hell out of the pool, am I right?"

"Yeah," William said, grabbing the handle above the window and gripping it tightly as they rounded a corner. "Do you swim competitively?"

"I just like the exercise, especially in the summer when jogging in the heat feels like breathing fire. Perfect time to hop in the pool. I wanna have one installed soon."

"You mean at home?"

"Yeah!" Tim flashed him a bright smile. "Why not?"

Because most people didn't have the money or room. William tensed up when the car braked sharply. He tried to focus on the conversation instead. "What sort of pool?"

"I was going to ask you that. You're the pro, right? From what Jason tells me, you're practically ready for the Olympics. No, the Coast Guard. Isn't that what you're training for?"

In the passenger seat, Kelly's head turned slightly, to better hear his answer.

"That was my original plan," William said carefully.

"What's your new one? There's got to be a reason you swim every morning."

"Why do you like jogging?" he countered.

"Because I like to stay in shape." Tim stretched out even more, hogging the backseat. Their knees touched, not that he seemed to notice. "More than that, it takes the edge off, you know? Like if I go without, I have a bigger chance of losing my temper or letting stuff get to me."

William nodded his understanding. "It's almost like a price you pay in advance. You get all of the day's tension out at the very beginning."

"I actually prefer jogging at night. I feel like it carries me through the next day, but maybe I should try it your way instead."

"Time to go," Kelly said.

William looked up, surprised to find the car had stopped. Outside the window was Kelly's home. His stomach turned at the idea of staying there, of running into disapproving parents, or having to listen to Kelly gloat. "I'm staying at my place tonight. I'm tired."

"You can be tired here," Kelly said.

William remained seated. "I want to be in my own bed. Besides, my mom misses me."

"Fine." Kelly opened the passenger door and struggled to get out, his crutches catching on something. This made William feel guilty. He didn't think Kelly was doing it on purpose. Those crutches got in the way constantly. William had seen that happen plenty of times, and he was partially responsible.

"I'll be right back," he murmured, hurrying to get out of the car and assist him.

Not that his efforts seemed appreciated. "I'm okay," Kelly said, waving him away. "Just go."

He wouldn't. Not like this. He walked Kelly to the door, his boyfriend's tone accusing when they faced each other on the porch. "He's a liar."

"You made that painfully clear at the restaurant."

"Can you blame me?"

Ouch. Maybe *everything* was obvious, not just what Jason had done, but why he thought he even stood a chance.

"Tell me you understand," Kelly pleaded. "Jason has a thing for you. All of this is because he wants to be with you!"

No sense in pretending otherwise. "I know."

"Then why get back in the car with those people?"

"I need to be home. I need my space."

Kelly looked hurt. William looked away, incapable of giving any more of himself tonight. He was worn down. Tired.

"I guess the apple doesn't fall far from the tree."

William's head whipped around. "Meaning?"

"That you're more like your father than you care to admit."

William felt like he'd been punched in the stomach. "That's not who I am," he growled. "I don't lie, and I don't cheat!"

Kelly shook his head. "Then what are you doing?"

Good question. Why did he invite Jason along to an event that had nothing to do with him? It was Bonnie's recital, Kelly's best friend, and he had asked a virtual stranger to tag along. William had fussed over his appearance, and when he saw just how hot Jason's "boyfriend" was, he had felt despair. Was this how his father had fallen? Had he taken so many small steps toward the cliff that he was surprised to find himself tumbling into the middle of an affair?

"Stay the night," Kelly said, the venom gone from his voice.

The change of tone wasn't enough, because tonight, the venom was in William's heart. "I'll see you tomorrow."

He turned and walked back to the car, hearing Kelly laugh as he went, like he was being foolish. Maybe he was. If so, it wasn't the first time. When he reached the car, he got in the passenger seat without thinking. No doubt he would hear about that tomorrow. He kept his attention on the road, watching for any potential hazards as he gave directions. When they pulled over in front of his house, he spared Jason a short glance, wanting to stare despite it all.

"Thanks for the ride," he said. Then he addressed the backseat. "And thanks for dinner. You didn't have to pay for us all."

"It was my pleasure," Tim said.

William gave into temptation, looking at Jason again before he got out of the car. He felt mystified when walking toward the front door, not comprehending how he could care so much against his will, especially when he worked overtime to care about Kelly. He stopped and turned around, as if he'd find the answer there. Funny then that someone was running across the lawn towards him.

"Wait," Jason said, slowing as he neared. What he had to say was reflected in his eyes, illuminated by the porch light behind William, even before he spoke. "I'm sorry."

"I don't like liars."

"It's a nasty habit," Jason said, trying a smile. When it wasn't returned, his expression became somber. "When I was growing up, I had to do certain things to get what I wanted. Or to get away from places I didn't want to be. I didn't lie exactly, not always, but I went to extremes to get my way."

William was reminded again of how little he knew of Jason's past. "Were you abused?"

"No." Jason kicked at the grass. "I lost my parents, so I was in and out of foster homes my whole life. That's not an excuse. I don't know what I'm trying to say, except that I know I'm messed up, and I'm sorry if I made things tense between you and Kelly."

"There's a reason I'm with him," William blurted out.

"I know. I'm sure there are plenty of reasons, and anyone with eyes could—"

"Just one reason," William said. "And I'm not sure it's a good one."

Jason went still. "What do you mean?"

William shook his head. "I don't want to talk about him. Remember what you said to me at the pool? How you felt when you first saw me?"

"Yeah."

"Was that a lie?"

"No!" Jason took a step closer. "I swear it wasn't. I only lied about not being able to swim. And about having a boyfriend."

"That's two strikes," William said.

"Do I get a third? I mean, I don't want another strike, but if I'm not out yet…"

"You're not," William said, even though he knew he shouldn't encourage him. Time to set the record straight. "I felt it too. When we first met. But I don't know what it means. Maybe we're meant to be friends. Maybe, if things were different, we could have been more. Either way, I don't have room for a liar in my life."

Jason's mouth opened, but he seemed incapable of speaking. This is the part where William would, both figuratively and literally, turn his back on Jason once and for all. He hated the idea though. The world was much too bleak without him.

"I'll see you at the pool," William said. "Monday morning."

"Monday," Jason repeated, leaping on the offer. "I'll be there."

William turned and went to his house, pressing his back against the door as he pushed it open. Jason still stood where he had left him. Maybe he would stay there all night, just to prove his dedication. William knew how that would make him feel. Not that it would matter. Story of his life. He was trapped.

His mother heard him entering, overjoyed that he was home again. She heated up some leftovers, which was welcome. William had barely touched his food at the restaurant. He wasn't in the mood to speak, but he could listen, which he did as she filled him in on what had been going on in her life and those of his brothers. Errol had a new girlfriend; Spencer was reenlisting. After an hour of this, he excused himself, saying he was tired.

Once upstairs, he turned on the light. His room now felt like a museum to his past. All the Beast Wars figures were exactly where he'd left them. He couldn't remember the last time he transformed one, so he grabbed Cheetor and let memory guide his fingers. Then he set it down in robot mode and moved to the dresser. On top of it was an application, the answers filled out in pencil. An application to the Coast Guard.

There's got to be a reason you swim every morning.

Out of the mouth of babes. Or super-hot and kind-of-drunk older guys. Tim was right. William wasn't just swimming to relieve tension, or to enjoy what little privacy he had. He could just as easily walk to school or take longer routes on his bike. Instead he was still pushing himself every morning, setting goals and reaching them before moving on to the next. Temptation had hounded him lately, but not even Jason Grant could compete with the allure of the Coast Guard. William wanted to be a rescue swimmer. He picked up the application, reviewed the answers and felt satisfied with most of them. Then he grabbed his old laptop, called up the Coast Guard website, and clicked on the button to apply. Soon he was looking at an electronic version of the same application. Without hesitating, he sat on the bed and started entering his answers.

Chapter Twelve

William felt like a bachelor. He had taken Sunday off from just about everything, including work and Kelly, sending a text that promised they would see each other in school. He also tried not to think about Jason. Instead he allowed himself a trip back in time, when his problems had been fewer and simpler. He dusted off his Transformers, helped his mother bake, and later sat on the couch to watch a movie with her while they crammed several cookies into their mouths.

The late afternoon took an exciting turn when a recruitment officer called. The woman sounded enthusiastic about his application and wanted to schedule an appointment for an interview. He had agreed. Wednesday after school. William kept telling himself it was just an interview. No promises had been broken—yet—but when he arrived at the YMCA the next morning, he felt more motivated than ever.

He didn't enter the building, squatting instead next to his bike to check the tire pressure. Or pretend to, when really he was waiting. William kept watching the parking lot until he saw Jason walking toward him. He seemed sheepish. No wonder, considering how tense their last encounter had been. William had decided to put that behind him too. Mostly. He wanted to find out more about Jason, but not through a Kelly-style interrogation.

"Ready for a serious workout?" William asked.

"I had a feeling that would be my punishment," Jason said.

William focused on his usual routine while keeping an eye on him. Not only to continue coaching Jason, but to log a list of questions. Before this obsession continued, he was determined to get to know the person who had managed to cause so much trouble. "Wanna hit the hot tub?" he asked, stopping earlier than usual.

"Yeah," Jason said, sounding uncertain. His tone changed once they were both shoulders-deep in hot bubbling water. "Oh man! Why don't we do this every morning?"

"I use it as a reward," William said. "I only come here at the end of the week if I meet all my goals."

"How often is that?"

Not very. William wasn't easy on himself, but he wanted to ask questions, not answer them. "So that Tim guy," he began. "He's your uncle?"

"Emma's uncle," Jason said. "Kind of. Look, I'm really sorry—"

William held up a hand to stop him. "I'm not judging. At least I'm trying not to. There's so much about your life that I don't get."

Jason looked exasperated. "You and me both."

"Tell me more about yourself."

"Okay, what do you want to know?"

William decided to make him squirm. "Let's start with your boyfriend."

Jason chuckled, taking it in stride. "Tim is taken, and even if he wasn't, he's way out of my league. He's not my uncle or my boyfriend. Like I said the other night, I was in foster care for most of my childhood. I never settled anywhere for long. Growing up, I blew through twenty-four homes. The place I live now is number twenty-five. Not that it's a foster placement exactly."

"What is it then?"

Jason considered the question. "My former case worker— she's really great. Her brother offered me a place to live, but sadly, he passed away a few years ago. His husband is still alive though, and when he found out I was in trouble, he offered to take me in."

"And that's who Tim is?"

"No, that's Ben. Tim is Ben's new boyfriend, but don't think he moved fast after his husband died, because it wasn't like that. Ben and Tim were high school sweethearts."

"I'm going to need a chart," William murmured. Maybe he needed to start with a simpler question. "Why were you in foster care?"

Jason was quiet long enough that William filled the silence for him.

"Sorry, that's too personal. I shouldn't have—"

"It's fine," Jason said. "Some of this is hard to summarize."

"Then don't."

"You have school soon. In fact, we should probably get going or you'll miss first period."

And delay returning to a life he could barely tolerate? For

what might have been the first time in his life, William felt rebellious. "So what?"

Jason seemed surprised but didn't try to talk him out of it. "Okay. Well, basically my real dad took off before I was born and died in an accident. My mother and grandma raised me together, and from what I can remember, they were doing a good job. Then my grandma passed away and my mom took it hard. She started drinking, which wasn't as big a problem as the abusive jerk she started dating."

William frowned. "Did he hit you?"

Jason's eyes unfocused, like he was staring into the past. "Yeah. He did. This is usually the part where I start defending my mom, but I've been thinking about that. Lately I try to put myself in her shoes, because before Ben and Tim came along, I was also struggling to pay my rent and bills. I felt alone, and it would have been nice to have someone—anyone—who was there for me, even if he had his faults. So I can get why she put up with him. But when I imagine myself having a kid and letting someone else hurt them—" Jason shook his head, too upset to continue.

"Sorry," William said. He wanted to offer something more significant, so he added, "My parents aren't perfect either. My dad cheated on my mom. That's what led to them getting divorced. It makes me angry, and I haven't forgiven him. All I can do is promise myself not to be like my dad. So in your case, when you have your own kids, at least you won't make those same mistakes. You'll be a better parent because of the bad stuff you've been through."

Jason laughed. "Me? Have kids?"

"Is that so unthinkable?"

Jason considered it more seriously. "No, but it seems awfully far away. I don't even have someone to help me raise one. I've been single for a long time."

"Really?" William asked, not hiding his surprise. "Are you just really picky or…"

"Not really," Jason said. "I keep finding guys I'm seriously into. The only problem is someone has always gotten there first."

"Oh." William felt flattered, because he was pretty sure Jason was talking about him. Still, there was no sense in leading him on. "You just have to keep looking."

Jason frowned and shrugged. "Maybe you're right. Anyway,

I'm still trying to get my life back on track. That's why I moved to Austin, for a fresh start. The idea of kids seems too far away to take seriously."

"But someday?" William pressed.

"Yeah. I guess. You?"

"Definitely! I grew up with two older brothers and always wanted a sister, so I'd like to have a little girl."

Jason nodded. "If you're willing to adopt, foster care is full of children who need homes. Just don't expect them to be grateful."

"I'd be the grateful one!" William said. "They can be whatever they want."

"You say that now, but you have no idea how much trouble us foster kids can be."

"I've got a pretty good idea," William retorted. "I've gained a lot of experience recently."

Jason grinned. "Oh yeah?"

"Yeah." William splashed him playfully, laughing when Jason retaliated by doing the same.

"So what's the deal?" Jason asked, the smile not fading. "Are you skipping the whole day? Because I could call in sick to work and tell them I've got a fever. A really bad one."

The breath caught in William's throat. He'd been dancing with temptation all weekend, but it had to stop here. "No. I better get going. You're so lucky to be done with high school."

"I wasn't a fan either," Jason said. "That's why I dropped out." He shook his head. "One more reason I'm single, I guess. Who wants to date a dropout?"

Me. Not that William could say so. "I think you're cool. And it's not like you've been sitting around all this time, right? Tim said something about you supporting yourself since you were sixteen."

"Seventeen. I emancipated myself from foster care, got a full-time job, and moved in with a complete stranger, thanks to Craigslist. Turned out he's a drug dealer. Super nice guy, but I eventually moved in with a friend of mine instead. Things were good for a while, but life has a way of pulling the carpet out from under you."

"Yeah," William said. "It sure does. I don't think you should be ashamed of dropping out of high school. Education isn't for everyone. I'm not going to college."

"No, but you're going to the Coast Guard, right?"

He hesitated, not wanting to be a liar himself. Then again, he did have an interview. "I want to, yeah."

"That's more impressive than a GED. Anyway, you've heard enough of my life story to know you should steer clear of me in the future."

William sucked in air, as if facing a difficult decision. "Your front crawl *is* atrocious, but I haven't completely given up on you. Not yet."

Jason laughed. "No?"

"Definitely not. You shouldn't either. Don't sell yourself short. I've seen how that can take a toll on a person."

"Have you?"

William nodded, thinking of Kelly. And of himself, because this weekend had shown him how good it had felt to set the past behind him and look to the future instead. He pushed himself up and stood, feeling lightheaded from the heat. "I better get going."

"Okay." Jason shot to his feet, which wasn't a good idea, because he swayed.

William reached out to catch him, a hand gripping each of Jason's deltoids, and his body reacted. Not down there, thankfully, but William still felt like an electric current had shot through him. Jason seemed equally stunned. Then they both laughed.

"Got a little dizzy," Jason said.

"Yeah."

"I'm okay now."

"Oh!" William let go of him, then turned around and focused intently on drying himself.

"Are we hitting the showers?" Jason asked.

"Um. No." The showers here were semi-private stalls without doors, which was better than the big open room at school, but he didn't think he could handle knowing that Jason was nearby and nude. "I mean, you can if you want. I have to get going."

He went to the locker room without waiting for Jason's response. William was dressed and ready to go, but still loitered there, feeling like he should say a proper goodbye. Jason wasn't by his locker, so William crept toward the showers, already chastising himself under his breath. He was only going to say goodbye when he got close enough to be heard. He definitely wasn't going to keep sneaking forward, just like he was doing *right now*, so that he could peek at a guy trying to wash chlorine off his skin. No, sir! That would be seriously messed up.

He was across from the shower stalls now, steam leaking from one of them in low clouds. From his current position, all William could see was an occasional elbow. And the ball of a heel, the foot pointing away from him. That meant Jason had his back turned. William stepped forward. He'd already seen most of his body, including a flash of his butt. Now he was able to stare at it. Those cheeks were soft, not rock hard from excessive training, and covered in light wispy hairs. Suds and water coursed over them and between them. Jason started to turn, which meant that the last remaining mystery was about to be revealed. It also increased William's chances of being spotted. The potential embarrassment brought him to his senses. He leapt backward, then spun around and hurried from the room.

"See you tomorrow!" he called over his shoulder, laughing afterwards because he had already seen quite a bit of Jason today. And yet, he still longed to see more. Dressed or naked. He didn't care. He just wanted more.

By the time William had biked to school and checked in at the front office, second period had already started. Luckily his calculus teacher was more interested in continuing her lecture than demanding an explanation. She nodded to William as he took a seat. It was Kelly who stared at him for the rest of the class, no doubt wanting to know where they stood. William didn't make him wait. As soon as the bell rang, he went to Kelly's desk.

"Hey," he said.

"Hey yourself." Kelly searched his face. "Late morning at the YMCA?"

"Yeah. I got a little carried away." Wasn't that the truth!

Kelly continued to evaluate him. "How about a kiss?"

"In the middle of class?"

"Class is over."

They were mostly alone, so William complied, but he kept it short. "Ready to get to next period?"

"Sure," Kelly said. "Do you mind?"

He was referring to his backpack, and even though Kelly was capable of carrying it himself, William hooked it over a shoulder.

"I missed you over the weekend."

"I needed the downtime," William said as they left the room.

"What did you do?"

"Mostly just hung out with my mom."

Kelly smirked. "Same here. What does that say about us? When we aren't together, we have only our mothers to keep us company."

"You have friends," William said. "You should have called Bonnie. She would have loved it."

"I tried," Kelly said. "She and Emma have hit it off enough that the rest of the world has ceased to exist. How was the ride home Saturday night?"

He already knew where this was going. "Uneventful."

"Jason didn't apologize?"

"He did this morning."

Kelly stopped dead, the flow of students forced to move around them. "This morning?"

William nodded. "Yeah. At the pool."

"You're still seeing him?"

The question was loud enough for everyone in the hallway to overhear.

William gritted his teeth. "I'm still his friend."

Kelly studied him anew, no doubt noticing his anger. His voice was quieter when he spoke again. "Did I do something wrong?"

"No," William said, the fight leaving him. "It's just nice to have a friend again."

"Jason doesn't want to be your friend," Kelly stressed. "He wants to be *with* you."

William shrugged. "That's been set straight."

"Has it?"

"Yes!"

Kelly shook his head and started moving forward again. "What about those girls you used to hang out with? Holly. Or Lilith."

"Lily," William corrected, "and if you'll recall, she wanted to be with me too. I can't help it if I'm irresistible."

Kelly ignored the attempt at humor. "Just tell me one thing. Honestly. I can deal with Jason wanting you, but how do you feel about him? Are you tempted? At all?"

William chose his answer carefully. "Everyone has thoughts. You told me that from the very beginning."

"You can look all you want, and you can fantasize about whomever you like. That's totally fine. What I'm asking is if you're tempted to do more."

"I made a promise." One that was becoming harder and harder to keep. When he saw how unsatisfied Kelly was with this answer, he amended it. "Temptation hasn't made me forget that promise, and it won't. There's a reason I'm standing at your side right now." Dedication? Maybe at one time. Lately though, all William truly felt was obligation.

"Do you have any questions for me?"

William sat across from the recruiter, or as she had introduced herself, Petty Officer 1st Class Mary Sheffield. He was in heaven, so excited by his surroundings that his nervousness had dissipated completely. He loved the patriotic posters, the boat model she kept on her desk, and especially the photo of her graduating company. William struggled to keep his happiness in check, which was the opposite of how he felt a mere two hours ago. When school had ended for the day, William parted ways with Kelly, using work as an excuse. After riding his bike to his mother's house, he showered and put on slacks, a button-up shirt, and a tie. Then he had borrowed her car. He abhorred driving, but the nearest recruitment office was more than an hour away. William had gone exactly the speed limit, no matter how many drivers sped past him on the highway, his hands shaky and palms covered in sweat by the time he reached his destination — a strip mall on the edge of San Antonio.

"I admire your dedication." This was one of the first things Officer Sheffield — or Mary, as she generously allowed him to call her — had said. "A phone interview wouldn't do?"

"No way," William had replied. "I'm way too excited. I also didn't expect to get called so soon. I admire your efficiency."

That had earned him a laugh. Then they had gotten down to business. They went over key points of his application together. Mary let William talk a little about himself, then she showed him a video. Afterwards she went into more detail about where a potential career with the Coast Guard could take him, but William knew it all by heart. That's what made her final question so difficult to answer. What else did he need to know? The truth was, Mary needed to know more. He figured it was better she hear it now rather than later.

"I was in a car accident," he said. "A pretty bad one. I was the driver, and my passenger… I was careless."

Mary leaned forward, hands reaching for the desktop keyboard. "Were you charged with anything? Manslaughter?"

"No," William said. "No!" he added when he realized what she was implying. "The passenger didn't die, but he did lose his leg."

"Did any of this go to court?"

"No. Does it decrease my chances?"

"That depends on the circumstances."

"It was just an accident. One I'd really like to make up for."

Mary sighed. "Many of us have extraneous reasons for joining the Coast Guard. I'm passionate about keeping America's waters safe, but that began when I was just a child and my older sister drowned."

"Oh my gosh! I'm sorry!"

"Thank you. After her death, I became obsessed with how I could have helped. I wasn't there when it happened, but I wanted to be prepared in case the same happened to someone else. I learned CPR, took extra swimming classes, and got a crush on just about every lifeguard I met." She laughed. "This eventually led me to the Coast Guard, and while my sister's death isn't the sole reason I joined, I'm not sure my life would have taken the same path otherwise. I have to ask, were you drinking during this accident? Or under the influence of drugs?"

"No." William shook his head. "I've always stayed away from all that. I wanted to join the Coast Guard before the accident, but now I also want to make amends by dedicating myself to helping others." That's what he had attempted with Kelly, but William didn't see what else he could do. If he was out there saving lives—helping tow stranded ships back to shore, or pulling people from frigid waters—surely that would be more valuable than carrying someone's backpack between classes.

"If you make it through the AST program, you'll have plenty of opportunities for redemption."

William nodded. "I'm determined to become a rescue swimmer. I won't let anything stop me. If I get accepted, that is."

Mary clicked her mouse a few times. "You seem like an ideal candidate to me. I noticed we have an application from almost two years ago with the same name but a different address. This one on Hillcrest. Is that you?"

"Yeah!" William said. "I didn't think it had gone through." That had been so long ago. He had filled out the form online, paced the room trying to work up the courage to send it, and when he finally clicked the damn button, the website had given him a timeout error.

"Nobody followed up with you on your initial application?"

"I didn't hear a peep," William said. "No email, no phone calls, nothing."

"Hm. Well, most of the information is the same. I could combine the applications. The only benefit would be that it demonstrates your early interest. There's no point in delayed enlistment, unless you have other plans after graduation."

"The sooner, the better," William said with a grin. On the edge of his mind, he was fending off images of Kelly, Jason, and his mother.

"Of course we shouldn't get ahead of ourselves. You still need to report to a MEPS and pass your ASVAB."

If this was part of the test, William wasn't intimidated in the slightest. "I've been training myself almost daily for years now. If I can't pass my Armed Services Vocational Aptitude Battery test at the Military Entrance Processing Station, then something's seriously wrong."

Mary smiled. "You certainly have the lingo down! You've either been paying attention, or you already know this all by heart."

"Both," William replied.

More forms had to be filled out. Then Mary helped him schedule an appointment with a processing station in Austin, one week from now.

"I'll contact you afterwards to see how it went," she said. "Unless you have any other questions, it's been a pleasure. Your enthusiasm is refreshing. You have the potential to go far!"

William thanked her, trying not to fawn too much, but he couldn't help it. In his mind, she was a rock star. He managed not to make too much of a fool out of himself when saying goodbye. William felt so giddy over the entire experience that he forgot to be nervous when driving home. At first, anyway. Once he hit the highway he resumed his death grip on the wheel, pulling over when he needed to call work to say he'd be late. None of this could put a damper on his spirits. When he arrived at the mall and stepped out of the car, he inhaled deeply and smiled, convinced he could taste freedom in the air.

"It's the only high you don't pay for the next day."

Errol had said this once after William asked him why he smoked pot. "Booze makes you feel crappy. Pills make you feel like shit when they run out. Don't even get me started on acid. With weed, you get a great night's sleep and wake up like nothing ever happened."

William was convinced that smoking dope *did* come with side effects. His brother didn't have the best memory, and he only got weirder as the years went by, but the essence of what he said rang true. Not just for drugs. Any high in life, no matter how natural, came with a price. William felt guilty after his visit with the recruiter. He worried he was betraying Kelly simply by entertaining the notion, and that he was wasting the Coast Guard's time by starting a process he couldn't finish. Hitting bottom only made him eager for the next high, and those came every morning when he spent time with Jason. That too had a price to pay, but at the moment, William was enjoying himself too much to care. He was sitting on a locker room bench, shoes beside him. That's as far as he'd gotten undressed because he was distracted by Jason, who was leaning against the row of lockers and retelling the story of their double date at Bonnie's recital, which was a lot funnier in retrospect.

"Tim made me switch colognes. Seriously. I finished getting dressed and went to their bathroom, because at the time I didn't have cologne of my own. I grabbed the coolest-looking bottle and sprayed some on. The second I came down the stairs, Ben got all starry-eyed and excited for me, but Tim, he walks a circle around me like a drill sergeant inspecting a uniform. Then he leans closer, sniffs, and freaks out. 'Is that my cologne? I will *not* be one of those couples who dress the same, talk the same, or smell the same. You hear me?'"

William shook his head. "But you weren't really a couple."

"Ben made sure to point that out! Well, actually he said,

'Don't worry, even your real boyfriend doesn't want to smell like you. Especially your socks.'"

William chuckled. "They sound cool."

"They are! You should totally meet them. Properly."

"That would be fun." William cocked his head. "Does Tim really have smelly feet?"

Jason rolled his eyes. "Are you kidding? He smells amazing. Even in the morning."

"Are you sure you don't have a thing for him?"

"Absolutely. You need to see them together to understand. Yeah, Tim is hot, but he and Ben are so right for each other that I can't even think of him that way."

"They must be really secure in their relationship," William mused. "Not many people are willing to loan out their boyfriend." Kelly certainly never would!

"I talked them into it. I'm good at stirring up trouble." Jason sighed theatrically. "It's just a matter of time before they realize that and boot me out."

William grew serious. "Is it hard for you to talk about your time in foster care?"

"Not really. Why?"

"Because you said you were in twenty-something different homes, and it made me wonder if foster parents are always that hard on their kids. It sounds like if you make them mad, they kick you out."

Jason shook his head. "It's not that simple. I'm just really good at what I do. I didn't want to stay with any of my foster families. I wanted to go back to my mom, and I thought that if they couldn't find a home for me, they'd be forced to return me to her. So I did whatever it took to get kicked out."

"Such as?"

Jason grinned. "Well, in foster home number three, the lady there collected jigsaw puzzles. Who does that, right? She had this room with box after box of puzzles and completed ones hanging on the wall like art. She was also a vegetarian, which isn't a big deal, except that she was fixated on lentils. She would use them to replace any sort of meat, so lentil burgers, or lentil hotdogs… And I don't mean a nice patty or sausage made from lentils. She would literally give you a hotdog bun filled with boiled lentils and expect you to put relish and mustard on top."

"Yum."

"I know. So anyway, one day when she wasn't home, I went into the collection room and dumped out every single box in the middle of the floor, making a giant pile of puzzle pieces."

"Was she pissed when she came home?"

"No, because after mixing the pile up, I put all the pieces back into random boxes. I told her I wanted to do a puzzle together that night. After a dinner of pizza with lentils on it, she let me choose a box, and we sat down at the table together. You should have seen her face as she slowly figured it out. She ran, literally *ran* to the collection room and started opening the other boxes there. I thought she was going to cry."

"You're such a bastard," William said with a grin. "Still, that seems like an unfair reason to kick you out."

"Oh, that didn't do it. I was still learning the ropes back then, so it took a few tries. A fake hunger strike is what finally got me out of that house. I used the allowance she gave me to buy cheap stuff like bread to live on. She thought I was starving myself, when in fact, I had a decent stash of food hidden under my bed."

"Any lentils under there?" William asked. "They're cheap."

Jason laughed. "No, for some reason I wasn't in the mood for those."

"So basically you've always been trouble," William said warmly. He noticed their surroundings again. "We should start swimming while there's still time."

Jason checked his watch. "Or you can let me take you to breakfast. A greasy diner somewhere, a huge plate of pancakes, and menus sticky with syrup. Sound good?"

"I already ate before coming here. Eggs. I boil them the night before and have them in the morning."

Jason looked like he was waiting for a punchline. When it didn't come he said, "Sounds kind of sad."

William shrugged. "It's better than eating breakfast with Kelly's mother."

"Why's that?"

"It's not worth getting into." William didn't like talking about Kelly. Especially with Jason, since it was a sure-fire way to skip directly to the guilt he'd feel later today.

"Let me take you to breakfast," Jason pressed. "If not today, then tomorrow."

"And miss another workout?" William shook his head. "No way." He bent over to put on his shoes, deciding they didn't have enough time for a swimming lesson. "Friday morning wouldn't be so bad. But only if we really push ourselves tomorrow."

"Deal. Hey, where'd you get that scar?"

William self-consciously touched his hairline directly above one eye. The place where he'd had stitches normally didn't show, but he'd had his hair cut for his recruitment interview, and the blood rushing to his head when he bent over probably made the white line show up against pink skin. "Just an accident when I was younger."

This wasn't a lie. Technically. He *had* been younger during the car wreck, but not by much. It seemed crazy that he could care about Jason so much and still hide one of the most significant events of his life. Part of William wanted to be more open, but pretending the accident had never happened felt too good.

"I've been telling you embarrassing stories all morning," Jason pressed. "You owe me at least one."

William finished tying his laces and looked up. "Your stories are funnier than mine."

Jason shrugged. "It's not a competition."

"There's not enough time anyway. Let's go."

Silence escorted them out of the building, the idea of them parting already causing his heart to ache. Oh yes, every high had its price, and even though he was paying it now, William knew he would be back tomorrow for more.

Chapter Thirteen

Each day began with dreams of a future that would never be—the Coast Guard and a life with Jason Grant. Then came school and work, which helped ground him in reality. By the evening he was firmly anchored there. In spite of his best efforts, William was feeling increasingly suffocated. While he and Kelly both accepted blame these days, the wreck of a bed they slept in each night had taken most of its damage from him.

He reported to the bedroom that night with a cowboy hat in one hand, his uniform shirt already partially unbuttoned. He just wanted to slip between the sheets, close his eyes, and—

"A letter came in the mail for you."

Kelly was sitting up in bed, an open book facedown next to him. Pinned between two fingers and held aloft was an envelope.

"Who's it from?" William asked, tossing his hat on the dresser.

"Take a wild guess."

William felt a jolt of panic, wondering if Jason had been crazy enough to send a love letter. "No idea."

"It's from the Coast Guard," Kelly said. "I think."

William walked over and accepted the envelope, glancing at the return address. It was from the military processing center in Austin.

"That's for your ASVAB, isn't it?"

William looked up in surprise.

"I pay attention to the things that matter to you," Kelly said. "I know you think I'm dismissive of them but… I guess it's getting close to that time, isn't it?"

William sat on the edge of the bed. He didn't need to open the letter. It was confirmation of his upcoming appointment. "I met with a recruitment agent earlier this week." He braced himself for anger and was met instead with silence. He looked over to find Kelly chewing his bottom lip, his brown eyes wet. "You don't seem surprised."

"I'm puzzled that you still need to meet with a recruitment agent. Is that to get the date you ship out?"

"No. It's to find out what my options are. Don't worry, I haven't enlisted."

Kelly shook his head. "How can you not be enlisted? I thought you were already accepted."

"Since when?"

"Since we met!"

They stared at each other. William was the first to laugh.

Kelly joined him. "You always made it sound like a sure thing. You haven't stopped swimming."

"No," William said. "I haven't."

"I wouldn't have stopped running either," Kelly admitted. "Now is about the time that I would have sought a sponsor for the Olympics."

"I know." William swallowed against the guilt. "I haven't been accepted yet. I honestly don't know what I'm doing by starting the process. Maybe I just want to know if I could have made it."

"I understand. If our situations were reversed, the temptation would have been too great not to try." Kelly's hand took his. "Part of me wants this for you. I really do."

"And the rest?"

Kelly bit his lip again, but not before William saw it tremble. "The rest is terrified of losing you." He swallowed and looked away. "Everything has been so weird lately, and I— If you do get accepted, what does that mean for us?"

"It doesn't matter," William said. "I won't go. I made a promise."

Kelly raised his head. "What's the alternative? We're close to graduating, and I've never heard you talk about college. Are you going to serve smoothies for the rest of your life? Or take classes with me just because I pretend to be dependent on you?"

"Pretend?"

"You know I can take care of myself. Physically, anyway. Emotionally is another matter, but I don't want this relationship to hold you back."

Wow. Were they breaking up? William squeezed his hand. "I'm glad we're finally talking about this. I wanted to, but I was scared."

"Of me?" Kelly said, sounding amused.

"Scared for you."

"I'm a big boy. I can deal with us being apart. I'll still be here when you get shore leave or whatever." Kelly looked amused. "Gosh, I'll be a sailor's wife!"

Not breaking up then. A long distance relationship. William

would have jumped at the offer a few months ago. Now he wanted more. He needed his freedom.

William struggled to find the best way to express these feelings. "Actually—"

"I know, I know. You're not a sailor. You're a coastie."

"Not yet," William said.

"I have no doubt that you'll be accepted. Maybe that's why I assumed you already had been."

"And if I am?"

"I knew the deal from the beginning," Kelly said. "But for now…" He pulled on William's hand as he leaned back and rolled over onto his side. William climbed the rest of the way into bed and held him, wishing—not for the first time—that he could stop hurting Kelly and start protecting him instead.

The next gay youth meeting was taxing. William normally enjoyed the lectures their group leader prepared, but this one was spent trying very hard not to look across the room at Jason. He gave into temptation a few times, the last of these resulting in eye contact. Jason smiled first. William couldn't resist doing the same, although he was pretty sure Kelly noticed. That's why, when the lecture ended, William purposefully ignored Jason. Perhaps understanding the situation, Jason ignored him too and went outside with others in the group. Including Kelly.

This made it difficult to relax, but William tried to put the issue out of mind as he listened to Lisa talk about an old Disney movie she had recently watched and felt conflicted about.

"The animals are so cute," she said in her mousey voice, "and I've loved the story since I was little, but it's not like you can ask a cat and two dogs if they want to be movie stars. Maybe they hated having to perform all those stunts."

William did his best to reassure her. "Dogs are happy when their owners are. They live to please, so I bet they liked it. The cat I'm not so sure about."

"Speaking of cats," Bonnie said, looking a little pale as she approached. "And fights."

William tensed up. "What happened?"

"Hurricane Kelly just blew through the parking lot." When she saw his reaction, she hastened to add, "Everyone is fine. Just some hurt feelings. Kelly and Jason exchanged words, that's all."

"About what?"

"You." This was said by Lisa, who hadn't even been out there. She covered her mouth as if embarrassed. "Sorry. I just…"

Saw the obvious, like everyone else. William felt his cheeks flush. Kelly would be upset, and rightly so. He probably felt like the laughing stock of the group, but he wasn't the one to blame. William was. "I'll go talk to him."

"Take him home," Bonnie said. "Or take him out. I think he just needs to be reassured that you still love him." She stopped short of asking if he actually did.

"I'll see what I can do." When he went outside, Jason and his friend Emma had already left. That was good. Smoothing things over would be easier with them gone. He saw Kelly surrounded by a few guys. Having an audience would only rile Kelly up more, so William waved him over, making a beeline for the bus stop when Kelly got near enough.

"We need to talk!"

"Let's get out of here," William said, glancing back at the church. "I'm done."

"That makes two of us," Kelly said, sounding somewhat appeased.

He prayed for a timely bus, but no luck. They were stuck waiting at the bus stop, Kelly with one topic on his mind. "I had an interesting conversation with Jason."

"Oh yeah?" William asked, making sure not to sound like he cared.

"He admitted that he's interested in you."

William remained very still. "That's not really news. We've known that since Bonnie's recital."

Kelly rolled his eyes. "Yes, but now he said that he's willing to wait until I'm no longer in the picture."

William scoffed. "He didn't."

"He did!"

"What was the context? Did he just walk up to you and—"

"I went up to him!"

"That's what I thought."

Kelly looked incredulous. "Meaning?"

"That if you ask someone how they feel, it's not fair to get angry at them for telling you."

"That's not the issue," Kelly said, straining every syllable.

"The problem is that you're spending every morning with someone who wants to sleep with you. How would you feel if I was regularly meeting some guy who—"

"I'd trust you," William said. "There's no point in doing otherwise."

"That's a very logical response," Kelly said, "but I asked how you would feel. I don't believe for a second that you would just shrug it off. You might not get angry like I do, but I bet you'd feel hurt."

William sighed. "I don't mean to make you feel that way. I'm sure Jason doesn't either." He saw the bus approaching. "Let's just drop it, okay?"

Not okay, because Kelly kept talking about the situation during the ride, intent on making William see things his way. Once they were home, they found Kelly's parents in the living room. Rather than letting them witness another argument, he went to the bedroom.

Kelly followed. "You're not going to do anything about this?"

"What can I do?" William said, spinning around to face him. "Jason can't help what he feels. Nobody can."

"No, that power belongs to other people."

William shook his head. "I don't understand."

"The other day, when we had that conversation about the Coast Guard, I could have made you feel ashamed, or guilty, or any number of things depending on how I chose to react."

"Okay," William said, still not following.

"I decided that your feelings are more important to me than what I want."

"Which is?"

"For you to stay here with me!" Kelly sounded exasperated. "I don't want you to go, but I know how strongly you feel about your dream, so I decided to make that sacrifice for you."

"And I'm grateful."

"Now the roles are reversed. There's something I need from you, and how you react has power over how I feel."

William clenched his jaw. "This is about Jason."

"Yes!" Kelly said.

The phone in William's pocket vibrated. He pulled it out, eager for an excuse to end this conversation. He wasn't entirely surprised to see whose name was on the display.

"Let me guess," Kelly said, lips pursed.

William pushed the button to answer, eyes locked on Kelly's as he lifted it to his ear. "Speak of the devil. Give me a minute and I'll call you back." He hung up and returned it to his pocket, still staring Kelly down. Or trying to.

"When you call him back," Kelly said, "I want you to end it."

"No."

"Excuse me?"

"I already abandoned my friends!" William said, voice rising. "I gave up everything for you without complaint, but this is too much! I like having someone else to talk to besides you. That's normal. It's healthy!"

"Not when that person has romantic feelings for you," Kelly said. "Bonnie—"

"—is a lesbian. It's not the same."

"But if she was straight and had feelings for me, I would break things off for her benefit as much as yours. Do you really think Jason is going to thank you for leading him on? Or maybe he's already getting what he wants."

"I'm not cheating on you," William snapped. "Feel free to come to the YMCA if you don't trust me."

"I will," Kelly said.

William glared. "Don't bother. There's nothing to see."

Kelly took a deep breath and sat on the edge of the bed, setting his crutches to one side. "Relationships always involve compromise, right?"

William remained standing. He nodded grudgingly. "I guess."

"Then think of it this way. I compromised on the Coast Guard issue. I'm not using it as leverage, but if you won't be in Austin much longer, then why is this friendship so important to you? Do you really think, as fledgling as it is, that it will survive you being gone the next four years? And I *really* don't like the idea of having to share when you're back in town to visit. Your mother? Fine. But not Jason. Not then, and not now. Please don't make me."

William sighed. "What am I supposed to do?"

"Call him back. Explain to him that your time is limited and that you want to spend it with those who matter most to you. Or find some even nicer way of putting it, I don't care. Just end it. Please."

William took the phone from his pocket and considered it. "I'll be out front."

"Okay," Kelly said, seeming placated. "Best of luck."

Once he was standing outside on the front patio, William considered the empty street. He was tempted to walk down it and keep going until he was far away. If he got accepted into the Coast Guard, that wish would be granted. Maybe Kelly was right. What point was there in any of this when he'd be living in a different part of the country later this year? He pushed the button to call Jason back, deciding to ease into it slowly.

"Hey!" Jason said, sounding eager.

"Hey. I heard what happened. At the group meeting. Bonnie told me first, and I've been hearing about it from Kelly ever since."

"Sorry," Jason said. "I didn't mean to—"

"I know, and it's not you who should be sorry." William checked to make sure the front door was still closed. "Kelly wasn't always like this, you know. Lately he's been getting more and more bitter, but I guess I'm to blame. For all of this."

"What do you mean?" Jason asked.

William nearly told him the truth. Learning about the accident would be enough to scare him off, but he didn't want Jason to remember him that way. "Nothing. He doesn't want me to see you anymore. At least not alone. He can't stop you from coming to the group meetings, but no more swimming together."

The line went silent. He thought it might go dead. He definitely didn't expect Jason to sound so determined when he spoke again.

"I think we should keep seeing each other. In fact, I want to see more of you."

William smiled. He couldn't help it. "Jason," he said warningly.

"So I guess you're the tiebreaker. Kelly wants us to stop seeing each other. I want you to come to my house, meet my friends, and then go on a picnic with me. So you tell me what you want, and whatever it is, I'll respect it. Just be honest with me, because I have no room for a liar in my life."

The very words William had used on him the night of the recital. He chuckled in appreciation, then considered the offer. If this was the last of his time in Austin, shouldn't he make the most of it? Kelly would be angry, but then, when wasn't he? They'd probably find something else to argue about if Jason wasn't around. William thought back to before all of this had begun. He hadn't been happy then. He wasn't happy now. Not all the time, but his mornings were pretty damn awesome thanks to a certain troublemaker.

"I do love a picnic," William said. "When?"

Jason didn't hesitate. "Right now?"

William laughed. "How about Saturday? I'll bike to your place as my morning exercise instead of swimming."

"We live outside of Austin."

"Sounds like a good workout. Text me your address. Right now, I have an argument I have to get back to, but uh… Swimming? Tomorrow morning?"

"Absolutely!"

William hung up the phone and steeled himself. Kelly would either yell or cry. Neither would be easy to deal with, but he had reached his breaking point. William couldn't stand the idea of things going back to the way they were, so he marched to the bedroom, cheeks burning. He wouldn't back down. Not this time.

When Kelly saw his face, his own fell. "I don't get it," he said, sounding defeated. "Explain it to me. You're in love with him? You don't love me anymore? Which is it?"

"I'm tired of not having my own identity," William said, the words ringing true. "I feel like the accident welded us together because ever since then, my entire world has revolved around you. At first I wanted that, but you're doing better now, so why am I still here every night? Why do I have a room at home that I never sleep in or friends that I never see? I'm sick of it! I still love you, but I'm so tired of us."

Kelly's voice was level, his chin raised high. "The accident didn't weld us together. Every relationship involves giving yourself up to the other person. That's how two lives become one. I'm sorry you feel like I'm suffocating you with my needs, but without you, I don't feel like I can breathe. One of us is going to run out of air. I guess it's just a question of whom."

William sat on the bed, placing his face in his open palms and rubbing weary eyes. Then he moved his hands away. "I just want to have a normal relationship."

Kelly remained eerily calm. "I'm not sure you do. I don't think you even know what a normal relationship is."

"We're in agreement there." William stood up and crossed his arms over his chest. "So what now? Do you want me to leave?"

"No," Kelly said. "That's the problem. Isn't it?"

Chop, toss, blend, pour. Smile at the customer. Process their payment. Take the next order. Chop, toss, blend, pour. The only issue with a job like William's is how much time it allowed him to think. During the first week of employment, he had been on edge, worried about messing up orders or handing back too much change. Now he knew the menu by heart, and the necessary actions had become second nature. That left him time to stew over the past, present, and future, entertaining alternate versions of each: A past where the accident never occurred, a present where he and Kelly were just friends—each having moved on to new relationships, and a future so idyllic that Jason was enlisted in the Coast Guard with him.

"Trouble down at the ranch?"

William looked up, switching from fantasy to reality. To his delight, both involved Jason. "Hey!" he said. "Wait, what did you say?"

"It was supposed to be a cowboy joke." Jason peered at him. "You look like someone ran off with your horse."

William managed a laugh. "I'm all right."

"I don't think you are. You need pizza. I can tell."

"I'm not really hungry."

"Now I'm really worried!" Jason scratched above one ear, offering him a crooked smile. "I don't suppose you have a break coming up?"

He didn't, but William turned a pleading expression on his coworker. She rolled her eyes but nodded. He looked back at Jason, grinning now. "You want a smoothie?"

Jason rotated one of his shoulders. "Have you got one for sore muscles?"

"I might. Meet me at our usual place?"

Jason nodded and turned away. That freed William to keep grinning like an idiot, which he did while preparing Jason's drink. Then he hurried outside. The sun had set, leaving behind a red glow on the horizon. Heat and humidity still hung in the evening air. William felt like stripping off his shirt. When he sat on the bench where Jason waited, he took off his hat to fan himself.

"Hot," he said.

"Extremely," Jason said, shooting him a sly smile as he accepted his smoothie. "Thanks." After sucking on the straw, he made sure to look impressed. Then he set it on the bench next to him. "What's going on? You were quiet this morning."

"Sorry," William said. "Everything has been crazy lately. Some of it makes me so happy I can barely cope. The rest has been hell. Hey, you know what would cheer me up?"

"What?"

"Another Jason Grant story."

Jason laughed. "Meaning?"

William leaned against him briefly. "From your foster care days."

"Ah. You mean the insane stuff I did to get booted out of each home."

"Yeah," William said, chuckling in anticipation. "Those always cheer me up. Start from the very beginning."

"The first home?" Jason shook his head. "That one wasn't so funny. I didn't have any tact yet, so I basically just screamed at the top of my lungs until they sent me back. I lost my voice for a good week after that, which is why the next time I got a little more creative."

"Then maybe we should work our way back," William said. "How did you get kicked out of the very last one? I wanna hear the grand finale!"

Jason coughed. "I guess you could call it that."

"You're blushing."

"Am not!" Jason pushed him playfully.

"Now I *really* want to hear this story!"

Jason stifled a yawn. "I don't know if I have the energy. There's this gorgeous guy I've been spending time with, even though he makes me get up at the butt crack of dawn. I can't remember the last time I got a full night's sleep."

William smiled at the compliment, then patted his left leg. "I'll be your pillow, but only if you tell me."

"Pillow talk?" Jason said with a smirk. He accepted the offer, twisting around to lay the back of his head against William's leg. "This is nice! Okay. You want a story? Instead of a wicked step-sister, this one involves a naughty foster brother."

"Was he hot?" William asked.

"Very. Dark wavy hair, bronze skin, amazing eyes. He was a

wrestler, but not heavyweight, so he had these lanky muscles…"

William frowned. "Is that your type?"

"One of many," Jason said shamelessly. "What about you? They say once you go black…"

William made a face. "That's such a stupid saying."

"Sorry. But some people have a strong preference in that regard."

"Race doesn't matter to me."

Jason's eyes were smoldering. "Good."

"Stop looking at me like that. And no more interruptions."

"Fine." Jason closed his eyes, brow furrowing as he continued. "His name was Caesar, and I didn't think of him as a brother or any other sort of relative. At first I steered clear of him because I had already learned the hard way that such things never work out. I don't mean I had affairs with lots of foster brothers or anything. Just that the guys I got crushes on always turned out to be straight. So anyway, we started getting friendly—"

"You mean sex?"

"Easy, horndog! You're rushing things. At first we just hung out, but yeah, eventually I lost control and made a move. I do that. When I like a guy, I reach a certain point where logic goes out the window, and I end up sneaking into his room late at night, overwhelmed by the urge to touch him."

William became aware of how close Jason's head was to his cock. "Is that what happened?"

"Something like that."

"I uh… I want details."

Jason smiled. "Really? Are you sure about that?"

William was on the verge of needing to adjust himself. "Maybe not. So you made a move and—"

"It didn't go so well. I was ready to pull another prank and get myself booted out, but then Caesar…" Jason swallowed, his features tensing. "He liked me back, and that was enough to make me love him."

"So you ended up together?"

"Yeah. At least I thought so." Jason opened his eyes and shook his head. "You don't want to hear this. It's boring. Did I ever tell you about the clam chowder? There was this lady who—"

"Wait," William said. "I want to hear the rest. What happened with you and Caesar?"

"It doesn't matter."

"It does!"

Jason looked confused. "Why?"

"Because relationships define you. They change who you are. They change your entire life."

Jason stared up at him. "I know it seems that way now. Kelly is your first relationship, right? I get it. I remember how the world feels like an entirely new place when you find someone you love. And when that person loves you back, it's empowering. Like winning the lottery. Like winning *everything*. Life seems perfect, you feel invincible, colors are brighter… Then they hurt you and it all comes tumbling down. Afterwards you feel like they've broken you, but it's not true. When that person goes away and you claw your way through the layers of heartache, you'll find who you used to be. Small and alone again, but still you."

"That's sad," William said.

"That's life," Jason countered. "I'm actually trying to be positive. You're right that relationships change everything, but that doesn't have to be permanent. You can always start over, find another person to make you feel big and invincible again, and if you're lucky, this time they won't leave. Or you won't need to leave them."

"Is that what happened with Caesar? You left him?"

Jason's eyes searched his, then he smiled. "You don't give up easily, do you?"

"Nope!" William said proudly. "You either tell me what happened now, or I'll bug you about it for the rest of your life."

Jason's tone was flirtatious. "Is that a promise?"

"I'm about to take back my leg pillow!"

"Okay, okay. What happened with Caesar is that someone else got there first. He had already found the love of his life, but they couldn't be together because… Well, whatever. I'm an idiot, so even that wasn't enough to discourage me. Eventually I forced him to make a choice. And he did. Just not the one I had hoped for." Jason covered his face and laughed. "I never learn."

"What's that supposed to mean?" When he didn't answer, William grabbed Jason's hands to move them away, loving the excuse to touch him. "Tell me!"

Jason chuckled again. "I keep meeting these amazing guys and not taking the hint when it turns out they're already taken."

William didn't know how to respond. Something had changed

between them. Ever since the phone call on Sunday, when Jason insisted they keep seeing each other, he hadn't been hiding his feelings. That was flattering, but also frustrating because William couldn't reciprocate. Doing so would be cheating. Already they were going too far. Having Jason's head in his lap—them having physical contact at all—was a bad idea. After today, he would make sure it didn't happen again.

The phone in his pocket rumbled. William pulled it out and saw an agitated text message from his coworker. "Duty calls."

"You could always quit," Jason said, sitting up. "Maybe I could get you a job at the pet store. We'd be coworkers. I'm pretty sure your poolside skills would qualify you to work in the aquarium aisle. You could teach the fish how to swim."

William laughed. "I'll keep that in mind. Sorry, but I've really got to go."

"It's fine," Jason said, standing and walking with him toward the mall entrance. "I hope my story didn't bum you out. The important thing is, no matter how bad the heartbreak, you will recover. Hearts can take a beating and *keep on* beating."

"You speak from experience?"

Jason smiled and held open the door for him. "Yes, but this most recent guy, he might be the one who finally does me in."

William licked his lips, which had gone dry. "I'll see you tomorrow?"

"Try and stop me."

That pretty much summed up Jason. He was unstoppable. But so was Kelly. William pictured them like two elemental forces, equally matched in power, a stalemate that only William could break.

William sauntered out of the Military Entrance Processing Station, head held high. As soon as the door behind him closed, he couldn't hold back anymore. He leapt, punching the air with a fist as he let out a "Yaaaaahooooo!" Then he remembered Kelly and worried about celebrating so openly. That is until he saw his boyfriend crutching across the parking lot, wearing a smile just as big as his own.

"You passed," he said, meeting him halfway.

"Yeah," William confirmed.

Kelly's face lit up. "I'm proud of you!"

"Really?"

"Yes! Why wouldn't I be?" Kelly stopped in front of him. "It's just a formality now. You're as good as accepted."

"We don't know that," William said.

"I have no doubt. I'm happy for you. You've earned this."

William took in the shining eyes, the goodwill between them almost tangible, and spoke without thinking. "I wish we could always be this way."

Kelly looked surprised, but not confused. "That wouldn't make leaving easier, would it?"

"No," he admitted. "If we could go back to this, I think I would stay."

Kelly chuckled warmly. "I don't believe that for one second. Even before the accident, you were already married to the Coast Guard. I've always been the other woman in this love triangle."

He had the geometry right. Just not the participants.

"I'm going to get my shit together," Kelly continued, moving closer. "When you're gone, I'll have to decide what I want to do with my life. That should help iron out the wrinkles. Oh who am I kidding? I'll always be a bitch, but I think getting my life in order will let it return to being an occasional eruption instead of never-ending lava."

"You've definitely got a way with words," William said, struggling to find any of his own.

Kelly smirked. "I've got more than just words for you. Not here though. These lips have the power to disqualify you, don't they?" He said this in good humor, not snidely, when normally the closeted nature of the military was a point of contention between them.

As for William, he was grateful for the excuse not to kiss. Doing so would feel like cheating... on someone other than his boyfriend.

Chapter Fourteen

Digital maps offer no solid frame of reference. Locations can be made to appear close or far apart just by zooming in and out, the terrain conveniently flat. When William went online and calculated a route to Jason's home, he realized that he would be biking for the better part of an hour. The map failed to inform him of the increasing heat, reckless drivers, or steady uphill incline. He missed his destination the first time, having to backtrack to find the long driveway. Once on it, the road wound through lightly wooded land that opened to reveal a house in the distance. The dwelling was two stories high with a separate garage off to the left. Considering that Tim drove a Bentley, William had expected a mansion.

He pedaled to the front door, leaned his bike next to it, and seriously considered ducking behind the garage to change clothes. His muscle shirt was soaking wet, as was much of his body, a problem fresh clothes would do little to hide. What he needed was a shower. He rang the bell, still trying to catch his breath as he waited. When it swung open, Jason was on the other side, looking much fresher in a navy blue T-shirt and white shorts.

"You weren't kidding about living far away," William said, sweat trickling down from his drenched hair. "Great workout, but I can't meet your family like this."

"My friends," Jason corrected, "and they won't care."

"I have a spare outfit with me." William unslung his backpack. "Maybe I could take a shower?"

Jason glanced back and grimaced. "I can't sneak you past them. They're all in the living room, desperate to meet you."

"Oh." William thought of the garage again. "Is there a faucet out here? I could hose off real quick. I'd rather meet them soaked in water than in sweat."

"Are you sure?"

"Yeah!"

"Okay. We'll have to go around back."

Jason led him around the house and opened the gate of a privacy fence. Then he crept ahead, attention on the sliding glass door. He waved William forward after making sure they wouldn't be seen. As soon as he saw the garden hose, William went for it, eager to feel the cool water on his skin. He ditched his shirt, kicked away his shoes, and peeled off his socks. Funny how often he and Jason began their time together by taking off their clothes, albeit usually in a locker room and not a backyard. William held the hose above his head, letting the water course over his shoulders and soak through the nylon shorts he wore, knowing they would dry quickly in the heat. Jason stood not far away, watching with a mixture of amusement and interest, so William pressed his thumb against the hose's nozzle, forcing the water to spray and playfully using it first on one armpit and then the other.

Jason's eyes darted away. Then he froze.

"Oh my goodness!" declared a husky voice. "Apollo has descended, and here I am without my camera! This is exactly the sort of scene that can't be faked!"

William spun around to discover a small audience. He instantly recognized Tim, who wore a puzzled expression. Next to him stood a large man, dark hair thinning in some areas and graying in others. He was currently clapping his hands like a delighted child. Was this Ben? The jeweled rings and sharp clothing implied money. Maybe Tim was a kept man, which would explain the Bentley. That just left a shorter guy with brownish blonde hair. His build was slight, his brown eyes friendly as he stepped forward. Unlike the larger man, he kept his attention above shoulder level.

William tossed aside the hose and extended a hand. "Uh, hi! I was really sweaty and… Um."

"William!" the shorter man said, expression bright. "Nice to finally meet you. I'm—"

A squelching noise cut him off, caused by William's wet palm. "Sorry!"

"—Ben," the man finished, letting go to wipe the hand off on his jeans.

"Oh!" William said, looking to the remaining stranger. "Then who is—"

"Marcello Maltese!" Ben was bumped aside by the larger man's bulk. "What a delightful way to make a first impression! The next time I meet a boy's family, I shall do exactly the same."

William stared, the blood rushing to his cheeks as Marcello continued to look him over while pumping his hand up and down. "I'm so embarrassed," he managed.

"No need to be," Ben said, gently stopping the endless

handshake and prying away Marcello's fingers. "Why don't we all go inside and let William finish getting refreshed. Do you need a towel or anything?"

"I think I'm okay," he replied. "Thanks."

Ben pulled on Marcello's arm, and when this failed to budge him, gestured at Tim to help. The extra muscle did the job, and the trio returned inside.

"I don't suppose we can make a run for it?" William said as he put on his spare clothes. "That was beyond humiliating."

Jason snorted. "You compete wearing less than that. If anything, you were over-dressed. Come inside and meet everyone properly."

He preferred to remain outside to dry out, but he could hardly follow this weird debut with an impromptu sunbath. "Who's the older guy?" William asked, stuffing his sweaty clothes into a plastic bag and then his backpack.

"Marcello?" Jason asked. "I don't think I could explain him even if I spent the whole day trying. Just think of him as a creepy uncle. That's close enough."

As soon as they were inside, a small bulldog greeted them. He was more prepared for this, having visited Jason at the store where he worked and choosing a present for each of the pets that lived here. "I've got something for you!" William said, sitting on the floor. "It's a…" he hesitated. "A dong?"

"Oh my!" Marcello declared, fanning himself in one of the plush chairs.

"It's a Kong," Jason said with a chuckle.

"Right," William said, his face feeling like he'd gotten too much sun on the ride over. "Anyway, you fill it with treats, which I already did, and the dog has to get them out."

"Chinchilla loves those," Tim said enthusiastically. "She took the old one with her everywhere. We lost it during a walk. I kept meaning to buy another. Whoa, watch your fingers!"

Chinchilla harrumphed and forcefully took the Kong from him, shaking it around to dislodge some kibble.

"I also have this," he said, holding up a bag of catnip.

"I believe I have rolling papers in my car," Marcello said.

"I'm pretty sure that's for Samson and not you," Ben said, joining him on the floor. "Try shaking it and I'm sure he'll make an appearance."

William did just that. A gray cat with orange eyes appeared

from under the couch and came toward him eagerly. Samson slowed a little when he got close, but after smelling William's hand, focused entirely on the bag. "I actually don't know how this stuff works," he admitted. "We never had pets when I was growing up. My mom has an aversion to poop."

"I know of at least one relationship cut short for that exact reason," Marcello offered helpfully.

Ben ignored him with practiced patience. "Just sprinkle some right on the floor. He'll want to roll around in it." Once Samson was gleefully twisting in the catnip, Ben looked up and smiled. "How considerate of you to bring presents! Thank you!"

"I wanted to bring a bottle of wine for you guys too," William said. "My mom didn't like that idea, but she did send some cookies along."

"Dibs!" Tim said, snatching the Tupperware container when William pulled it out of his backpack.

Ben looked exasperated. "If you were worried about making a good first impression, don't be. I wish I could say my boys aren't usually this ill-behaved, but I'd be lying."

"He loves us," Tim said, mouth already half-full of oatmeal cookie.

"I wouldn't put up with them otherwise," Ben said, tickling Samson's tummy. "Jason says you live on the other side of the river. That must have been some bike ride!"

"It was." William still felt hot from the exertion. "I probably stink. Do you mind if I finish getting cleaned up?"

"Not at all!" Ben said. "There's a bathroom by the front door, or if you need more than a sink—"

"You can use mine," Jason said. "I'll show you."

He guided them to the other side of the living room, where a door led to an enclosed stairway. Once upstairs, Jason pointed out his bathroom, the first door on the right.

They stopped outside of it, like they were on a front porch, jittery as they tried to negotiate a goodnight kiss.

"—fresh towels under the sink," Jason was saying. "You can use my body wash if you want. Not that you need a shower. I think you smell fine. Ha! God, that sounds weird. You know what I mean, right?"

"No," William teased, glad to see he wasn't the only one feeling nervous. "I'll call if I need any help."

Jason perked up at this. "You do that!"

"So I'll meet you downstairs when I'm through?"

"Oh! Right. Yeah. See you soon."

Jason wavered a second longer, then walked toward the stairs. William shut himself in the bathroom, taking in the cluttered counters. He noticed a bottle of cologne, sniffed it and recognized Jason's scent, or at least the one he'd bought after Tim refused to share his. The neat-freak in him checked the shower next, happy to see it was clean. Then he made himself presentable. Hosing off outside preempted the need for a shower, but he put on fresh deodorant and switched the nylon shorts for a denim pair and some boxer briefs. The underwear was an expensive brand, a Christmas present from Kelly. William paused, thinking of the argument that had started the day. Kelly had pulled every trick to stop him from going on this picnic.

"I won't abandon any more friends for you," William had snapped at one point.

Kelly responded by insisting he hang out with Lily instead, but that's not what William wanted. Not today. He wanted to spend time with the guy downstairs. He hurried to finish, washing his face in the sink, and just before he left, sprayed on a puff of Jason's cologne. That made him feel naughty, a smile on his lips as he hustled down the stairs. The living room was empty. Nearly.

"The sun may disappear," Marcello said, "but it is always destined to shine again. One must simply wait."

"Hey," William said, not having a clue how to respond to something like that.

Marcello was still seated in the same plush chair. He raised a narrow glass, the liquid inside an orange color. "Care for a mimosa? Ben insists they are healthier, but I can't agree since I find myself drinking twice as much for the same result."

"Does it contain alcohol?" William asked.

Marcello smiled. "I never answer that question truthfully. Not when handsome young men are involved."

William took note of the nearest exits. Just in case. "Where are the others?"

"Preoccupied." Marcello gestured to the nearby couch. "Won't you keep me company until they return?"

William took a seat, trying to remember if Jason had

mentioned this person previously. That might help him figure out how to make conversation. As it turned out, Marcello was willing to do the work for him.

"I remember the first time I was introduced to the masking qualities of orange juice. Are you familiar with screwdrivers? I don't mean the tool. No? Well, when mixed correctly, the cocktail involves a fair amount of vodka. I wasn't as fond of drinking back then, being nearly as young as yourself. When I told my date I didn't care to drink, he offered a screwdriver as an alternative. Despite his ruse, I could still taste the vodka, but not enough to mind. Or complain. He was a very rich man with influential friends, and I found that enviable back then. The party my date had brought me to was in a mansion filled to the brim with beautiful people. Funny then, that I should find myself so taken by one young man. He wasn't handsome exactly. I don't remember his name, and my memory of his face fades with each passing year. What I *do* recall is how much I enjoyed his company. He was delightfully clever, making me clutch my sides in laughter. I snuck away as often as I could to spend time with him. I knew he found me attractive, but sadly, I was still burdened by the ideals of youth and wanted to remain loyal to my date. Even alcohol couldn't loosen my convictions."

William found himself leaning forward. "So what happened?"

"I'm not entirely sure. My head was spinning by this point, having had one too many. I might have kissed him. Perhaps I only wish I had. I do know that I went home with my date that night, and well, that's not a story worth telling. Unlike my mystery man, I *can* remember all the relevant details about him, but it seems terribly unfair because he meant nothing to me. I only think of him in context of this story. Why can't I remember the name of this other person or see his face when I close my eyes? Decade after decade, I've thought back to a man I can't truly remember. Isn't that silly? I blame myself. That night I took a road that led to a dead end, all because of a false sense of nobility. I can't help but wonder what would have happened had I listened to my heart instead. Would he and I still be together? Would I be any happier now? I've met so many people since then. Why does this one stay with me?"

"Have you ever tried to find him?"

Marcello shook his head, jowls matching the motion a split

second later. "No. What I know now, and failed to understand then, is how transient these things are. When opportunity presents itself, it never waits long for an answer. I failed to act that night, or the next day, or the next week. I wouldn't know where to begin to find him now, or if we'd even still find each other's company so pleasing. No, that road is closed to me. All I can do is learn from my mistake. Or perhaps you could learn from it instead. Consider it a cautionary tale. The next time your heart asks such a question, remember this old man filled with regret and—"

"Ready to go?" Jason walked into the room, a backpack in one hand.

"Just a sec." William looked back at Marcello. "Finish your story. Please."

"That story ended a long time ago," Marcello said easily. "It's the future that interests me more. Yours and mine. Let's meet again someday and compare notes. Shall we?"

William nodded, but only because he didn't want to be rude.

"You okay?" Jason asked on the way out the door.

"He's really strange," William whispered.

"You mean Marcello?" Jason laughed. "Yeah, but I like him."

"Ben's really nice. Should I say goodbye to him?"

"You're my date, not theirs," Jason joked. "I was about to serenade you and Marcello with some music. Things looked pretty cozy in there."

"We did almost kiss," William said to get a rise out of him. "Maybe we should invite him along?"

"We don't have enough bikes," Jason said, nodding to the person they saw outside.

Tim was rolling a bicycle toward them, a smudge of grease on one cheek. "Chain is oiled," he said. "Brakes are tight but could use some new pads, so stop early. If you mess with the gears, do so at your own peril. I can never figure them out."

"I'll make sure to bring it back with a full tank of gas," Jason said.

"Just be careful." Tim eyed the helmet William was strapping on. "We really need to buy a couple of those."

"They make your head look like a mushroom," Jason said.

"Better than it looking like a pizza," William countered. "You really don't have a helmet?"

"I could tie a pillow to my head," Jason offered.

"I'll get some rope," Tim said, heading toward the garage again.

"He's probably not kidding." Jason hopped on the bike. "Let's go!"

Together they puttered down the drive, their pace not increasing when they reached the main road. William usually tried to match speed with cars when he rode, but neither he nor Jason felt a sense of urgency. The traffic was minimal enough to let them remain side by side. They grinned at each other and indulged in banter, a perfect blue sky above them. The world felt as though it was theirs alone, especially when they reached their destination. St. Edwards Park was more like a nature preserve. No playground or baseball diamond awaited them. Just unpaved paths that wound through woods and fields. After consulting the map posted near the parking lot, they aimed for Bull Creek to the south, which widened considerably due to the small dam.

They dismounted as they neared this target. The canopy of leaves above filtered the sunlight and shielded them from heat. The water ahead helped cool the air too. They pushed their bikes along the creek until they reached the place where it was restrained by a small stone wall—water cascading over it—and agreed they were unlikely to find anywhere more scenic to have their picnic. After shaking out the blankets they had both brought along, they settled down and began arranging the food. While setting up everything, they looked at each other more often than they did the plastic containers. Jason seemed wistful.

"You okay?" William asked him.

"Yeah," Jason said. "Just a little hungry."

"Me too. Let's see what you've got."

Jason opened a container of potato salad. He had made it himself and was clearly nervous about the results. "It's heavy on the mayo," he said, sounding apologetic as he scooped portions onto two plates.

"Perfect." William grabbed a plastic fork and shoveled some into his mouth. It was good, but even if it had been over-salted or flavorless, he would have loved it anyway. "The great thing about exercising so much is all the calories that get burned. I get to eat like a pig. Speaking of which, my mom made cookies for you too."

William pushed the container toward him.

Jason opened it, eyes lighting up. "These look awesome!"

William's mother had been pretty emotional while baking. She had heard Jason's story, and knew he didn't have family of his own. Homemade cookies were no doubt a rarity for someone like him. "She made them especially for you."

"Really? She knows about me?"

"Mm-hm." William held back a smile as he consumed another bite. "She kept asking if this was a date."

Jason shook his head. "Doesn't she know about Kelly?"

"She knows all right! That's why she's hopeful that I'm moving on." She often told William that he was too young to settle down. "Kelly and my mom don't see eye to eye. They never have."

"Oh." Jason nibbled a cookie, chewing distractedly. Then he swallowed. "So… *is* this a date?"

I wish! The words almost escaped his lips, but they were knocked back by more bites of potato salad. He focused on eating, not trusting himself to speak. Being out here felt too good. The park was neutral, free of any memories he had made with Kelly. Best of all, they were alone. No prying eyes or interruptions. He hadn't realized how tempting that would be. Here they had a little too much potential.

Jason passed him a bottle of water, then opened his own, attention still on William even as he drank. "This is probably none of my business," he said, "but do you and Kelly get along?"

"No." William clenched his jaw, then took a swig of his water, wishing it were vodka instead. Or one of those screwdrivers Marcello had spoken of. "He probably feels otherwise, but then Kelly likes to argue."

Jason seemed hesitant. "The other night, when we all went out together… You told me that you love Kelly but for the wrong reasons."

God that seemed so long ago, but he remembered the conversation on his front lawn, word for word. "I said there's only one reason I'm with him."

"You don't love him?"

William didn't usually discuss Kelly with Jason. Doing so seemed disrespectful and would inevitably lead to the accident. Not only was it a difficult subject to broach, but if he told the whole truth, Jason would reject him. Then again, that would probably be for the best. Jason would lose interest, and William could focus on counting down the days until it was time to leave. He pulled his legs up to his chest. "I like that you like me. I really do, and I hope it's obvious that you're not alone in your feelings."

Jason breathed in sharply. "I wasn't sure—"

"You don't know me." William sighed. "I mean you do. This *is* the real me, but there are things you don't know, and if you did, I don't think you'd like me so much anymore."

"Try me."

William faced him. "You never ask about Kelly's leg. Why is that?"

Jason worked his jaw. "I figured it was the sort of thing everyone asks about. That must get old. Besides, I don't want to feel sorry for him."

"Why not?"

Jason shrugged. "I guess because I wouldn't want people to feel sorry for me."

William laughed humorlessly. "I don't think that's how Kelly feels at all."

"Sorry, I just—"

"No, it's a good thing. You both have pride, but I don't think Kelly has dignity. Not anymore." William scowled. "Maybe that's why he's still punishing me, because I stole that from him. It's my fault Kelly lost his leg."

Jason already seemed lost. "What do you mean?"

William took a deep breath, casting his mind back to a year ago, a grey morning that had changed his life forever. He raised his face to the sky, almost expecting to feel rain on his cheeks. Then he told Jason everything. How his relationship with Kelly had started out well, how it had slowly deteriorated, and how the greatest transgression had been committed by William himself. A simple twist of the wheel followed by blood, screams, and sorrow.

"You didn't mean to," Jason said.

"I told you I wanted to scare him," William snapped. "I could have calmly pulled over and told him he was walking to school. Instead I put him in the ICU. *That's* the kind of person I am. That's who you think you have feelings for, but I bet you're not so certain now."

Jason became very interested in his paper plate, head lowered as he picked at it. He would find an excuse to cut the picnic short. Or maybe he would change the topic and act like nothing had happened, just to get through the day. Their final day, because no way would he want to see William again. Jason looked up and met his stare, expression calm. "So what happened next?"

William was too taken aback to respond.

"I want to know everything," Jason pressed. "Tell it all to me. Then I'll decide how I feel."

Fair enough. He had heard the worst of it, but William told him anyway, talking about how difficult Kelly's recovery had been, and how bitterness had slowly set in, leaving William confused, because at times Kelly seemed to need him more than anyone else, and at other times—all too often, in fact—he felt like Kelly couldn't stand him. At the end of the story, Jason only had one question.

"Do you love him?"

William honestly didn't know. He was pretty sure he had in the very beginning. Kelly had helped him come out, had been there for William when his parents had gotten divorced. Everything had been so painful and confusing, but Kelly had remained solid and certain, always patient, which seemed unthinkable now. When he thought of that portion of their relationship, his heart swelled with love. When he considered the previous year, resentment crept in. William felt trapped, like the credits to a bad movie had rolled but he wasn't allowed to leave the theater. No, not a theater. He was stuck in a vehicle, just seconds before everything went wrong. "That argument in the car? I was breaking up with him. I didn't want to be with him anymore. If the accident hadn't happened, I wouldn't be."

"But you feel obligated," Jason said, searching his eyes. "That's why you're still with him."

William grimaced. "Please don't tell him that. I would hate for him to know. It would kill me to do him any more harm than I already have. So I won't leave him. Ever." That was the gist of it, and what Jason really needed to understand. Even though William was allowed to leave for the Coast Guard, he would still be there for Kelly in spirit, and eventually return to him in the flesh. He explained this promise to Jason, being honest enough to admit that he wished he hadn't made it. Too late, because William owed a debt that he couldn't possibly repay, but he had to try.

Jason listened carefully. Then he responded. "Do you really think me knowing all this is going to mess with how I feel about you?"

So much for scaring him away. William shouldn't be surprised. If the confession had been Jason's instead, if Caesar had lost his leg due to Jason maliciously jerking the wheel, William wouldn't have disowned him. Hell, Jason could probably confess to murder and it wouldn't matter. But they couldn't be together. Jason's feelings hadn't changed and neither had the situation. William shot to his feet in frustration. He walked toward the dam, heading for a tree with the intent to punch it. Instead, when he reached it, he leaned against the trunk and exhaled. He'd had enough of anger. What he needed was love. He wanted to give it and feel it in return.

William tensed when he heard footsteps approaching. "I want to be with you," he said, but he couldn't look at Jason during this confession. "You have no idea how bad I want to just… do the things we should be able to do. Even something small, like holding your hand. But now you know everything. You know it's impossible. Or would you really ask me to turn my back on Kelly and hurt him all over again?"

"Maybe we don't need to touch," Jason said. "Love is more than holding hands or kissing or sex. It's more than just the physical, right? If that's what this is, maybe we don't need those things."

William turned to face Jason, feeling a sudden burst of hope, but one look at those eager eyes and all he wanted was to kiss him. Lately he had made sure they never touched. Not since Jason had rested his head in William's lap. At this point, even a hug would feel like cheating. William could imagine it lasting an hour, their arms around each other as they basked in the closeness. That was the dream. In reality, an insurmountable void separated them. "What are we going to do?"

Jason tried a smile. "If I wasn't such an honest man these days, I'd suggest you stay in your loveless relationship with Kelly while secretly going elsewhere for what you really need."

"An affair?" William nearly laughed. "No. You're too good to be the other woman. I won't do that to you."

"My feelings don't hinge on you being so noble."

William shook his head. "There's got to be a better way."

Jason considered him, those blue eyes burrowing into his soul. Then he changed tactics. "A picnic is a failure if any food is left over," he said. "Did you know that?"

"No," William said, "but I'm relieved, because I'm still starving."

They agreed to let the subject drop. If either of them had a solution, they wouldn't be bothering with food right now. Still, it could provide a different sort of comfort. William allowed himself to pig out more than usual. He soon regretted this decision. He felt weighted down and groggy but knew an easy solution.

"Ready to hop back on our bikes?" he asked.

Jason stared. "I can't believe you're not in a coma. Even Tim doesn't eat that much."

"A coma is what I'm trying to prevent. Let's go."

They didn't speak of the past for the rest of their time in the park. Instead they reacted like two children exploring the world for the first time. They stopped to watch butterflies fluttering above a patch of wildflowers, or left their bikes behind to chase each other through a dense nest of trees, ducking branches and slipping on muddy earth, all while laughing. When they grew tired of exercise, they found a field flooded with sunlight, made a bed of their picnic blankets, and stretched out next to each other, feeling as content as they could without touching. William even dozed off briefly, returning to a dream that so often haunted him. Once again he was behind the wheel, but there was no sign of the rainy weather. When he turned his head, he didn't find Kelly sitting in the passenger seat. Just a guy with a mischievous expression, trying to feed him potato salad, heavy on the mayo. When he woke, he felt the prickle of too much sun on his face.

"We should probably head back," William said. "I'm going to burn if we stay out any longer."

Jason groaned. "Next paycheck, I'm going to buy you one of those big floppy sun hats. That way we can stay out here forever."

"I should have brought my cowboy hat from Juicy James."

They got on their bikes, looking around at their surroundings longingly before they rode away, as if they would both miss this place. They weren't as talkative on the return trip. When they arrived back at the house, Jason took his bike to the garage. William walked his, along with Jason, to the front door.

"I should go," he said. "I'm sure Kelly is getting more nervous by the hour."

Jason's eyes widened. "He knows we're together?"

"Of course. Nothing like an early morning argument to start the day."

"Sorry."

"Nah," William said. "It was worth it."

"Hey! Before you go, there's something I wanted to show you." Jason tilted his head toward the house. "Come up to my room real quick."

William raised an eyebrow, imaging exactly what Jason might want to show him. "Yeah, okay."

Being in Jason's room felt too personal, and he was sure Kelly wouldn't approve, but he didn't care. He took note of the cluttered dresser top and the dirty clothes that Jason tried to kick under the bed. Then Jason shrugged apologetically and grabbed a guitar from a stand in the corner and sat on the mattress. Not knowing what else to do, William sat next to him. He remembered Jason mentioning that he played, but a lot of people made that claim. Spencer could "play" the clarinet, which really just meant he owned one and knew how to force notes out of it.

Jason plucked at his guitar, twisting the tuners. Then he shot William a sheepish grin and started strumming. More than that, he started singing! He wasn't bad, either. William couldn't focus on the words at first, too fascinated by the way Jason's fingers moved and the creases of concentration on his face. Then he caught a line about there being fifty ways to leave a lover and started laughing. Jason grinned back before continuing his song. He looked so cool, sitting there on his messily made bed, fingers summoning up music like a conjurer. Nobody in William's family had musical talent, not even Spencer, despite how hard he tried. Jason made it look easy. He made other things seem easy too, like the idea that they could still have what they wanted without Kelly ever finding out.

"Very interesting song," William said when Jason was finished.

"Yeah, it's fun." Jason stretched forward to set the guitar back on the stand. Then he leaned back, resting on his elbows.

William wanted to tell him how handsome he looked, how kissable his lips were, but settled on something harmless. "You're really good."

"Thanks. Honestly, that's not the best song for me, but—"

"I thought it was awesome," William interrupted. "And it gives me something to think about on the long ride home."

"Yeah." Jason eyed him, expression serious.

"I should go," William said. Should. Instead he reached over, placing his hand on top of Jason's, as if by accident. He didn't try to hold it, but just touching him, even briefly, sent electric currents though William's body. Jason sat upright, as if wanting them to kiss, so William squeezed his hand and stood before anything else could happen. Jason stared up at him with transparent longing.

"Fifty ways, huh?" William asked.

"At least," Jason said, breaking into a smile. "I can make you a list if you want."

If only it were that easy! He'd love to choose from a menu of convenient excuses and gentle letdowns, but in essence, William knew the truth. There was only one way to leave your lover, and that was by doing so.

No Heaven without Hell, no high without a low. This theme continued in William's life. The picnic with Jason? Awesome. Kelly's reaction? An absolute nightmare. William's biggest mistake was spraying on Jason's cologne. Even after the sweaty bike ride home, Kelly had still smelled it on him, and that had triggered everything that followed. Swimming in privacy together at the YMCA was out. Kelly was there each morning, scowling and grinding his teeth at Jason. He didn't even pretend to participate—the only person in the pool area who was fully dressed. William was so frustrated with this that he skipped a morning, preferring to miss out rather than witness Kelly's anger or Jason's discomfort.

His work was no longer safe either. Kelly started showing up more often at the mall, once with his entire family in tow. Serving them had been a real treat. Jason visited him there too. Not at the same time, thankfully, but William warned him away. They no longer had access to a safe haven. What would they do even if they did? Feeling frustrated one night and not wanting to return to either of his homes, William biked across town, ending up in front of an apartment door.

"Hey!" his father said, looking genuinely happy to see him. "What a nice surprise! Come on in."

William strained his neck to see into the apartment. "Where's Gina?"

"She's working." Lewis grabbed his shoulder and pulled. "Now stop being an idiot and get in here."

His father hugged him, gesturing to the living room before ducking into the kitchen. William sat on the sofa, looking around the room and not recognizing much of anything. His father had never cared how the house was decorated, and that hadn't changed. Everything here represented Gina.

"You're not driving, are you?"

William looked up and saw a frosty bottle of beer angled toward him. He didn't normally drink, but tonight he felt like he needed a keg. "Thanks," he said, accepting the bottle. His father plopped down on the couch next to him. After clinking bottles, William took a swig, wincing at the taste.

"It gets better after the first sip," Lewis assured him. "What's going on? You don't look so good."

"Girl troubles," William said. "Or at least the gay equivalent of them."

He expected his father to change the subject, and while he did look a little uncomfortable, he at least tried. "Tell me what's going on. Maybe I can help."

William forced down more of the beer. "No thanks. I can guess what your advice would be."

His father drummed his fingers along the bottle he held, digesting these words. "There's someone else you like. Someone besides Kelly."

William raised his head. "I'm surprised you know his name."

"Your life is important to me," Lewis replied. "I'd like to be a bigger part of it."

Then you shouldn't have abandoned Mom. That was the sort of response he usually gave, but he was no longer in a position to judge.

"Talk to me," Lewis pressed.

William took another swig and nodded. "Things aren't so

good between Kelly and me. They haven't been for a long time. And yeah, I met this new guy, and he's really sweet. He makes me feel good about myself."

"And Kelly doesn't." Lewis nodded in understanding. "All he seems to do is criticize, and no matter what you do, you feel like you can't make him happy. And that makes you unhappy, but then you meet this person, and suddenly you feel cool again, like you're a real catch and not some unholy burden."

William stared as the truth of his father's words sank in. "Is that how you felt with Mom?"

Lewis leaned back and sighed. "Those last few years weren't good. We both were to blame. I'm sure I wasn't fun to be around either. And yeah, when I met Gina, suddenly there was this beautiful woman who I could make laugh instead of glare. Maybe I'll wear out my welcome with her too. I hope not, because I love her. I know people see us together, and with her being so young, they probably think I'm some old pervert. Or her dad. Even if she was my age, I'd still be just as into her because I can make her happy, and she makes me happy." His father took a swig of beer, looking a little embarrassed by his confession. "So this other guy, do you love him?"

"It doesn't matter." William scowled at his bottle. "I can't do what you did."

"You could leave Kelly."

William shook his head. "I made a promise. And you should have left Mom. If that's what had to happen, then fine, but sneaking around behind her back was low."

"I made a promise too," Lewis said. "A vow before God, and I had more than just your mother to think of. We had a family together. A house. Our entire lives were intertwined, and while I could imagine saying goodbye to most of it, you kids were the sticking point. I didn't want to lose you. I never wanted any of you boys to be hurt by a divorce. But at the same time, I was miserable, and I'm sure you probably don't want to hear it, but I had my needs too, and they weren't just physical. So yes, sneaking around on your mother was wrong, but I thought it would be easier to end things if I waited until you boys were out of the house and on your own." His father sighed. "Even then I pictured your mother by herself, husband and sons having flown the coop, and I kept asking myself if that would be any better for her. That's why I tried to do both—be the husband and father I had promised while still…" Lewis shook his head.

They nursed their bottles, William taken aback by how similar their situations were. "Do you regret what you did?"

Lewis jutted out his chin. "No. I wish I hadn't got caught. I still love your mother. I miss her as a friend. I miss the house, spending time with you, and sharing holidays together. I also love Gina and wouldn't want to miss out on what we have. Greedy as it sounds, I wanted to have my relationship with her while everything went on as normal at home. That way nobody would have gotten hurt."

"But that's wrong," William said.

"Maybe, but you need to understand that it wasn't my first choice. Your mother and I tried working it out. We talked. We argued. When I brought up the idea of separating, she broke down into tears. She didn't want me to go. Part of me didn't want to either. Maybe I should have let things remain the way they were and stayed unhappy. I guess I'm just selfish."

"I know how hard it can be," William said. "Especially when you've been unhappy for a long time."

His father nodded. "I thought I had found a solution where nobody would get hurt. That's how it was supposed to be, anyway."

William shifted uncomfortably, wanting to change the subject. "I got my acceptance letter."

"For the Coast Guard? Wow! This calls for another round!"

William wasn't done with the first, but celebrating instead of agonizing over his love life felt good. Lewis grabbed more beers from the refrigerator and conversation remained light, his father telling funny stories about his own enlistment and the trouble he had gotten into. They hadn't talked like this since the divorce. Maybe even before. As upsetting as William still found the situation, at least they were being honest with each other. Strange to think of his father having the same urges and emotions. William wasn't sure it justified his actions, but it made them understandable. He could see things from his mother's side too; being hounded by suspicion and the misery of discovering she had been right. Like his own situation, he couldn't see a happy resolution unless, by some miracle, his father and mother started getting along again. That seemed as likely as him and Kelly patching things up.

"I hope it all works out for you," his father said when walking him to the door. "With Kelly, I mean. And who's the other guy?"

"Jason," William said, the name alone making him grin. It didn't hurt that he was also tipsy.

"You're leaving though, right? You ship out when?"

"Not too long after graduation. My recruitment officer managed to get me on the early enrollment list because my first application slipped through the cracks."

Lewis appeared stunned. "That's soon!"

William nodded. "I know."

"Then I don't understand why you wouldn't leave Kelly now. You'll do so anyway in a couple months, and at least then you could have your time with Jason before you go."

"Kelly wants a long distance relationship."

"Ah. Tough break. Are you sure you don't want a ride home? Gina will be back soon. Or I could call a taxi."

"I'll be fine," William said. "I'll walk with my bike and let my head clear, maybe think through some stuff."

Lewis hugged him. "I have faith in you. You'll make the right decision."

William appreciated his confidence. He just didn't share it.

Chapter Fifteen

I thought I had found a solution where nobody would get hurt.
These words haunted William over the next few days because he had too. Was it moral? No. But unlike his father, he wouldn't need to maintain a lie for entire months. A handful of weeks shouldn't be too difficult. He could be with Jason, and at the same time, try to give Kelly whatever he needed. When William left for the Coast Guard, the rest would sort itself out. Kelly would be forced to move on in his absence as they slowly grew apart, and Jason—maybe he could relocate to Connecticut. Be closer to where William was stationed so they could still see each other.

He was sitting on the bedroom carpet, pulling on his shoes, when the sheets behind him rustled.

"Going swimming today?" Kelly asked. "Give me a minute. I'll take a quick shower."

"Go back to sleep," William said.

"Where are you going?"

"For a bike ride."

"Training for this year's triathlon?"

That sounded like a joke. He looked over his shoulder to see Kelly snug in bed, a twinkle in his eye. Handsome as ever and probably amorous, but he knew if he stuck around, a foul mood would appear. "I won't be long. It's Sunday. Go back to sleep."

Kelly yawned, nuzzling his head against the pillow. Then he closed his eyes. William thought back to the first time he had seen Kelly sleeping. He had woken up in the middle of the night, confused about where he was because Kelly had taken him in, listened to him agonize over his parents' divorce, then done his best to make William's first time special. Despite how messed up everything was, that night had been perfect, and when he lay next to Kelly and watched him sleep, he swore they would be together forever.

"Hurry back," Kelly murmured. "I miss you already."

"I miss you too," William said, the truth of the words making his throat ache. What they once had together had been real. Even if it hadn't lasted. He missed the guy he had fallen in love with. William rose, quietly made his exit, and padded through a silent house. Taking a deep breath once he was outside, he went around to the side where he kept his bike. The garage door made too much noise, so he had planned ahead, knowing what he wanted from this morning.

Doubt took a swing at him regardless. As William pedaled his way toward Jason's house, the same cyclical debates went round and round his mind. He should leave Kelly, but he couldn't, but he would anyway, just not like that, but no matter what he couldn't have Jason. Oh yeah? Well fuck you everything ever! He was sick of being miserable! Like a fox stuck in a bear trap, he'd rather gnaw off his own leg than remain captive any longer. He needed this. *Needed*. Not just wanted or desired. William pushed himself, dodging traffic, hunching closer to his bike when the first hill appeared. Nothing would stop him.

And yet, when he reached the entrance to the long drive, he did stop. What he planned to do couldn't be undone. He wouldn't be able to take it back. Going through with this would change everything, even if Kelly never found out, because William was compromising his integrity. He would be one of *those* people. Like his father. He had spent so long shaking his head in judgment, and yet here he was, about to commit the same transgression. He should leave, return home, and focus on Kelly until it was time to go. That would be the decent thing.

"What are you doing here?"

William turned at the sound of that voice, saw the unadulterated joy in Jason's eyes, and all doubt evaporated. He swung a leg over his bike, letting it clatter to the ground. William placed a hand on each of Jason's shoulders, squeezing because it felt so damn good to touch him, to have this tiny moment for them alone. "I told him I wanted to bike today instead of swim. I don't have long."

Jason scrunched up his nose, not understanding. "Then why are you down here instead of at the house?"

"I was trying to decide if I was going to do it or not."

Jason's lips twitched happily. "Do what?"

"This."

Then they were kissing, but not an innocent peck, nor was it the only part of them that touched. Jason's hands moved up his back, clutched at his hair. William responded by wrapping his arms around him like a python, not ever wanting to let go, because the situation might be fucked up, but this… this was *right*. He pulled back to look, cupping Jason's head in his hands.

He was so damn cute! William was torn between wanting to stare at him and kiss him again. He settled for a quick smooch, but Jason leaned forward as he tried to back away, demanding more. William was all too glad to comply. Eventually he felt lightheaded from lack of oxygen.

"Okay!" William said, placing a hand on Jason's chest to hold him back. "Holy shit… That felt even better than in my fantasies."

"You've been fantasizing about me?"

"You have no idea!"

Jason's expression became conflicted. "Did something happen?"

"Nothing has changed," William said. "Sorry. I guess I should have told you first, but I think maybe you're right. Until we figure out something better, we just… uh…"

Jason grinned. "Have a sultry affair."

William grimaced. "I hate how that sounds."

"A sweet affair then," Jason said, making doe eyes at him. "I'm okay with that. I hated the last few days—not being able to be alone with you."

"It's only going to get tougher to see each other." William looked down the street, almost expecting to discover Kelly there. "Like I said, I can't stay right now."

"Come back later," Jason offered. "Or I'll sneak over to your place. You guys don't spend every night together, do you?"

William frowned.

Jason was aghast. "You do? Even on school nights?"

"I never thought I'd say this, but unfortunately, I have very liberal parents. He does too. I took care of him when he was recovering, and that meant us staying together, even at night. Somehow that became the norm."

"Lucky bastard," Jason said, shaking his head. "What are we going to do?"

William smiled at him. "You're a clever boy. I'm sure you'll figure something out."

"Your mom's house. Make an excuse to go over there, and I'll meet you."

William chewed his lip and thought about it. "She gets off work before school is out. I don't mind introducing you to her, but she's always so glad to see me these days. Like I said, I'm not home much. It'll be weird if I show up and insist on privacy."

"But we dropped you off there after Bonnie's recital. You must spend the night there sometimes."

"Not since Kelly has been on the warpath."

"Skip school."

"I share most classes with him. He'll notice."

Jason growled. "Then call me when he goes to sleep, and I'll break into his damn house!"

"He's a light sleeper."

"You aren't making this easy!"

They shared the same frustration, that much was clear. "You'll figure it out, and when you do, I'll make it worth your while."

Jason grabbed his hand and tugged on it. "Come inside. Tim is home, but he's cool. He won't care."

"Your boyfriend is home?" William said, pretending to be scandalized.

"Ha ha. I'm serious. Let's go."

William laughed. "I can't stay!"

"Five minutes! I swear that's all it will take."

"I want way more than that. Come here."

Jason complied, pressing against him and making the most of the kiss. Once they parted ways, William waited for doubt to return, for the same debates to march across the battlefield of his mind. As he biked toward the city, the certainty never faded. What he was doing might be wrong, but somehow, it was also right.

Very little separated clever from crazy. William was starting to think Jason leaned in one direction more than the other. He had come up with a plan, which is why William was currently making the rounds in a crowded ballroom, wearing nothing from the waist up but a bow tie. The palatial home belonged to Marcello, who apparently liked to host fundraisers so much that his house included a ballroom. What shirtless waiters had to do with donating to charity had baffled him, but not once he was officially on duty. Then he understood. Most of the guests were older, successful, and gay. They certainly didn't mind letting their eyes wander. All for a good cause, William kept telling himself, but he wasn't really thinking of charity. The real goal was to earn time alone. With Jason.

"This is nuts." Jason paused next to him, equally

underdressed and overwhelmed. He balanced an empty tray in one hand. "You doing okay?"

"Yeah," William said, looking him over hungrily. Better than okay! The past week had been great. That first kiss had carried him to the next day and each that followed. They were forced to hide in Jason's car during work breaks, and William had once snuck over to the pet store where they made out to an audience of exotic birds. He had nearly suggested they make use of one of the restroom stalls at the mall, but then Jason revealed his plan.

William hopped from foot to foot, nearly dropping his tray. "How much longer?"

"Until the shut-in?" Jason got the attention of one of the guests, asking him the time. "Ten more minutes. Better make an appearance."

William nodded. "Right."

The shut-in. Soon the festivities would grind to a halt, and he, Jason, and the other waiters would be sent away and the ballroom locked. Everyone remaining would watch films about the charities they were asked to support. Donations would be collected, and at the end of the hour, the doors would open again, food and drink pouring back in to reward everyone. The idea was fun, but what really mattered were those locked doors. A fire marshal was on hand to make sure everything met safety standards. The whole affair was pretty official, which hopefully meant it didn't look like a ruse.

William returned to where he'd left Kelly, who could have given any of these waiters a run for their money. Except maybe Tim. Finding him in the crowd wasn't difficult. William only had to look for where the largest number of guests were gathered around someone. Tim was playing waiter too, and was apparently experienced in doing so. Seeing his bare torso on display, a blue metallic bow tie shining against dark Latino skin, only increased William's appetite. As hot as Tim was, Kelly managed to turn heads while fully dressed. Anyone would think William was crazy for breaking up with a guy like that. Then again, this wasn't about who was hottest, but who he felt the most for. Jason, despite all his imperfections, drove William wild. Even just looking at him was enough to cause a reaction. And to think, in mere minutes they would… He forced the image from his mind and approached Kelly. He was sitting alone at a table, just as tense as he'd been when William first mentioned the fundraiser, predictably insisting on tagging along.

Trying his best to cheer him up, William sauntered over and bent to offer Kelly an *hors d'oeuvre*, making upbeat conversation. None of this was forced. William had been in a great mood all week. That had everything to do with Jason, but Kelly was benefitting too. William felt reenergized, able to handle bad moods, slights from Mrs. Phillips, and lack of privacy or personal time. So much was easy now, thanks to a single star that burned brightly for him alone.

"Your attention please!"

Marcello had taken the stage, dressed in a white tuxedo and looking every bit the ringmaster. "As you all know, the intent of this little soirée tonight is to benefit those who are unable to leave their homes, be it due to illness or other unfortunate circumstances. In order to understand how that feels, let's bravely go an hour without food, drink, or charming company. I'm going to ask all my waiting staff to kindly leave the room. As they go, please place any remaining beverages on their trays."

The time had finally come. William went rigid, taking the tray from the table. "Sorry. You'll have to finish these later."

He could feel Kelly watching him, and braced himself for an argument or protests as he adjusted his balance, scarcely believing his luck when silence reigned. "See you soon."

He hurried for the door, wanting to search the crowd for Jason but not allowing himself. Once safely in the kitchen, he found Jason looking repulsed. William followed his gaze and saw a waiter draining half-empty champagne glasses by chugging the contents down.

William snuck over to him and whispered, "That's one way of doing the dishes."

Jason turned in surprise, expression affectionate. Then he seemed to remember something and pulled out a piece of paper.

"Where are we going?" William asked, leaning over his shoulder to look. His chest touched the bare skin of Jason's back. They definitely needed some privacy or the other waiters were going to get one hell of a show!

Jason consulted the paper, a crude drawing of a floor plan on it. A giant black X marked one area, a description beneath, which he read out loud. "To a 'love nest.'"

"Let's hurry," William said, grabbing his arm. "I want the entire hour alone with you."

The house was a virtual maze. Jason stopped repeatedly to check the map. William was about to suggest they choose any of the rooms and lock the door when Jason turned the paper forty-five degrees and seemed to understand it better. Then he rushed forward, leading them through a spacious bathroom to another door.

"The love nest," Jason announced, pausing to stare. William did the same. The décor was dark, from the walls to the floor, but the gloom was chased away by candles covering every surface. On a nearby dresser sat a bottle in ice.

"Think the champagne is for us?" he asked.

Jason didn't seem to hear him. He was too busy shutting the bathroom door, sealing away artificial light. After locking it, he turned around, pressing his back against it while wide-eyed.

"An hour," William said, understanding. "All for us."

Jason continued to stare. "What do you want to do?"

He nearly laughed. Was he seriously nervous? The guy who wouldn't take no for an answer? William reached for him and squeezed. Jason hugged back, some of the tension leaving his body as they breathed together in silence. He didn't want to rush. He wanted to spend the entire night here. They would open the bottle, get a little tipsy while talking, and then they'd let their bodies take over. Afterwards they would hold each other, talking again until morning. That's what Jason deserved. Not this ridiculous deception.

"I'm sorry," William said, taking a step back. "We shouldn't have to resort to this. You're too good to have to sneak around. You deserve better."

Jason squared his jaw. "You deserve better than Kelly."

"I ruined his life," William said. "I took his leg and ruined his dream. He's the one who deserves better. I know I'm not the right guy for him, but until that person comes along, he's not going to be lonely. At least not until I join the Coast Guard, but I have to. It's the only way I can make up for it."

"For what?" Jason asked, not hiding his frustration.

"I ruined one life, but maybe if I save another, it'll kind of equal out. You know?"

Jason swallowed. "I wish you wouldn't be so hard on yourself.

And you're right that Kelly deserves to find someone who loves him, but if you're going to be out of his life eventually… Why not now?"

Could he explain it well enough to make him understand? "My parents are divorced. I hardly see my dad anymore, but I'll never forget what he put my mom through by leaving. I don't want to be that guy, so I'm hoping Kelly will leave me. I keep pushing for us to go to the youth group, hoping he'll meet someone. That way I won't have to break my promise." A promise to stay with him, not to be faithful. He could spin it a million different ways, but the bottom line was that William was finished with talking.

He unclipped his bow tie and set it on the dresser. Jason remained motionless so William helped him remove his bow tie too, stepping into his personal space to do so. Jason's eyes were searching his. He still seemed worried, so William smiled reassuringly and got to his knees. He worked Jason's shoes loose, then sat to take off his own. He casually let his eyes dart to the crotch directly in front of him, checking to see if the bulge there was getting bigger. William swore that if he didn't get out of his own pants, his cock would rip a hole right through the front.

He stood, placing a hand on his belt. "At the same time?"

"Sure," Jason said, eyes even wider now.

William took his time, tugging the leather strap from the metal buckle and yanking on it playfully before letting it slip loose. Jason was scrambling to get his open, so William decided to pick up the pace. After unbuttoning and unzipping, he pulled it all down, his cock flexing in the open air. Jason did the same. Beneath the tangle of brown pubic hair, his cock and balls were both hanging loose.

"You're not hard," William said. "Are you sure you're really gay?"

"Shut up," Jason said, face turning red. "I'm a little nervous."

William kicked off his pants. "We've spent weeks around each other in nothing but swimwear, and you're nervous about the last skimpy piece of clothing being gone?"

"I wish we had more time," Jason mumbled. "I want to spend the entire night with you, but the clock is ticking, and there's so much pressure."

"There isn't any pressure," William said, offering his hand.

Jason accepted it. William walked with him to the bed, then crawled in first because the frame was huge. They practically needed a ladder. They didn't need the blankets though, since the room was toasty warm. William stretched out on his back, then pulled Jason on top of him.

"Lay on me," William said. "All of your weight."

Jason complied, their legs brushing, chests and stomachs pressing together. Wrapped in each other's arms, they kissed and murmured gentle words. William felt comfortable. The first few times with Kelly had been good, but he'd been so self-aware and overwhelmed by everything he had wanted to do. With Jason, he felt like they had skipped past those early fumblings and had done this a thousand times already. The smell of Jason's skin as William's nose nuzzled against his neck, the curls of brown hair around his ears, even the reassuring beat of his heart—all this felt familiar despite it being their first time. Judging from what was pressed against his hip, Jason was feeling more comfortable too.

"Not so nervous now," William joked. Then he flexed his muscles and rolled so Jason was on his back. William slid off him, moving a hand over that chest, enjoying being able to touch what he had stared at so many mornings in the pool. Jason's body was so different from his own, the ribs more pronounced, the muscles still untrained, but the contrast drove him wild. William and Kelly were different too, but they were both athletes. Jason felt rawer, less trimmed and shaved. William wanted to tickle the dark armpit hair, trace his tongue down the treasure trail running from his belly button down to—

He shifted his attention, seeing Jason's cock hard for the first time. He wasn't disappointed. William was bigger, but that didn't matter to him. He liked the way it curved upward, a drop of precome calling to him like dew for a hummingbird. He scooted down, darting his tongue into the slit, listening to Jason hiss with surprise and moan as William went down on him. Then Jason started laughing.

"Hey!" William complained after freeing his mouth. "This is serious stuff!"

"Totally," Jason said before cracking up again.

William hopped to his knees. "I see there's only one way to shut you up."

"Oh yeah?" Jason pushed himself up on his elbows, the grin

sliding off his face when William straddled his chest. He stared with rapt attention as William brought his cock near, waving it tantalizingly back and forth. Jason seemed mesmerized, looking up with shining eyes.

"That's got to be the most beautiful dick I've ever seen," he said.

William smirked, then his eyes rolled back when Jason took him in his mouth. He felt like he could come right then and there, but he managed some control as he started thrusting, changing the speed and angle to make sure he wasn't pushed over the edge. Jason's blue eyes were trained upward, watering when William went too deep, but he couldn't help himself. It felt too good. He arched his back, groping behind himself to find Jason's dick and pumping it to the same rhythm. Just when William was about to shoot, he pulled out and stooped so they could kiss, swatting away Jason's hand to make sure this wouldn't end too soon. William wanted to go down on him again, but Jason grabbed his arm when he tried to pull away.

"Keep kissing me," he said.

"But how—" William noticed a bottle of lube and had an idea. He grabbed it and squirted some on Jason's dick, sliding his hand up and down a few times before shifting downward so their hips were lined up and their cocks pressed together. William stroked them, Jason placing a hand over his to help. As William started moving his hips, adding extra motion, he remembered Jason's request and started kissing him again. He never wanted this to end. The sex was great and all, but it was the freedom he reveled in—that he was finally able to be with Jason. They still had so much to learn about each other, and after tonight, they would return to fighting for any scrap of privacy they could get, but William would never give up because this was the real deal. He was in love.

William pulled back, tempted to speak this revelation aloud.

"You okay?" Jason asked.

"Yeah," William said, the physical reasserting itself. He was on the verge. "Great. Are you close?"

"I was getting there," Jason said.

"Sorry," William started pumping again, loosening his grip to buy himself time. He placed his forehead against Jason's. Their eyes locked, short breaths puffing against each other. Jason gave him that doe-eyed expression again and bit his bottom lip, looking too adorable. William couldn't hold back anymore. He felt like he'd go crazy from the effort, so he stopped holding back, kissing Jason while he came, his mind humming with pleasure. He kept his arm pumping, Jason growling a second later, shooting all over his stomach.

Drained of strength, William collapsed onto to him, his breathing ragged. Worried he was crushing Jason, he rolled off to one side. Once he had caught his breath, he propped himself up on an elbow. He let a fingertip wander aimlessly over Jason's body, ending up at his bellybutton, which was full with the mess they had made.

"Like a little hot tub," William said.

"Ew," Jason replied. "How can sex be so appealing one second and so totally gross the next?"

"It's not gross," William said, laughing happily. "We better get cleaned up. It'll be obvious if we return to the party all sweaty."

"I guess so." Jason sighed, his expression still longing. "How much time do we have?"

William groped around on the dresser where he remembered seeing a small clock. "We've got about twenty minutes," he reported. "Plenty of time. Come on."

He went to the shower first, getting it to the right temperature. As soon as he stepped in, Jason was behind him, grabbing for the body soap.

"Let me wash you," he said.

"Be my guest." William turned around and raised his arms, laughing as Jason sudsed him up.

"Why do you shave everything?"

"Swimmer," William reminded him.

"Yeah, but everything?" Jason moved his hand downward. "Does being smooth down here really make you faster?"

"It makes it easier getting a tight suit on, and it's more hygienic for the pool. I want my skin slick like a seal so I can glide through the water. You don't seem to mind. When is that thing going to go down? First you couldn't get it up—"

"Hey!" Jason scowled. "I don't have any trouble with that!"

"You will if you walk into the ballroom with a perma-boner!"

"It's bound to increase donations," Jason said. "Wanna wash it for me?"

"Gladly." William squirted soap on him, rubbing his body with one hand, pumping with the other. If they had more time, he was certain they could manage another round. Checking the clock after leaving the shower helped them regain their focus. They hurried to dress, looking each other over for any telltale signs, Jason patting his hair dry like mad. They paused in the doorway before leaving the room, both of them somber.

"I hope Marcello doesn't take a black light to that comforter," William said.

Jason shrugged. "Probably the first thing he'll do. You ready?"

William nodded. They walked down the hall together, Jason remembering the way. He almost wished they would get lost and be forced wander the halls together for the rest of their lives. After so much build-up and anticipation, the night should have been nowhere near his expectations. Instead it had exceeded them. William's insides still sizzled with raw emotion.

Jason took his hand as they neared the kitchen. "Do you regret it?"

William shook his head. "I just forgot what sex feels like when it's with someone you love." He saw the waiters heading for the doors and shook his hand free, using it to gently guide Jason forward. "Come on. We're running late."

The breath felt short in his lungs, his heart against the idea of going back to the way things were. The situation had seemed so impossible just earlier today, but now that he understood how he really felt… "This is the last time."

Jason spun around to face him, misunderstanding. "Why?"

"Because you deserve better," William said. "The next time we're together, we won't be sneaking around. I'll figure something out. Okay?"

Jason nodded, looking misty-eyed, but they didn't have time for that now. William grabbed a tray of sandwiches and entered the ballroom, heading to where he'd last seen Kelly. If he got away with tonight, he would end their relationship. That he promised himself. Hurt feelings were inevitable, but the damage would be worse if he and Jason were caught in the act. Hormones and emotions had driven William off the path temporarily, but only because he hadn't allowed himself to be honest. He prayed for a chance to correct that on his own terms.

Kelly's table was empty, making William's stomach sink. He knew. Of course he did! Kelly was smart. Even if he didn't realize they would be allowed free access to Marcello's private rooms, surely he would imagine William and Jason in one corner of the kitchen. Unchaperoned. A hand reached for a sandwich, but William didn't stop long enough for the guest to take it. He kept walking, ending up at the very back of the ballroom. Then he turned and saw a familiar outline.

"There you are!" William said, walking around the table to face Kelly. He seemed relaxed, swirling a glass in one hand. Was he drunk? "Is that wine?"

"Sure looks like it," Kelly replied, words a little sloppy.

"You're going to get in trouble!"

Kelly smirked, and in a deep voice he croaked, "So be it."

William studied him with concern. "I'll get you some water. Or maybe a Coke and something to eat." He turned and hurried back to the kitchen but was stopped short of his destination, a large stomach blocking his path.

"Ah!" Marcello purred. "There you are. How did everything go?"

"Great," William said with flushed cheeks. "Thank you."

Marcello looked expectant. "I was hoping you'd be more descriptive. Love is poetry. So are adjectives and verbs. Pantomime is fine too. Whatever you need to get the picture across. Oh! Should I grab a pencil and paper?"

William stared. "I can't tell if you're serious or not."

"I'm rarely certain myself."

"Sorry, but can we do this later? I need to get to the kitchen and help my friend sober up. When did you start serving wine?"

"We haven't yet."

"But my friend— Sorry, my boyfriend…"

"Kelly," Marcello said patiently.

"Right! He's definitely drinking wine." William turned to look at the table. It was empty. The entire back of the room had cleared. People were moving to the front where live music had started. He looked back at Marcello. "Where did he go?"

"Perhaps he never existed," Marcello said, patting him on the shoulder. "In which case, you shouldn't bother sneaking around anymore. Imaginary boyfriends are rarely the jealous type."

William spun around, nearly losing the tray of sandwiches. Then he stumbled forward, searching the room. He didn't have any luck. He resumed his duties, just in case Kelly was watching him from afar. William should at least appear natural, when in truth he was freaking out. He kept looking as he walked the ballroom, eventually spotting Tim and approached him.

"Have you seen Kelly?"

Tim shook his head, preoccupied with organizing the checks he had collected.

"I can't find him."

Tim shrugged. "He couldn't have gone far." Then his head shot up. "That's not a joke about his disability. I'm his ride. Yours too. He'll turn up. Now get back to work."

"Okay." William hesitated. "You put your shirt back on."

"Yup."

"Can I put mine on again?"

"Nope."

"Why?"

Tim thwacked him over the head with the checks. "Seniority. I'll let you know if I see Kelly. Hey! How did everything go?" He held up a palm. "Never mind. Don't answer that. All I want to know is if Jason's okay. Is he happy?"

William nodded. "He sure seemed like it!"

Tim smiled. "Good. I'll see you at the end of the night. Or in the morning. These things can drag on."

He was right. The hour was nearing three in the morning before the last of the guests left. The ballroom was mostly empty, enough to be sure that Kelly was no longer there. William found Tim and Marcello standing with a broad-shouldered guy in a tuxedo, the one who had been in charge of the waiters.

"Nobody's seen him?" William pressed, feeling concerned.

The heads around him shook. Marcello turned to the large man. "Nathaniel?"

"Crutches with attitude?"

William nodded in confirmation.

"He isn't here," Nathaniel grunted. "Or elsewhere in the house. I reactivated the security system as soon as you were back from your little tryst. Maybe he wised up and left."

William scowled. "What's that supposed to mean?"

"Gentlemen!" Marcello said, raising a hand to silence any retort. "Let's end the evening on a civilized note, shall we? William, go to the kitchen. You'll find Jason hiding there in an attempt to appear casual. I'll make some inquiries and see if I can't find your friend. Yes?"

"Okay," William said, shooting Nathaniel a glare before he

left. What did he care about any of this? His words were effective though. William felt like a sleazebag as he slunk into the kitchen. Seeing Jason there helped cheer him up but didn't chase away his concern.

"What's wrong?" Jason asked, seeing his expression.

"Kelly's gone AWOL."

"Do you think he knows?"

Before he could answer, Nathaniel barged into the room. He used a key to unlock a cabinet and grabbed a basket, the waiters gathering around him to collect their cell phones. William jostled for position to get his, pacing impatiently while he waited for it to power up. Then he used it to call Kelly.

No answer.

He sent a text message, deciding on a casual, *Time to go! Where are you?*

No answer.

What if Kelly had done something extreme? He could have tried walking back to Austin, but it was a long way, especially with crutches. And he'd been drinking.

Tim entered the kitchen, shaking his head. "Marcello says the grounds are clear. Maybe he got a ride back, or called a taxi. What do you want to do?"

William didn't have a clue.

"If he did leave," Jason said, "where do you think he would go?"

"Home," William said. "Or maybe over to Bonnie's place."

"Then I'll take you home," Tim said. "If he's not there, we'll keep trying until we find him."

"Thank you," William said. He felt like he would go crazy while Tim slowly said goodbye to a variety of people. When they were finally in the car, he kept his attention on the window, just in case he spotted Kelly on the side of the road. He asked Jason to do the same, unable to worry about how this might make him feel. His stomach was filled with dread when they reached Kelly's home. William hurried through the house and opened the bedroom door. A sleeping form was in the bed. He bent over it, relieved to see Kelly's face, his breathing deep. William pulled out his cell phone and sent Jason a text, letting him know that everything was okay. He didn't know if that was true, and wouldn't until tomorrow when they were both awake. Only then would he find out what Kelly knew, and that feeling of having lost him would return, because one way or another, William's actions had brought their relationship to an end.

Sleep was brief and unsatisfying. William woke, expecting to find Kelly looming over him accusingly. Instead he was softly snoring. That was unusual. Just how much had he drank? William rose, trying to imagine how the day would play out. Whenever Kelly woke, an argument was sure to follow. He should probably be dressed when that happened, just in case he was kicked out of the house.

William showered and put on his clothes, then checked the clock. He couldn't have gotten more than three hours' sleep. Kelly was still snoozing, so he decided to take the edge off his anxiety by returning to his previous routine—a bike ride to the YMCA and a vigorous swim. The decision proved to be just what he needed. He couldn't remember the last time he'd been at the pool alone or had the luxury of focusing on his workout without having to coach Jason or reassure Kelly that everything wasn't falling apart. Even if it was.

After climbing out of the pool, William felt ready to return to the house, to confront the inevitable instead of avoiding it. He got dressed without bothering to shower and biked back there. Kelly's family was awake, gathering around the breakfast table. This included Kelly, who greeted him pensively. Just a quick hug, no kiss, but that was more than William had expected. He pulled him aside so they could talk privately.

"Where'd you get to last night?" William asked. "You had us all worried."

Kelly averted his eyes. "I caught a ride home. I didn't want to stay any longer."

"Okay," William said, "but you could have told me before you left."

"I got a little drunk," Kelly said, "which explains why I'm now tempted to drink bacon grease straight from the pan."

The words sounded lighthearted, but Kelly delivered them without humor. William waited for him to continue, but he didn't. Kelly sat down at the table, as did the others, and they ate. He was disappointed. While he hadn't been looking forward to an argument, the confrontation would have been a natural transition to a break-up.

The bad mood, the loss of patience, the cutting comments…

they never came. The day wore on, a sluggish Sunday spent in the living room. Two more meals came and went without words between them. That definitely wasn't normal. Kelly either knew or suspected enough that he was beyond anger. The battle cry had been raised. All that was left was to charge into war.

He waited for Kelly's family to retire for the night, then went with him to the bedroom, even though he couldn't imagine sleeping next to each other anymore. Kelly seemed to sense this too, perched on the end of the bed while still dressed. The time had come.

William sat next to him. "Kelly—"

"I'm ready to talk about it. Just promise me you'll be honest and we can get through this."

William glanced over at him. Kelly was sitting upright, his expression open and earnest. This wasn't going to be as easy as he hoped. "I don't make you happy anymore."

Kelly shook his head adamantly. "That's not true!"

"Are you sure? Because we can't seem to get through a day without you snapping at me or rolling your eyes or—"

"I'm a bitch! I get pissy. You take it too personally."

"That's not how it was when we first met. I don't remember you getting so grumpy with me. Not all the time."

Kelly exhaled. "Since the accident, I've been a little—"

"Not since then," William said. "It started *before* then. That's why I wanted to break up. I was tired of feeling like I constantly pissed you off. I didn't make you happy then, and I know I don't make you happy now."

Kelly frowned. "You're wrong."

"I'm not." The evidence was right before him. William felt like holding up a mirror so Kelly could see his own expression. "Just think about it. Open yourself to the idea and ask yourself if it's true."

Kelly took a deep breath and quietly considered the possibility. His response was grudging. "Maybe we're not the most compatible, but they say opposites attract."

"They might attract, but they don't stick together."

Kelly balked. "What are you saying?"

"That I don't make you happy anymore." The words were hard to force out. "And if I'm honest, I haven't been happy for a long time."

"If you're honest," Kelly said, getting worked up, "all of this is actually about Jason Grant!"

"Not all of it, but yeah." William licked his lips. "Meeting him made everything complicated. I promised you I would stay. In the hospital, I swore I would never leave you because I wanted to do the right thing. And I still do, but now I'm worried that if we keep going like this, I'm going to do the wrong thing."

"With Jason," Kelly said with disgust.

"Yes, with Jason! I'm through denying it. I love him."

Kelly looked like he'd been slapped. Repeatedly. His mouth hung open and he shook his head inadvertently like he wanted to deny what his ears had just heard. Witnessing his shock didn't feel good, but William couldn't turn back now.

"I never wanted to hurt you," he said, "and I didn't do this on purpose, I swear. Just… just think about the morning of the accident and pretend I didn't screw up and cost you your leg. If none of that had happened, do you really think we'd still be together?"

Kelly remained fixated on one detail. "You *love* him? How far have things gone?"

William met his accusing stare. "Isn't that far enough already? I want to be with him, but I also made a promise to you. I can keep that promise, but it seems insane because you're not happy and I'm not happy, and now that you know the truth, do you really think that's going to get better? Is there anything we can say or do to fix this? Because if not, I'm scared I'm going to end up hating you."

He braced himself for hellfire. What he didn't expect was the angry expression to shift to one of pained acceptance. Kelly's voice became a whisper. "Okay."

"Okay?" William repeated. "What do you mean?"

"You kept your promise to me long enough. You stayed by my side." Kelly's hands clutched at the blanket they were sitting on. "You're free. Go be with him."

William didn't feel like leaping up and racing from the room. Years of memories—a shared history together—were about to come to an end, and to his surprise, not all of him wanted that. "I hope we can be friends. I still want you in my life."

Kelly laughed, as if he was being foolish. "Well, we don't have much choice. We share almost every class in school, so for the next few months, you're stuck with me."

"I can ask to be transferred to other classes. If you want."

"No," Kelly said with a resigned sigh. "I really don't." He looked at William, the longing in his eyes familiar because it matched what he felt deep inside. "I hate that everything ended up this way."

"Me too. I wish we had quit while it was still good, before it got tarnished by… *everything*."

Kelly nodded, looking around at a bedroom that was meant to belong to his parents. They had gotten used to a life suited to people twice their age and stuck in an unhappy marriage. William wouldn't miss that aspect of their relationship. Not one bit. He couldn't wait to sleep in his own bed again.

"I need your help," Kelly said. "One last favor."

As in one last night together? William bent over to start putting on his shoes. "I should probably head home before it gets too late."

"I don't mean tonight. Tomorrow. Maybe the next day too."

"Oh."

Kelly rolled his eyes. "Just a couple more afternoons with me. Then you can spend your entire life with that floozy. That's right, I called him a floozy, and you know that's me being nice. I can think of numerous other terms that would be more appropriate, such as—"

"All right, all right," William said, holding up a hand. Kelly would be okay. His anger would serve him well in that regard. "I'll help you."

William stood and stretched, sorrow pooling in his stomach and rising upward, invading his heart and wanting to get at his eyes. "I guess this is it."

Kelly nodded glumly. "I guess so."

William looked at him, the tears blurring his vision and making it easy to pretend he was seeing the guy he had fallen in love with. Kelly, king of his own world, the best runner, the man with enough attitude to not care about what anyone else thought. Kissing him the first time had been so terrifying. William hadn't been sure if he was worthy or even capable. Never had he imagined what would follow, or that he would ever want to leave this amazing person behind. Despite all the bitterness and anger, Kelly was special. Strong and sharp, funny and sexy. William had been lucky. "You were my first everything," he said.

Kelly pursed his lips, summoning up some of that attitude. "From the sound of things, I won't be your last. Good night, William."

"Kelly, I really did lo—"

"Good night," Kelly repeated, looking away.

Fair enough. William had lost the right to say such things. He had failed to make Kelly happy and whole again, but despite it all, William really did love him. Part of him always would.

William unlocked the front door, setting down his backpack and straining to hear if his mother was still awake. He saw the flicker of television from deep in the house but didn't hear any studio laughter or jarring commercials.

"Willy?" His mother appeared, tying a robe over her nightgown. Her face lit up when she saw it was him. "Are you staying the night?"

"Permanently."

"Oh!" She brought a hand to her mouth. "You're moving back in?"

"Yeah," William said with a chuckle. "Someone needs to keep an eye on you."

"This is wonderful!" She switched on the living room lamps. Then she turned around suddenly. "Isn't it? Did something happen between—"

"Yes," William said, not ready to talk about it. Not with her, or even Jason, who would have to wait to hear the news. "And yeah, it is a good thing. I guess."

"I'm sorry, baby."

"You never liked him," William said.

"I don't care. You're my child, and I know how bad this sort of thing hurts. I'm sorry for both of you."

"Thanks," William said, feeling emotional again.

"How about something to eat? Ice cream?"

William shook his head. "I'm tired. I think I just want to crash, if that's okay. We can talk tomorrow."

His mother smiled. "Tomorrow it is! I'm just happy knowing you're home again."

He felt a little better when she hugged him and kissed him on the cheek. Then he trudged up the stairs, switching on the lights in his room and surveying it. Nothing had changed. He could pretend that he and Kelly had never met. Externally, at least. When William shut off the lights and crawled into bed, he lay there with his eyes open, despite his exhaustion. Too much was missing, such as a warm body next to his and the sound of Kelly breathing. Not to mention a piece of his heart, which William had known he would have to leave behind. He just hadn't expected that piece to be so big.

Chapter Sixteen

For the first two days after his breakup with Kelly, William didn't see Jason. They didn't speak or even text. William had already suggested they keep their distance so he could deal with the fallout of the charity ball. Once he was finally single again, William found himself needing space to nurse his wounds. He mourned the good memories they had made together, which were easier to remember now that they were getting along.

The favor Kelly had needed, his final request, was for his bedroom to be restored to the way it had been before. William didn't mind. Returning to his own room had felt like a way of turning back the clock. He wanted Kelly to have that too. During the process of carrying furniture up and down the stairs, they remained on friendly terms. He even found talking to Laisha possible again, explaining to her how he had tried to make up for his mistakes. She admitted that she had her own regrets, apologizing for how she had treated him. Burying the hatchet was easy now that the past was in the past—as much as possible, anyway—and he and Kelly were a couple no more.

Having finally accepted that, William sent Jason a message, not telling him what had transpired but asking if they could meet during his next break at work. As usual, Jason didn't approach the counter when he showed up. Kelly had put an end to that. Normally, after catching his eye, Jason would retreat to the parking lot. William would meet him there in secrecy, their limited privacy fleeting. That's exactly what happened today. Jason nodded once to get his attention and walked away, except this time, William followed. He grabbed Jason in the mall corridor, spun him around, and locked lips with him right there where everyone could see. Kissing him before had felt great, but doing so without the added guilt took it to new levels.

When William explained that he was finally free, Jason's glee was contagious, but he needed to clear the air on one point. "I won't betray anyone like that again. Not you or anyone else. It's better to hurt someone with honesty than to hurt them with lies."

Lesson learned, he hoped. They made plans to meet the next night for their official first date. Then he returned to work, and afterwards, went back to Kelly's house for the final time. But did it really need to be? He hated the idea of losing someone he cared about forever. He didn't want that, and by the time the bus dropped him off, he had convinced himself they could still be friends.

Once he reached Kelly's house and finished helping out, he discovered that his former boyfriend had other ideas. William was by the front door, holding a box of his possessions under one arm as he waited for his mother to pick him up.

"Don't forget this."

He turned around to find Kelly holding a bright red helicopter. Of course William hadn't forgotten it! He just thought he had lost the right to keep it.

"It's a good luck charm," Kelly said, thrusting it out.

"Are you sure about that?" William replied. "The night you gave it to me we were both arrested."

"Who knows how the night might have played out otherwise. We might have gotten drunk, thought it was a good idea to dive off the bridge, and ended up drowning. No, it was sheer luck that I got us in trouble."

William laughed, accepting the Transformer and placing it in the box. From outside the house, headlights moved across the room, signaling that his mother had pulled in the driveway. "The last few days have been nice," he said. "We should do it again."

Kelly raised an eyebrow. "Interior decorating?"

"No. We should hang out."

"I don't want to be your friend, William." Kelly closed his eyes briefly. "Sorry. That sounds terrible. The problem is that I still wish you were my boyfriend. I need space so I can move on. If that ever happens, then we'll see. For now, get the hell out of my life."

He said this with humor, but the essence was true. They could only be friends once the love between them had died. William wasn't sure that would ever happen.

"Okay, well, I guess—"

A horn honked outside.

Kelly smiled. "Our families, always getting in the way of those tender moments."

"Yeah. I shouldn't keep her waiting."

Kelly nodded cordially and turned away, but just before he

did, William saw his face crumple. The image remained with him for the rest of the night. His freedom had come at a cost to them both, but Kelly was paying the bigger price.

Life returned to being blissfully normal. William had a curfew again. His mother began sticking her nose into his business, wanting updates on his grades and plans, and she constantly worried he wasn't eating or sleeping enough. He even had privacy in the mornings, since Jason no longer needed to wake up early to see him.

"Forbidden fruit," Errol had said during a visit home, affecting age and wisdom. "Now that you guys are allowed to be together, I bet the chemistry doesn't last."

His brother's expertise didn't extend beyond illegal substances, because he was wrong. William was even more into Jason now that guilt was no longer clouding the love potion. Their first official date proved this. Tim had loaned them his Bentley to make the night extra special, Jason driving them to an art gallery, and even though William wasn't into such things, they had a great time. Jason made everything fun, except maybe at the end of the evening when another car dinged the Bentley. Just a scratch, but Jason was certain he would get booted out of the house because of it.

Tim took the news well. Kind of. First he rushed out to meet them in the detached garage, and yeah, he did freak out. And no wonder! A Bentley wasn't a cheap car! But before he could get too worked up, Ben had showed up in the garage. That changed everything. Tim was suddenly cool with it all, clearly seeking Ben's approval, which he got. They were adorable together. William wanted to spend more time with them. He had mentioned the idea of a double date to Jason earlier in the evening, and now was his chance to ask. Ben and Tim were heading back inside the house when William called after them.

"Hey, you guys want to go on a double date sometime?"

"Again?" Tim called back. "Ow!"

It looked like Ben had pinched his nipple, but when he spun around, Ben's face was angelic. "Just tell us when!" Then they disappeared into the house.

William grinned. He turned to Jason, who seemed amused too. They were standing outside the garage, a small pool of light pouring out and shielding them against the night. "You *so* need them to adopt you!"

"Jason Wyman?" His boyfriend cocked his head, trying the name on for size. "Or Jason Bentley. Neither sounds right."

"Not as good as Jason Townson, anyway." William said with a wink. "No, wait! If they adopt you, and you take Tim's name, and *then* we get married, I would be William Wyman."

Jason laughed. "Seems like a lot of effort just for a name change. I'm surprised you're so crazy about Tim. I got the impression you didn't like him the first time you met."

"That's back when I thought he was dating you. It's not just Tim. I like them both. I get what you mean now. They're a package deal! I really envy what they have together. They're so adorable! If you really made me choose, maybe I like Ben a little better, but it depends if you mean emotionally or physically because—"

"Breathe," Jason suggested, shaking his head. "And if you want adorable, you should see pictures of when they were younger."

"Like right now? Yes, please!"

Jason chuckled, then pivoted to face the house. "Let's go!"

A few minutes later they were seated side by side on the couch. Ben and Tim where nowhere to be seen, which meant they had retired to their bedroom. The thought alone had his heart fluttering, even before Jason opened the laptop.

"Ben had all their photos digitized," Jason was saying. "Personally, I like the old-fashioned printed kind. More romantic, you know?"

William nodded, not really having a preference but eager for the show to begin. "Is this Ben's laptop?"

"Yup!"

"And you have the password?"

"He has mine too," Jason said easily. "We trust each other." He clicked a few times and an image appeared on the screen.

William practically shoved him aside to see. "Is that them?" The image was of two teenagers sitting on a bed together, looking baby-faced compared to the men he had just spoken to. Ben's hair was a lot blonder, Tim's muscles not quite as big.

"Yup!" Jason said, anticipating his next question. "Sixteen, maybe seventeen."

"Wow! They've been together for that long?"

"No," Jason said, "because if you'll remember…" He skipped past photo after photo, William tempted to reach out and stop him. Not all were of Ben and Tim. Most showed Ben with people who looked like family, including a black girl who aged along with him as the years flew by. "—there's also this guy."

The image was of a kitchen table, the room fairly small. Seated in front of poker cards and a half-empty bottle of booze were two guys. Ben's hair was closer to the darker shade it was currently, his expression surprised as he looked toward whoever was taking the photo. The guy next to him must have seen it coming. He was older than Ben but still handsome, his smile warm. He had reached over to put a possessive hand on Ben's shoulder, or maybe to get his attention for the photo.

"Who's that?" William asked.

"Jace. The guy Ben was married to."

"I don't like him," William said dismissively.

"Hey!" Jason shoved him playfully. "He was nice! He's the one I met after things fell apart between me and my last foster family. Caesar and I were history, and I was hopelessly depressed. Then I met this guy, and honestly, it was the first day after all the bad stuff that I felt happy again."

"Maybe I like him a little," William conceded.

"You should. He gave me his number, and Ben's. That's how I reached him after Jace died."

"Now I feel bad."

"It's fine. Just remember that if it wasn't for him, I wouldn't have met Ben or ended up here. I probably wouldn't have met you!"

William leaned his head on Jason's shoulder. "Thanks, Jace," he said. "But still, it's hard to picture Ben with anyone but Tim. They're a perfect match."

"It is hard for me to imagine too, I guess because I never saw Ben and Jace together."

"Show me more photos of them."

"Of Ben and Jace?"

"Ummm…"

Jason laughed. "Fine. More Ben and Tim."

William witnessed a progression of images that made his heart swell: Ben and Tim posed in front of monuments, behind birthday cakes, next to each other on beaches or in the snow. The ordinary nature of the photos is what made them poignant. William hadn't grown up with any gay role models—just celebrities living glamourous lives he couldn't relate to. Had there been a couple like this in his family, or even just in the neighborhood, maybe accepting his own sexuality wouldn't have been so hard.

"I love them," William murmured. "I know I barely know them, but…"

"I get what you mean," Jason said, smiling as he continued scrolling. "It didn't take me long to love them either." He reached the first image again, two teenagers sitting on a bed and just beginning their history together.

"Do you think they knew?" William asked. "Way back then, do you think they realized they would be together all these years later?"

Jason thought about it. "Tim? No way. He couldn't even admit he was gay. Ben probably hoped for it though."

"That could be us," William said, pointing at the screen. "Maybe we'll look back years—*decades*—from now, and shake our heads at how young we were."

"Maybe," Jason said, not sounding so certain. "They had to go through a lot to get to where they are now. Like I said, you should ask Ben about it."

"I will." He nuzzled Jason's neck. "On one of our double dates with them."

"There's only going to be one," Jason said. "I don't plan on sharing you that often! I'm selfish."

"Are you?"

"Yup. I'm keeping you to myself from now on."

William nodded at the screen. "How much action do you think that mattress saw?"

Jason shut the laptop and set it aside. "Enough of their story. I want to get back to ours. It's time for bed."

"I have a curfew," William said. "I can't stay the night."

Jason smiled, taking his hand as he stood. "Who said anything about sleep?"

Another sign of William's return to normality was that he had a social life again. When he looked back on the friendships he once had, he realized there was only one person he was eager to reconnect with. As it turned out, she was equally fond of double dating.

"This brings back memories," Lily said when she walked into his bedroom.

William glanced over to see a naughty smile, then hurried to pull on his shirt. A pale yellow polo, which made him feel rebellious because Kelly had hated it. "Don't try making out with me," William teased. "It's not that kind of double date. You aren't swingers, are you?"

Lily shrugged innocently. "Wait until you see Isaac before you dismiss the idea. He's gorgeous."

"So is Jason," William said proudly. "You're going to love him."

"He can't be worse than the last one. Ding dong! The witch is dead!"

"I liked Kelly!" William protested, grabbing a belt and shutting the closet door.

"Even though he scared us off?"

"That sucked," he admitted, weaving leather between loops of denim. "I'm still bummed that Abby moved away."

"To Iowa, of all places," Lily said with a grimace. "Holly is doing the born-again thing. I tried hanging out with her once, but I really don't like her new friends. If I'm honest, all we really had in common was our friendship with Abby."

William exhaled. "Man… I missed out on so much."

"But now you're back," Lily said, shaking invisible pompoms. "And just in time for prom! Has Jason asked you?"

"I asked him," William said, cheeks flushing. "He's not in school anymore so—"

"Hey hey, an older man!"

"Just by little, but yeah."

"Show me some photos!"

"He'll be here any second," William said. "Besides, I don't have any."

"Not even on your phone?"

"None at all." He thought of how important those early photos of Ben and Tim were now and promised himself to correct the oversight. "I haven't taken any because—well, just think of how Kelly would have reacted."

"Good point," Lily said. "Describe him to me."

"Jason? Brown hair, blue eyes, cute smile."

Lily pantomimed a yawn. "Fascinating."

"Fine, let's hear you describe yours."

"Deal. Isaac is John Cusack hot, say from around the *High Fidelity* era. He's got that black hair and pale skin combo that drives me wild, a hairy chest, and down below…" She held out her index fingers, both pointed straight up and moving farther apart, like describing a fish she had caught. And boy was it a whopper!

"You're so bad!" he said, shaking his head.

"It's a perfectly natural interest," Lily said unabashedly, sitting on his bed. "So what about Jason?"

"What about him?"

"How big is his thing?"

William shook his head. "Don't even go there! And I'm pretty sure Isaac wouldn't like you telling everyone about his!"

"You clearly haven't met him yet."

The doorbell rang. They looked at each other.

"Yours or mine?" Lily asked.

They listened to his mother giggling happily.

"Mine," William said. "She's crazy about Jason."

"You weren't kidding!" Lily said when they heard more tittering. "Sounds like she's the one going on a date!"

William grinned and waited by the bedroom door. He felt a little intimidated about introducing Jason to Lily, especially since she was in a naughty mood, but when he heard the stairs creaking and footsteps approached, he threw open the door and all doubt dissipated. Jason wore a pair of tan cargo pants and a dark brown dress shirt, the top button undone. His hair was mussed to perfection, the chestnut tangle covering his brow. This only made his blue eyes stand out more. Currently they were locked onto him like he was the only man in existence.

"Hi," William managed. "You look cool."

Jason made a face, then started laughing. "You're adorable," he responded, giving him a quick peck on the lips. Then he noticed they weren't alone. "You must be Lily!"

"Hello there!" she said with a wave. She used the same hand to fan herself theatrically when Jason turned to face him once more.

"Am I late?"

"You're right on time," William said, checking his watch. "That's worth extra points."

"Score!" Jason said. "So am I driving? I couldn't get the Bentley. No surprise, considering what happened last time."

"Isaac will drive," Lily said. "He has a nice car. Wait, did you say a Bentley?"

"I'm a millionaire," Jason replied. "William didn't mention that?"

"He's a liar is what he is," William said. "I thought we were past this!"

Jason's face fell. "I was joking!"

"So was I."

Jason recovered, playfully nudging him. William counterattacked by tickling his ribs, their faces getting nearer. Then he remembered Lily and looked over at her.

"Pretend I'm not here!" she said. "I'm totally into this. Oh!" She pulled out her phone. "Isaac is out front. Says we should meet him there."

They piled down the stairs and outside. Parked alongside the curb was an old Mustang in serious need of restoration. On one corner of the hood sat a guy with swept-back black hair. William shook his hand when they were introduced, trying very hard not to think of something very large while doing so. Unlike Jason's innocent smooch a few minutes ago, Isaac and Lily's kiss involved tongue and lasted the better part of a minute.

"So," Jason said, "I take it you guys have met before?"

"Yeah," Isaac said with a dry chuckle. "Lily's my girl! How long has it been now? Three weeks?"

"Yup!" She shot William a wink. "We go way back."

Their date continued in the mundane style that William had been enjoying lately. They went to a pizza place, and while they ate, mostly listened to Isaac talk about the thrash metal band he hoped to start. He only needed willing participants.

"Jason can play guitar," William supplied helpfully.

"Really?" Isaac asked, leaning across the table. "Man, that's great!"

"Acoustic only," Jason said hurriedly, playfully slugging William's leg under the table. "And I'm really slow. I couldn't thrash to save my life. Sorry."

Afterwards they went to the movies, the ticket agent selling them on a special advance screening. None of them had heard of the movie, not that it mattered because Lily and Isaac spent most of it making out. William found this distracting, but the movie made him uneasy too, since it was about an orphan who gets adopted by a family and starts doing horrific things to them.

Halfway through the film, Jason shot to his feet, moving down the aisle. William hurried to follow. "Hey," he whispered. "I'm sorry. I didn't know it would be so offensive."

Jason looked over his shoulder in puzzlement. "Are you kidding? This is the greatest movie ever made!" He plopped down into an empty seat. "I can't hear half the words over their slobbering, that's all."

William sat next to him, stifling a laugh. "So the movie is accurate? This is what your life was like?"

"Absolutely," Jason whispered back. "Especially the stuff about seducing hot dads. I used to do that *all the time.*"

He took William's hand, attention on the screen until the next scene ended. Then he tilted his head closer. "I freaking love horror movies!"

I freaking love you! William thought, wishing they were in the kind of seats made for cuddling. He settled for shooting the occasional glance in Jason's direction, adoring his easy smile and quiet chuckle each time something really gruesome happened. When the movie ended and they stumbled out into the parking lot, Jason seemed eager to discuss the plot, but clearly he'd been the only one really paying attention.

"You guys suck," he said. "That was an advance screening! We should feel honored!"

"I felt something!" Isaac cackled.

"Yourself," Lily said, "and that's all you'll feel if you keep bragging."

"Sorry, babe."

"So what's next?" William asked before they could start making out again.

Isaac tossed his keys in the air and caught them again. "Let's go for a drive!"

Lily and Jason both seemed eager, so William agreed, hiding his reluctance. He soon regretted this decision. The backseat of the Mustang was so cramped he had to sit at an angle, and Isaac drove like a maniac, picking up speed as they left the city and headed east. Between the roar of the engine and the thrash metal pumping from the speakers, conversation was impossible, leaving William with nothing to distract him from the potential accidents he kept imagining. He was embarrassed by his sweaty palms when Jason took his hand, and was relieved when Jason patted his lap, inviting William to lay his head there. This involved some serious twisting and squirming, but he managed, feeling much better when he could close his eyes and focus on the gentle stroking of his hair.

He sat up again when the car stopped, the engine and music shutting off simultaneously. Not much could be seen outside the windows besides shadows and trees.

"Where are we?"

"The middle of nowhere," Isaac replied, leaning forward to peer up through the windshield. "Check out the stars."

William couldn't see the sky from the backseat, but he was glad they were no longer in motion. He was about to ask what they were doing here when Lily murmured something to Isaac and they began kissing again. He looked over at Jason, who shrugged as if to say *why not*? Even though he felt a little awkward kissing so close to another couple, he still reveled in tasting a hint of buttered popcorn on Jason's lips and the tang of his cologne when nipping at his neck. Another smell soon overpowered those he had been enjoying, and man was it pungent!

William pulled away in confusion and saw a glowing ember being held out toward him. A joint! Isaac was fighting against exhaling, trying to communicate with facial expression alone.

"Oh. Uh…" William was tempted to indulge, but his urge to be a normal teenager stopped when it came to compromising his career with the Coast Guard. "I can't. Not that I mind! You guys go ahead." He looked at Jason, the joint offered to him now.

"I'm feeling pretty high already," Jason said, beaming at him. "No thanks."

That was sweet, and had William feeling all bubbly inside, but it also triggered another thought. The car interior wasn't exactly airy. What if being in here was enough to actually *get* high? Isaac had turned to Lily again, so William moved closer to Jason. When they kissed, he held his breath at the same time, not wanting to inhale. Pretty soon he was gasping.

Jason pulled back in puzzlement. "You okay?"

William moved his lips to Jason's ear, keeping his voice down. "Do you think a contact high would show up on a drug test?"

"No idea," came the whispered response.

"I really *really* can't get high. Seriously!"

Jason searched his eyes, then thunked the seat in front of him. "Hey, let us out. William and I are going for a walk."

Isaac was happy to comply, smiling at them like he knew exactly what they wanted to do. William had no such plans. Once free of the vehicle, he sucked in fresh air eagerly. Then he glanced up. Away from the glow of the city, the sky was filled with hundreds of tiny pinpricks, lights beaming through a dark void and offering hope.

"That's crazy beautiful," Jason said. "I haven't seen the stars like that since I went camping ages ago."

"It's gorgeous," William breathed. "I've heard it's always like this in the middle of the ocean. At night, anyway."

"You better hope so or you won't be able to steer your ship."

He laughed. "The Coast Guard has more modern navigation equipment than that."

"Oh yeah?"

"Yeah. They have rolls and rolls of maps, and a pocket telescope we all get to share."

"Very impressive," Jason said, grinning at him. He nodded to the car, the interior getting foggier by the second. "That's why you needed to leave, isn't it? Because of the Coast Guard."

"Yeah," he said, waiting for Jason to roll his eyes or chastise him for being square.

Instead he looked back to the sky. "Cool. I thought you got accepted already."

"I did, but random drugs tests are… random. You can get high if you want. I don't mind."

Jason shook his head. "I've never been into that sort of stuff. I've tried a few times, and yeah, it's fun, but I could never afford it. Cigarettes, booze, and drugs are for people with money. More money than me, anyway."

William could think of plenty of people who couldn't afford those habits but managed anyway, but he liked that Jason had priorities. "So what now?"

"Let's go for a stroll."

William glanced around. Isaac had parked on a dirt road

next to a line of thick trees. To their left was a barbed-wire fence and farmland. Only a waning moon provided useful light. The idea of walking in any direction made him feel spooked, but Jason had his hand extended in invitation, and that was all the encouragement he needed.

"Where are we?" William asked.

"No idea," Jason admitted.

"How long do you think it would take to walk home?"

"Hours." Jason looked over at him. "You don't do so well in cars. I thought it was my driving that bugged you the last few times, but it's not. Is it?"

"No," William admitted. "Ever since the accident— Ugh! That's the last thing I want to talk about right now."

"We don't have to," Jason said, swinging their arms playfully. "I'm just confused because you're the guy who wants to jump from helicopters, which sounds way worse than driving around Austin. And then there's boats. I'm picturing waves. Really big ones. It'll be like a roller coaster. Hey! Do you like those?"

William sighed. "I don't know. I haven't been on one—"

"Since the accident," Jason finished for him. "If I were you, I'd figure out how well I do with all that stuff before I make any promises to the Coast Guard."

"How?"

Jason thought about it. "Face your fears. Start driving again every day. Or maybe just go for a helicopter ride to see if they make you nervous too. If not, then you'll probably be fine. You can get away with not driving, right?"

"Maybe." William thought about it as they went around a curve in the road. "In a way, it doesn't matter if I'm scared or not. I have to do this. It's the only plan I've got. You know what I mean?"

Jason was quiet.

"You probably think I'm kidding myself," William said.

"No," Jason replied instantly. "I believe in you." Then he stopped and pointed toward the trees. "First fireflies of the year!"

Deep in the shadows, greenish-yellow lights blinked on and off, slowly drifting on the warm night air. The lazy movements were hypnotic. Soothing.

"There must be a creek in there," Jason said. "Or maybe a pond. Fireflies always live near water."

"Really?" William said. "I remember them being in my

backyard when I was a kid. We don't have a pool or anything."

"They must have found water somewhere. I wrote an essay on them once. Come on, I'll show you."

Before William could react, Jason pulled them toward the trees, unconcerned about not having a clear path. He stopped occasionally to make sure William was aware of some obstacle—a low branch or a spider's web he'd seen reflected in the moonlight. Aside from that, he didn't seem to share William's nervousness, or flinch at any unusual sounds.

Then Jason halted, extending an arm to make sure William did the same. "There you go!"

William pressed against him, looking over Jason's shoulder. The ground dropped away, rising again a few yards ahead of them. He couldn't see the water at the bottom of the ravine, but he could hear it.

"You're amazing!" William said, hugging him from behind.

"Eh," Jason replied. "It was only a school paper."

"I don't mean just that. The rest of you is amazing too."

Jason was silent. Then he gently moved William's arm away so he could turn around. "What I was saying earlier about not having money, that probably won't change."

William stared, not understanding where the conversation was leading. "Okay."

"I just don't want you to get the wrong idea about me. You've seen me driving around in a Bentley, but it's not mine. The house I live in is nice, but it doesn't belong to me, and I won't be there forever. I need to get my own place, and when I do, it'll be just an apartment."

"That's not why I love you," William said. "My feelings don't—"

"It's more than that. I don't have a plan like you do. I'm not enlisting or going to college. I work at a pet store. I'm a retail grunt. That's all I'll ever be."

"You don't know for sure," William said.

"I've got a pretty good idea," Jason said. "Most people have dreams of what they want to be. Mine revolve around what happens when the work day is over. I just thought you should know upfront. I might hang out with successful people, but I don't want you to confuse me for one of them."

William laughed. "I'm not in this for the money."

"I'm not calling you a gold digger," Jason said hurriedly. "I guess I just don't... Never mind."

"What?"

"I don't get what you see in me."

William's mouth fell open. "Wow. Okay, if you want to start with the superficial, you're smoking hot."

"I'm not fishing for compliments! I only—"

William covered Jason's mouth with his hand. "I also like how positive you are. Whenever I tell you one of my deep dark secrets, you always find the silver lining. And all those obstacles keeping us apart? You plowed right through them. Give yourself credit." Jason tried to move William's hand, but he was outmuscled. "I'm not done. I like that you play guitar, especially the face you make when you're really into it, because it's the same one you make when you're about to come."

Jason pulled away and looked aghast. "You're messing with me!"

William shook his head. "I'm not. I like your crazy history, and that you always know how to make me happy. I was miserable before you came into my life."

"Having met Kelly, I can imagine why."

"Stop." William laughed. "He wasn't that bad. And besides, this is about you."

"Fine," Jason said, feigning exasperation. "Praise away!"

"You're fun to be around, you're always sweet to me, and unlike a lot of people, you're genuine. And I'm glad the Bentley isn't yours."

"If it was, I'd sell it, buy the cheapest car I could find, and put the rest in the bank."

"Now that's what I call sexy!"

Jason laughed. "You're weird."

"Yup. If it helps, I'm just as surprised that you're so into me. I come with a lot of baggage, but you still put up one hell of a fight. I don't deserve that."

"Maybe that's how it works. When two people really love each other, they each feel like the lucky one."

Jason moved in slowly, eyes locked onto William's as they kissed. When their bodies pressed together, he could feel they were both hard. He slid a hand down the front of Jason's jeans and kissed him more intently. Unfortunately, this ruined Jason's balance and he stumbled back, almost sliding down the ravine. William caught his arm just in time and pulled him in.

"Maybe this isn't the best place," William said.

"I disagree," Jason replied, stepping close again.

William walked backwards to avoid him. "Seriously. It's kind of creepy out here."

"You said you like how persistent I am."

"Did I?" William said, bumping up against a tree. "I take it back."

"Too late."

Jason kissed him again, then slid down to his knees, getting William's pants open with surprising speed. William exhaled in pleasure, feeling the warmth of Jason's mouth. He wanted to do more, to pull Jason back to his feet and return the favor, but this felt too good. William stared into the darkness, the fireflies blurring and doubling in his vision. Then he closed his eyes and reached behind to hug the tree for support as his body convulsed, fingers running along the bark.

Jason refused to stop, head still bobbing, one arm pumping until he hissed in pleasure and rested his forehead against William's hip. Then he got back to his feet.

William helped him. "Add that to the list of things I like about you."

Jason laughed, zipping up his jeans. "Think Lily and Isaac were that quick?"

"Only one way to find out." Part of him wanted to remain, the darkness more like a sanctuary now. He imagined they could stay the night there, talking about their feelings until the sun came up. "So what do you like about me?"

"You?" Jason said, sounding surprised. "Nothing."

"What?"

"I don't like anything. I *love* everything."

"God that's cheesy," William said, "but it so works for me!"

They loitered awhile longer, basking in the afterglow, before making their way back to the dirt road. They joked about the car rocking back and forth, but when they rounded the bend, they saw it was motionless. Lily stood next to it, arms crossed over her chest.

"Everything okay?" William asked when they approached.

She jerked her head toward the interior. "He fell asleep."

"Oh." William stifled a laugh. "Before or after…"

"We didn't have sex," Lily said, sounding tense. "Let me ask you something. Have you ever been stoned?"

He shook his head. Jason nodded in the affirmative, so she turned to him. "When you're high, does that make it hard to…" She raised an index finger, making it go from a hook shape to pointing straight up.

"Oh." Jason rubbed the back of his head sheepishly. "I actually have the opposite problem. Like it won't go away."

William made a mental note to buy a joint from Errol and get Jason high. "So Isaac couldn't…"

Lily blew the hair out of her eyes with a huff. "Right. I said we could cuddle instead, because that's what they always say on TV. Then he fell asleep."

"Maybe he's narcoleptic," Jason said.

"And impotent," William added.

"Or just really high." Lily seemed lost in thought. "Then again, so am I. One of you better drive."

"No problem," Jason said. "I'll—"

"I'll drive." William turned to him with a meaningful expression. "Can't be worse than flying in a helicopter, right?"

Another double date, this one even better than the previous because it was with Ben and Tim. William was pretty sure he had a crush on both without actually wanting to be romantic with either of them. He loved how Ben seemed to be in charge, even though Tim was the brawnier of the two. William could relate to that. He also loved that when they bickered, it was never long before their smiles reappeared. Or before they made bedroom eyes at each other. He couldn't imagine their relationship not lasting, detecting no sign of the stagnation his parents' marriage had gone through before their divorce.

When they returned home from dinner and a movie, Ben fed the cat and asked Tim to take the dog with him to the mailbox. Normal and boring, but they made it all so enviable. Being around them was an inspiration, but also bittersweet because he realized he wasn't ready yet. Not long ago, he'd had a similar life with Kelly, albeit not as happy. He was still enjoying the freedom resulting from leaving that behind. Jason was the best perk of all, but their relationship could easily become a similar trap. He was certain sharing a life with him would be harmonious, but it would still limit what he could do.

"We're about to retire," Ben announced, returning from the kitchen.

"Okay," William said. He was seated on the couch, Jason to one side of him, Tim on the other, and debating which of them he'd rather snuggle up against.

"*You* might be going to bed," Tim said. "*I'm* watching the game."

William's eyes flitted to the TV screen where athletes were throwing a ball around. Yay. Then he looked to see what Ben's response would be.

"You can watch it in our room."

Tim grunted. "On that tiny screen? No way. You go ahead. I'll be up later."

Ben didn't budge. "They need their privacy."

Tim put an arm around William. "They're watching the game with me! Besides, Jason has his own room. They can go up there if they're in the mood for shenanigans."

"Shenanigans," William repeated, giggling madly.

Ben sighed. "Remember when we were their age, and we'd be in my room, except we couldn't do anything fun because we never knew if my mom was going to interrupt us? Only once my parents had gone to sleep were we able to relax. And besides, maybe they aren't the only ones interested in shenanigans."

Tim hopped to his feet. "Good night, gentlemen!"

William, much to his embarrassment, stood up with him. "Good night. Thanks again for dinner. And the movie! It was awesome. Can I get a hug?"

Tim humored him, patting him roughly a few times on the back while doing so. Ben was gentler, William tempted to pick him up and run for the door. He grinned while watching them go upstairs.

"Now I see why you're with me," Jason said. "After a bigger prize?"

"No!" William said, happy expression still in place. "They're just so hot! I love them. I want to start a fan club and be the president of it." He noticed Jason's raised eyebrows. "You don't think so?"

"I remember feeling the same when I first met them, yeah. These days, they're more like... I don't know."

"Family?"

"Hard to say." Jason reached for the remote and turned off the television. "It's been a long time since I've had a family. I'm not sure I remember what that feels like. I mean, I think I do, but maybe it's just a fantasy I invented, or something I learned from watching TV." He looked at William. "No need for the sad eyes! I'm okay. Really. Let's go outside. It's too nice to be in here."

"Only if you play for me."

Jason agreed, ducking upstairs to fetch his guitar. Once they were outside, they pulled two of the lawn chairs to the very edge of the patio. Jason set the guitar in his chair and stripped off his shirt.

"Should I take mine off too?" William asked, staring in appreciation.

Jason laughed. "I wouldn't mind. I just like how the guitar feels against my skin. The vibrations, more than anything."

"Too easy," William murmured. He adjusted the lawn chair until it was almost flat. Then he lay on his side and faced Jason, ready for a private concert. The music was random, shifting in shape, beautiful chords ascending and descending between periods of repetition.

"Did you write this?" William asked.

"Just freestyling," Jason said. "Some is from songs I know, the rest I'm making up on the fly."

"You're a rock star," William said affectionately.

"More like a wedding singer. I also take requests."

"Play something that makes you think of me."

"A song that represents you," Jason said, nodding musingly. Then he started strumming while singing, "Bicycle! Bicycle!"

William made a face, but started laughing because the song was about a guy who wanted nothing more than to ride his bicycle. "That's not a real song," he said when Jason was through.

"That's Queen! You're not serious…"

William shrugged. "I've never been into music. I just listen to whatever's on the radio."

"What station?"

"Anything that plays pop."

Jason groaned. "That's not music. That's fast food. Disposable forks and spoons. People use it and throw it away. I'm talking about timeless classics."

He launched into another song, this one about wanting to

rock all night and party all day. William had heard it before and thought it was cheesy, but his laughter only encouraged Jason to play it up even more, banging his head to the music and making heavy metal faces. At the end he stuck out his tongue as far as he could. William looked confused. Jason shook his head. "Gene Simmons? Kiss! No? You're hopeless."

"At least I knew that one. Now play something softer."

"Okay." Jason resumed plucking at the strings, freestyling again or maybe searching for the right tune.

William watched him, wishing their time together would never end, but it would. Sooner than he liked. They still had good times ahead, one in particular he was especially looking forward to. "I'm excited about prom. Are you?"

"Honestly?" Jason cocked his head while strumming. "I'm a little nervous. I take it you're out at school?"

"Yeah," William said, propping himself up. "Since forever."

"And nobody gives you shit for it?"

"People have called me names…" William pulled back his shirt sleeve and flexed an arm, loving how Jason looked impressed. "But for some reason, no one's tried to pick a fight."

"In that case, I hope your muscles are still visible beneath your tuxedo."

"Did you rent yours already?"

Jason nodded. "Ben wanted to buy me one, but I insisted I could handle it on my own."

William flopped back in the chair, feeling as melancholy as the night sky above them. "This dance will be our grand finale. For now, at least."

The guitar let loose an ugly note and went silent. "What's that supposed to mean?"

"My enlistment in the Coast Guard," William said, swallowing against the words.

"So? That's still months away." Jason sounded panicked. "Isn't it? I figured it was like school. You get the summer off and…"

William sat up. "I ship out to Cape May the week after I graduate."

"I don't even know where that is."

"New Jersey."

"And how long will you be gone?" Jason looked hurt, maybe even betrayed.

"You've known about this since the beginning."

"How long?" Jason said, voice raspy.

"Four years."

Jason carefully set down the guitar. "You'll come back though, right? You'll have—I don't know—shore leave or whatever."

They should have talked about this sooner, or at least in more depth. William explained how he'd be back only for the occasional holiday, which only made his heart ache more because it wouldn't be enough to sustain a relationship. "I know four years is a long time, Jason. Too long for me to expect you to wait."

"I don't care. I'll wait."

William felt a surge of affection for him. "I won't let you."

Jason scowled. "You don't have a say in it!"

"I do. Becoming a rescue swimmer is going to be the hardest thing I've ever done. It's going to take absolutely all of my willpower and attention, and frankly…" William's throat ached, not wanting to speak the truth, but he had to. "After all that time with Kelly, trying to make someone else happy instead of taking care of myself, I need a break. I can't go to the Coast Guard and think about how sad you are, sitting here for years and years while waiting for me. What if you meet someone or just want to screw around? I can't worry about any of that. Not if I'm going to do what I need to do."

"So don't join the Coast Guard." Jason crossed his arms over his chest and jutted out his chin. "If it's a choice between me and leaving, then stay here."

"This is my dream we're talking about. You know that, right?"

Jason nodded, once and final. "Yeah."

William thought about it, returning to a mental space he had once shared with Kelly. No more dreams. They had both abandoned them at one point, which had felt like a prison, but surely it would be easier to share that cell with Jason. "Okay. If you want me to give that up for you, I will. That's how much I love you."

"Good," Jason said, looking away, his jaw clenching a few times. "I'll remember that when you're gone. When it hurts the most, I'll remember that you would have stayed for me."

William leapt to his feet, pulling Jason to his so he could hold him. "I'm sorry."

Jason shook his head against his shoulder. "Don't be. You just become the best rescue swimmer they've ever had."

"I'll try. I promise."

"Four years!"

"I know." William sighed. "Of course, you could join too. Be my bunkmate."

Jason disentangled himself. "I've never done well with authority, and I doubt I'd even pass the physical. I don't think I'd make it."

"We will though," William said, feeling the force of his conviction. "Just like Ben and Tim. All those years went by and they still found each other again. And if some hot guy sweeps you off your feet in the meantime, I'll be happy because I'll know that you're loved. But someday, even if we're both in an old folks' home and have lost our husbands, we'll find our way back to each other."

Jason forced a smile. "So what now?"

William took a deep breath and released it. "Now we make the best of the time we have left."

Jason turned to pace the patio. "We've got two weeks left, maybe three. I can quit my job. We'll rent a cabin. No, never mind, a hotel room. A suite! We'll have everything we need. Room service, a bathroom, a bed." He spun around. "Don't worry about laundry because you're not going to be wearing any clothes. I'll pay for everything. I have a little saved up. I think it'll be enough. If not I'll get a loan, probably from Marcello. Hey! Maybe he'd be willing to let us stay in that room again."

William laughed. "You're not serious!"

"Try me!" Jason said, expression earnest. "Why not? If I'm barely going to see you the next four years—"

"I still have to graduate."

"Home schooling," Jason said. "I'll be your teacher."

"With an emphasis on physical education?"

Jason grinned. "You read my mind!"

William walked to him, grasping his shoulders so he'd stop pacing. "What I want most is for things to keep going the way they are. I want to see my family and friends. I definitely want to see you as much as possible, but not at the expense of avoiding everyone else. I've tried that, and it doesn't make me happy."

Jason frowned, looking him over like he wouldn't have another chance to do so. "Whatever you want," he said. "I'll take what I can get."

"It's not just about me," William said. "What do you want? I mean now. Say it and it's yours."

Jason bowed his head and gave it thought. "I want to hold you. Actually, I don't want to stop touching you at all. Not for the rest of the night. We can go inside and eat ice cream or watch TV, just so long as you stay close to me."

William smiled. "That's an easy wish to grant."

"You say that now," Jason said, "but just wait until you need to use the bathroom. It's going to get weird, but I don't care. I'm not letting you out of my sight."

"We could leave the bathroom door cracked and hold hands through the gap."

"Not good enough. If you've gotta poop, I'll be sitting on your lap."

William made a face. "That's disgusting."

Jason was shameless. "Do we have a deal?"

"Here's my counter offer. I get private bathroom breaks, and in return, I'll call my mom and tell her I'm spending the night. If she won't let me break curfew, I'll officially run away from home."

"Deal," Jason said. "Are you a light sleeper?"

"No. Why?"

"Because I'm going to brick up the door to my room from the inside. I'm not letting you get away." He made it sound like a joke, but his grip on William's hand was tight, his eyes earnest. They loved each other. If only time wasn't so precious and scarce. William wished he could rewrite their story, find Jason when he was still on his own in Houston and begin there. That way they could have had years together instead of mere months. He felt cheated, even though his own decisions were to blame. All he could do is remind himself that it wasn't over. Not quite yet.

Chapter Seventeen

"Look at my little man! He's so handsome!"

William stopped on his way down the stairs to roll his eyes at his mother's words. Even if he did feel handsome. This was his first time in a tuxedo, and he was having visions of being in a high-end casino, rolling dice and flirting with hot waiters. His mother calling him "little man" made him feel considerably less cool. Spencer and Errol snickering from the couch didn't help either. He stomped down the rest of the stairs, glaring at his brothers.

"Wait, honey!" his mother said, hurrying forward. She had her camera out. "Go back up the stairs for me and pose."

William glowered, then did what he was told.

His mother snapped photos, gasping in delight. "Okay, now walk down the stairs, but slowly."

"Like one of those girls from the Deep South," Errol said. "What are they called?"

"Debutantes," Spencer supplied helpfully, nudging Errol. "Willy is our own southern belle!"

They both went into fits of laughter, Errol toppling over and practically weeping.

William shifted his glare from them to his mother. "This is embarrassing!"

"Won't Jason be thrilled!" she replied, oblivious to it all. "You look so beautiful."

"I'm not a girl!"

Kate lowered the camera. "No, but I've never had a daughter, so humor me and smile while you walk down the stairs. I want a video of this."

Errol and Spencer lost it, howling now. William stomped down the stairs, not hiding his misery. Then he heard a car outside and hurried forward to check the window. A black stretch limo!

"He's here!" William said, bad mood vanishing. He turned to his family, who would no doubt spoil the magic. "I'll meet him outside. See you later!"

"No!" his mother cried. "I need photos of you together!"

He jabbed a finger at his brothers. "Then make those two leave the room!"

"We'll be good," Spencer said, elbowing Errol so he would stop snickering. "I know what a big night this is for you."

They had no idea, but explaining it to them would only make them laugh harder. For William, this wasn't just about going to prom. He wanted tonight to be the memory he and Jason held on to while they were apart. His recruitment officer had called with his departure information. The remaining time he and Jason had left together was slipping away.

"Just one photo," his mother pleaded.

"In and out," William replied.

Errol snorted. "That's usually what happens on prom night!"

"I just don't want to be late!" William snapped at him.

"Then you better make sure he wears a condom," Spencer said, shoulders shaking.

"You guys suck." William raised a fist. "And if you make that into a joke, I'll beat the living—"

The doorbell rang, and suddenly he no longer cared about his brothers. William opened the door, imagining Jason in a tux similar to his own, his hair slicked back. Instead Jason's hair was unruly as ever. He hadn't even shaved, the scruff a stark contrast to his formal attire, although the metallic blue bow tie, the gray piping lining the lapels, and the jacket tails all asserted his nonconformity. William looked him over, feeling a little weak in the knees. Currently Jason was holding out a flower.

"Is that a corsage?" Errol called from the couch.

Jason's eyes flicked to him and back, then remained on William as he stepped forward. "It's a boutonnière," he said, voice low. "The florist said a red tulip would be best, since it symbolizes romance, but I thought the white would look better on you."

"What does white symbolize?" William asked, cheeks flushing as Jason pinned it to him.

"Purity."

Their eyes met, then they both snorted.

"Should I have gotten you a bouton—What was it?"

"Boutonniere, and no. I don't do flowers." Jason smiled. "I'm not even sure I do dances."

They became aware of a camera clicking, Kate moving to capture them from multiple angles. When she looked over the lens, tears were in her eyes. "Could you stand by the fireplace?"

"Sure," Jason said, offering his arm.

They paused on the way so William could introduce his brothers, bracing himself for more dumb jokes, but Errol seemed a little emotional too. Spencer remained composed, shaking William's hand after Jason's. "You look great together. It's going to be a magical night." No repressed amusement or leering smile. Just sincerity.

"Thanks," William said, nodding his appreciation.

His mother took an ungodly amount of photos, but he was glad, since he wanted them too. Just not as much as he wanted to be alone with Jason.

"We should probably get going," he said.

"You boys have fun." Kate followed them to the front door. "Don't drink. Or do drugs!"

"Mom!" Spencer said, putting an arm around her. "He's an adult now. Let him be."

His mother seemed unwilling to accept this, but she nodded, breaking free to kiss William on the cheek. Then they were outside. Jason hurried to open the limousine door for him. William slid inside, amused by the long seats and mini-bar.

"Just so you know," Jason said, sitting next to him, "I didn't pay for this. I asked Tim if I could borrow the Bentley, and he offered to rent us a limo instead."

"He's so nice!"

"He didn't want me dinging up his car again," Jason said. "But yeah, he's also nice. I couldn't talk him into stocking the bar with real booze, but I'm willing to share a Mountain Dew with you."

William tried his best to look debonair. "I take mine on the rocks."

Soon they were sipping neon green liquid from wine glasses, one of which had ice in it, and that felt about right. Neither of them had an appreciation for the finer things in life, and a couple of rented tuxedos and a limo wouldn't change that. They goofed around, Jason stretching out on one of the seats in an attempt to hog all the space. William played bartender and combined a number of drinks to make the grossest possible combination. Then he dared Jason to drink it. Which he did.

"What was in that?" Jason asked, eyes watering.

"Tomato juice, Coke, black pepper, grape juice—"

"I don't want to know the rest. Here, you try it."

"Uh, no."

"Then come give me a kiss," Jason said, taking another sip of the brew.

"So you can spit it in my mouth? No thanks."

Jason shook his head adamantly, expression innocent, but he didn't speak, proving his true intention. Then he swallowed and stuck out his tongue. "Blech! Holding it in was even worse!"

William laughed and pulled out a pack of gum. "Here. I *will* be kissing you tonight, but not until you chew one of these. Actually, make it two."

They felt more reserved when they reached the hotel ballroom where the dance would take place. Limos were everywhere, the parking lot filled with teenagers trying to look their best, and for the most part, succeeding. The energy was frantic, but in the best way possible. William felt like he was going to a mass wedding. Jason seemed a little less enthusiastic, eyeing the crowds warily and standing stiffly at his side when they had their photo taken. He relaxed when they entered the actual ballroom.

"This brings back memories," Jason said.

"Of your own prom?"

"This *is* my prom. I dropped out before I could go to my own, not that I would have had a date. No, I was thinking of Marcello's fundraiser and what that night led to."

"Play your cards right and you might get lucky again," William said. "Wanna dance?"

Jason looked around, brightening up when he spotted someone. "Hey, there's Lily and Isaac! Let's go say hi."

William was happy to do so, pulling Lily aside so they could squeal in excitement.

"This is so hot," Lily said. "I didn't give a crap about prom for all those years, but with us graduating soon and everything coming to an end…"

"It's epic," William agreed. "Is it wrong that I want to skip ahead to after the dance?"

"If I can wait, so can you," Lily said. "Savor the night. They don't do stuff like this in college. This is our last hokey high school experience, and between you and me, I'm loving it."

"Me too!"

"Mind if I butt in?" Isaac said, shooting William a wink. "I think it's time we hit the dance floor."

Isaac offered his hand, and when it was accepted, he led Lily toward the growing number of shaking bodies. William looked to Jason hopefully, but his date was casting around for another excuse.

"Where's the punch bowl you always see in movies?"

"I don't think they do that anymore," William said. "It's not hygienic. Besides, after everything we drank in the limo, you can't be thirsty."

Jason tried again. "Maybe I should use the restroom. I think I saw one over there. Let's go."

William stayed where he was. "You don't dance?"

"Do you?"

"Not really, but all you have to do is move to the rhythm. You're the music guy. That shouldn't be too hard."

"Yeah, but maybe instead we could—"

"We're at a *dance*. You knew this was coming."

"I know, but—"

"Do you love me?"

Jason peered at him. "If I say no, does it mean I don't have to dance?"

"Yes, but I'll break down in tears. I'll be *wailing*. Really loud. It'll cause a scene."

"Fine," Jason said, sounding resigned. "Lead the way."

"Just stay close to me," William said. "It'll be fun. You'll see."

For a guy who protested too much, he did just fine. They found their goofy mood again, shaking their hips and not trying to impress. Jason even managed to look cool, his tails catching the air when he spun around. All around them drama erupted, but William ignored it, only having eyes for Jason. He longed for a slow dance, but when that didn't happen, decided they could be just as close during a fast song, their bodies grinding against each other. That was sexy, but it didn't last long.

Someone jostled into them, forcing them apart, and it was no accident.

"Oh sorry," a guy said, breath reeking of hard liquor. "I thought this was a high school dance, not a gay bar."

William recognized him. Mack Tucker, one of the popular kids. He and the two guys flanking him were on the football team. "You sure you're not looking for a gay bar?" William retorted. "I don't see any ladies with you."

Mack didn't find this funny, his sneer becoming a snarl. "Shut your mouth, faggot!"

Jason pushed past William and swung. Not the best combination, because he stumbled and missed completely. Two of the guys laughed. Mack looked deeply offended. Nobody in school was dumb enough to mess with him. He had too many friends and muscles, but the high school cliques no longer mattered, and William was in better shape, thanks to his fitness regimen. When Mack lunged for Jason, William stepped between them.

"You're drunk. I'm stone-cold sober. Do you really want to find out who has faster reflexes right now?"

Mack sized him up. William stared him down and prayed that Jason wouldn't start swinging again.

"Whatever," Mack said, pushing past them. "Have fun sucking each other's dicks."

"We will!" Jason shot back. His chest heaved with indignation, fists clenched at his sides.

William placed a hand on his shoulder, noticing how tense it was. "Just forget about it."

Jason spun around. "I won't let anyone mess with you!"

"Thanks," William said gently, "but I don't need another hothead in my life. Let it go. The opinion of some random jerk isn't worth ruining our night."

Jason exhaled. "You're right. I just hate when—" He shook his head. "You're right."

"Are you guys okay?" Lily had reached them, concern on her face. She wasn't alone. Many of the other students around them, mostly the girls, were equally upset.

"We're fine!" William said. "We're here to dance, right? So let's dance!"

Doofy, but it worked. He started shuffling his feet, smiling at Jason to encourage him to do the same. In truth, adrenaline was still shooting through his system, but this was a good way of shaking it off. He was relieved when a slow song played and he had an excuse to pull Jason close.

"About time," William said. "If I got any sweatier, we would have stuck together."

Jason remained somber. "You were amazing. How you handled yourself, I mean."

"Thanks," William said.

"You really know how to keep your cool. That's important in an emergency. The Coast Guard is lucky to have you."

William squeezed. "And you really know how to make a guy feel loved."

"Can we go?" Jason murmured. "Not because of those guys. I just want to be alone with you. We don't have much time left."

William felt a lump in his throat. "I want my slow dance. Afterwards…"

Jason complied, holding him throughout the song and not pulling away when the next one was slow too. They kissed, chasing away any thoughts of homophobic nitwits, but William swore he could hear the clock ticking. When the song ended and was replaced by one with a funky beat, Jason pulled away, expression questioning. William nodded. It was time to go home.

Home in this case wasn't his own. The limo drove them to the outskirts of Austin and down a long drive. Jason was quiet for most of the ride. William understood why. They had spent a lot of time together lately, and even though William said he wanted a normal life, he had thrown himself into the relationship, savoring every minute they had left. As the big day neared, Jason became more and more preoccupied with William's inevitable departure. He never tried to stop him, or change his mind, but their impending separation was clearly taking its toll. One of them was embarking on a new adventure. The other would wake up to his usual life, except the bed beside him would be empty.

And speaking of empty, they had the entire house to themselves. Jason announced this as he unlocked the door, but he didn't say it with gusto. He still seemed pensive.

"Where are they staying?" William asked.

"Somewhere on the West Coast. I don't remember. Ben wanted to go shopping and Tim wanted to see some museum. Watch out, Chinchilla is faster than you'd think."

The bulldog leapt around their feet, not getting very far off the ground. This helped cheer Jason up. He scratched her rump, talked to her in a baby voice, and led the way to the back yard so she could go outside. Samson came out of hiding when they returned indoors, leading them to the kitchen. Jason took off his jacket and rolled up his sleeves to get a plate of cat food ready. Then he set Samson on the counter so he could eat. Only when they retired to the living room did his somber expression return. He put on light music, then moved to the couch, staring off into the distance as if he could already see the lonely future.

"Maybe you should get a pet of your own," William said. "Ben and Tim each have theirs. You should too." A companion so he wouldn't feel so alone. These words seemed to fall on deaf ears. "Jason!"

His head snapped around, expression still pained. "Sorry!"

How could William possibly leave him like this? "You're breaking my heart."

"You broke mine first." Jason's smile was more than a little sad.

"I know what'll cheer you up." William scooted closer to him, murmuring against his neck. "Do you want to do it in Ben and Tim's bed?"

"What?" Jason looked incredulous. "Why?"

"They're so hot! We can pretend we *are* them."

Jason chuckled. "You're way too into them."

"I don't care. They're an awesome couple. I envy them."

"Yeah, me too. The answer is no, by the way, but if I had said yes, who would you pretend to be?"

"Ben," William said instantly. "I figure he's the—you know. I mean, Tim has that aggressive side to him, so he must be the top."

Jason thought about this, his response careful. "So you would want to be the bottom?"

"Yeah."

"But you're huge!"

"So? Oh I see. Bottoms have to be slight and feminine, is that it? Don't judge a book by its cover."

Jason grinned and moved closer. "But it's such a pretty cover." The kiss didn't last long, Jason pulling back again. "So Kelly is a top?"

"No!" William laughed. "No no no. That's just one more thing I did to make him happy."

"So you've never actually…"

"Nope."

Jason remained confused. "Then how do you know you're a bottom?"

"Because the whole time I was topping Kelly, I was thinking how bad I wanted someone to do that to me. Maybe not Kelly." William poked him in the chest. "Maybe someone like you. Wait, are you a bottom?"

Jason seemed excited. "So there's still a first for you."

"I told you I was saving myself for prom," William said. They'd been joking about it for weeks, although they had done plenty of other things in the interim.

Jason grinned. "I guess I was too."

"No! Seriously? Oh my god!" William felt like bouncing up and down on the couch and clapping. Thankfully, he managed to restrain himself. "This is so momentous. I mean, if that's something you want to do."

"Yeah!" Jason said. "Desperately. Uh, but not in Ben and Tim's bed. In my room. I want it to happen there."

So the memory would remain near, even when they were far apart. The notion was romantic and had William ready to go. He kissed Jason, mentally questioning if he was really ready for this. The answer was a resounding yes. He stood and offered his hand, pulling Jason to his feet and leading him upstairs.

"I just need to grab a few things," Jason said as they were passing the bathroom. "Meet you in my room? Emphasis on the *my*. Don't go sneaking down the hall to the master bedroom!"

"Shut up," William chuckled.

He went into Jason's room, impressed that it had been cleaned since he saw it last. It still wasn't as organized as he preferred, but he appreciated the effort. He decided to surprise Jason by being undressed, so he hurried to get his clothes off. Then he noticed the guitar and inspiration struck. He grabbed it, sat on the corner of the bed, and pretended to play. He didn't actually touch the strings, but instead made guitar noises as best he could with his mouth, sounding more like a boat engine. "Brummm brum brum."

Jason started laughing the second he walked in. "I normally just take off my shirt."

William set aside the guitar, exposing himself. "Maybe you should take it a step further."

"Hey, there's a flute behind the guitar!"

"Know how to play it?" William asked, opening his legs.

"I'll do my best."

Jason kept his distance, undoing his bow tie and tossing it at him. That was cute. Having to dodge his shirt, socks and pants wasn't. "If you throw your underwear at me..." William said warningly.

"You'll what?" Jason said. He stood there naked, arm primed with undies crumpled up in his fist.

"I'll put them on."

Jason cocked his head, considering the threat. "Would you take them off again eventually?"

"Only after I'd gotten home. First I'd put on the rest of the tiny man clothes you threw at me so I could leave."

"I'm not tiny!"

William grabbed Jason's shirt and put it on, trying to tug the front closed. The buttons wouldn't meet the holes.

"This isn't good for my self-esteem," Jason complained.

"You don't like my muscles?" William asked.

"I love them," Jason said, letting the underwear drop. Then he did his best to flex. "Do you like mine?"

"I love your body," William said, shrugging out of the shirt. "I think. Bring it closer so I can double check."

Jason strutted forward, already hard. That was exciting. William adored all of him, but of course some parts were more alluring than others. He stooped to take Jason's cock in his mouth, running his hands up his back. Then he placed his palms on the bed to support himself because Jason had started thrusting. He felt something beneath one hand, using his fingers to identify it. The bow tie.

"Hey," William said, leaning back. "Put this back on."

Jason laughed. "We're not playing waiter again."

"No, but I think it's hot."

He held it out, and Jason complied, looking suspicious as he wrapped the ribbon around his neck and struggled to get it tied. "You know this is the one Tim wore that night."

"Is it?" William asked innocently.

"You're such a perv."

"Says the guy who chose to wear it to prom."

"Maybe I was hoping some of his sex appeal would rub off on me. Now then, if I'm going to be a topless—and bottomless—waiter, I might as well serve you."

Jason got to his knees, returning the favor, and while the blowjob felt great, William focused on his messy hair, running his fingers through it and feeling a little melancholy, because he was going to miss it and everything else about this person.

"Come here," he said, tugging on Jason's arm.

He crawled into bed, Jason doing the same. Then William rolled over onto his side.

Jason scooted close behind, wrapping an arm around him.

"One of these days I'm not going to let go again." He pressed his lips to William's shoulder and ran a hand up and down his thigh, tickling him.

William rolled over to face him so they could kiss. Jason wiggled his hips, making their cocks bang together. "Sword fight," he said with that mischievous smile of his. How he could be tender one second and so goofy the next was baffling, but William added it to the list of the things he liked.

"I'm ready," he whispered.

"Okay. Um."

William smooched away his concern. "I've got a lot of experience you can learn from."

Jason looked relieved. "I'll need all the help I can get."

"Get on your back. It's always easier if you let the bottom, I mean me, be in control. That way I can set the pace. At the beginning anyway."

Jason rolled over, groping for the condom on the nightstand. "Want to do the honors?"

"Sure." William sat on Jason, bouncing up and down to make him laugh. Then he twisted around to get Jason suited up, which was trickier than he thought it would be. The bottle of lube came next. He poured some on his finger and slid it inside himself. William had been practicing, fantasizing about this happening without knowing if it would.

"Okay," he said, making sure Jason's cock was drenched in lube. "Let's find out if this is something I really want or not."

He sure liked the idea when Jason was rubbing against his butt. That felt good in its own way. Actually getting it to go inside was a lot trickier. After a few false starts, he went for it, instantly regretting his brashness because it freaking hurt. He thought of Kelly, having been on the opposite side of this situation, and used the same phrase he always had.

"Play with me."

Jason started stroking him. Everything changed. Pain shifted to pleasure, and while William still had to proceed with caution, this no longer seemed impossible. They moved slowly, Jason going deeper a fraction at a time. Then William was sitting on him completely, butt cheeks touching hip bones. He rose up and down again, moaning in pleasure. His fantasies had always been a little different though.

"Let's roll over, but try to stay inside because that was harder than I thought it would be."

William lowered himself, pressing their torsos together. This took some doing, but they managed to roll over. Jason pushed himself up, palms to either side of his head. William's legs were in the air, the position alone making him wild, but when Jason carefully pumped his hips…

"Is that okay?"

"Yeah." William rasped. "Oh man… Go to town!"

Jason put a shoulder under one of William's legs. That seemed more comfortable for him, but he still moved slowly. William grasped at him, wanting him to pump faster—harder—but knowing they should play it safe. They got there eventually, Jason's cheeks flushed, his eyes glazed over with pleasure. He leaned close to kiss William, hissing against his lips at times. Then he pulled back, eyes questioning. William nodded. He'd been on the verge since they rolled over. He didn't want to hold back anymore and didn't. Jason growled in ecstasy as he came too. William struggled to breathe. He knew it would feel good, but this was off the charts!

Jason moved out from under his leg and collapsed onto him. William caught him in his arms. Jason remained inside, which was fine with him.

"I love you," William whispered.

"I know. I could feel it. I love you too."

They held each other, the heat of their bodies keeping each other warm. Then Jason pulled away, but only to get a towel so they could clean up. Once they had, William rolled over on his side, wanting to be held again. He crossed his arms over his chest, feeling like his heart was going to explode, words insufficient to express the depth of emotion he felt.

"I can't go," he said, swallowing against the tears, but they came anyway. "Not after that. There's no way. I can't."

Jason tightened the arm around him. "You have to. It's your dream."

"That's not my only dream," William said. "I've been waiting for you without even knowing it."

Jason was quiet, his voice hoarse when he replied. "I'm not going anywhere. I'll still be around when you need me. You'll see."

"This isn't goodbye," William promised. They would make it work somehow. Four years was a long time, but he couldn't imagine these feelings ever fading. Their love would keep them together. Ben and Tim had proven it was possible. If they could do it, he and Jason could too.

"I always pictured you getting on a boat." The tone was humorous, and Jason wore a brave smile, but William knew him well enough to see through it. "This feels wrong."

That they were at the airport? Or that they were about to say goodbye? "I have to take a plane to where the boats are," William said. He knew Jason understood this, but with their time at an end, all that remained were superficial words that failed to mask how much this hurt.

"I know you're freaking out," Spencer said. "And it's only going to get worse during boot camp, but stick with it. After a few weeks, you'll feel like you've found a new family. You won't depend on us anymore."

That couldn't be true. William considered the people surrounding him. Errol was present and trying to flirt with Lily, getting a cold shoulder in return. Lewis had met them at the airport, insisting on seeing him off, which felt like a miracle and a gift because Kate was also there, and so far, they had remained civil to each other. His family and friends gathering around him made William realize just how lucky he was. He wanted that for Jason too, and hoped that Ben and Tim would take care of him in his absence.

"Knock em' dead, baby brother," Errol said, giving him a hug.

"Come back to us," Lily chimed in, doing the same.

His mother clutched him tightly, her tears leaving wet marks on his cheek. His father was misty-eyed too. "I'd rather you joined the Marines," he teased, "but other than that, I couldn't be prouder."

His mother insisted on another hug. "If there's one thing I did right," she whispered, "it's you. Go help people."

Great, now he felt like crying, which sucked because the most difficult goodbye was yet to come. Jason shuffled forward uncomfortably, searching for the right words. When he found them, they weren't meant for William. "Could you guys look away for a second?"

Everyone suddenly became interested in their surroundings. After winning that small bit of privacy, Jason embraced him, his kiss meant to express how he felt inside. William understood, but in case he hadn't…

"I won't stop loving you," Jason said, face hard with determination. "Even if we never see each other again, I won't stop. Ever. I swear."

William stared at him, unable to speak, certain it would make him cry. Jason took a step back, hand sliding over him and down one arm until only their fingers were touching. Then he let go and turned away. William did the same, knowing if he didn't go now, he would never find the strength. He looked back only once—at the same time that Jason just happened to. He took some reassurance in that. This wasn't the end of their story. He wouldn't let it be.

Part Three
Cape Cod, 2011

Chapter Eighteen

Transitioning between vastly different worlds was never easy, but over the past two years, William had become something of an expert. The first return home to Austin was accompanied by a sense of pride. Basic training was behind him, and thanks to his ASVAB score and hard work with his first unit, he was officially an E-3 and on the waiting list for "A" school. Even just relaying these most basic of facts was enough to confuse most people back home, including his mother. By the time he explained it all, she was past excitement or surprise, but she managed to be proud of him anyway.

Seeing Jason again… That felt good, although the communication problems only continued. They were in a familiar environment—Jason's bedroom—but they might as well have been speaking a different language.

"I had this amazing conversation with a petty officer," William said, "and he assured me that if I keep going the way I am, I'll make rescue swimmer. He says the biggest obstacles are psychological and that I'm determined enough to see it through."

"Sounds like a nice guy," Jason replied.

"He is."

"Then why'd you call him petty?"

William laughed. He couldn't help it. "Chief petty officer, actually. That's just his rank. I know it sounds weird, but this guy is an AST and thinks I can be too."

"AST?"

"Aviation Survival Technician."

Jason shook his head. "I thought you wanted to be a rescue swimmer?"

"I do! That's just the name of the rating."

"Ratings like movies have?" Jason grinned. "Rated R for restricted! Rated AST for awesome sexy tankman!"

"Tankman?"

"I made it up on the spot. Give me a break."

"I'll give you something!" William said, leaning closer.

"Again?" Jason asked, but he clearly wasn't averse to the idea. Regardless, after a few kisses, he pulled back. "I was worried I'd never see you again. I barely even heard from you."

"Sorry. They keep us busy. *Very* busy."

"Did you get all my letters? I only got one from you."

"Yeah, sorry. But when I've got liberty, I mostly just want to sleep."

"Liberty?"

William tried not to smile. "Time off."

Jason looked exasperated. "Then why don't you just say that?"

"Because active duty means never having time off."

"But you just said—"

"I know, but if they need me now, I'm expected to respond."

Jason scrunched up his face. "Better put your pants back on then."

"No time. When the call comes, I'll have to make a beeline for the airport, even if I'm buck naked."

This had earned him a laugh. "Let's talk about something else. The Coast Guard already gets most of your time. I'm tired of sharing. Within the confines of this bedroom, the Coast Guard doesn't exist."

Most people he knew felt that way. They might not be open enough to say so, but when he spoke of the Coast Guard, the conversation quickly reached the point of polite interest. No follow-up questions, no shared excitement. Spencer was the only person he found it easy to talk to since they could compare notes. Being a Marine was different, but they were both enlisted in the service. Civilians simply didn't understand the finer details of military life, so William drew a line in the sand. When he was home, he learned to talk mostly about whatever the big movies that year had been, or news events that everyone followed. This was hard though, because the Coast Guard *was* his life. Before too long, it began to feel more like home than Austin did. When he finally did start "A" school, entire weeks went by without a single thought of his life back in Texas. He no longer had time for pop culture or long emails and was too focused elsewhere to bother with texting.

Training to become a rescue swimmer nearly broke him. William gave all of himself—more than he realized he had—to graduate. He did though! He walked away from the experience feeling as though he had survived a war, especially considering that half of those entering the program didn't make the cut. When he visited home again, he was greeted with celebrations, but once the parties were over, he found himself even more alienated from his friends and family. He didn't care about Charlie Sheen's simultaneous meltdown and comeback or that Oprah had broadcasted her final talk show episode. All he could think about was putting what he had learned to good use.

He didn't stop caring about people though. When he did focus on the past, Jason was the first he thought of, and when making brief trips to Austin, the person he most wanted to see. As William settled into the routine of his new life, he began to miss what he had left behind. Such as now. He was at the place where he both worked and lived, Air Station Cape Cod, and while he had once imagined he would spend most of his rescue swimmer days dangling from a helicopter, currently he was engaged in the less glorious task of checking PFDs for flaws.

William smiled as he worked, imagining Jason's response to this task.

"I thought a PDF was a type of file?"

"PFD," William said out loud. "Personal Flotation Device, and no, that doesn't just mean an airline seat."

PFDs ranged from life jackets to ring buoys and even full-body flotation suits. One of William's jobs was to make sure inventory was up to snuff, any flawed equipment either repaired or replaced by him. At the moment, he found himself hoping a cruise ship full of tourists would capsize so he would have something more exciting to do. After feeling guilty, he quickly amended his wish to a search and rescue drill, which would at least get him out into the warm night. Summer was here, and the last place William wanted to be was indoors. Maybe he could leave the PFDs for now and head back to the main hangar. There he could do a routine inspection on the aircraft assets, which gave him an excuse to be near the helicopters he loved so much. The hangar door would likely be open enough for him to step out briefly and watch the breeze shake the nearby trees.

A nice idea, but William remained where he was. His personal desires and his duty were two separate things, and the latter had priority. For the next hour, he systematically worked his way through the equipment and logged his findings. Only then did he leave the storeroom and go to the hangar. Despite all his training, he still felt a child-like glee when he actually saw the MH-60T

Jayhawk helicopters. He wasn't alone in his enthusiasm. A little girl was skipping around the nose of one and smiling up at it. Not far away, AMT Christie Patel was engaged in her own inspection, although her hands weren't tweaking an engine. Instead they were moving down the back of her husband to squeeze one of his butt cheeks. William discretely moved out of sight, waiting until their murmured goodbyes were completed. He greeted Max and Jenny on their way out, then laughed when he saw how starry-eyed Christie still was over their visit. Her russet skin was a shade redder around her cheeks, her raven-black hair slightly mussed. She looked like a teenager who had just played spin the bottle, which only made him laugh harder.

"Shut up!" she said, punching him lightly on the arm. "You're just jealous."

"Hopelessly," he confirmed.

"Are you hungry? There are leftovers in the mess hall. Don't worry, Max cooked, not me."

"I'm fine."

"You're not!" Christie said. "You've lost a lot of weight since boot camp."

His weight wasn't so different. AST school had simply atomized what little fat he'd had and made his muscles leaner. Not to mention he wasn't a teenager anymore. He had thought he was in great shape when arriving at boot camp, but he and many others had learned otherwise. What surprised him more was that Christie still remembered what he looked like back then. They hadn't been close, only interacting a few times. Ending up stationed together and on the same crew had changed that. William was grateful, since his mechanical skills weren't the best, and she often helped him out. Christie came from a family of coasties, some of them very high up. If he had thought his knowledge of the Coast Guard was comprehensive, that changed when he met her. She was a virtual encyclopedia, and William was always asking her questions. As for what she got out of the relationship, he wasn't so sure. Maybe she just needed someone to scarf down all those leftovers.

"Fried chicken and potato salad," Christie said seductively.

That did it. His stomach grumbled and they both laughed. "Okay. Hook me up."

They went to the mess hall—a glorified breakroom—

where food from Max's visit was still out. Her husband was a phenomenal cook. Crispy skin surrounded the fried chicken, and the potatoes were so soft that they had nearly dissolved into the mayonnaise.

"You're so lucky!" William said around a mouthful of food.

Christie smiled from across the table. "That I am. You can be too."

William shook his head. "I need to—"

"I know, I know. Focus on your duty, but we've been here almost two months. I don't know about you, but I'm settling in nicely. I don't feel so overwhelmed anymore."

"Me neither," he admitted.

"Then why not find a nice girl who will bring you food? You owe me leftovers. Believe it or not, it's possible to get sick of Max's cooking. It would also get you out of those horrible bachelor barracks."

Now she was talking marriage! To a woman, naturally. Necessity had forced William back into the closet. He tried busying himself with the food, but only a few bites were left. "Maybe once hurricane season is over."

"You have days off," Christie pressed. "You have time."

"I really don't. I train every single day and still have so much to learn, especially if I'm going to make—"

"I'm sure you could spare a few hours in the evening. You have to eat. Why not do so with a nice… with someone nice?"

He didn't like what her hesitation implied. Did she know? "I'm fine."

"You have someone already, don't you?" Christie continued trying to read him. "You've always got a spring in your step when you get back from Austin, and I don't think it's from kissing your mother on the cheek."

William chuckled. "I don't know what you're talking about."

Christie tilted her head to one side. "Really?"

"Really."

"Well, in that case, Sheila Banks was asking about you. Again. She's not the only one."

William stared at his empty plate. "Sheila isn't my type."

Christie remained quiet until he looked up. "I know we're not supposed to ask—"

"Then don't!" William snapped. He felt bad for doing so, not wanting to hurt her feelings or betray his training by losing his cool, but no other topic made him this uneasy. He had a secret weakness, an Achilles heel, and he hated how easily it could ruin everything. "I've worked really hard to get where I am," he said. "We both have. I can't throw all of that away for a relationship. Does that make sense?"

Christie nodded. "I think so. It's not always easy balancing duty and a personal life, but sometimes Max and Jenny are the only things that keep me going. I want you to have that too."

"Okay."

"A support network is important."

"I know," he mumbled.

"You've always got us! My home is your home. And my family… I don't think you'd want them, but we're there for you. I hope you know that."

"Thank you," William said.

He thought the discussion was over, but as they were cleaning up, Christie had one more thing to say. To her credit, she did so as casually as possible.

"It sounds like DADT will be repealed soon."

Don't Ask, Don't Tell, the official policy allowing gay people to serve in the military while also ensuring they could never do so openly. If William merely spoke of his sexual orientation, regardless of all the time and money the government had invested in him, and no matter how much he had achieved, his military career could be over.

"I have a cousin," Christie continued. "He's gay, and he says he'll enlist if that comes to pass. I hope it does. Not just for him, but for anyone serving who is forced to live a lie."

William didn't express his agreement. "If they're smart, those people will keep their mouths shut until it's official."

"I guess you're right."

They walked side by side back to the hangar, Christie finally changing the subject. "You have some time off soon, don't you?"

"Just a long weekend really, but yeah. I'm flying to Austin."

"Better get that liberty in while you can! Like you said—" Christie nudged him. "—hurricane season."

"I'm a little nervous about that," William admitted. "As in I'm trying not to freak out."

After a brief silence, Christie exhaled. "Yeah. Me too."

* * * * *

William returned to his quarters after forty-eight hours of duty. His mother had practically fainted when he first told her of his weekly schedule, how he was often on the clock for two days at a time. It wasn't as bad as it sounded. He wasn't expected to go without sleep for two days. Bunk beds in the overnight berth provided a place to sleep during the late hours. He just needed to be on standby in case an SAR or any other emergency happened in the middle of the night. Still, it felt good to return home to his own bed. Usually.

Christie's words remained on his mind as he entered the bachelor barracks. They weren't so different from what many people his age experienced in college. A three-story building with public recreational areas, communal restrooms, laundry machines, and other essential facilities located within. William had a room to himself on the third floor, which he went to immediately. He only had a few hours to pack before his flight. After entering, he closed the door behind him and surveyed his living quarters.

Empty, tidy, and efficient. He had a bed to sleep in, a dresser to stow his belongings, a small refrigerator for food, and a desk and chair to work at. From the doorway, it was difficult to tell that anyone lived here. All part of the rules. Their rooms weren't supposed to be messy with personal belongings. William took this to an unnecessary extreme, keeping flat surfaces clear except for a laptop and a small collection of books. He allowed himself to imagine the room cluttered with toys, Jason Grant sitting up in bed, placing a finger to his lips so William wouldn't wake the sleeping child next to him. Wouldn't that be something?

Of course a small room like this was no place to raise a family. Nobody was expected to. Married couples in the Coast Guard were provided with larger housing. Heterosexual couples, at least. Even though two men could get married in Massachusetts, this didn't mean the military recognized such relationships. That wouldn't change even if DADT was repealed. Still, it was a nice fantasy.

William dropped the duffel bag he was carrying, grabbed a carton of juice from the fridge, and sat on the edge of the bed while drinking from it. Then he considered the lifeless room again and sighed. Maybe Christie was right. The hardest part was behind him now. While the future still held challenges, he had made it this far. He had become a rescue swimmer. Dream achieved. What about the next one? William wasn't selfless. He felt honored to serve, but he also wanted more for himself. A husband. A family. He read the news whenever DADT appeared in headlines and knew the hateful policy might be on the way out. If so, that meant an end to two years of secrecy. He could be with Jason again and would actually have time for him during his days off.

In a different world, maybe.

William stood, tossed the empty juice carton in the trash, and turned to the dressers to begin packing. The first drawer he opened gave him pause. There, next to his socks and underwear, was a red helicopter. He took the Transformer out, spinning the propeller and thinking of Kelly. To his surprise, he felt an ache of sorrow, missing what they once had. Jesus, that showed how lonely he was feeling! William never imagined Kelly as being part of this world. They had never planned on it, at first because Kelly had his own goals and later… On some level they both knew it wouldn't last. Jason was different. They had only gotten started before they were forced to part again, but now that William had more or less settled down, they could at least discuss the possibility. Jason couldn't live on the base with him, and they definitely couldn't be open, but behind closed doors was the potential for love. Setting down the helicopter, William started packing, mind still whirling with possibility long after the toy propeller had stopped spinning.

"How do I look?" William said. He stood in the living room, arms spread wide. His mother scrutinized the tight jeans and even tighter navy blue T-shirt before she stood up from the couch and moved toward him with a concerned expression. Errol remained on the couch, peering at a laptop. He was living at home again, having left his most recent girlfriend and the apartment they shared. Funny that William intended to do the opposite. By the end of the night, he hoped he and Jason could—

"Blech!" he said, leaping backward, but too late. His mother's saliva was smeared on his cheek, her thumb reaching toward him again. "Just tell me what I have on my face, and I'll get it off myself!"

"Looks like shaving cream," she said, still reaching for him.

He held up a hand to ward her off. "Mom! Please!"

"Oh fine," she said with a resigned sigh. "You look very nice. Do you always wear cologne these days?"

"No," he admitted.

"So you're wearing it for Jason?"

He shrugged sheepishly. "Yeah."

"Are you back together? I thought you broke it off before shipping out."

"We did."

"Then why do you keep spending the night at his house? I'm not asking for details but… Are you sexually active?"

"Sexually active?" William repeated incredulously.

"She wants to know if you and Jason are doing it," Errol supplied helpfully. "Hey, we need to discuss more important issues. It says here that the Coast Guard confiscated over a hundred thousand pounds of marijuana last year. What's up with that?"

William ignored him, addressing his mother instead. "I might not be home tonight. Does that answer your question?"

"No, because you often spend the night over there and claim to be single." Kate put her hands on her hips. "I like Jason. If you *are* together, you could at least invite him over so I can see him. Stay here instead! Or are you ashamed of your mother?"

William shook his head. "We're not together. We can't be. But when we hang out, all the feelings and uh—everything else—is still there."

She narrowed her eyes suspiciously. "So it's an open relationship?"

"No! It's not anything. But I'm working on it."

"What I'd like to know," Errol said, raising his voice, "is what happens to all that weed? People need it! For medicinal reasons!"

"He lost his stash," Kate explained. "And if I have to hear about it one more time, I'll be the one getting stoned!"

"Best of luck with that," William said. He hugged his mother, promised to have the car back in the morning, and went outside. Only once in the driver's seat did he use the rearview mirror to wipe off the remnants of shaving cream.

He gripped the wheel while on the road, still preferring not to drive. He would rather be on his bike, but he didn't want to show up sweaty for their date. Reunion! That's what it was, not a date.

After he arrived at Jason's house and parked, he wiped his palms on his jeans, pulse picking up in anticipation when he rang the bell. The guy who opened the door was cute, but definitely taken. That didn't stop him from flirting a little.

"William!" Ben declared, opening his arms wide. "It's so good to see you!"

"And seeing you has me feeling good," William said, accepting a hug. "Ready to go?"

Ben disengaged and batted his eyelashes. "Tempting offer, but I think that would break a certain someone's heart."

"Jason? Or Tim?"

"Both." Ben gestured behind him. "Come on in! Jason will be down soon. He's dealing with something."

"The pimple of doom?" Tim said, showing up in the entryway and offering his hand.

"He's getting ready," Ben said a little tersely. "That's all."

"He bought makeup," Tim countered, checking William out as they shook hands. "Wow! The Coast Guard looks good on you. Maybe I should enlist myself." He flexed casually. "See what boot camp can do for me."

"There's still time," William said. "You've just got to make it through before you're forty. That leaves you what? A year? Maybe less?"

Tim pretended to be offended, even swiping at William, but only to get him in a hug. "You should go upstairs," he advised. "It's pretty bad up there. He's not coming down unless you make him."

"Tim!" Ben said in protest.

"It's fine," William said. "I can't wait any longer anyway."

He hustled through the living room and up the stairs. Jason was in the bathroom, face close to the mirror. When he saw William, he gasped and tried to shut the door. William put a hand on it to stop him. Then he laughed, because Jason's face was covered in a thick layer of powder and base. Through it he could still see the small bump to one side of his chin.

"It's not funny," Jason complained.

"It is," William said, "but only because you think a pimple could make me love you less."

Jason stared for a second. Then he looked back at the mirror and sighed. "I look ridiculous."

"Wash that stuff off so I can kiss you," William said.

Jason's eyes met his again, intense as always, like they could see straight through to his soul. "I'll be out in a second."

William nodded and went to Jason's room, which would definitely not pass inspection. He walked around, breathing in familiar scents and entertaining treasured memories. William didn't blame his mother for being confused. The truth was, he and Jason often tried to distance themselves. They didn't text much, since it wasn't as satisfying as being in person. On the rare occasions spent together, they would start out platonically, asking casual questions to see if the other person was still available. It wasn't an open relationship. William would have backed off immediately if he learned that Jason had found someone else. He never seemed to, and William didn't have time to look. That paved the way for all the old feelings and urges to return, if only for a few days. And nights. God, how he loved their nights together!

"Try not to stare at it," Jason said, reappearing. His face was still damp. He looked a lot better with the makeup gone. As for the small pink bump, William couldn't care less. There were plenty of other attributes worth staring at, such as the hint of skin revealed by the torn jeans that contrasted with the black dress shirt. He moved forward, stroking his fingers across Jason's cheek to his ear. Then he pulled away. "Sorry, are you—"

"Hopelessly single," Jason said, taking the initiative and kissing him.

William's body responded instantly. He had changed so much, inside and out, but these feelings were eternal, forever a part of him.

"That was a fantastic evening," Jason said, pulling William toward the bed. "Let's call it a night."

"Not so fast," William said with a chuckle. "I plan on enjoying our time together."

"That's what I had in mind," Jason said, but he stopped tugging and was smiling. "Where are we going?"

"Dart Bowl."

"Is that a soup place?"

William snorted, then put on a southern drawl. "You're not from around these parts, are you?"

"I guess not!"

"Dart Bowl is the most magical place in the world. Let's go."

They had made it to the front door when Jason stopped him. "I need to grab the car keys. Ben and I are still sharing."

"Not a problem," William said. "I'll drive."

"*You'll* drive?"

"Yup! I've got my mom's car."

Jason looked him over. "That explains why you're not sweaty. Are you sure you're okay with this?"

William thought back to three days earlier, when he had been dangling from a helicopter over the coastline cliffs, rescuing a teenager who had gotten stranded while trying to climb down them. "I think I can handle it."

On the drive to Dart Bowl, they chatted, mostly about other people. William always loved hearing about Ben and Tim's relationship, and Jason was polite enough to ask how his parents and brothers were doing. They didn't discuss their own lives, maybe waiting until they could focus on each other better. Besides, what William had to say was too important to take place in a car.

"Here we are!" he declared as they pulled into the parking lot.

Jason stared out the windshield, not looking too impressed by the long squat building. "Is this a bowling alley?"

"Yeah!"

"You spoil me," Jason deadpanned.

"Do you know how?"

"To bowl? Not really. I've only been once or twice, and that's when I was a kid."

William grinned. "Then you're in for a treat!"

Once they put on their rented bowling shoes and went to the lane William had reserved, he spent the next ten minutes choking down laughter as Jason landed gutterball after gutterball. His face grew redder with each failure, but that didn't make him any less handsome. William sat after taking each turn and reveled in simply being able to watch him. Back on the base he often fantasized about Jason showing up as a surprise. Or Jason being the person who needed rescuing, which in their current situation, wasn't far from the truth. William rose, hugging Jason to chase away the grumpy expression, and then taught him a few techniques. When Jason managed to wing the pins, knocking down three, he leapt around in excitement like he'd gotten his first strike.

"Good job," William said. "Now watch the master in action."

He made sure to "accidentally" get two gutterballs in a row, which thrilled Jason to no end. Totally worth it.

By the time the first round was over, William was tired of them being apart. "Are you hungry? We're only really here for dinner."

Jason scrunched up his nose. "Really? The food here is good?"

"More of a guilty pleasure," William said. "Hey, grab that table over there. I'll be right back."

The dining area, like the rest of the bowling alley, looked like a throwback from the seventies. The chairs were plastic with metal poles for legs, the carpet patterned with squiggles and swirls to hide any stains—resulting in ALL of it appearing stained—and against one wall was a bar with neon lights shaped like pins and other bowling paraphernalia. William found the waitress and placed an order with her.

"Again," Jason said when William joined him at the table, "you take me to the nicest places."

"If you want fancy, go on a date with Marcello."

Jason smiled. "Is that what this is?"

"Why not?" William replied, finally ready to admit it himself. Besides, this was the perfect segue to what he really wanted to talk about. *Move to Cape Cod and be with me.* He would approach it with a little more tact than that. "Jason—"

"Your drinks," the waitress said. "An iced tea and a Mountain Dew."

Jason grinned at him like he'd ordered champagne when in truth William had only remembered his favorite soda. William made small talk, not wanting to be interrupted a second time. He became antsy while waiting for the waitress to return, grateful when she came and plonked down two plates.

"Two orders of enchiladas, one sunny side up. Enjoy!"

Jason's stared, aghast. "Enchiladas? From a bowling alley?"

"Don't knock it until you've tried it," William said. "They're the best!"

Jason didn't seem convinced. "That's a lot of cheese. And grease. I see that wasn't enough for you."

"Gotta have the eggs too," William said, pulling the plate toward him. "Good source of protein. Are you on a diet or something? You haven't put on a single pound since I met you."

"Because I usually don't eat things like this! I'm sure you don't have to worry about it. You'll probably burn the calories by towing a boat back into port, you swimming with a rope between your teeth."

William laughed. "I'm still working on that trick."

"Have you saved any lives yet?" Jason asked, poking at his food.

"I've rescued people, but I wouldn't say that I saved any lives. Just because someone's boat is taking on water doesn't mean they would have drowned. We'll help them get to another vessel, or airlift them if the situation is a medical emergency, but saving someone is different than saving a life."

"Still pretty awesome though." Jason took a bite and looked surprised. "And so are these!"

"I knew you would like them!"

"It just so happens I saved a life," Jason said.

William leaned forward. "Really?"

"Yup. Someone brought a squirrel to the animal shelter I volunteer at. We do pet adoptions, not wildlife rehabilitation. This was just a baby someone found while out hiking. I did some research online and found you're supposed to make it possible for the mother to get the baby back, but these people weren't sure they could find the spot again. Long story short, I hand-fed that little bugger until it was big enough to be released into the wild." Jason laughed as if he was being funny, but William was enraptured.

"That's amazing. Seriously."

"It's nothing," Jason said. "Not compared to what you do."

William disagreed. "I love that you volunteer now. Animal lives are just as important as human lives."

"I sure love them," Jason said with a wistful sigh. "I'm trying to improve things at the shelter. We're doing good work there, but the cats are stuck in tiny cages. The dogs at least have pens, and those can be improved too, but the cats are the hardest. I saw this shelter online where each cat has its own space. There's enough room for them to move around, and they even have access to a small outdoor enclosure. It's going to take a lot of money, but I've got some fundraising ideas."

William was torn between feeling impressed and concerned. "It sounds like you're really setting down here."

Jason shrugged. "I guess so. There's still a lot I don't know about Austin, but it already feels more like home than Houston ever did."

William took a few bites, considering the implications. "Do you ever feel like trying other places? Or are you going to spend the rest of your life here?"

"I haven't thought that far ahead. I don't know. I've never really traveled, but I also don't feel like I'm missing anything. Some people can't wait to see the world. I guess I'm more concerned with trying to find a home."

"A family is important too. Do you feel like you've found one?"

Jason seemed overwhelmed by the question. "Sometimes. Ben and Tim… I love them. I know I should get a place of my own. I'm way too old to be— See? I was going to say living at home! That's crazy. They aren't my parents, but a lot of the time, it feels that way. I know they want me to stay, and I don't want to leave. I'll have to eventually, but for now…" Jason clenched his jaw and wiped at his eyes. "Spicy!"

He'd had one whole bite and that had been minutes ago. The enchiladas weren't making him tear up. Jason becoming so emotional at the mere thought of getting his own place had William worried about his own hopes. "I'm really glad you're doing so well," he said anyway, when really a little part of William wished Jason wanted to escape from Texas. As it stood now, asking him to move to Massachusetts would be akin to asking Jason to leave behind the only family he'd had since he was a child. "It's good that you're with people who love you."

"It's nice having someone there," Jason agreed. "When I come home, I'm not alone."

Something else William couldn't promise. They wouldn't see each other for days at a time due to his schedule, and he might be deployed elsewhere for entire weeks.

"What about you?" Jason asked. "I picture you living in a big room full of bunk beds. Sort of like you always see in movies. Is it like that? Because my first thought is how any guy finds time to jack off. Especially since the showers are public too."

"Public might not be the right word," William said, "and I have a little more privacy than that. I still manage, although Internet pornography is strictly forbidden in the barracks."

Jason was appalled. "Seriously?"

"Yup! Don't ask me why. Magazines and such are still okay, oddly enough."

"Now I know what to get you for Christmas."

They tackled their food, William not tasting much because his plans were steadily unraveling. Uprooting Jason for two years when he'd only been in Austin a little longer than that wouldn't make him happy. Not when he realized how often he would be on his own in a strange new town and an entirely different state.

"I wish you could stay," Jason said wistfully, pushing away his half-finished plate of food. "Every time you're back, it makes everything better. You have no idea."

"I do," William said. "It gets harder and harder to leave."

"What happens if you go AWOL? The Coast Guard won't find you here. There's no water around for the ships."

"You mean vessels, and you're forgetting about the air assets."

Jason snorted. "You talk weird."

"I'm about to use the head," William said.

"Huh?"

"That's how we say restroom."

Jason laughed. "What else? Say more."

"Aye-aye. We're in the mess right now, I buy my groceries from the commissary, and I berth on the third deck of the barracks."

Jason was laughing and shaking his head. "Why don't you speak like normal people?"

"Because we like to pretend we're on a boat, even when we're not."

Jason grew solemn. "You're halfway through. Do you realize? Only two more years to go."

"Assuming I don't make a career of it."

"What? I don't like the sound of that!"

"Nothing has been decided," William said hurriedly.

Jason looked sullen. "So you have a choice?"

"Aye-aye. That's how we say yes. Just in case you haven't caught on."

Jason continued to frown. "Do you want to stay longer?"

"I don't know. I'm just getting started as a rescue swimmer, so it's weird to talk about quitting."

"Okay," Jason said, "here's the deal. If I beat you in a game of bowling… Forget that, I don't stand a chance. If I get a strike, or what's the other thing called?"

"A spare."

"Right. If I get either of those, you have to come home after four years."

"Okay," William said.

"Say it like you mean it," Jason said.

After a moment, he caught on. "Aye-aye."

He used the restroom and finished his food. Then the game began. He thought he had nothing to worry about, but Jason was determined. His concentration was unwavering, his motions controlled. At first this didn't help much, but he started hitting pins with most throws. Jason insisted on another round after the first, and in the middle of it, he got his spare and flipped out, leaping toward William and grabbing him in a hug. "Yes! You saw that, right? You'll keep your promise?"

"I'll try," William murmured.

"Don't just *try*! This is legally binding! I'll take the entire Coast Guard to court if I've got to."

"Okay, okay," William said with a chuckle. "Just leave the lawyers out of it."

They finished the game and decided to go elsewhere. William felt a strange mixture of happiness and sorrow as they strolled across the parking lot. "You know that you're free," he said. "Don't you? If you find someone else, a guy who can be there for you, I don't want you to push him away because of me."

Jason groaned. "I know! You make sure to tell me that every time we see each other. I get it. We're not together. At least you think we're not."

William looked over at him sharply. "Is that really how you feel?"

When they reached the car, Jason sat on the trunk. "Does it matter? You've made up your mind."

William sat next to him. "It does because I don't want you to be alone."

"I'm not. I've got Ben, Tim, Emma, Marcello, Chinchilla… And a bunch of furry orphans. We're like a club. I'm not alone."

"You know what I mean."

"I do," Jason said, "so drop it. It's up to me if I move on or not."

"Okay." William poked his finger into Jason's ripped jeans, tickling his knee. "I can fix these for you."

"You know how to sew?"

"All part of my training."

Jason shook his head. "You're full of it."

"I'm not! It's the second phase of becoming a rescue swimmer. The sewing classes were really intense."

"Needle and thread," Jason said incredulously. "That kind of sewing?"

"We have machines too, but yes."

"During all your time training, I pictured you swimming against waves or doing endless pushups, not sewing curtains!"

"I needed to learn how to repair parachutes and other safety equipment, but I did plenty of pushups too."

"I don't buy it," Jason said. "The truth is out. I bet you made your own uniform."

"Maybe I'll sew something for you."

Jason laughed. "Do it! That would be so funny." He narrowed his eyes. "You're messing with me, aren't you?"

"Wait and see. So where to next?"

"We could go back to my place," Jason said innocently. "Maybe watch a movie. Or something."

"Or something?" William asked. Then he smiled and leaned over for a kiss. "Aye-aye."

William walked down the stairs of his mother's house. He had left Jason's house early in the morning, yearning for exercise. The lawn needed cutting, so he had done so while pushing the mower along at a jog. Now that he was cleaned up, he hoped to find his Kate making pancakes as she so often did when he came home for a visit. The kitchen was silent, meaning she had gone to work. After grabbing a bowl of cereal, he found his brother sitting on the living room floor, feet pulled close so he could clip his toenails.

"Do you have to do that here?" William complained. "I'm trying to eat."

"Then go back to the kitchen," Errol said. "This is the living room. It's for living. That's all I'm doing."

"That's debatable." William sat on the couch. "Shouldn't you be looking for a new place to live?"

"I'm on it, believe me. After two months of being here, I might as well be eight again from the way Mom treats me."

William watched as a crescent-shaped toenail soared through the air and was lost in the carpet. Maybe their mother had a good reason for treating him like a child. "Please tell me you're going to vacuum afterwards."

Errol shot him a glare. "Why are you so grumpy? Usually when you come back from Jason's place, you've got your birthday face on."

"My what?"

"You know, like you've got piles of unopened presents and a cake loaded with candles in front of you. That sort of face."

William stabbed at his cereal with his spoon, forcing the multi-colored loops to submerge. "You wouldn't understand."

"Baby brother, if it's lady problems… No, *love* problems, then you're talking to the right guy. That's all I've got!"

William considered him. Bad advice was better than no advice, he supposed. "I feel like I'm holding Jason back. I'm hardly ever around, but he's still waiting for me. He doesn't see anyone else or even try to date, as far as I can tell."

"And that's a problem?"

"I don't want him to be lonely. He deserves someone who can be there for him every day."

Errol sighed wistfully. "Man, does that sound nice. I hate being single."

"That's probably how he feels most of the time. Instead of going on dates and having fun, Jason is stuck at home because he's committed to me. Even though I keep telling him not to be."

Errol set aside the clippers and stretched out his legs. "Then maybe you should take the lead."

"Huh?"

"Remember Nicki? I think you met her once. Anyway, she broke up with me, and I was definitely not willing to say goodbye. I talked her into us staying friends. Things stayed platonic, but occasionally we'd sleep together or whatever. That was enough to string me along. I don't think she was doing that on purpose. Like you said, people get lonely, and me being there was convenient. Only when she started dating a new guy—" Errol grimaced. "That hurt like hell, but you know what? I stopped waiting around for her. I went out to a bar that night and met this completely crazy chick who helped me get over Nicki completely."

"Are you still friends?"

"Me and Nicki? I guess so, but more like 'Hey, we're at the same party!' friends instead of 'Come over to my place for pizza and a movie.' Your situation though… If Jason is willing to wait, why not let him?"

"Because he deserves better." William sighed. "I want more for him and I'm not sure we're compatible anymore. We are as people, but our lifestyles are too different now."

"You're married to the Coast Guard," Errol said, nodding his understanding. "I feel the same way toward my art sometimes. But I tell you what, I'd rather have a girl in my bed at night than a bunch of my drawings."

William frowned, remembering that old saying about loving someone and letting them go. He had always thought it was some weird test to see if they came back, but maybe it was more about loving someone enough to want them to be free. If William allowed himself to be selfish, he wanted both the Coast Guard *and* Jason. Not a guy in every port. Just one. But when he asked himself what was best for Jason, he knew what needed to be done, even if he didn't like the solution. In fact, he hated it.

Chapter Nineteen

William was performing a routine inspection on one of the Jayhawk helicopters, making sure the oxygen system was operating correctly, when he noticed an odd sound. A hissing noise. No, that wasn't quite right. More like sharp inhalation of air that kept repeating. He remained still in order to locate it and realized it was coming from outside the aircraft. He found Christie leaning against the helicopter, wiping her eyes.

"Are you okay?"

Christie snapped to attention. Then she leveled a wrench in his direction. "I'm perfectly fine! Understand?"

"Aye-aye!" he said, raising his hands in the air. "Just don't hit me!"

She lowered the wrench and her posture relaxed. "It's just been a shitty day. That's all."

"What's going on?"

"Max ate some bad fish and is puking up his guts. Jenny doesn't have food poisoning—thank god—but she does have a fever. Max is taking care of her between bouts of barfing, but they need me there."

"When's your shift end?"

"Another thirty-six hours."

William winced. "That's rough. You can't get leave?"

"During hurricane season?"

"Right."

Christie looked him over. "I take back what I said previously. You're lucky that you can focus on your duty now. You'll still have time for a family someday. I don't wish I hadn't met Max or had Jenny, but sometimes I wish it had all happened after the Coast Guard." She pinched the bridge of her nose. "Forget I even said that. I don't mean it."

"I get what you're saying," William said. "It's hard being pulled in two different directions. It's not that you don't love them or your job. You just wish you didn't have to choose between them."

"Exactly!" Christie said. "Somebody clone me because I want to be both places at once."

"I've only got another twelve hours to go," William said. "I can check on them when my shift is over. Cook dinner for Jenny or read her a story. I'm guessing Max won't be up for either."

"You sure?"

"Yeah!"

"You're the best! You'll make a wonderful father, you know that?" She poked him in the stomach and smiled. "Just don't rush into anything."

"I'll try not to."

They turned to face fast-approaching footsteps. Lieutenant Francis Peck. His name might not sound macho, but Francis's build was compact and hard, his jaw often flexing while he fidgeted, waiting for the next call to action. Then his bright blue eyes would light up, like now. "We've got an SAR!" he said, brushing past them.

The call came over the radio seconds later. William and Christie sprang into action. All thoughts of his personal problems fled as they geared up and got into the zone. Search and rescue missions required focus, not just to save the victims, but to ensure proper protocol was followed to minimize risk to themselves and others. With impressive speed, William and his crew were soon in the air.

"Aviation hobbyist called it in," Francis said over the radio built into their helmets. The nose of the helicopter dipped as it cruised out over the Atlantic. William was already scanning the waters below for anything unusual. "Pilot spotted an inflatable dinghy taking on water. No engine, just paddles."

"Number of survivors?" William asked.

"Two reported," Francis responded.

"Last known whereabouts?" Christie inquired.

"Fifteen miles out to sea."

She exchanged a look with William. "They paddled that far out?"

The crackle of the radio mixed with Francis's laughter. "We haven't had any distress calls from vessels, so it looks that way."

William returned his attention to the water. How the hell had they managed to get so far, and what was their goal? None of that truly mattered. Locate and rescue. Questions could wait. They were fighting against time, or more accurately, the fuel remaining in the helicopter, always needing to calculate how much they needed to return to base. They were in luck today. The aviation hobbyist was making repeated passes over the survivors, reporting on their location as it slowly changed. William and his crew were able to arrive on scene with minimal diversions. As soon as he had visual confirmation, he assessed the situation. The raft was useless, half of the yellow plastic submerged, the rest flat and floating on the surface. He saw two men clinging to a flotation device, but he couldn't determine what variety. When he saw they weren't wearing life jackets, he decided risk of exhaustion was the greatest threat, since neither person seemed to have much grip on whatever was keeping them afloat.

"I'm jumping," William informed his crew. No time to be lowered down on the hook.

"Aye-aye," Christie confirmed. As flight mechanic, they were a team. Of all the crew, he relied most on her competence to keep him safe, but he already knew from experience that he was in capable hands. William sat on the floor by the open cargo door, legs dangling over the edge until the helicopter had lowered enough. Then he leapt, plummeting fifteen feet through the air. He felt no fear, nor did he pay heed to the sensation of his stomach being left behind. He shot into the ocean and allowed the water to slow his descent naturally before he kicked his way to the surface. Once he emerged, he raised an arm to signal to Christie that he was okay. Then he oriented and started swimming, cutting a line toward the survivors.

He reassessed the situation when close enough: two men, both younger than himself, their faces red with sun and taut with fear. They were definitely not old enough to drink from the small silver keg they clung to. William's initial assessment had been incorrect. They did have a life jacket, but only one between them. They had wrapped it around the keg to increase its buoyancy. He couldn't decide if this was inspired or stupid, but he didn't have time to deliberate.

"My name is William," he said as he approached the survivors. "I'm a rescue swimmer with the United States Coast Guard. You're going to be okay."

The skies were clear, the waters warm, and the ocean calm aside from choppiness caused by the helicopter. This was simply a matter of getting both men to the basket that Christie had surely deployed by now so they could be hoisted to safety.

"I'm going to take you back with me one at a time," he

explained. "Before you know it, you'll be on dry land."

He reached for the survivor closest to him, but the man let go of the keg to knock his arm away. This caused the survivor's head to dunk beneath the surface. William groped in the water and grabbed the man's shirt to get his head above water again.

"Not me!" the survivor spluttered, still fighting against him. William could smell the beer on his breath. "Take my brother first!"

"I'm the better swimmer!" his sibling protested. "I'm fine. Go with him!"

The first survivor managed to slip out of William's grasp, grabbing for the keg, which bobbed dangerously. "Damn it, Richie! I'm older! If anything happens to you, Mom will—"

"I'm not going first! I was a swimmer in high school—"

"Junior high!"

"*And* freshman year," Richie growled. "You just never went to my swim meets!"

"I'm your older brother! You have to listen to me."

"Screw you, Tony! Go with him or I swear I'll swim away and—"

"Don't you dare!" Tony swiped at his brother, losing his grip on the keg.

Richie let go of it too, arms waving and legs kicking to propel himself backwards and away from them both. The situation was getting out of control!

"Stop!" William shouted, but it didn't sound very convincing. He thought of Kelly—how he so easily harnessed anger—and did his best imitation. "If you morons don't shut up and listen to me, I'll leave you both here to die! Understand?" That got their attention, so William continued in this manner. "Richie, get your ass back here and put the life jacket on. Keep hold of the keg. You'll be fine. As for you…" He grabbed Tony around the neck in a maneuver that had been drilled into him during "A" school. At the time he couldn't imagine a survivor resisting their own rescue, but now he was grateful for the training. William started moving sideways through the water, dragging Tony along with him. Any protests were silenced by each yanking motion and the water lapping over them as they neared the helicopter. The basket was ready and waiting. It could fit two people in a pinch, but he didn't trust Tony to remain there while William retrieved his brother. He'd probably swim after him in the name of drunken heroism. Once Tony was inside the basket, William instructed him to hold on tight and signaled Christie to hoist him up. He waited long enough to make sure Tony wouldn't try jumping or anything stupid like that. Then he headed back for the other brother.

When he got there, Richie's mouth was open wide as he gulped in air. His head was barely above water, chin sinking into the life jacket. "Cramp," he managed to gasp.

"I've got you," William replied, putting an arm around him. "You can let go."

"There's still a few beers left in that keg," Richie said as they abandoned it. "You should come back for it. It'll be your reward."

William slowly began the return swim. "After what you two put me through, I'll need something stronger."

"Thanks for taking him first," Richie said. "I really am the better swimmer, even if it was just junior high. I lied."

"That's okay," William said. "We're not actually with the Coast Guard. We're pirates. I hope you like swabbing decks." Then he got serious about swimming, heading for the basket that had just splashed down. Once he made sure Richie was secure, he signaled Christie again, exhaling with relief when the second survivor was safely aboard. As he waited for her to drop the hook that he would connect to his suit and ride up with, he decompressed enough to feel a sense of pride. He had made a lot of sacrifices to get here, but when he did something useful like this, it all seemed worth it.

"Two more lives saved," Christie said when they were back at the base. She held up a fist so he could bump it. "Well done."

"Well done yourself," William replied. "Two more rescues though. I don't know if we saved their lives."

Christie laughed. "Not this again! You really think they would have been okay without our intervention?"

William shrugged. "They could have floated there long enough for a fishing boat to pick them up. They were smart to hold on to that keg."

"They were stupid to have it in the first place," Christie retorted. "As usual, you hold yourself to an impossibly high standard."

"It's a rescue swimmer thing."

"I guess. When I finally get to go home, I plan on telling my family that I helped saved lives."

"I'll tell them for you," William said. "That'll be the story Jenny hears before bed. Her mother the hero."

Christie patted his arm affectionately. "You're something special. If you do have someone, I hope they realize how lucky they are."

He didn't reply to that. He couldn't, but he appreciated her kindness. For the remaining hours of his shift, he thought again about what it must feel like to have a spouse and child waiting at home—one full of life, not a minimal barrack, empty and silent. He imagined such a place for himself, replacing Max with Jason, although he would gladly keep Jenny. His fantasy soon fell apart. William was required to live on base. Jason wouldn't be allowed. And if his boyfriend did need him—if he was the one with food poisoning—Jason would be sick and alone. No child to keep him company, no Ben and Tim either, just Jason shivering on a bathroom floor after throwing up, William unable to carry him to bed because of his duty. Twelve hours, forty-eight hours, two entire weeks. The idea of leaving Jason on his own for so long— even if he wasn't sick—made his heart ache. Then he realized that's what he had been doing all along, except worse, because William had abandoned him for months at a time. Entire seasons! He couldn't let that continue.

He knew their relationship needed to end, but he wasn't entirely sure how. They couldn't break up because technically they weren't dating. Jason never took William seriously when he said he should move on, and no wonder since when they were together again, they always picked up where they had left off. Words had become ineffective, leaving action as the only option. No more cruising into town and pretending that nothing had changed between them. No more stringing Jason along.

He pulled out his phone, sending a text. *I'm glad we've managed to stay friends.*

With benefits? Jason texted back, adding a smiley face.

Just friends, William replied.

If that's what you want to call this, then I'm okay with it.

William sighed. He thought of the two brothers, both so desperate to do the right thing for each other that they only made the situation worse. Words definitely wouldn't be enough this time. One of them would have to be the first to swim away.

* * * * *

Don't Ask, Don't Tell was all but dead. A federal appeals court had forbidden the military from further discrimination against openly gay service members, the president himself certifying that by the end of September, DADT would be no more. This was cause for celebration. William came out to Christie right away, since she had always expressed interest in his personal life. She hadn't been surprised, but her response had caught him off guard.

"Does this mean the guy in Austin will be moving up here?"

"No," William had replied. "We're not together anymore."

They hadn't been together for years, but only now did that statement feel true. He hadn't contacted Jason for nearly two months. No letters, calls, or texts. William was slowly feeling like he had moved on, but then DADT died, and suddenly those discarded dreams were found washed up on the shore. They still couldn't share a home, and the Coast Guard still wouldn't recognize a marriage between two men. The love William felt would no longer have to be kept secret, but that didn't change the demands of his job, or how often Jason would be left alone.

Faced with three days of downtime, William decided to get away from it all. He took a Greyhound bus north to Boston and checked into a hotel. The first day he spent sightseeing, visiting the New England Aquarium and exploring the Boston Harbor. The next day he did some window shopping, walked the Freedom Trail, and ended up at the USS Constitution Museum. So much for getting away from it all. He kept finding himself drawn back to the water. It didn't help that, while at the museum, he saw two guys standing close together, their voices a murmur. Occasionally one touched the other in ways much too intimate to be platonic.

William decided he needed a little assistance when it came to forgetting. Booze should do the trick. As he walked back toward the city, he kept his eyes open for a welcoming bar. Preferably one without televisions blaring sports. Eventually he noticed a door with a rainbow sticker on it, and if this wasn't indication enough, a stack of the local gay newspaper was just beyond the entrance. He'd never been to a gay bar, or *any* bar for that matter. He wouldn't be twenty-one for another two months, but he'd heard other guys talk about how a military ID could open a lot of doors, so he decided it was worth a try.

The bar interior was dim, and while it did have a television, it was currently broadcasting a talk show. Not many patrons were inside, probably because it was a weekday afternoon. The few there turned to look in his direction. William felt his cheeks flush. He hurried to the bar and ordered a beer.

"ID," the bartender said without much interest. He didn't seem too awed by the military identification, but the math must have been close enough because he nodded and grabbed a tall glass. William glanced around while he waited. An older man with gray hair sat at the corner of the bar. A table by the window was occupied by two middle-aged guys sharing an animated conversation. Deeper in the interior was an empty dance floor and more tables, only two of them in use.

"Here you go," the bartender said, sliding the glass toward him.

"Thanks." William gave the guy a ten-dollar bill and told him to keep the change, mostly because he wasn't sure how much a beer cost or how tipping worked at a place like this. The bartender took it in stride and went about his business, leaving William alone. He had never been a big drinker, although he was a lot more experienced these days. He still had to hide his revulsion during the first few sips, but he knew if he kept going, the beer would start to taste better. Before long he had reached the bottom of the glass. His head hummed with a nice buzz, his troubles already distant.

"Can I get you another one?" the bartender asked.

William nodded. "Please."

"Another for me too," a voice said, someone sliding onto the stool next to his.

He glanced over in apprehension, his nerves increasing when he saw how hot the guy was. His dark hair was short and brushed to one side, a hint of copper highlights bringing color to the brown waves. He was gangly, although not in an unappealing way. He had broad shoulders, a hint of stubble on his chin, and eyes the golden color of honey. Or beer, which was soon set before them.

"Mind if I join you?" the stranger said.

William shrugged. "Fine by me."

The man continued to study him. "Sorry," he said. "I'm just trying to decide which of my pick-up lines would work best here."

"Bottoms up?" William suggested, raising his glass. The other man laughed. William joined him. They drank from their glasses, eyes locked while doing so.

"What brings you to Boston?" the man asked.

"How do you know I'm not from here?" William challenged.

"You don't have the accent."

"Neither do you."

"Case in point. I'm only here on business." That explained the salmon-colored dress shirt he wore, and the dark gray suit jacket resting on the next stool over. "What about you?"

"Pleasure," William said. Was he flirting? He didn't exactly mean to. He turned his attention to the television, which was now on a news channel. A woman celebrating her one-hundredth birthday was smiling for the camera. Then it changed to the weather, making him sit upright.

"I come up here once a month," his companion was saying. "Still haven't gotten used to the crazy streets. I spend most of my trips here lost."

"I know what you mean," William murmured, still focusing on the television as he sipped his beer. The meteorologist was making his predictions, which William ignored, since the media loved to make people think a hurricane was always imminent. Instead he paid more attention to the satellite time-lapse of cloud movement.

"This time I decided to rely solely on taxis. More expensive, but less time wasted, don't you—"

William held up a hand, the weather forecaster pointing to a swirl over the Atlantic that he felt was a potential hurricane. At the very least, another tropical storm was blowing their way. When a commercial for pizza replaced the weather map, William blinked and looked over at the man next to him.

He seemed amused. "You're a coastie, aren't you?"

William took another drink. "That obvious?"

"I've known a few through my line of work. The only people who take weather more seriously are meteorologists and my grandma."

"What kind of work do you do?" William asked.

"Aviation industry. I'm not familiar with the local bases though. The nearest one I've been to is down in Cape Cod, so don't worry, your secret it safe with me. But hey, I guess that's not an issue anymore now that what's-it-called has been repealed."

"Don't Ask, Don't Tell," William said, attempting to wash away the bitter taste in his mouth. "Can we pretend it's still a thing? I don't feel like talking about my career."

"Neither do I," the man said, eyes sparkling. "Why don't we make a game of it? We'll promise not to be honest with each other from here on out. Starting with our names. What's yours?"

William opened his mouth to answer, then clamped it shut again. "Umm…"

"Scott," the man said. "You look like a Scott. Or maybe an Adam. Yeah! I like that better. You'll be Adam. What should I call myself?"

"Steve," William said, the joke intentional. He was definitely flirting!

"Adam and Steve," the man said musingly. "Why not? Nice to meet you, Adam."

"Nice to meet you, Steve." William clinked glasses with him again, surprised that only a small amount of liquid remained at the bottom to swish around. "So what is it you do for a living?"

"I'm a ringmaster at a circus," Steve said, puffing up his chest as if he were talking about repairing cars. "Yep. That might sound like glamorous work, but when I'm not in the spotlight, I spend most of my time wrestling tigers back into their cages and trying to get the elephants to take their vitamins."

"Sounds rough," William said with a grin. He nodded when the bartender pointed to their near-empty glasses. "I'm a movie star."

Steve looked suitably impressed. "I thought I recognized you from somewhere!"

"Probably from the movie about the bottled-water addict. My character can't stop drinking it, which isn't so bad until his increasingly frequent bathroom breaks start to interfere with his personal and professional life."

"*Watered Down*," Steve said. "That was the name of it!"

William grinned. "You're quick on your feet!"

"I'm quick even when I'm not on my feet," Steve replied. Then he made a face. "That sounded better in my head."

He felt grateful when the bartender set down another round because it gave him something to focus on. Steve was cute, but William hadn't thought this through. He either needed to leave at the end of this drink, or start pretending he had a boyfriend.

"So what brings you to Boston?" Steve asked.

"I'm studying for my next role." William nodded to their surroundings. "Right now, in fact."

"You're going to play a bartender? Or a drunk?"

William leaned close and whispered, "A homosexual. I'm not gay."

Steve sighed dreamily. "Those three little words always get my heart pumping!"

"You have a thing for forbidden fruit?"

"Apples in particular. Wanna take a bite?"

They laughed together, Steve looking him over. "You're not really straight, are you?"

"Adam Beefcake is."

"Your last name is Beefcake?"

"Yup! Don't look so surprised. Very common name. It's Danish in origin. What's yours?"

"Ironrod."

"That's…" William narrowed his eyes thoughtfully. "Scottish?"

"Exactly," Steve said. "I've got a kilt on beneath these slacks. It's a tight squeeze down there. Enough about me! I want to learn more about Adam Beefcake. Who is the man behind the legend? What's his life like?"

"Not as perfect as you might think," William said. "Being a movie star is very time-consuming, and that's rough on my personal life. My girlfriend and I just broke up, in fact. We've been on the rocks for years, but now it's really over. In theory."

"How so?"

William shrugged. "I'm having a hard time moving on."

"I see." Steve nodded thoughtfully. "I might have a cure for that."

William's chest felt tight. "Oh yeah?"

"Yeah. We could get out of here. If you want."

He did. And he didn't. Jason returned to his thoughts, as he so often did, but maybe only out of habit. Jason had been his lover for more than two years now. William had once thought of Kelly just as often and couldn't imagine sleeping with anyone else until he actually had. If he was going to move on, that meant being with other people, and what better way to start than with an anonymous encounter? That would help wipe the slate clean.

"Can we finish our beers?" William asked. "I don't uh... I don't usually do stuff like this."

"Perfectly fine," Steve said easily. "I understand. So without getting too real, if you could have any profession other than what you actually do, what would it be? An actor?"

"No," William said. "A firefighter, maybe. I dressed up like one for Halloween once. Actually, I dressed up like a Dalmatian wearing a fireman's hat. Man, I haven't thought about that for years!" He rambled about a long forgotten dream. Steve did the same. This took the pressure off, enough that by the time he pushed away his empty glass, William was relaxed enough to ask a time-honored question. "My place or yours?"

Steve smiled. "Mine's just down the street."

They settled their tab and stumbled outside. The sun still hadn't gone down. In the brighter light, they sized each other up again, laughing when catching each other in the act. The dimness of the bar hadn't hidden any flaws. Steve was a good-looking guy. The dressy clothes brought back warm memories of Kelly, although he had never worn a full-blown suit. That was kind of hot. Maybe he could talk Steve into leaving it on while William blew him.

The thought made his face flush as they walked. Were they really going to do this? Would it be hot? Or awkward? They were in a hotel lobby now. Last chance to bail. He didn't. When the elevator doors closed and Steve pressed him up against the wall, William met his lips, the taste sweet, like they had been drinking different types of beer. He inhaled through his nose, taking in the musky scent of cologne. A tongue slid against his own, a hand gripped his pec, and something hard pressed against his hip. Then Steve pulled away, facing the opening elevator doors as if nothing had happened. He looked over with an innocent expression that was betrayed by a smirk.

"I hope you don't have any plans tonight," Steve said.

"None," William answered, his breath still short.

"Good."

As they walked down the hallway together, a number of

concerns rose in William's mind. This was a stranger! What if he was a murderer? Did this make him a slut? What about STDs? Each worry that bobbed to the surface was soon drowned in a sea of beer, no rescue swimmer in sight. Steve used a card to unlock one of the doors, flicked on the lights, and gestured for him to enter. William looked around the generic room for hints of who this person really was, seeing only luggage and a closed laptop on one corner of the queen-sized bed.

"Care for something to drink?" Steve asked, gesturing toward the minibar fridge.

"No," William said. "I'm good."

"That remains to be seen. But first, a couple of ground rules."

"Rules?"

Steve nodded. "You military types like structure. Right?"

William shrugged. "I'm not into being dominated, if that's where this is going."

Steve stepped into his personal space. "Have you ever tried?"

"No."

"Then how do you know?"

"Because instead of licking boots, I'd rather be licking other things."

Steve laughed. "I'm with you there. My rules are simple. I'll follow them too. Number one—" He took hold of William's hands. "—these are for touching me, not yourself."

"Okay." That was easy enough to agree to.

"Rule number two, you don't come until I say you do."

"What if it just happens?"

"Leave that to me. Rule number three is my favorite. Keeping the first two rules in mind, do whatever you want."

William acted on that one immediately. He kissed Steve again, helped him out of his jacket, and started unbuttoning his shirt. Once he got it open, he kissed Steve's neck, his chest, his stomach… Then he was on his knees and working the belt loose.

"You're hungry," Steve commented.

"Yeah," William said, rubbing a hand over the dark gray fabric of the pants to feel the hard mound beneath. "Starving."

He got the pants unzipped, pulling them and the underwear down at the same time. The cock that sprang free was—not Jason's. That was his first thought, but hormones helped banish it. He focused on bronze skin just as dark as the rest of Steve's body, which implied he sunbathed in the nude. He took the cock into his mouth, the scent slightly different than what he was used to, as was the taste and everything else. That was the point.

"Take it all," Steve was saying, a hand on the back of William's head as he slowly slid his dick deeper inside. It reached the back of his throat and didn't withdraw. William had mastered his gag reflex, but deep throating? The head of Steve's cock pressed against his tonsils, cutting off his air supply and making his eyes water. Uncomfortable, but also hot as hell. If he ever had to choke to death, this would be the way to do it! Steve pulled back, sliding all the way out before his dick pressed against William's lips to open them again. He went deep, then pulled out, slow and deliberate as the cycle repeated over and over.

"Rule number two," Steve said. "I won't come until you say I can, but right now I want to blow a load straight down your throat."

Already? William found himself nodding, his nose buried in pubic hair when the cock in his mouth throbbed and let loose warm liquid. He couldn't swallow—couldn't take in air—until Steve finally pulled out. William scrabbled at his jeans, craving relief.

"Nope!" Steve reached down to grab his wrists. "I'll take care of everything. Stand up."

William did so, urge replacing thought. He wanted everything. All of it. Steve was undressing him, William interrupting the process to kiss him, to grope the semi-flaccid erection, to touch the taut muscles of the bare torso in front of him.

"There's rock hard…" Steve said, squeezing William's dick. "And then there's steel! I'm guessing it's been a while?"

He nodded, pressing down on those broad shoulders and wanting the favor to be returned. He felt frustrated when he met resistance.

"Get on the bed," Steve instructed, guiding him toward it. "Just relax. I may have rushed, but I won't let you."

William lay on his back, but he didn't relax. He tensed and writhed as fingertips moved softly across his skin, tracing the lines of his muscles, brushing against his lips, grazing his balls. He was on the verge of insanity when Steve scooted down, using his tongue to tease him instead, tip meeting tip. William might be forbidden to touch himself, but that didn't mean he was without options. He grabbed Steve's head with one hand, his neck with the other, and thrust his hips forward. The shaft of his cock moved along that warm wet tongue until it reached its goal and plunged inside. Sweet relief! He started pumping, not intending to let rule number two stop him, but Steve was a good judge. As soon as William got close, Steve twisted free of his grip with surprising finesse.

William groaned, his dick throbbing once, but not enough to come.

"Easy," Steve whispered. "We're not finished yet. Either of us."

He looked down to see that Steve was hard again. No wonder he hadn't worried about coming so soon! He intended to do so more than once. William pleaded for the same right, but Steve shook his head and started caressing him. He used his hand to bring William close again, then backed off. Next he did the same with his mouth. William tried to hide any sign that he was on the verge, but failed. Steve backed off at the last second, squeezing William's cock with an upward thrust before he let go.

"That's what I'm looking for!"

William raised his head. A clear strand of liquid stretched from the head of his cock to his stomach. Precome. That didn't happen very often. Steve treated it like a treasure, not breaking the strand. He stroked William more carefully, bringing him to the edge once more. Then a break, more translucent liquid pouring out, Steve never disturbing the growing puddle. He kept his hand pumping, scooting down to lick William's balls, or moving upward to tease his nipples. During some of the forced breaks they would kiss, or he would make William suck his dick. This stretched on for what felt like hours. William basked in the pleasure at times and at others was tempted to shove Steve away so he could finish on his own.

"Please," William whimpered at one point.

"Still hungry?" Steve said. He held himself above William, running the head of his cock through the pool of precome and coating it. Then he moved upwards, bringing this close to William's mouth. Fucking hormones! They made everything sound like a good idea. William opened wide, sucking it clean and savoring the sweet flavor. This was repeated a second time,

Steve not moving away as his hips pumped faster. "Rule number two?" he hissed.

William nodded, taking his second load of the evening.

"Got room for a third?" Steve asked when he pulled out.

William balked. "How many times in a row can you come?"

"I wasn't referring to myself." Steve smiled wickedly, then got out of bed. He stood and tugged on Williams legs. "Put them over your head."

"I'm not a gymnast!"

"You can manage this. Trust me. I've done it tons of times. Scoot down a little first."

William did as he was told. With a little help he swung his legs over his head and came face to face with himself. Steve didn't waste any time. He started pumping William's cock, and when he said to open wide, William was so desperate for release that he complied. The first splash hit his cheek before Steve adjusted the angle. The second, third, and fourth shots…. William lost count as his lips and tongue were coated.

"Damn!" Steve exclaimed. "Where's a video camera when you need one?"

William couldn't respond. He let his lower body flop back down, swallowed, and tried to catch his breath. He had never done anything like that on his own or fantasized about the possibility. He felt his cheeks burn, but it was a little late to be bashful. He looked over at Steve, who was grinning from ear to ear.

William wiped his mouth against the back of his hand. "I think I'm going to need that drink now."

Chapter Twenty

William woke in the morning feeling like a dried-out husk. Steve was next to him, as were a number of empty bottles from the minibar. They had done a couple of shots, hopped into the shower together, and then gotten dressed and hit the hotel bar. They had even started doing it again once they had gotten back, but exhaustion had won out and they fell asleep before anything serious happened.

He rose as quietly as possible, crept to the restroom, and drank from the sink. Then he used the toilet, sitting to make less noise because he was pretty sure he wanted to leave before Steve woke up. He liked the guy, but he wasn't... William frowned, unwilling to even think the name. Not yet. The last thing he wanted was to get emotionally vulnerable in front of a stranger.

He didn't flush, deciding stealth was more important. He was back in the bedroom and pulling on his jeans when Steve rolled over and smiled. "Good morning, sailor!"

"I'm not a sailor," William murmured.

"Sorry, movie star or whatever. Let me guess. You're sneaking out so you can surprise me with donuts."

William's only response was a guilty expression.

"I get it," Steve said, stretching and sitting upright "There's somewhere you need to be."

"Yeah. Sorry."

"It's fine. I had fun last night. I hope you did too."

"Definitely," he said. He still hadn't considered the emotional implications, but he couldn't deny that he had enjoyed himself.

"Good. I wouldn't mind doing it again sometime. I'm in Boston once a month."

"I'm not."

"Where are you stationed? I travel a lot for business."

William shook his head. "I'm not looking for a relationship."

Steve didn't seem offended. "It doesn't have to be. No strings attached."

William grabbed his shirt and put it on. "People don't choose when they get attached."

"You're that irresistible?" Steve asked, expression amused. "You're convinced I'll fall in love with you so easily?"

"It's guaranteed," William said, sitting to put on his socks and shoes. "I'm doing this for your own good."

"Thanks for looking out for me. For the record, I'm okay with your decision. I won't try to change your mind. That means you can stick around for breakfast if you want."

"I really have to get going."

"How about a quickie?"

"Seriously." William stood and patted his pockets to make sure he had everything. "I have a flight to catch."

"At least tell me your name."

"Adam."

"Your real name!"

William paused by the door. "See what I mean? You're infatuated."

Steve laughed, threw a pillow in his direction, and flopped back down into bed. "Thank you for a ridiculously hot night."

"My pleasure," William said, opening the door. "I definitely won't forget you."

They stared at each other. Then William stepped into the hallway, closed the door behind him, and breathed out. Jason. The name came unbidden. As he left the hotel and walked down the street, he realized that he hadn't found a cure. He still loved Jason and wanted him. All that had changed was that William had now gone too far for them to be together again. He couldn't imagine returning to Austin and letting them fall into their old habits without telling Jason where he had been. They might not be committed—they had clarified over and over that they both had the right to wander—but he could still picture Jason's hurt expression when he learned what William had done. Rather than have that discussion, William would finally do what he had been promising himself. He would move on, whether he truly wanted to or not.

"Hey, look who's back from his mystery trip."

William entered the mess hall, surprised to find much of his unit there. Francis, Christie, and a handful of the other pilots and mechanics who he regularly went on missions with. They all seemed amused, and he automatically matched their smiles, but this didn't last.

"I wonder where he went?" Francis said, rubbing his chin theatrically. "San Francisco?"

"New York," said another of the pilots, "to see Broadway. You know how his kind love musicals."

"I think he was at one of those Turkish bathhouses," a mechanic chimed in. "The kind where men give each other massages. *Naked* massages."

William looked to Christie for support, feeling hurt when he saw her eyes shining with amusement. "I guess the secret is out," he said to her. "Is that what this is about?"

She opened her mouth to explain, but Francis cut her off. "We all pitched in and got you a present." He grabbed a small package off the table and handed it to William. The wrapping paper was pink and patterned with white kittens. "Go on, open it."

William kept his head down as he did so, torn between embarrassment and anger. Inside was a transparent bag full of gummy bears. No, that wasn't quite right. He looked closer. Gummy penises. Really? This is how they were going to treat him? He had served alongside these people, performed his duty to the best of his abilities and suffered through the same trials to achieve his position. And now they were going to turn their backs just because of his sexuality? He looked up with a scowl. Then he stared. Everyone around him had hastily put rainbow bandanas on their heads. And they were saluting him.

Francis spoke, voice loud and clear like a drill sergeant. "We, the proud members of the First District, would like to formally express our support for our fellow Guardsmen, AST William Townson. We are pleased that you now have the freedom to be who you truly are. We've got your back. Just stay away from our back doors. Hoo-rah!"

"Hoo-rah!" his unit shouted in unison.

William grinned. Then he started laughing. "Thanks, but from what I've seen in the showers, none of you guys are packing anything impressive enough to interest me."

This started a chorus of boos and hisses from all but Christie, who stepped forward to hug him. "Sorry. It slipped out in conversation. I didn't mean to—"

"It's fine," William said, squeezing her back. Then he addressed the room. "Family shouldn't keep secrets from each other. The only reason I did is out of dedication to my duty. I hope you understand that."

"Nobody wants to hear about your doodie," Francis said,

pushing his way in for a hug, albeit the manly kind followed by slaps on the back. "Between you and me, I'm glad. A lot of hearts were broken when the news leaked. Now I'll be there to comfort all those beautiful women."

"Assuming any of them will have you," William said, looking around at a room full of supportive faces. "Thanks for being so cool, everyone. From now on, whenever a CO tells me to eat a bag of dicks—" He tore open the gummies and popped one in his mouth. "—I'll think of you guys."

William had never been lucky in love. Lately he was starting to wonder if he was cursed. His relationship with Kelly had been a disaster, and Jason was a perfect example of the wrong place and time. Since them, he hadn't done much better. He wasn't the only member of the Coast Guard to come out. Hurricane Irene kept him too busy to think about relationships, but in the lull afterwards, he was approached by a handsome boatswain and asked out. They dated for a few weeks, and while the other guy tried his best to win him over, William felt as though he was going through the motions and called it off. The same happened later in the fall when Christie introduced him to her cousin. William treaded more carefully, since he didn't want to strain his relationship with her. Luckily her cousin was only visiting from out of town, and when he left, William didn't feel any pangs of sorrow or an urge to stay in touch.

His heart wasn't cold though. His insides still glowed whenever he thought of Jason, but he was determined to do the right thing. As the holidays approached, he realized his convictions would be tested during his usual trip to Austin. Instead of flying there, he decided to invite his mother to New England to show her the world he now inhabited. She was thrilled, and while her visit felt nothing like a traditional Christmas, they both enjoyed themselves immensely.

He couldn't avoid his home state forever. His mother's birthday was in mid-February, which meant he would be in Austin during the most dreaded holiday of all. This didn't go unnoticed.

Do I get to see you tomorrow? Jason texted. *It's been forever.*

William checked his phone to be sure that tomorrow was the fourteenth. Valentine's Day. *Not the best time for me,* he texted back. *Day after?*

I have work. You're really busy the whole day? Doing what?

Nothing. His brothers had plans with their girlfriends, his mother was going on a date, and William was left without an excuse. *Okay.*

Is that a yes?

Yes. William chewed his lip. *I don't have a lot of time though. Sorry.*

Cool! Do you want to come over?

God that would be amazing! He could see Ben and Tim again, lounge around their awesome house while talking to everyone, and then go up to Jason's bedroom for privacy. But those days belonged to the past. *Let's grab lunch somewhere.*

Okay. Might be hard without reservations.

Because happy couples would be cramming their faces full, grinning at each other over their plates while celebrating Valentine's Day. *Let's meet at Whataburger.*

Fast food?

William thought quickly. *Yeah. They don't have those up north. I miss them.*

Okay.

They finalized plans. William was certain he could hear the despondence in Jason's voice, even though he was reading emotionless text. He dreaded the next day, which was crazy, because seeing Jason was usually the highlight of each trip. He didn't allow himself to be picked up, or offer Jason a ride. They met at the Whataburger like two strangers from Craigslist who had a transaction to complete. "Here are the antique bookends I advertised. Twenty bucks, please."

He at least waited to order. William was standing inside, staring at the menu above the counter, when a wonderfully familiar voice said his name. Jason was dressed nicely—a freshly ironed shirt, jeans too pristine to be anything but new, and a whiff of designer cologne. Even his messy hair had been freshly cut. When Jason came near for a hug, William thrust out a hand instead. Jason stared at it like he wasn't familiar with the custom. Then his face fell and he accepted his consolation prize. They shook hands, their arms limp, their grip lacking commitment.

"You look good," Jason said, expression still pained.

William was wearing a crappy T-shirt that even he didn't like. No haircut, no cologne. Just some stuff he'd found in his old closet. Jason was stunning, and not just by comparison. Surely an army of guys were competing for his attention, only to be turned away. Maybe this miserable day would change that. "Hungry?" he asked, forcing himself to look at the menu again.

"I guess," Jason said, sounding confused. "Is everything okay?"

"Everything but the green chili burger," William jested. "Tastes fine, but trust me, you'll regret it the next day."

Jason didn't respond. William felt his gaze but couldn't bring himself to meet it. When he stepped up to the counter to order, he did so solo, feeling like an asshole. He could at least buy Jason a meal, but he was determined that the message be perfectly clear this time. Actions. Not words. When they carried their trays to a sloppily wiped table and sat, William noticed that Jason had opted for nothing but french fries and a vanilla shake. That brought back memories. Jason liked to combine the two, using the shake like a condiment for his fries. Watching him dip the first one in made his throat tight.

"I was thinking of you the other day," Jason said. "We all watched *The Guardian*."

William snorted.

"What?"

"Sorry. That movie is kind of a joke among coasties."

"I liked it." Now Jason seemed hurt. "I was trying to understand your life better."

"It's a good movie," William hurriedly amended. "I saw it in the theater. Twice. I think it just makes us self-conscious. There aren't many movies about the Coast Guard. Hardly any, so of course when Hollywood finally makes one, we scrutinize it to death."

Jason resumed dipping his fries. "Is it inaccurate?"

"Not terribly. They made some mistakes with uniforms, and the part with the bar fight is stupid. Unless you're being extremely obnoxious, someone in the Navy is more likely to buy you a beer than attack you. The same when they visit our haunts. We're all in the same boat, more or less. No pun intended. It's a good movie. Really. And hey, who does Ashton Kutcher remind you of?"

Jason shook his head. "Demi Moore?"

William laughed. "Tim! You don't think they look alike? They could be brothers!"

Jason made a face. "Cousins, maybe. Second cousins."

"I can't believe you don't see it," William said. "How are they doing?"

"Good. They ask about you all the time."

The smile left William's face. He missed being a part of that world. His loss. He picked up his burger and took a bite.

Jason continued to watch him. "I don't know what to say because I never hear from you anymore."

William swallowed. "Remember how being a rescue swimmer ruined Kevin Costner's marriage in the movie?"

"Yeah," Jason said. "I understand why, but it's not like you couldn't— Never mind. I missed you. That's all."

William missed him too. He supposed that would never change. Especially now.

"But I get it," Jason added.

William looked up. "You do?"

"Yeah. I'm embarrassed it took me this long, but…" Jason sat up, putting on a brave expression. "Anyway, I noticed there was absolutely *no* sewing in that movie. I still think you're messing with me."

"I'll prove it!" William said. "Somehow."

"It just so happens I have needle and thread in the car," Jason said, "and some underwear I found on the street. They're full of holes and so dirty that they're completely stiff, but I'm sure your rescue sewing skills will have them fixed up in no time."

He was kidding, of course, and his banter felt a little forced, but William appreciated the effort to make this easy on him. He didn't deserve that. The rest of the meal passed in a similar fashion. They avoided serious topics, or any mention of love and relationships. When all that remained on their trays were crumpled wrappers and empty paper cups, Jason stood. "I won't keep you any longer." He paused, perhaps considering how these words had a much more poignant interpretation. "I know you're busy."

"Yeah," William said, standing and taking both their trays to the trash can. One final act of chivalry. Pathetic.

"Walk me to my car?" Jason said.

William wasn't sure how hopeful this suggestion was, but he complied. When they were standing beside Ben's old car, William struggled to find the right words. Or at least any he would allow himself to speak. Jason seemed to be waiting too, but then he gave up and opened his arms for a hug. William wanted nothing more than to pull Jason close. Instead he kept their bodies distant, angled away when they embraced. An unsatisfying end to what had been the best relationship of his life. He felt like apologizing, or explaining, or making promises he couldn't keep. Instead he settled on a single word that broke his heart to say.

"Goodbye."

Hell was often painted in flames, or sometimes dressed in ice, but for William, Hell was a lurching sea at night, the sky filled with torrents of rain. In other words, the very weather the helicopter was currently flying through. His version of paradise was the flipside of this environment—sapphire skies, gentle clouds, and a warm sun keeping watch over a calm ocean. God how he wished that's where they were now! Not for his sake, but for the poor soul stranded somewhere down below. The fishing boat had sent a distress signal more than an hour ago. Just one man was aboard, Captain Gonzalez, who radioed to tell them his engine had lost power. The storm had moved in quickly to claim his vessel, contact lost soon after.

The helicopter interior was quiet as they made repeated sweeps over his last known coordinates. Occasionally one of them would call out, believing they had spotted something in the turbulent waters below, but they were always mistaken. The dark made their mission all the more impossible, even with night vision and heat-sensing technology, but they couldn't quit. Not when a person's life depended on them.

"Mark, mark, mark!" Francis said over the radio. "We have visual!"

The helicopter slowed to a hover, the searchlight illuminating an object below. William saw the hull and keel, waves lapping over both. The boat had capsized! "Get in closer," he said, but he didn't need to because Francis was already bringing the helicopter as low to the water as they dared, the searchlight moving over the waves. Debris was everywhere. He scanned the area for the blinking light that was built into higher-end life jackets. Nothing. Not even a flare. They circled around the boat, still searching. The captain might have taken shelter from the storm and still be trapped inside. If so, they were unable to help him. The waves were merciless, washing over the vessel. From the way it bobbed, it had taken on a lot of water. Enough that the captain would have abandoned ship by now.

"No signs of life," Francis said. "Thirty minutes to bingo."

Meaning that they only had so much fuel left and would need to start back to base. William tried to put himself in the mindset of the captain, who had radioed for help and been expecting them. He would have watched the skies for their approach, ready to shoot a flare when he saw them coming. Most likely that would put him above deck when the boat capsized, or when the first waves washed over it. Maybe he was down there now, staring up at them and unable to signal his whereabouts, praying that they would see him and come to help. William could also imagine his desperation when his one hope turned and flew away.

"Might be a lost cause," Christie said from next to him, tacitly seeking his permission.

"Twenty-five minutes," Francis said. "We'll have to come back out or—"

"I see him!" William lied. "Survivor at eleven o'clock." He pointed to the biggest cluster of debris. "Lower me down."

As the helicopter moved closer to the proposed target, he began to doubt this gambit, but he would gain a new vantage point when actually in the water. His crew expressed their confusion, no one else seeing what he had because of course he hadn't seen anything. Jumping in these conditions was too dangerous, especially with so many obstacles below, so they chose an area on the edge of the clutter. William was attached to the pulley and slowly lowered. Winds buffeted him, making him spin in the air. He could tell from their chill that the water would be even colder, late March showing no signs of spring. He ignored the conditions as best he could, still searching as he neared the water. Just before he splashed down, he thought he saw a figure bobbing in the water, one arm raised skyward. He did the same after detaching himself to show he was okay and free. Then he started swimming in what he hoped was the right direction. The helicopter's spotlight illuminated him and followed his progress.

Despite all the cutting-edge gear he was provided with, salt water still soaked into his suit, got inside his snorkel, and did everything to drag him down. That was his first battle: resisting the elements. The next was fighting against his emotions. Fear, desperation, doubt—these things might plague his personal life, but he couldn't afford them now. He shoved his feelings aside, focused on his training, and prayed the odds would be in his favor.

A straight swim was impossible. Metal barrels surfed on the heaving swell, threatening to knock into him. The Styrofoam coolers weren't as worrying, the dead fish that had been the vessel's catch that day merely unpleasant. Other artifacts from the ship made his search more difficult. More than once he swam toward what he thought was a person, but turned out to be only random equipment. He ignored the cold seeping into his body and pressed on, trying to keep track of time. He couldn't stay out here forever. Not without putting his crew at risk. If the helicopter ran too low on fuel in these conditions—

William saw a hand shoot into the air before disappearing again. He summoned all his strength and raced toward it, hope exploding from his heart when he finally found what he was looking for: Captain Gonzales, eyes wide in panic, but very much alive due in large part to the life vest he was wearing. "I'm a rescue swimmer," William shouted as he got near. "Everything is going to be—"

A wave crashed over him, his body spinning like a spool with its thread being yanked. William rode this out and kicked to the surface, only to find that everything had changed. He had been playing a game of chess and someone had upended the board and put all the pieces back in the wrong places. He spun around in the water, searching for the captain. The spotlight above found him, and after signaling he was okay, he moved through the water. Time was precious, not just because of fuel concerns, but because he had no idea how long Captain Gonzales had been in the water and if he was suffering hypothermia. The spotlight stopped moving, focusing on a point ahead of him. William swam toward it. The captain was there, his head listing to one side, his body low like he no longer had the strength to kick. The captain was dangerously close to the hull of the ship and likely to be sucked under.

William cut a line toward him, mind counting down the minutes and trying to calculate how close he could get to the hull without being pulled under himself. He felt the suction just as he reached the captain, grabbing him and swimming them both away from the capsized vessel. He stopped when he felt they were at a safe distance, but they weren't out of danger. Another wave washed over them, this one smaller. William was prepared, not letting go of the survivor. As soon as it had passed, he quickly assessed the captain. He was no longer conscious, his skin pale, a laceration just beneath the hairline. Worse than that, Captain Gonzales was no longer breathing. William signaled the helicopter, relieved when he saw the basket already on its way down. The wind was blowing it around, causing it to spin. They might need to lower the hook instead. Did they have time for multiple attempts? Or was this it? The basket splashed down, farther away than he liked. He swam for it, pulling Gonzales with him. When he reached it, William growled with effort to get the man inside. Usually he would send a survivor up on their own, the lighter weight meaning they would get to safety quicker, but unless he acted fast, all they would be bringing back with them was a corpse.

William climbed into the basket, already pulling off his mask and snorkel before the helicopter lifted into the air. Once it did, he arranged Gonzales as best he could and started resuscitation. Chest compressions. A lungful of air forced past frozen lips. More compressions. A silent prayer to God. Another lungful of air. The chopping sound of the helicopter above was nearer now but Gonzales still wasn't responding. William tore open the lifejacket and tried again, pressing the base of his hands against the chest, touching his lips to those of a dead man and trying to breathe life into him.

Christie was shouting at him, pulling at the basket, trying to get it inside, but William ignored her. One more set of chest compressions, one more borrowed breath… Salt water splattered his face, followed by a wheeze and rough coughs. William pulled back, saw the captain's eyes shoot open, then squeeze shut again against the rain and light. He was alive! William didn't allow himself any relief or satisfaction. Now his survivor had become a patient, and what mattered most was getting him aboard and warm again. After a flurry of activity, he had the captain seated inside the helicopter and was piling every available blanket on him, even the one Christie tried to wrap around William's shoulders. Then he fell into one of the flight seats, the adrenaline receding and leaving him exhausted. He sucked in air, trying to calm himself. William looked over and saw Christie checking on the captain. She met his gaze and gave him a thumbs up. William smiled in return as the helicopter flew toward the coast. Soon they would be home again. And safe.

The ambulance had gone, a weeping wife climbing into the back with her husband. William's cheeks were still wet from her kisses. His crew had jostled him with congratulatory hugs, all of them sharing in the credit for this rescue. It felt good, and yet, part of him felt like crying. Maybe from relief. Or because this was the one. Of all the missions he had been on, this was the first rescue that convinced him he had saved a life. Had he not been there, that wave would have crashed down over Gonzales, debris would have knocked him unconscious, and the captain would have drowned. Hell, a smarter man wouldn't have pretended to see him down there in the first place!

Once showered and partly dressed, William stood at his locker and pulled out his phone. His first instinct was to tell Kelly, of all people. He had finally done something big enough to make up for the horrible accident, but in truth, he knew that wasn't possible. He couldn't give Kelly back his leg. Pretending otherwise was unfair. Then he thought of Jason, how he had loved William enough to let him go. Not just once, but every time he left town again. Especially the most recent, when he had reacted with grace to an ugly situation. Jason hadn't yelled or tried to hurt him back. He had simply let go. Jason deserved part of the credit too.

William's thumb moved over the keyboard on the screen, sending him the news.

I saved a life tonight.

He looked away as someone patted him on the back in congratulations. After a quick conversation, he returned his attention to the phone to read the reply. Still none. He finished getting dressed and checked again. A response!

Wow. All I did tonight was go to a gay bar.

William swallowed against the pain that rose up. Jason probably thought he was boasting, or maybe he wanted to be clear that he too had moved on. William wished he could explain how their sacrifice hadn't been in vain. Instead he decided to tell Jason the only thing that really mattered to him.

I want you to be happy.

The response was much quicker this time. *I'm proud of you. So crazy hugely proud of you! You're my hero. You always will be.*

"Thank you," William said out loud, wiping away the sudden tears. Then he spoke the words he wouldn't allow himself to send. "I love you, Jason. You have no idea. I love you so much! I always will."

Chapter Twenty-one

William sat at the table, waiting for his date to return from the restroom. The lighting was low, the walls decorated with repurposed antiques, and a jazz band played at the far end of the room. The perfect place for falling in love. Or for charming the socks off a married woman.

Christie Patel reappeared, the orange sherbet-colored dress complimenting her hazelnut skin. Her dark hair fell in waves over her shoulders, which he wasn't used to since on the base it was always pulled back for practical reasons. She smiled demurely as she sat down.

"I love my family," she said, "and don't you dare laugh, but I haven't felt this liberated since prom."

William laughed anyway. "It's not like you and Max don't get out on your own. How many times have I babysat Jenny over the years?"

"True, and don't take this the wrong way, but I spend most of those dates worrying about her."

"Hey!"

"I knew she would be safe with you," Christie added hurriedly. "I was more worried that she missed me, or resented us for having fun without her. That she's at home with her father allows me to enjoy myself. Speaking of which, where's the waiter with that wine?"

William was eager for him to return too, since alcohol would help soften the blow. Over the past two years, he and Christie had become a team. They didn't always work the same shift, but when they were on missions together, they understood each other's needs without having to voice them. They were often teased about this—that they were either long lost twins who looked nothing alike, or that they were having a secret affair. Neither suggestion was taken seriously, but the connection they had together was real. And it mostly took place on the base. Considering their homes were there too, this might be the first time they had both been away from it together.

Christie eyed him and sighed. "I hope I'm wrong."

"About what?"

"The reason for this meal. Four years is up. For us both. I've been talking about my plans nonstop, and you've been awfully quiet. You're going reserve, aren't you?"

The waiter arrived. William made a grumpy face at him when he was busy filling Christie's glass. He made sure his expression changed when the waiter turned to fill his. Christie laughed, but she was shaking her head by the time they were alone again.

"Your plan was to get me drunk before telling me."

"Damn right," William said, lifting his glass. They clinked them, then took sips before setting them down again. "Are you drunk yet?"

"You worked so hard to get where you are!" Christie said. "Too hard to leave after so few years. You could easily make chief petty officer, get that C added to your title. Zimmerman is retiring next year, did you know that?"

"No," William admitted. "And I agree, it's way too soon for me to leave, but if I don't, I'll miss out on other things."

Christie took another sip and leaned back. "Is there someone I don't know about?"

"Jason."

"Your guy in Austin?"

"Yeah." He didn't have to explain further. He had long ago confided their entire history to her. "He's the main reason I want to go back. The only one, really."

Christie betrayed her opinion with a shake of her head. "Is he still single after all this time?"

"I think so. He visited my mother recently and was asking about me. He wanted to know if I was coming home."

"Really? That's so sweet!"

"I know. So yeah. I'm going home."

Christie considered him over another sip. "Don't take this the wrong way, but how long were you together?"

"Hard to say. Either a few weeks, a few months, or more than two years. We were together before we should have been, and it took a lot of tries before we managed to really break up."

"Right, but you haven't really been in a stable relationship with him for a significant amount of time."

"I guess not, but—"

Christie raised a hand to stop him. "I'm not questioning your feelings for each other. Look at this though." She picked up her purse and pulled out her phone. After poking at the screen, she showed it to him. The picture was from boot camp. A group shot, two other recruits standing between Christie and him. Her hair was short and she looked awfully lanky. As for him, his build was bigger, not at all optimized for the job he did now, and he appeared a lot younger.

"Your baby cheeks were so cute!" Christie teased. Then she swiped at the screen until it displayed a photo of them together from last week. The difference was significant. "You're a man now. I'm sure Jason has changed a lot too. I'm not saying you shouldn't find out if you still have potential together. Just don't shut down your career to do so. Take leave, and if the spark is still there, bring him back with you."

William wasn't convinced. "A lot has changed for the better, but he still wouldn't have the right to live on the base with me, and I wouldn't be allowed to live off of it. Would you be okay if Max and Jenny had their own place and all you could do was visit them?"

"Of course not!" Christie scowled, but her anger wasn't directed at him. "When is this country going to wake up and start treating everyone equally?"

"I don't know," he said, "but I'm not going to wait around until it does."

"Just…" Christie took a deep breath. "Just don't burn all your bridges yet. Treat this like any other SAR. Examine the intel, assess the situation, and formulate a plan. Do you need me down there with you? I'll be your wingman!"

William imagined himself being lowered from a helicopter until he was dangling outside Jason's bedroom window. "Tempting, but I need you to hold down the fort here."

"It won't be the same without you," Christie raised her glass, "but I hope you find everything that you're looking for."

And William hoped that someday he would no longer need to say goodbye to the people he loved, because his heart broke a little more each time.

Home. As much as William had begun to think of Cape Cod that way, standing on the doorstep to his mother's house proved just how wrong he was. So many memories had been made here. Crying in the living room when he didn't want to return to kindergarten. His father teaching him to ride his bike, his mother setting up a tent in the backyard and camping with him, his brothers helping him climb onto the roof so they could pretend they were kings of the neighborhood, ruling from on high. So many happy times. Plenty of tears too. Even though the house had changed over the years, and not as many people lived there anymore, this place was his home.

He turned to consider the neighborhood, then the driveway again, which was filled with cars. Most of them he didn't recognize. What was up with that? He went inside to find out. The door was unlocked, the aroma that greeted him reassuringly familiar. He saw someone dart from the living room to the kitchen. Smiling to himself, William followed and found a small crowd gathered there.

"Welcome home!" they chimed in unison. So many familiar faces were present—his mother, his brothers, even his father and his new wife. Lewis had married Gina. This made it easier to forgive him. If it had just been an affair, a mere fling that tore their family apart… Then again, William didn't hold a grudge about any of it anymore. Both his parents were happier, even if part of him still wished they could have felt that way while together. He barely got a word out before he was being hugged by one person after another. Then someone stood in front of him that he didn't recognize. Or did he?

She was tall. The tan skin and athletic build implied she spent a lot of time in the sun. Her brown hair was short, a pixie cut, and the freckles… those he definitely remembered!

"Lily?" he said disbelievingly.

"Surprise!" she said, brown eyes twinkling.

"Where in the world—"

"I ran into her at the grocery store," his mother said. "I was buying ingredients for this very cake!"

He glanced over at it, seeing blue frosting shaped like waves, a toy boat riding them. A little figure swam below yellow words that said *Welcome Home, Willy!* The cake was both impressive and embarrassing, but he was more interested in the woman standing before him. "Where have you been?"

"I could ask you the same thing," she said.

They had lost touch years ago. After he had left for the Coast Guard, they traded a few emails, but he had been so distracted. More likely than not, he had been the one to stop replying. "It's good to see you again!"

"I knew you would be happy to see each other!" his mother

said. "What were the odds? Shopping for your welcome home party, and there she is. Of course I invited her!"

"I'm glad you did!"

They didn't have time to catch up yet. His mother wanted him to cut the cake, taking photos while he did so and crying with happiness. Lewis put an arm around her, and Kate didn't push him away. Gina seemed fine with this too. So much had happened while he was gone. Peace had been made and old friends had grown up. Spencer was engaged, proudly introducing his fiancé, a shy girl with bright red hair. Not everything had changed. Errol slipped him a small baggie and winked. "For later," he said. "Now that you're free from the system."

"Thanks," William said, pocketing the weed and making plans to flush it down the toilet later.

More than cake awaited him. Food, music, laughter… He was definitely home again. As good as it was to see his family all together like this, he kept looking across the table at Lily. All grown up. That she had become a beautiful woman was no surprise. She'd been gorgeous when they were younger. They managed to exchange a few sentences here and there, but only once the party had wound down did they sit on the living room couch to talk.

"Where to begin," he said, chuckling nervously. "I can't believe my mom ran into you like that. What were the odds?"

"Slimmer than you realize," Lily said. "I live in Houston these days, so I'm only here on vacation. And before you make fun of me like everyone else does, there's something to be said for returning home for a couple of weeks and letting your parents baby you."

"That's how most of my off time was spent too." William stared at her in wonder and shook his head. "This is so wild."

"I know," she said. "God… You're a man!"

"You're a woman!" he echoed.

They laughed again.

"Okay, the basics," Lily said. "Who's the lucky guy? No way are you single."

"Hopelessly," William replied. "Hey, do you remember Jason? The guy I was dating before I left for the Coast Guard?"

"Of course! He was sweet!"

"Well, I'm hoping he still remembers me."

"Very nostalgic," Lily said. "Any time I see one of my high school boyfriends, I run the other way."

"Speaking of which, I don't see a wedding ring."

Lily reached for her left hand, touching an empty spot there. "I have one. It's in a jewelry box at home."

"I don't get it."

"We got divorced a few months back."

"Oh." William grimaced. "Sorry."

"I'm not!" Lily said. "Dave wasn't a bad guy. We had chemistry. Just not the kind that lasts."

"How long were you together?"

Lily jutted out her bottom lip and blew, the air moving her bangs. "Three years? I think that's right."

"Wow. Do you have kids?"

"Nope. Corn won't grow in this field."

"Oh. Uh. I…"

Lily laughed. "It's still ridiculously easy to make you blush! I'm fine. Not being able to have biological children just means there won't be any surprises. When I'm ready, I can adopt and give a home to a child who needs one. That's nothing to feel sad about. Although, if I could have had children with one person, it would have been with Dave. They would have been so pretty."

"Someone's full of themselves," William teased.

"Not me. Him." Lily took out her phone, navigated to an image, and held it up.

William stared. When she moved the phone away, he almost grabbed it so he could look longer, because the guy was gorgeous. "Model?" he asked.

"Elementary school teacher."

"Aw!"

Lily sighed. "I know. He was a dreamboat. Most of the time. At others he was a garbage barge."

William laughed.

"I thought you'd like that joke," Lily said. "Mr. Coast Guard! Tell me about that."

He did so grudgingly. William was proud of helping other people, but he never felt like boasting about his rescues. Instead he felt honored to be of service.

"You really jump out of helicopters?" Lily asked.

"Only when I want to show off," he joked. "What about you?"

"Financial advisor. Glamorous, I know."

"It sounds impressive to me," William said. "Is that what brought you to Houston? Or was it—"

"Dave? No, I met him there once I relocated for the job."

"I'm terrible with numbers, but I do have a little money saved up. Can you make me rich?"

"Maybe." Lily cocked her head and smiled at him. "Are you really back for good?"

"I think so," William said. "A lot of that depends on Jason."

"If he's anywhere near as happy to see you as I am, you won't have any trouble. And if it doesn't work out..." She put a hand over his, "I've got a shoulder you can cry on."

William flipped his hand over so he could squeeze hers. "Thanks," he said. "That means a lot to me."

They spent the next hour dredging up old memories and laughing at how young they had been. Then they made plans to meet again. After he had said goodbye to Lily, William went to the kitchen, determined to help clean up the mess. He found the food put away, the dishwasher running. His mother was leaning against the counter, sipping a cup of coffee.

"I didn't want to disturb you," she said. "Did you have fun?"

"Yeah! I never should have lost touch with her."

"I'm glad. I wasn't sure if I should invite her, but I couldn't resist. I thought about inviting Jason too."

"It's good you didn't," William said. "I want to surprise him. He doesn't know I'm back in town, does he?"

"I kept it secret, just like you requested." Kate set aside her coffee and moved forward to hug him. "I'm so happy you're home! I know you're probably sick of hearing it."

"Nope! I feel the same way."

"I hope you stay. I know you're a man now and need to live your own life, but I like having you here."

"We'll see." He went to the sink to fill a glass of water.

"There's someone else I thought about inviting," his mother said.

"Who?" He turned around when she didn't answer and saw her biting her bottom lip. "You're with someone? I know you've been dating, but... Is it serious?"

She nodded. "Very. You'll be seeing a lot of him. That is, if you're comfortable. Otherwise—"

"I think it's great!" He thought about it and guffawed. "Gosh, pretty soon I might have a new dad!"

"It's no joke," Kate said. "I love him."

William put on a more serious expression. "Why didn't you mention this sooner?"

"I wanted to be sure before I told any of you children. I didn't want to— Oh, it doesn't matter. I like Gina. Did I tell you that? She's a decent person."

"So are you," William said. "Forget that, you're amazing! I'm proud of how far you've come."

"Stop," his mother said, cheeks rosy.

"So when do I get to meet this guy?"

"Soon. He's around the house a lot these days."

"What's his name?"

"Buck."

William snorted.

His mother scowled. "What?"

"He's got a porn star name."

"Laugh all you want. He has the equipment to back it up."

"Mom!"

"Well it's true!" She smiled. "It's not just that. He's sentimental. I don't want to say anything bad about your father, but he never wrote me poems. Or showed up at my work with flowers. Or asked for a lock of my hair." Kate covered her mouth and laughed.

"Buck does all of those things?"

"Yes."

"Then I like him already."

In truth, the idea of his mother being with someone besides his father was a little odd, but he had gotten used to Gina, and he was sure he would get used to this Buck person too. "So much has changed," he murmured. "I feel like I've been gone for ages."

"There's still a place for you here," Kate said. "That hasn't changed. Neither have Jason's feelings for you."

"Are you sure?"

"I am. Just you wait and see."

William awoke feeling warm nostalgia, remembering days gone by and selectively choosing which ones he allowed his mind to drift back to. A narrow sliver of history between Kelly and the

Coast Guard, when all that he and Jason had was each other. If he was lucky, he would return to that world today. The morning was for getting ready, the time beyond for meeting his mother's new man. After a nice lunch, she urged him to try his luck. William ignored the car, hopping on his bike like he always had. He'd arrive sweaty and disheveled, but that had never stopped Jason from kissing him or pulling him close for a hug.

He grinned while pedaling to the edge of town, laughing when he imagined bugs getting stuck in his teeth like they did in the grill of a car. Then he reached a private drive that was easy to miss, but he hadn't forgotten where it was. He rode down it at a leisurely pace, butterflies filling his stomach. They were welcome to stay there. Soon, if all went right, he and Jason would be together again.

A moving van was the first thing to shake his optimism. Were Ben and Tim relocating? Had they already gone, the new owners moving in? Then he saw a guy jump down from the loading bay. Even from behind, the lanky frame and broad shoulders were instantly familiar to him. As was the sweaty mop of perpetually messy hair. Jason crouched, picked up a cardboard box, and disappeared behind the van again. William rode closer and saw him yanking on the door to close it, which was funny, because a box still sat on the ground, waiting to be loaded.

"You forgot one!" William called out, bringing his bike to a halt.

Jason stuck his head out of the van, eyes widening in disbelief. William set the bike on the ground and picked up the box, handing it to him with a smile. Jason placed his hands on the cardboard but didn't pull it away, still staring.

"Moving?" William asked.

"Very," Jason replied. Then he blinked a few times, looking slightly panicked. "I mean, yes." He finally took the box and loaded it into the van. When he turned back around, he had recovered somewhat. "Home for a visit?"

William shook his head. "Home for good."

Jason was clearly overwhelmed. He slowly sat down on the edge of the truck's loading platform, speaking carefully. "You're moving home?"

William nodded. "More accurately, I moved home already. I'm back."

"No more Coast Guard?" Jason asked, making it sound like William had been fighting cancer and was finally in remission.

"I'm considering my options, but no more active duty. I decide what I want to do now. Please tell me you aren't moving away from Austin."

"No!" Jason said hurriedly. "I finally got my own place in town. With Emma, actually."

"Emma? Wow. Is she—"

"Eighteen," Jason said, as if he couldn't believe it either. "Time flies by. She's starting college in the fall."

"Wow. How long was I gone?"

"Four years!" Jason finally returned his smile. "I can't believe you're back!"

"Feels like a dream, doesn't it?"

Jason looked him over, as if it might be and William would disappear at any second. As much as people kept telling him he had changed, Jason looked exactly the same. Still the intense eyes, the sun on his nose and cheeks, and his over-due-for-a-cut hair that wouldn't meet Coast Guard standards. William wanted nothing more than to run his fingers through it, or to taste the salt on his lips, but first he had to be sure.

"So," he asked as casually as possible. "What's going on in your life?"

Jason understood the question. His mouth opened and closed again, like he couldn't find the right words. Was that a good sign or bad? Was he simply excited that they could finally be together again, or trying to find a way of explaining why they couldn't?

"Ready to go?" said a familiar voice. "Oh hey! Look who's here!"

William turned. Another sweat-soaked guy. Like Jason, he wore an old T-shirt, this one pressed against a lot more ridges, because time hadn't made any of Tim's muscles sag. William had seen plenty of bodies in top condition while in the service, but something about Tim still made him both nervous and giddy. "How's it going?" he managed.

"Excellent, my man! Is this it? You're back?"

"That's the idea!"

Tim offered him a hand. "I'd hug you, but…" He gestured at his damp T-shirt. "So is it like other branches of the military where you're still on reserve?"

"Yeah." He turned to include Jason in the conversation, wanting to reassure him. "That just means I'll get called in during really big emergencies. I have a couple days of training every month and two weeks' active duty per year. Other than that, it's back to a normal life."

Jason's reaction to this news was hard to gauge, especially since Tim had more questions. "But you'll be living in Austin?"

"I think so."

"Doing what?"

William exhaled. "Taking some time off! Then I have to figure out the rest of my life. Easy, right?"

Tim laughed. "Best of luck. I'm still trying to figure out mine."

"What's all the—" Ben appeared at the front door. Then he hurried forward. Even though William had managed to work up a sweat too, Ben hugged him. "Look at you!" he said, taking a step back. "How long has it been?"

"A couple years," William answered sheepishly.

"You're all grown up," Ben said with shining eyes.

"People keep saying that like I joined the Coast Guard when I was a toddler."

"Just wait until you're my age," Ben said. "You were a baby in my eyes."

"You're not that old," William said. "You look… Twenty-three? Am I right?"

Ben pointed at him while addressing the others. "I love this man. Seriously." He turned back to William. "Now that your four years are up, we won't let you escape again. Move in with us."

Jason made a choking noise.

"I guess there's a free room now," William joked. "I can't believe you're letting *him* get away."

"Don't start," Tim said in exasperation. "We've begged and pleaded for Jason to stay. Maybe you can talk some sense into him."

"Yes!" Ben said excitedly. "If anyone can convince him to stay, it's you!"

He liked the sound of that. He looked to Jason, who seemed dazed. "What do you say? I'll help move everything back inside."

"The lease is signed," Jason said. "I'd be letting Emma down. She needs to live close to campus. And I need to keep an eye on her."

"Sorry," William said, addressing Ben and Tim again. "I tried my best. I'll help with the rest of the move. It's the least I can do."

"Yeah!" Tim said, playfully jostling him. "We could do with an extra set of muscles."

"That rules me out," Ben said. "I'll hold down the fort here."

"Sounds like a plan," Tim said. "You guys ready to go?"

They climbed into the moving van, Jason taking the middle seat. The truck was wonderfully cramped, meaning their arms were touching. William wanted more than that. A hand on his leg, a kiss on his neck. Tim kindly provided a diversion from these urges, asking him about his service time. William tried to make his answers funny or interesting. Jason remained distant despite his best efforts.

They arrived at an apartment complex, the kind with a dedicated entrance to a campus of buildings. Jason's was at the very rear. They parked the truck, then each grabbed a box before heading up to the third floor, setting them down on the carpet in an empty living room.

"What goes where?" Tim asked.

"You haven't seen the place?" William asked. When Tim shook his head, he added, "Give us a tour!"

"Okay." Jason gestured around. "Living room. I figure the couch Emma is bringing will go on that wall. We'll put my TV across from it." He pointed to the end of the room. "Kitchen is over there. We're thinking of making the dining room corner an office area instead, because the bedrooms are too small for desks, but at least we each have a private bathroom. Emma's bedroom is on that side." He pointed to a door, then faced the opposite direction. "I'm over here."

He led them to it, turning in a circle once, considering the possibilities. He seemed proud. William supposed Jason hadn't been on his own for quite some time. "Oh yeah, check out the balcony!" The land behind the building wasn't developed, providing a nice view of a wooded area. "The other apartment we were considering was bigger and cheaper, but no balcony, only one bathroom, and it was right next to a busy road. This is nicer."

William thought so too. He could already imagine sitting out there at night, a candle burning on a small table between two chairs, but only one would be occupied because Jason would be on his lap. Or maybe the reverse.

"Okay," Tim said. "Let's get this over with."

Moving sucked. As much as William liked to stay active, hauling boxes and furniture up flights of stairs wasn't fun. It also limited how much he and Jason could interact, since anything that required two people to lift was handled by him and Tim. Still, being apart from Jason provided plenty of motivation to get things finished as quickly as possible. William worked his ass off, chest heaving by the time they were finally through.

Then they sat on the floor, letting tense muscles relax. William's back was killing him.

"I'm starving," Tim moaned. "Let's order pizza."

"Better call Ben first," Jason said. "He might have fixed something for us."

"Good idea." Tim groaned as he got to his feet, grabbed his phone from the kitchen counter and went outside to make the call.

Alone at last! William looked at Jason, who also seemed to realize that they finally had privacy. The tension was thick before they laughed to dispel it.

"I wish we were at your old place," William said wistfully. "I'd like to hose off out back again."

Jason grinned at him. "They have these new things called showers, you know. Very cutting edge. There's one here. Two, in fact."

"Sounds amazing." William put on his bedroom eyes. "We should try it out." When Jason appeared more concerned than interested, he hastily added, "Not together, of course. That is unless… We have a lot of catching up to do, verbally, because I don't even know what your situation is."

"My situation?"

"I noticed you're not moving in with another guy."

"Oh." Jason looked away. "There is someone, actually."

"That's great!" William forced himself to sound upbeat, when really he felt like he'd been punched in the stomach. "That's what I wanted for you."

Jason's brow knotted up. "What you wanted?"

"Everyone into the truck!" Tim said, holding open the front door. "There's lasagna waiting for us! I just hope he made two, because I swear I could eat one all by myself." William didn't budge, wanting to see the conversation through. Jason didn't move either, still wearing an incredulous expression. "Sorry, boys," Tim said, "but Benjamin is going to have hurt feelings if we don't show. Especially since this is your last night with us, Jason."

Jason nodded, attention still on William. "We'll catch up later."

"Right," he managed to say. "Of course."

William dragged his feet on the way back to the truck, not just because he was physically tired, but because of what he had learned. Jason had someone. Of course he did. William had done his best to make sure Jason would move on, and he had. If William was smart, he would get on his bicycle and leave as soon as they were back at Ben and Tim's place, but he didn't want to be a sore loser. And he was curious to know who Jason had ended up with. He prayed the guy was decent and kind.

"I'm sure Ben will let us take a quick shower before dinner," Tim said as they turned down the drive.

"Might be a tight squeeze with all of us in there," William joked.

Jason seemed not to hear him, staring wordlessly out the windshield.

When they were back at the house, Ben greeted them and made sympathetic comments about their pain, but he also seemed happy to have avoided the heavy lifting. They trudged upstairs as a group, Tim disappearing into the master bedroom. That left him and Jason alone in the hall.

"Do you want to go first?" William asked.

"No, go ahead. I have a few things to take care of."

William hesitated, wishing he knew what to say besides, *Forget the other guy and get in the shower with me. I promise I'll never leave you again.* "Thanks," was all he uttered. Once shut into the bathroom, he stripped off his clothes, remembering how he and Jason had once squeezed into the tub together, water sloshing onto the floor. Or the time they left the bathroom lights off, shut the door, and held each other under a stream of hot water.

He stepped into the bathtub, the showerhead already steaming. He smelled the body wash before applying it to his skin. William felt like crying. Sometimes he still wished he was a hothead like other guys, the sort of person to get angry, hurl insults, punch walls, and do whatever it took to feel anything but vulnerable and sad. That wasn't him and never would be. Not again. Once had been enough.

When he was finished, he considered his sweaty clothing, realizing he didn't have anything else to put on. Feeling daring, he wrapped the towel around his waist and went to Jason's room, planning on asking for something to wear while casually showing off his body. The room was empty. Jason had moved out. Moved on. Same thing, he supposed. All that remained was the old dresser. He opened the top drawer despondently, surprised to find a little black box, the kind normally reserved for a ring. He opened it, the inlay still there, the slit empty. Where was the ring? On Jason's finger? Had the new guy proposed when giving the ring to him? Were they that far along? Envy made him clench his jaw. The box snapped shut, William's fist enclosing it. Then he shut the drawer without putting it away. He was stealing, wanting a piece of the life that Jason now had with someone else.

William returned to the bathroom and put on his old clothes. He pocketed the ring box, and after shaking his head at his own reflection, went downstairs. Ben was setting plates on the table. Tim played in the backyard with Chinchilla, but William saw no sign of Jason.

"Sorry if I still stink," he said. "I don't have anything to change into."

"It's fine." Ben smiled at him. "I can't tell you how good it is to have you here."

"You sound like my mom," William joked. "Need any help?"

"Just sit," Ben insisted, sliding into a chair across from him. "How did the move go?"

"Fine. I accidentally shoved the mattress too hard when we were carrying it upstairs and knocked Tim over. Aside from that, it went okay."

"That's fine," Ben said, "but I was referring to you and Jason."

"Oh."

"He told you?"

"That he's seeing someone? Yeah."

Ben studied him. "What about you?"

"Why do you think I showed up here unannounced?"

Ben sighed. "I thought as much."

William swallowed. "This new guy, is he nice?"

"He's…" Ben hesitated. "I don't know if charming is the right word, but he has a certain magnetism."

"So it's serious?"

"Well, they do have a history."

Another gut punch. They had probably been together for years now. Ever since William had been dumb enough to invite Jason to Whataburger, of all places, for Valentine's Day. "I'm glad," he managed.

"You're not, but you're a good man for wanting to be." Ben's finger tapped the surface of the table nervously. "I probably shouldn't mention this, but Jason still loves you. He might have found someone else to be with, but his feelings for you haven't changed."

"Thank you," William said hoarsely. "I'll try to take comfort in that."

"You're both still young," Ben said. "Tim had to wait a long time to be with me again, but eventually the stars aligned just right. I'm not saying I want Jason to go through what I did, but the relationship he's in might not last. Maybe you'll get a second chance someday. If it were up to me—" He checked the doorway to make sure they were still alone. "—I know who I would rather have as my son-in-law."

This made William feel better. Tim entered soon after, complaining that he was starving and that he would be dead by the time Jason came downstairs. Ben rolled his eyes but went to fetch a piece of lasagna. He chastised Tim for not waiting, but his expression was pure love when Tim started shoveling food into his mouth and making happy noises.

Then Jason walked into the room, bringing shadows with him. He didn't look happy. When William insisted on serving, using a spatula to slop lasagna on Ben's plate and then Jason's, it didn't earn him any warmth. Instead Jason ignored the food, staring a hole in his head. William sat across from him and offered a smile. It wasn't returned.

"Eat up," Ben said, looking concerned.

Jason did as he was told, but not for long. After a few bites, he let the fork drop to his plate and shot an accusing glare across the table. "What the hell!" he shouted. "You *wanted* me to be with another guy? How could you even say that?"

William looked at Ben and Tim, wishing for privacy to explain himself, but he had a feeling it was now or never. "I didn't want you waiting for me. I wanted you to have your freedom."

Jason crossed his arms over his chest. "Why? What's the use?

Did you really think that would stop me from loving you?"

When he put it like that, it did sound lame. "Eventually."

"*Really*? Simple as that?" Jason clenched his jaw, head shaking. "Well, I don't work that way. Maybe you do. Took you about two years to stop caring about me, didn't it? That's when it really ended!"

William couldn't meet his gaze. He felt ashamed. He wanted Jason to move on, and yet he had shown up again. Sure he had waited two years this time, but it was still the same bullshit William always put him through.

"Maybe we should give them some privacy," Ben said, pushing away from the table.

"I'm not done eating!" Tim complained.

"It's okay," William said, taking the napkin off his lap and setting it next to his plate. "I should head home. My mom will be getting worried. She hates it when I ride my bike at night."

"We can give you a ride," Ben offered.

"No, really. It's fine. Thank you for dinner. It was wonderful seeing you again." He looked to Jason, who was glaring at the food in front of him. "All of you."

Jason met his gaze, his anger wavering, but William didn't stick around because he knew the reaction was justified. This time really would be the last. Even if he had to move far away. Whatever it took to stop tormenting Jason's heart. William fought against tears as he left the house, not allowing himself the right to cry, because this was his fault. He had brought this upon himself and everyone involved.

Once outside he grabbed his bike and started walking it down the drive. He fought the urge to look back. Then he got onto the seat, put his feet on the pedals, and started picking up speed.

"Wait!" Jason cried out.

William looked back to see him running behind, pumping his arms and trying to catch up.

"Please! I'm sorry!"

William squeezed the brakes, tires skidding to a halt. "I'm the one who should be sorry."

"No." Jason bent over, hands on his knees to catch his breath as he shook his head. "Let's just forget everything, okay? That was no way to welcome you back. Let's just move on."

The phrase stung, and although he was sure it wasn't meant to be a barb, he didn't like having his own advice thrown back at him. "I really do have to get home."

Jason grasped the handlebars as if to stop him. "We're having a housewarming party. Emma and I. We can make it a homecoming party too."

That was sweet, and more than he deserved. "Do I have to wear a corsage?"

Jason grinned. "Not that sort of homecoming. It'll be a welcome home party for you. Saturday. Seven o'clock. Please."

William nodded. "I'll be there." He studied Jason, recognizing what he had lost. Then he offered a halfhearted smile and resumed his ride home. He forced himself to calm down and not be so emotional. He had made a decision when leaving for the Coast Guard, and again two years ago. Both times he had been aware of this possibility and had chosen his dream over his love life. It hurt. Part of him regretted it. A big part, but he wasn't going to torture himself over it like he had the accident. This was different—intentional—and he was man enough to accept the consequences. He would never forget Jason or stop loving him. If Ben was right and someday William was lucky enough to get a second chance, he would take it. Now it was time to consider the future and decide what he wanted to make of it. But first, he wanted to get blitzed.

Chapter Twenty-two

William placed the empty beer bottle on the dresser next to his bed where he had set all the others. When he realized he had enough, he arranged them into a bowling pin formation. Ten empty bottles. At least he hadn't consumed them all, although he struggled to remember how many he had downed compared to his drinking partner.

"Two more," Lily said, pulling the cardboard box across the mattress toward her. "They must be there for a reason." She peered blearily at the nutritional information label. "Six bottles is a single serving, right?"

"I think so," William said. "Let's finish them."

After twisting off bottle caps and clinking bottle necks, they drank and gasped. "This is good," William said, gesturing at their surroundings. "Twenty-two years old and I'm sitting in my childhood bedroom, getting wasted. No, I *am* wasted. How far I've come!"

"I'm so proud of you," Lily said. "Of both of us!" Then she burst out laughing.

"We're pathetic."

"Eh, you're too hard on yourself." She pointed a bottle at him. "As usual! This is exactly why I came here for vacation. I'm Little Miss Responsible three-hundred-something days out of the year. I *want* to be stupid and reckless. You need it too. More than me. Did you ever let yourself get wasted when we were teenagers?"

"No," he admitted. "I was too worried about everything."

"And I've been stuck in a relationship where we couldn't eat anything that wasn't organic or gluten-free or had any flavor or fun. Polenta, almonds, and grapefruit for breakfast. Somebody shoot me."

"At least he was hot," William said. "Let me see his photo again."

"For real?" Lily didn't wait for an answer. She set her bottle on the side table, flopped back on the bed, and started messing with her phone. Then she held it up.

William leaned near. This photo was hotter than the previous because in it Dave was shirtless, droplets of water on his long torso, the camera held low and pointing upward—probably right where his cock would be—to take a selfie. "Wow. Are you sure he's not the one? Because he sure looks like the one."

Lily laughed, then turned the phone so she could see the picture. "He's pretty, but *way* too controlling. Everything has to be done a certain way. The first time he invited me to his apartment, I thought he must have hired maids to make it look that nice, but no. He's anal as hell. I didn't like his attitude about the baby situation either, like I was failing him by not producing an heir."

"That bad?"

"Pretty much."

"Jason was sweet," William said. "I never should have…" He took a swig of his beer, annoyed that it was already half-empty. Why did they make them so damn small? "I ruined everything."

Lily sat up. "Living your own life isn't a bad thing! It's healthy! When we were teenagers, and you two hadn't been together long, you would have been crazy to give up your dreams for someone you barely knew. I would have kicked your ass."

William felt a surge of affection for her. "You're right. What about your dreams? Do you feel like Dave got in the way?"

She shook her head. "I wouldn't let him. My career is too important to me. I didn't get in the way of his either. In a healthy relationship, you come back home at the end of the day exhausted but satisfied and enjoy the afterglow together. Or make your own afterglow."

William's eyes moved back to her phone. "Was he good like that?"

Lily smirked. "I know exactly what you're asking." She tapped and swiped and held the phone up again.

William squinted at the screen and saw the typical image of a shirtless guy taking a photo of himself in the mirror, face twisted up in concentration. The dark tuft of hair on his chest matched the one down below where— "Whoa! Hey! I can see his… Jesus, Lily!"

She laughed, not the least bit embarrassed. "So what do you think?"

"You're terrible!" William glowered at her. Then his attention moved back to the screen. "How big is that thing anyway?"

"I don't know," Lily said. "I never got around to measuring. He knew what to do with it too. We definitely had chemistry in that department." She started moving the phone away, but William grabbed at it because he wasn't finished looking.

They both laughed at his behavior, then Lily studied him. "Can I ask you something?"

"What?" he said, finally pulling his eyes away.

"When we were teenagers…"

William covered his face in embarrassment and groaned. Their makeout session. In this very room, on this very bed. "I knew you would bring that up!"

"It was confusing as hell!"

He dropped his hands. "For us both."

"Really?"

William shrugged. "Yeah."

"Were you just pretending you liked me because you didn't want anyone to realize that you're gay?"

He sighed, trying to remember what his thoughts had been. "I honestly don't know."

"Because the one thing that bothered me—" She shook her head. "Never mind."

"Don't keep me in suspense!"

She grabbed her bottle and took a generous swig. "I'm pretty sure you were hard. I *know* you were, because my hand brushed against it, and unless you had a banana shoved down there…"

"It's not that big," William said, cheeks flushing.

"No?"

He thought about it. "Depends on how big of a banana we're talking about."

"So you were?"

A lot of time had gone by, but he was pretty sure she was right. "Yes."

"How? Were you thinking of a guy?"

"No." He shook his head, trying to make sense of it. He used to look at straight porn when jacking off. He forced himself to. Sometimes no guys were involved, and it still worked. Somehow. "I guess there's an exception to every rule."

"And I'm it?"

He looked up at her. "Yeah. You're pretty."

"So are a lot of girls."

"But you've got a great body. I love that you're athletic, and that you never wear much makeup because you really don't need to. Your personality is part of it too. I hate saying it, but with some girls, I had to guess what they were really thinking or feeling but—"

"I have no filter."

William laughed. "Yeah. That can be a good thing."

"I only wish everyone agreed with you." She scooted toward the edge of the bed and stood. "I gotta use the ladies room." Lily walked to the door, then turned around. "Do you think it would have worked? Do you think we could have…"

William looked her over. He was drunk, but even when sober he thought she was an amazing woman. If anyone could have coaxed him into that situation, it would have been her. He nodded. "Yeah."

She stared at him, then left the room.

William finished his beer. He tried to remember that day in more detail and imagine what would have happened if he hadn't met Kelly. Would it have been so bad? Right now the idea of being with anyone was a comfort. He couldn't have Jason, and that sucked, but he also didn't want to be alone. He wanted to feel loved.

The door to his bedroom opened. Then it shut again, Lily pressing her back against it. "It's getting late," she said.

"Yeah."

"Mind if I crash here?"

He wondered what she was really asking and then realized he had a preference. "I want you to stay. I think."

"You think?"

He nervously passed the bottle from hand to hand, the glass growing warm. "This is outside my comfort zone."

Lily smiled. "It's well within mine. I can show you what to do. If you want."

He nodded. Lily flicked off the light switch. The room went dark except for the orange glow of distant streetlights outside the window, which was enough to gently illuminate her as she came near. He stood to meet her, uncertainly rising with him, but as their lips met, it dissolved. Kissing her was soft, devoid of the coarseness he was used to. Even when guys shaved every day, the difference was between abrasive sandpaper and one with a fine grit. He found he didn't miss that, or the aggression he was used to, because Lily wasn't passive. She took control, helping him out of his shirt, taking off her own, along with her bra. If he was honest, the breasts pressing against his chest didn't do anything for him, but he did like how strong he felt compared to her. Even though she was athletic, her frame was still much smaller than his. The contrast was beautiful, and he found himself eager to explore it. His pecs were hard, her breasts soft in the palm of his hand. He was heavy, and lifting her in his arms was easy.

He gently placed her on the bed and climbed in. He started undoing her pants, stalling when he realized he wouldn't find what he was used to. Lily seemed to sense his uncertainty, pulling him close for more kisses and then pushing him over onto his back. She got his jeans open, her mouth feeling like any other. William was responding, enough that the drunken confusion of his mind gave up and handed the reins to his body. Lily got out of bed briefly, pulling off his jeans. He looked up and watched her finish undressing. Then she climbed over him, kissing him, rubbing against his stomach. She took hold of his cock and sat upright.

William held his breath. Then exhaled once he was inside her. He thought of Kelly, how good that had felt despite not being his preference, and how this wasn't so different. The pleasure was enough for his body to perform, his mind deciding to participate after all, throwing erotic imagery his way. He thought of Dave's dick, of how it had been where he was now. Lily's body leaned close to his. No doubt it had writhed against Dave's muscles as it now did his, the same gentle moans whispered in his ear. William stopped being passive, his hips moving, hands exploring her back or gripping her hips. He grabbed her tightly, rolling them both over so he could take control. Her hands reached up to touch his face. His eyes closed as he focused on the pleasure. He was getting close, not understanding how to tell if she was or how to even get her there, but her light moans became words of encouragement. William lost control, becoming an animal, thrusting with increasing urgency and then growling with release. He kept moving, the pleasure so overwhelming it became unbearable, but he wanted to make sure she was satisfied too.

A giggle made him open his eyes, meeting a pair half-lidded and brown. "You can stop," Lily whispered. "You look like you're in pain."

"I just wanted to... Are you done?"

"I'm happy," she said, pulling him near. "An old forgotten dream just came true."

"Really?"

"Yes," she said. "We're at the part when you would hold me throughout the night. Any chance of that coming true?"

"Yeah," William said, rolling over onto his side. He felt a little conflicted, and confused, but having a warm body to press up against helped silence these doubts. The alcohol and fading endorphins in his bloodstream calmed him further, as did the words Lily murmured next.

"We're okay," she said, as if sensing he needed reassurance. "Beats being lonely, right?"

"Definitely," William said, pulling her closer. "I'm glad we've got each other."

William awoke, taking what felt like his first breath and his last. He hadn't made it through his years in the Coast Guard without getting drunk occasionally, usually at the behest of his crew. Nothing like good ol' peer pressure to make him do something stupid, or a killer hangover to ensure he didn't do so again any time soon. The events of the previous night came back to him, his stomach sinking. Lily was on the opposite side of the bed, their bodies no longer touching. Currently she was gently snoring. That amused him. He didn't know girls snored. He didn't know much about girls at all, although he supposed his expertise was broader now.

He carefully untangled himself from the sheets, then crept across his room to the door. He peeked outside to make sure the coast was clear. The upstairs was empty, his brothers' old bedrooms no longer occupied. Then he looked back to make sure Lily was still sleeping before he slipped out and went to the bathroom. He drank from the sink, used the toilet, and got in the shower. Once beneath hot water, he allowed himself to consider it all.

Was it bad, what they had done? No. They were both single adults and had been equally drunk. Still, that sinking sensation… He followed it and realized it had less to do with regret than it did his fear that Lily would get hurt. William liked her. That's as far as it went. His heart still longed for the guy he couldn't have, his hormones conjuring images of men when he soaped himself down there. Last night had felt good, but didn't change anything for him. He worried that Lily wouldn't be able to say the same. She had described him as a dream come true!

Once clean and wrapped in a towel, he returned to the bedroom. Lily was awake, sitting on the edge of the bed and looking just as rumpled as the day-old clothes she wore.

"Hey," she said.

William remained where he was. "Hi."

"I slept great."

"Are you okay?" he blurted out. "I'm sorry. I shouldn't have done that to you."

Lily's eyebrows shot up. "Don't be a sexist dick. I'm not some virgin you tricked into deflowering. This lily lost her petals long ago."

"Sorry, it's just… Sorry."

She studied him, then laughed and shook her head. "You're too sweet. You know that?"

"I am?"

She didn't answer the question, asking one of her own. "So was last night an epiphany for you? Or are things still the same?"

"I'm gay," he said.

"Could have fooled me." Lily raised a hand to stave off any response. "Sorry. That wasn't fair. Could you get me a water?"

"Sure." He went downstairs, towel and all, and grabbed a bottle of water from the refrigerator. "For Lily," he explained to his mother, already praying that would be the end of the conversation.

When he was back upstairs, he got dressed while Lily slowly rehydrated herself. He supposed there was no point in being modest now.

"I slept with a girl once."

William turned around in surprise, tugging a shirt down around his hips. "What?"

"I slept with a girl," Lily repeated. "The circumstances were similar. We were high instead of drunk, and I had just signed the divorce papers. She was my attorney. Ugh. Anyway, I was horny, vulnerable, and needy, so I figured what the hell. It felt great too, but the next morning, I wasn't looking for a repeat. Humans are physical creatures, and in the right situation, we're capable of doing things way outside our norm. So if that's how you're feeling right now, I understand."

William nodded. "Yeah. That's where I'm at. What about you?"

Lily sighed and stood. "I was planning on proposing."

William's stomach dropped again. Then he felt foolish when she started laughing. "Okay. You got me."

"The truth is," she said, stepping close and kissing him on the cheek, "I would happily call you my man if you were straight. But you're not, and I accept that. Getting to steal your virginity was pretty awesome though."

"I wasn't a virgin!" William protested.

"Your straight virginity then," Lily said, heading for the door. "I'm going to use the restroom. Then I'm out of here."

"You can stay," he said hurriedly. "We can go out for breakfast or something."

"Tomorrow," Lily said. "As cool as I'm playing this, it is a little weird. I need my space to think it all through."

"Okay," he said, feeling unhappy. "I know we haven't seen each other in forever, but I hope this doesn't ruin anything."

Lily smiled. "I have a lot to think about, but I already know I'm not letting this come between us. Nothing has been ruined, I promise. I'll see you later. Okay?"

William wouldn't let her get away that easily. "Come here." He grabbed and hugged her, squeezing twice. Then he returned the kiss to her cheek. "I'm glad it was you."

She pulled away, nodding in understanding. "So am I."

"You'll call, right?"

She laughed. "Maybe. You'll definitely see me again."

"Jason has a housewarming party on Saturday," he said. "Wanna be my date?"

"You're not making this easier on me," Lily said, shaking her head. "You're really going?"

"I agreed to," William said. "He was really insistent. After everything else I've done, I don't want to break a promise."

"Fine. I'll be your plus one, but that doesn't mean I'll put out!"

He laughed. "My loss. I mean that."

"You better." She looked at him with longing, then turned and walked out of his room, but hopefully, not his life.

William knew he should stay away from Jason. He promised himself he would. Not out loud, thankfully, because that made it count. He tried his best to distract himself regardless. He took Lily out to breakfast the next day, and to his relief, their friendship mostly felt the same. She kept teasing him about his O face, doing what he hoped was a very exaggerated imitation, but there were no longing glances or lingering tension. They were friends, the experience bringing them closer rather than causing a rift.

William spent time around the house and got to know Buck better, mostly to make his mom happy. He went shopping with his father and Gina, who insisted on buying him new clothes. He even contacted Kelly, wanting to make sure he was doing okay. From the sound of things, he was doing great and about to have his first photography exhibition. They made plans to meet there. Despite all of this, he was left with time on his hands. He went to his old YMCA every morning and swam, picked up around the house, helped run errands, and yet still found opportunities to dream about Jason, miss him, and think of excuses to see him.

That's how he ended up at a pet store, and when that didn't pan out, the animal shelter where Jason volunteered. He had no way of knowing if he'd be there, but Jason wasn't at his day job, so he had to be either there or at home. Unless he was visiting Ben and Tim. Or was on a date with his boyfriend. Ugh.

William's heart pulled out of a nosedive when he saw a guy in a field near the animal shelter, holding on to a number of leashes as he was yanked around. Was it Jason? Surely he'd be better at walking dogs at this point. By the time William parked the car and got out, the field was empty, so he went inside.

"Can I help you?" asked an older woman working the front counter. "Are you looking to adopt?"

"I'm definitely searching for an orphan," he said. The joke fell flat, so he added. "I just wanted to look around. A friend of mine works here. Jason Grant?"

"Jason!" the woman said happily. "Of course."

"Is he working tonight?"

"Yes. Should I get him?"

"No! No, like I said, I just wanted to have a look around."

"Okay." The woman pointed him in the right direction.

William walked to a wall of large cages, expecting to find an equally large animal inside of one. Instead he saw a cat tree, a number of beds and toys, and a litter box off to one side, but no cat. A photo of an orange tabby hung on the cage, a printed explanation below the name and description: *Privacy gives our animals a sense of security. If you're interested in seeing a potential pet that is shy, please ask a member of staff for assistance.* The next cage was the same, and the next, except the fat tabby there steadily glared at him from the highest bed.

A door squeaked open, attracting his attention. Jason walked in and turned in the opposite direction, attention on people browsing other cages. William strode over to him as quietly as possible. "I'm looking for a housewarming present," he said.

Jason spun around, William tense because he was uncertain what his reaction would be. Surprise, but then what? Anger? More harsh words? Nope. A smile! When William saw it, he felt like grabbing Jason and nuzzling noses... or maybe not, because something smelled gross.

"Oh!" Jason said, noticing him sniffing. He lifted one of his feet. "I had a little accident. A dog, I mean. Not me. Ha ha!" His cheeks became redder. "So what are you doing here?"

"Like I said, I'm looking for a housewarming present."

Jason shook his head, not satisfied with his answer. "But how did you know I'd be here?"

"Just because we've been apart four years, doesn't mean we haven't spoken. We kept in touch a fair amount, didn't we?"

"Yeah, of course. It's just that there's more than one animal shelter in Austin and—"

William cut him off. "All those text messages you sent me? Every email and letter? I read them all. Multiple times. I never stopped caring about you. My leaving wasn't about that." This outburst was greeted with silence, but he felt better for having said it. He wished it would turn into a discussion, but Jason's mouth had clamped shut. "So anyway, what sort of pet do you think my friend would like? He's about your age, your size. Just got himself a rockin' two-bedroom apartment."

Jason tore his eyes away, considering the cages as he started walking. "Hm. I'd imagine he likes big dogs. Not really into puppies because they take more effort and get adopted easily. He's probably the type who likes ugly mutts with problems, because he knows they'll have a hard time finding a home."

"So something big, ugly, and weird. Have anything like that here at the moment?"

Jason stopped. "Honestly, I bet your friend is a little too overwhelmed with all the changes in his life to take on a pet right now. It's a nice idea. I'm sure your friend will appreciate the thought."

"I hope so," William said, wishing he hadn't introduced the word friend, even though it was probably accurate. They had been so much more once, but that's how these things went. When romantic relationships come crashing down, in the best-case scenario, the only thing you can pull from the rubble is a friend. Speaking of which… "Hey, I called Kelly the other day."

Jason's face became a little strained. "Really? How did that go?"

"Fine. He said you guys had lost touch."

"Yeah. Sad but true. We actually got along pretty well after you were gone."

"I heard. Anyway, his photography has really taken off. He has his first exhibition next week, and look—" William pulled out a folded brochure he had picked up, pointing at the address. "That's Tim's gallery, right?"

"Yeah," Jason said.

"So do you want to go with me?"

"To the opening?" Jason hesitated. "Is that a good idea? If you're trying to get back with Kelly…"

William laughed. "No. And even though that bridge has been thoroughly and completely burned, I still want to show my support."

"Yeah." Jason nodded. "Okay. It'll be good to see him again."

"I wonder why Tim didn't mention it to you."

"Probably didn't make the connection. You'd be surprised how many artists try to get their stuff shown at the gallery. It's getting national attention."

"Cool. Hey! Did he and Ben tie the knot yet?"

Jason looked exasperated. "Nope. They haven't even set a date. They're too happy or superstitious or who knows what. I think they're being silly and should get it over with."

"Hm. Maybe we should have a preacher meet us there one morning, march up to their room, and make them go through with it before they can even get out of bed."

This made Jason laugh. "Yeah, we should! That might start a new trend. People can get married in bed and consummate the marriage right then and there."

"Would make being a preacher a lot more interesting."

They laughed, walking past a few more cages. William tapped one of the signs defending an animal's right to privacy. "Is this your work? I remember you talking about wanting to improve conditions here. Looks like a nice setup."

Jason nodded. "It's better, but still not what I want. Do you remember Marcello?"

William made a face. "How could I forget?"

"No kidding. I think I want to get his help. He's good at fundraising. I've been doing all right, but we'll need real public awareness and support to make this shelter into what I'm dreaming of."

"I imagine the cages going completely," William said. "You'll train the animals to run the place. A Doberman will open the door and greet people when they arrive. A sheep dog will work the counter, and that grumpy-looking cat back there will be the security guard."

"You read my mind," Jason said. "For now, I'd just be happy to find them all homes. Speaking of which, we have work to do."

"We?"

Jason nodded happily. "You're walking the dogs with me."

"I can do that!"

"And picking up any poop we find."

"Oh."

"There'll be treats at the end."

William perked up. "Really?"

"For the dogs." Jason nudged him playfully. "Let's go."

Once they were outside, the light of the day slowly fading, William expected the conversation to turn serious. Now they would tackle unresolved issues of the past, discussing why they shaped the present and what that meant for the future. He remained silent so Jason could broach whatever subject he most needed to, but all he seemed interested in talking about was animals.

"That's basically you," he said, nodding to the dog William was walking.

"Gosh, thanks."

"I mean it. If you were a breed, that's the one it would be."

The dog had tight curly hair, not unlike that of a poodle, its fur charcoal gray. "We don't look much alike."

"No, but a Portuguese Water Dog is bred to be a good

swimmer. They even know how to dive. Traditionally they used to go out with fishermen, so they're very hard-working."

"Cool!" William said, a little more spring in his step. "In that case, thank you."

Jason laughed. "No problem. If you ever want to adopt, that would be a good match."

"And what about you?" William asked. "I'm not really planning on getting you a dog, but which breed would you be?"

Jason shrugged. "I'm not sure. I don't think many dogs know how to play guitar or enjoy horror movies."

William chuckled. "How about dogs that are nurturing?"

"Nurturing?"

"Yeah. Like they help take care of others. That's what you're doing here. I think it's awesome."

Jason smiled at the compliment. "Maybe one of the sheep herding breeds then. Like a Border Collie."

William looked over, trying to imagine Jason as a dog. The eyes would be alert, the hair rumpled and messy. God that would be cute! If William found him in a shelter cage, he'd instantly fall in love and bring him home. Just the idea made his heart swell.

"Here," Jason said, handing him a plastic bag. "Pick that up for me, would you?"

Obviously he was the only one feeling the romance. He realized then what he was witnessing. This was Jason having moved on. Past William leaving him and the emotional turmoil that must have caused, Jason had picked himself up, sought a worthy cause to fill his days, and even found a new boyfriend. Job, family, friends, and lover. He had everything he needed. No wonder Jason had been so upset when William showed up out of the blue and threatened to ruin it all again.

"I'm proud of you," William said. For everything, but he didn't want to make things awkward so he focused on the current situation. "It's really cool what you're doing here."

"Thanks," Jason said. "I just wish there was an end in sight. You find a home for one animal and feel good for about two seconds, then you turn around and three more are on your doorstep."

"I can relate," William said. "Although we never had to keep our survivors in cages. A few of them I would have liked to."

Jason laughed. "Really?"

"The drinkers, definitely. Or this one guy, who threatened to sue because I forced him off his sinking boat. I get that it was his home, but me letting him stay wouldn't have saved it."

"Wow. That's messed up."

"Yeah."

Jason looked amused. "Maybe we could team up somehow. Your original idea wasn't bad, but instead of training animals to run the place, we'll enlist them in the Coast Guard and have them play fetch with people instead of balls."

"You're joking, but we've had a few."

"No!"

William nodded emphatically. "Mostly on cutters. The boats. Sinbad was the most famous. They enlisted him and everything. He even saw combat!"

"Was he hurt?"

As William continued telling the story, Jason listened with rapt attention. Once they were back at the shelter, William pulled up photos of Sinbad on his phone, like the one of him sleeping in a hammock, two coasties watching over him affectionately.

They walked another pair of dogs together, the mood remaining light, but clearly Jason had plenty more work to do, so William made an excuse to leave.

"You'll be at the party, right?" Jason asked before he went.

William nodded. "I'll be there." He was pretty sure he'd go anywhere Jason asked him to, even though he wasn't truly needed anymore. William took a deep breath, forcing himself to accept the truth. If they did have a future together, it would only be as friends.

Jason didn't seem to sleep much. Between managing the pet store, helping at the animal shelter, and enjoying his love life, he still somehow managed to make his new apartment look finished. The furniture had been moved from where William had last seen it, finding ideal spots among more possessions that must belong to Emma. Nary a cardboard box remained. The walls were decorated with pictures and an impressive flat-screen television. Currently it was playing music videos, not that many of the guests were paying attention. The little apartment was currently full, mostly with women, quite a few of whom were checking out his date.

"Are you sure you're not gay?" William said. "Because you'd have your pick."

"Shut up," Lily said. "Although I do see at least one exception to the rule."

He laughed at this, then shot a nervous glance to where Jason stood. William had made sure to arrive an hour after the party began, hoping the place would be crowded. And it was. A total stranger had opened the door when he knocked, and so far, his presence hadn't been detected by Jason. William watched him from a distance and sized up the guy hovering around him. The new boyfriend. His replacement. The guy had dark hair and was good looking. He was sort of familiar too. William kept going through a list of celebrities, trying to find one who matched. At first he was thinking actors, but now he was considering rock stars, because Jason's boyfriend had that kind of vibe.

"Aren't you going to introduce me?" Lily said. "Or are we going to be wall flowers all night?"

"You've met him before," William said.

"Years ago. Come on. This is awkward."

She didn't wait for a reply. She walked straight toward Jason, thrusting out a hand when close. "Hi! Remember me?"

Jason's expression was blank, but when he saw who she was with, it clicked. Sort of. "Holly?"

Lily pulled back her hand before he could take it. "Oh, so close! But no. Holly was the blond. I'm Lily."

"Of course!" Jason said. "Sorry!"

"It's fine." Lily extended her hand again. "I can't blame you for not remembering. At the time, you only had eyes for William."

Her drawing attention to that was humiliating. Or a stroke of genius, because Jason looked him over as if those days weren't so far behind. "I'm glad you came."

Before William could respond, a figure stepped between them. The boyfriend. He was smiling and offering his hand, and for a split second, William found himself back at a bar in Boston, already buzzing from drinking beer on an empty stomach. That's when a guy had sat next to him and flashed the same smile.

"Hi! Nice to meet you. I'm—" *Steve.* "—Caesar."

William took his hand numbly, doubly confused now, because that name was loaded. Jason's first boyfriend, the foster brother who had broken his heart, also shared that name. But this couldn't be him. This was Steve! His mind took three separate people and merged them into one. The new boyfriend was also the fabled guy from Jason's past and *also* the guy from his own past. The smile on Caesar's face faded, either because William had failed to respond or—

"Don't I…" Caesar's eyes widened. He let go of William's hand as if scalded. He recovered quickly enough, focusing on Lily and introducing himself. "Nice to meet you. Great smile! If I had a genie lamp, my first wish would be to make it my own, although it probably looks better on you than it would me."

Charming. And infuriating. William was trying to figure out how he could be both when a familiar voice said hello. Ben was there with Tim, offering him a hug, William grateful for the comfort.

"Nice to see you here," Ben murmured.

"You too," William said, nodding at Tim over Ben's shoulder.

As glad as he was to see them both, he needed to get away to make sense of the situation.

"Let's grab a drink," he said to Lily, but she was still happily chatting with Caesar. "Lily! I'm thirsty."

"Okay," she said, putting on an exasperated expression. "It's hard being so loved. He wears me out!"

Ben grinned. "I know the feeling."

"Yeah, well, get used to it." Tim draped a possessive arm around him.

Even this couldn't make William smile. "Excuse me," he said, eyes meeting Caesar's once more before he retreated to the open kitchen.

"You okay?" Lily said, hurrying to catch up with him.

"No!" he hissed once they were at a safe distance. "I slept with that guy!"

"I hope so! You used to date!"

"Not Jason. The guy he's with."

She snuck a glance over his shoulder. "Are you sure?"

"Believe me, that night is impossible to forget."

"Wow, that good? He's really handsome!"

"Thanks," William said bitterly.

"Sorry. You're handsomer. Way *way* handsomer."

William exhaled. "Maybe we should go."

"Why?" Lily's eyes darted around the room. "Don't tell me you've slept with everyone here."

"No!"

"Seriously, I think I'm on to something. You've slept with Jason, Caesar, me… You're a player, William! Admit it."

He clenched his eyes shut. Then he started laughing. He couldn't help it. The situation was too absurd! "I'm not a player, I swear. This is so awkward!"

"So how? And when?"

"That's the craziest part! This was years ago in Boston. Nowhere near here!"

"And you're absolutely positive?"

"Yes."

Lily exhaled. "Where's that drink you promised, because if I need one, I can only imagine how you're feeling right now."

They each filled a disposable plastic cup with white wine and retreated to the other side of the apartment where they had privacy. From there they observed Jason and his crew.

"Do you think Caesar has said anything?" Lily asked. "Or will say anything?"

William frowned. "I don't know. Jason looks calm. Maybe he won't care. We weren't together at the time, so it's not like I cheated. It just feels *weird*."

"I bet."

"Maybe I should tell him."

Lily was quiet as she weighed the pros and cons. "Are you trying to break them up? Because that might backfire."

William shook his head. "No. At this point, I just want Jason to be happy."

"Ignorance is bliss. I hate to say it, but if Jason wasn't with either of you at the time, then I don't see why he needs to know. Are you going to tell him about me?"

William looked over at her. "Do you think I should?"

Lily took a sip of wine. "Imagine that you and Jason were together and things were moving along nicely. Then I show up and tell him all about our drunken night together. What would you think?"

"That you were trying to break us up, because you're right, outside of a relationship, that sort of thing is private."

"Then I believe you have your answer." She stiffened. "Don't look now, but here they come."

He looked anyway, expecting to see Jason and Caesar. He got it half-right. Caesar was moving through the room toward them, but Ben, not Jason, was at his side. He and Lily went unseen. Ben had car keys in hand as they headed for the door. Regardless, William didn't want to interact with Caesar again, so he moved along the wall to avoid them.

"Maybe he's leaving for the night," Lily said.

"Not with Ben. That doesn't make sense. They must be doing a beer run."

William looked over to where he had last seen Jason, but the spot was empty now. He didn't have to search far, because Jason was making a beeline toward him.

"Hey," he said when close enough. "Can we talk for a minute?"

"Yeah!" William said.

Jason looked at Lily. "Do you mind if I steal him away?"

"Be my guest!" she replied. "I'll get us some refills."

William handed her his cup, then followed Jason. To his bedroom. His heart was thudding. Caesar must have said something, and now Jason wanted confirmation. Right? Maybe not. This wasn't the first time they had snuck away from a party and hid themselves away in a bedroom. Ha! He only wished…

"This brings back memories," William said, looking around the room, which was still too new to have Jason's trademark clutter. "Although last time we were playing waiter."

Jason grinned, leaning against the closed door. "That's right. Uh, but I didn't bring you in here—"

"I know," William said, holding up a hand. "Those days are behind us. No more cheating." He sat on the edge of the bed, his chest painfully tight when Jason sat next to him. "I'm glad we have a chance to talk. There are things I want to set straight."

"Okay."

William took a deep breath. "Two years ago, when we stopped sleeping together or being affectionate, that wasn't because I stopped loving you."

Jason looked over at him. "Then why?"

"Because I felt like I was holding you back. I was never okay with making you wait four years, but every time I returned to Austin, all I wanted to do was see you and be with you, and I knew that kept you hanging on. So I made the decision to let you go. Properly. And it worked. I knew it would hurt you, but you finally moved on."

"No, I didn't." Jason sighed. "I didn't stop loving you. Ever."

William met his gaze, sensing the truth of his words. He couldn't help smiling in response, but it was tinged with sorrow. "That's different than moving on. We'll always love each other. That's how it works. But there's more I want to say because I'm not a saint. I'm human, and I've been with other guys. There were situations I found too tempting, or that I simply wanted. So two years ago, that wasn't an act of self-sacrifice. I needed that freedom, and I needed you to have it too."

"I've also been with other guys," Jason said easily. "After you and before Caesar. Guys who didn't mean anything, and a few who I thought could be something special. But none of them even came close to what you are to me. None of them changed how I feel."

Fair enough. Lily was right. They both had a life away from each other. Nothing was wrong with that, no matter how awkward the situation might be, and regardless of who the other person had been. "The guy out there, he's the one from your past, right? There aren't too many people named Caesar, so I figured…"

Jason nodded. "Yeah. It's him."

"Knowing that makes it easier," William said. "And harder."

"What do you mean?"

He could vividly imagine, due to firsthand experience, Jason and Caesar sleeping together. The pain this caused was overwhelming, and proved he hadn't practiced what he'd been preaching. He hadn't moved on, and he wouldn't be able to resist finding excuses to see Jason. Not while he was so near. "I'm thinking of leaving Austin."

"What?" Jason stood up, turning to face him. "Why would you even say that?"

"I need to figure out what I want to do with my life. Coming home felt good, but I guess that old saying is true. You can never go home again."

Jason sounded exasperated. "Is this because of me?"

"No. This isn't a childish ultimatum. I get that you and Caesar have a history together. It's a blessing and a curse, because if he was some guy you'd been with for just a few weeks, I'd chase him off in a heartbeat. But he actually means something to you.

And you're happy. I want to be happy too, so I'm exploring my options. That's all. The Coast Guard was great, and I'm not sure I'm ready to leave it."

Jason frowned. "And Austin doesn't have a coast that needs guarding."

"That's right," William said. "So it's not your fault. Even if we were together, I'd still have to decide what my future will be."

Jason plopped down next to him again, posture slumped. "I don't want you to go."

"I know."

"Isn't there some sort of civilian job you can take? Ultra-lifeguard or something?"

William laughed. "There are a lot of possibilities. I'd like to keep saving lives, so originally I was thinking of working as an EMT."

"What, like a paramedic?"

"Yeah. I am one already, technically. I had to get my certification as part of training."

"For real?" Jason started laughing. "You're a paramedic?"

"Yes. There's more to rescuing someone than dragging them out of the water. Why is this funny?"

"It's not." Jason got himself under control. "I used to know a guy who wanted to be a paramedic, that's all. You should do it."

"Think so?"

"Yeah! You won't always be young enough to jump out of helicopters, right? Sounds like a good choice." Jason's shoulder bumped against his. "And by the way, I love how casually you say 'I'd like to keep saving lives.'"

"Just doing my duty," William declared with a country twang. Jason's eyes sparkled. Lord, how he had missed them! Going without was just a sliver of the sacrifice they had both made. "When I saved the first guy… You remember that? I texted you."

"Of course I remember."

"That was such a high. I felt so good, like I had paid back a debt. I don't know if that makes sense, but anyway, when it was clear the guy was going to make it, I thought of you. If you hadn't told me to go, that guy might have died. Sure, maybe someone else would have been there in my place, but then again, maybe not." He looked over, wanting to make sure Jason understood the significance. "Either way, you made it possible. By letting me chase after my dream, you saved his life too."

Jason's smile was sheepish. "Cool as it sounds, I can't take credit for that."

"Sure you can," William said. "Him and all the others."

Jason perked up. "How many?"

"It's hard to say, since some of them could have survived on their own, maybe been picked up by boaters eventually, or—"

"How many?"

Of all the rescues, only a handful wouldn't have survived if he hadn't been there. "Five."

Jason's mouth dropped open. "You're a freaking superhero, you know that?"

William smiled, love filling his chest. "So are we good now? You understand what the last few years were about and absolve me of all my sins?"

Jason nodded. "We're good."

Someone knocked on the door, then coughed. Jason looked to it with concern. William ignored the door, staring at Jason instead. They didn't have many moments like these left. If this wasn't the last, it was close to it. He was leaving Austin, but before he went, he wanted to study that face so he would never forget. Not a single detail. There was one more thing he wanted too, a selfish wish he decided to grant himself.

"Time's up," Jason was saying, turning to look at him. "Caesar probably jumped out of the car and ran back to—"

William leaned forward and closed his eyes as their lips met, breathing in Jason's scent and resisting the urge to cry. What they once shared had been beautiful. He forced himself to pull away, saw the affection in Jason's eyes, and was comforted that those feelings hadn't been lost. "For old times' sake." He stood and walked to the door. "From now on, I promise that you're all his."

Throat constricted, William turned and opened the door. Tim was standing just beyond it, quickly looking away to give him privacy. This allowed him to casually wipe his eyes. He hoped Lily really had refilled his wine. He found her in the kitchen, deep in conversation with Emma, Jason's roommate.

"Excuse me," a voice said. "Delivery coming through."

Caesar was squeezing his way into the kitchen, a twelve-pack of beer in each hand. He noticed William, face registering surprise. Then he checked to see if anyone else was near enough to overhear before addressing him. "Long time no see… Adam."

"How's it going, Steve?" William said without humor.

They sized each other up, Caesar speaking first. "Did you tell him?"

"No. I don't plan to. You?"

Caesar shook his head. "I don't want him to get hurt."

"See that he doesn't." William left the kitchen, retreating to the far side of the apartment and tempted to keep running all the way out of Texas, but moving halfway across the country hadn't let him escape these feelings, nor had four years worn them down. The past would always be a part of him, and for that, he was grateful. He couldn't have Jason, but at least the love William felt for him would never fade.

Chapter Twenty-three

"So this is it."

William stood in the driveway of his mother's house. Lily was leaving town, her vacation at an end. He had made her promise to stop by before she returned to Houston.

"Back to the real world," Lily said, sounding wistful. "Part of me can't wait to get back to my routine, but mostly, I could use another two weeks of waking up at ten in the morning and vegging out on the couch all day. What about you? Have you made any decisions? Will you be in Austin the next time I visit my parents?"

"I don't know. I talked to my dad about it the other day— what I want to do with my life. He says I can either treat it like a problem or an opportunity. I guess he felt trapped sometimes, having to stay in Austin and work a steady job to provide for us. He's learning to play the drums. Says he always wanted to be in a band."

"Don't join a band," Lily said in dead seriousness. "I don't see that working out for you." She reached up and rubbed his buzzed hair. "I'd love to see you grow this out. Just once. All the way down to your butt."

William laughed and shook his head. "No way! It was good seeing you again. Let's stay in touch. No matter where I end up, I don't want us to lose track of each other."

"I don't either. Now give me a hug. I've gotta get going."

He was happy to comply. He stood in the driveway, waving at her as she drove away. Then he dragged his feet to the front step and sat, letting the heat warm him inside and out. A neighbor mowed her lawn, kids chased each other with water guns, and overhead a plane traced a line in the sky. He wasn't used to sitting still like this and letting the world move around him. He preferred action, which made his recent lack of direction all the more frustrating. He thought of Cape Cod and longed for his work there—not just the rescue missions but the humdrum chores like maintaining inventory or helping with special events to engage with the community. He missed his crew, especially Christie and her family. He felt like he had gambled it all and lost.

His pocket rumbled. William leaned back to get at his phone.

He expected a text from Lily, one last goodbye. He sat up straight when he saw it was from Jason.

Need a ride to the gallery tomorrow?

A nice offer, but the last thing he wanted was to be stuck in the car with Caesar. *Thanks, but I'll drive myself.*

On your bike? You'll be all sweaty and stink up the place.

He grinned. *A car. I might drive like a granny, but I'll get there.*

Think of the environment! Jason responded. *Car pool with me. You like pools.*

Ugh. Why did he have to be so cute? *What time?*

They confirmed details. Then William put the phone back in his pocket. He considered stealing Jason away by doing anything necessary to force Caesar out of the picture. Would that be so wrong? If William made sure to treat Jason well for the rest of their lives, wouldn't it be worth abandoning his morals briefly? He didn't know, but he was done sitting around. He would make himself useful. Cleaning up the house, taking out the trash, weeding the lawn—anything but feeling sorry for himself. He was finished with that.

Jason picked him up the next night, alone except for Emma. That increased the evening's potential. No need to avoid awkward conversations with Caesar, or see him and Jason being affectionate together. He felt genuinely excited as they made their way into the gallery, pausing to consider the photos on display in the window. Kelly's art! How long had it been since they had seen each other? Four years, at least. Would he look different? Better? Worse?

Definitely better. Kelly strode toward him, and while his appearance hadn't changed that much, something else had. William needed a second to figure out what. No crutches! Kelly walked on two legs! No limp, no struggle. He seemed perfectly fine.

"Surprise!" Kelly said, doing a little dance to show off.

William didn't understand how it was possible, just that one of his greatest wishes had come true. He hugged Kelly, clutching him close and struggling to keep his emotions in check. "You're walking," he managed to say.

"I am." Kelly's voice was soft. Forgiving. "No harm done. It's like it never happened."

William leaned back to look at him, tears escaping his eyes. He knew Kelly well enough to know he was on the verge of crying too. That's probably why he turned his attention to Jason and Emma. "Prosthetic leg," he explained. "It's amazing what they can do these days. When Marcello found out I was looking into them, he insisted on flying me to Germany where they have the very best prosthetics in the world. All paid for by the company."

"I love that man," William blubbered, releasing Kelly and feeling happy beyond belief. "I love you!"

Kelly rolled his eyes and smiled. "Someone fetch William a drink. He gets so emo!"

"Guilty as charged," William said proudly, "and drinking only makes me more emotional, so we'd better stay sober. Unless you want to see a grown man cry."

"Tempting." Kelly looked him over, expression warm. Then he addressed Jason and Emma again. "I didn't expect to see you two here. Thanks for coming."

"It's good to see you again," Jason said. "Sorry for not staying in touch."

"It's fine. Modeling kept me busy. Then I got tired of the scene and ran away from home. What about you?"

"Me? Oh, I've been…" Jason stalled, looking somewhat downtrodden. "Honestly, I'm right where you left me."

William opened his mouth to disagree. Jason had done plenty with his life! His best friend had him covered though.

"You never did know how to sell yourself," Emma said, placing a hand on his shoulder and addressing Kelly. "Jason has been volunteering at the local animal shelter and keeps coming up with fundraising ideas, enough that the shelter has been able to expand. He also trains new volunteers."

"That's really cool," Kelly said, "and much more worthwhile than what I've been doing. Trust me."

"I don't know about that," Jason said. "People seem to be enjoying your art."

"They feel sorry for me. But if you'd like to look around, I'd be interested in your opinion."

"Yeah! Of course!"

William's attention remained on his ex-boyfriend. "I'll catch up with you guys."

Kelly seemed a little surprised that he would want to stay behind, but then said, "Walk with me?"

"Gladly."

They strolled to the nearest photo—a broken-down pumpjack in Colorado—Kelly explaining how he hoped someday all oil refineries would be retired in favor of cleaner energy sources. William knew from their recent phone conversation that Kelly had spent the last few years traveling. The second photo was taken at a school cafeteria in South Carolina, proving he hadn't limited himself to just one region.

"Did you ever make it up to Cape Cod?" William asked.

Kelly seemed distracted, his attention on the gallery patrons. Maybe he was worried about what they thought. "Cape Cod," he repeated. Then he blinked. "No. I'm in New York now. That's the closest I've gotten."

They moved on to the next photo, and the next, and as impressive as they were, William couldn't help but look at Kelly's legs, letting his eyes drift over the rest of his body too. There was a reason William had been so drawn to him when they first met. Kelly noticed his glances, but they had been too intimate for this to feel awkward. "You look good."

Kelly's eyebrows shot up. "If you hadn't shown up with Jason tonight, I'd think you were flirting with me."

William chuckled. "Don't worry, I wouldn't be so cruel as to subject you to dating me again."

"Oh it wasn't all that bad," Kelly said generously. "I've had worse."

"Really? Just how many prosthetic limbs do you have?"

Kelly laughed. "Just one, and when you put it that way, you do sound absolutely villainous. But you're not. You've always been a good person."

William swallowed. "I'm trying to be. I really am."

"You already are." Kelly poked him in the stomach. "I'm disappointed. I expected the Coast Guard to make you more confident."

"That was the plan. And yeah, most of the time I feel like I've gotten my life on track. Funny how temptation can sneak up on you though."

Kelly didn't miss a beat. "Spill it," he said.

William exhaled. "I came back to Austin hoping to sweep

Jason off his feet, only to discover that someone else got there first. He's with another guy, and I want to wedge my way between them, but we both know that can lead to disaster."

Kelly's sympathetic expression turned to one of amusement. "I can't decide if this is karma or not, but I'm pretty sure you deserve it."

William couldn't help smiling along with him. "You're such a bastard."

"I know. But you'll be fine." Kelly took his arm, guiding him farther along. "From what I gather, Jason is still madly in love with you. Give it a few weeks and I'm sure things will shake out in your favor."

"I hope you're right."

They stood in front of the next photo, but they were both too lost in the past to see it. "Ever regret leaving town all those years ago?" Kelly asked.

William tried to imagine being with Jason the past four years instead. Then he thought about everything the Coast Guard had given him, and what that had allowed him to give back, and he knew his answer. No regrets. William hadn't been at peace with himself before the Coast Guard and wouldn't have been a good boyfriend to Jason. He felt complete now, and was certain he was ready to settle down, even though the opportunity wasn't there. He explained this to Kelly, who had turned to look at the entrance. William wasn't sure he was listening, so he asked, "What about you? Do you regret leaving?"

Kelly didn't answer at first, his attention still elsewhere. Then he breathed in sharply. "I can't say I feel complete… But no, I don't regret it. Leaving was the right thing to do." He turned his full attention on William. "So you came back for Jason."

"Yeah. I guess so."

"And it didn't work out."

"Right. Now it's one big nostalgia tour until I decide what to do with myself."

"That's what I am?" Kelly said, the hint of a smile betraying his serious tone. "Nostalgia?"

"I'm pretty sure it's a compliment," William said.

Kelly laughed, but for a different reason. "We were two of a kind when we first met. Both driven and focused on our dreams. Funny that after all this time we would share the same motivation again."

"So you—"

"Came back into town, hoping for another chance with a special guy."

"Me?" William said, even though he knew it wasn't true. "I'm flattered but…"

"No, not you!" Kelly squeezed his arm affectionately. "I met mine while working for Marcello. No doubt you've seen some of my critically acclaimed modeling photos and are crippled by regret."

"When I think of our failed relationship," William retorted, "all I feel is regret."

Kelly reappraised him. "Nicely done! A little more of that fire and we would have made it together. Seriously though, this guy got to me. I fell hard for him, and for a while, it was good. We split up for different reasons than you and Jason, but I find it ironic that we're both in the same boat now."

"So what are you going to do?" William asked. "Lately I feel lost."

"I'll return to New York," Kelly said without hesitation. "I'm broke and struggling, but at least I'm doing what I feel I was meant to. And honestly, I can't imagine you not being in the Coast Guard. I've read about your exploits."

"You have?"

"Google-stalking," Kelly explained. "Some of your rescues made the news. You know that, right?"

"In that case, I don't mind admitting that I've looked at plenty of your modeling photos. Some more than others. If you know what I mean."

"Masturbation is the highest form of flattery," Kelly said. Then he appeared concerned. "That sounds like something Marcello would say. I hope he isn't rubbing off on me! No pun intended. Oh god! Is debauchery contagious?"

"I'm not sure," William said, laughing. "But I do know that I missed you."

Kelly's smile was demure. "On rare occasions, I've missed you too. But don't get used to having me around. Like I said, after this exhibition, I'm returning to New York. Think you'll stay here?"

"No," William said, finally feeling confident about his answer. "I'm not sure where I'll end up, but it won't be here."

"Giving up on Jason already?"

"Yup. Don't say it's a lack of confidence! I've seen the new guy. I could compete, but I've been around them when they're together, and Jason didn't seem too broken up over me."

"I told you he was bad news," Kelly teased. "You should have listened."

William put an arm around him affectionately. "You're right. As always."

Kelly sighed and leaned against him. "You used to say that all the time, just to shut me up. Good times."

"Yeah," William said, matching his sigh. "We had some good times. Definitely."

Jason was missing. The Eric Conroy gallery wasn't huge. It only had three rooms that didn't take long to explore. William had even checked the sidewalk out front, and after seeking permission, went into the back room and poked his head out the rear entrance. Jason wasn't there.

"I'm your ride home."

William spun around to find Ben. "Oh. Hi. Any idea where Jason is?"

Ben chose his answer carefully. "He had something he needed to take care of."

"Is he okay?" William said. "He's not answering his texts."

"I'm sure he's fine." Ben had his keys in hand. "Whenever you're ready—"

"I couldn't find Emma either."

Ben smiled. "She left with Bonnie. I realize it's your occupation, but I promise there's no need for a search and rescue right now."

William's shoulders relaxed. He looked around the gallery, the crowd having thinned out somewhat. So far he had spoken to Marcello, met the famous Allison Cross, and made his peace with Kelly. Those were all the boxes he'd be checking tonight. "I'm ready whenever you are."

Ben turned toward the entrance. "Let's go. All I can think about is a hot mug of tea and an even hotter bath."

"Rough day?"

"No. I just like to spoil myself."

"I thought that was Tim's job." William sought him out in the crowd. "Shouldn't we get him before we go?"

"He'll be here until the gallery closes," Ben said, holding open the door. "If you want to stay that long, you can."

"No. That's okay." He normally thought of Ben and Tim as a package deal. If forced to choose, he liked Ben a little better. Tim was hotter and more exciting, but Ben was more like a comfortable old friend. "New car?" he asked when they walked up to a brown sedan.

"Not for me, it wasn't," Ben said. "I bought it used after we gave Jason my old car."

William waited until they were both inside the vehicle before replying. "I'm surprised Tim didn't buy you something ridiculously expensive and new."

"Oh he had a few ideas! But I wouldn't let him. I still have an independent streak. I even financed it on my own, which drove him nuts." Ben flashed an embarrassed smile as they pulled out of the parking space. "To be honest, he was probably right. My credit isn't great, and I didn't get the best deal."

"Then why'd you do it?"

Ben navigated in silence, considering his answer. "At the time I was still uneasy about using his money. I wanted to prove that I was with him out of love, not because I was struggling to make ends meet when we reunited."

"And now?"

Ben briefly considered the car interior. "Maybe I'll ask him to pay it off as my birthday present."

William laughed. "You two are adorable. I'm going to miss you guys."

Ben's head whipped around. "What's that supposed to mean?"

"That I'm just passing through."

"You're leaving Austin? When did you decide this?"

"Tonight," he admitted.

Ben seemed genuinely distraught. "Because Jason left so suddenly?"

"No, because I can't have him." William looked out the window, the shopfronts of downtown Austin whizzing by. "That sounds petty, doesn't it? I just mean that it hurts too much to be around him when all I want is to be *with* him."

"That doesn't sound petty at all," Ben said. "Jason loves you."

William exhaled. "My ex-boyfriend said something similar.

He and I were terrible together, but I still love the guy. That doesn't mean I want to be with him again. I'm guessing that's how Jason feels about me."

"Have you told him what you want?"

"Jason?" William thought of the stolen kiss. "He knows."

"And have you asked what he wants?" Ben checked his blind spot and switched lanes. "Actually, it doesn't matter if you have, because the answer has probably changed since then."

"What do you mean?"

"Have you ever been in love with two people at once?"

"I guess so," William said, thinking of Kelly again.

"Did you find that confusing?"

"God yes. I obsessed over what would be the right thing to do."

"Which probably wasn't what you really wanted to do, or it would have been an easy decision."

William looked over at him. "Are you having an affair?"

Ben laughed. "No. This was ages ago. My point is that Jason might be in a similar situation. If I were you, I would give him a little more time."

"I feel like I already gave him too much."

Ben nodded. "True, but maybe stick around so he sees that you're actually an option."

"You're saying I should settle down here and hope he dumps this guy?"

"Is there somewhere else you need to be?" Ben glanced at him. "I don't mean that sarcastically. If you can spare a few more weeks, maybe a month… Just in case."

William shifted in his seat. "I can stay, but I need something to do or I'll go crazy."

"Know anything about drywall? Or insulation?"

"No."

"Neither does Tim. Maybe you can figure it out together. He bought this huge shed he wants to use as a studio. I'm sure he could use your help."

"Yeah!" William said, never needing an excuse to be around them. "Is this on your property?"

"Yup," Ben replied. Then he grimaced. "Actually, you're about to see for yourself because we're nearly there. I totally forgot about dropping you off!"

"I didn't even notice!" William said.

"I'll turn around." Ben shot him a smile. "Unless you want to crash at our place for the night. You're welcome to. A change of scenery might do you good, and it's not like you haven't stayed with us plenty of times before."

"I'd like that," he admitted. "Tim and I can start work on the shed tomorrow."

"Then you've got a deal!"

"Awesome." He settled back into the seat, loving the idea. The only thing that would make it better was if Jason still lived there, but maybe he would stop by. Ben could be right. If William proved that he was going to be around, Jason might start to see him as an option instead of just a memory.

William didn't see Jason during the next few days, but the hours passed pleasantly enough. He and Tim worked on the shed, spending much of their time watching instructional YouTube videos or undoing previous attempts so they could redo them correctly. Ben kept them fed, or encouraged them to take breaks by cooling off in the pool that had been installed in William's absence. Often they raced each other for fun. William even let Tim win on occasion. He sometimes stayed the night, Ben having converted Jason's old bedroom into one for guests. Even though the furniture and decorations were different, William always thought of him while drifting off. On some days, when he felt too mopey, he would distance himself from these memories by returning home to his mother's house again.

At the end of the first week, Jason finally showed up. He walked into the kitchen while they were eating lunch, stopping dead when he saw William seated there.

"Hi," Jason said, sounding more than a little puzzled.

"Hey," William replied casually. Then he resumed eating chicken casserole, pretending not to hear the quiet conversation that ensued between Ben and Jason.

"What's he doing here?"

"Helping out around the house."

"What? Why didn't you—"

Ben interrupted, their whispers too low to hear now. Tim winked at him from across the table, causing William to miss his mouth with his fork and poke himself in the cheek.

"Anyway," Jason said in a normal speaking voice, "where's the mail you wanted me to pick up?"

"Oh! Right here."

He glanced over and saw Ben hand him a single envelope.

"That's it?" Jason said.

"Afraid so."

"This is junk mail."

"Is it?" Ben said innocently, moving toward the kitchen counter.

"It's from a pizza place."

"Maybe you have a pen pal who works at Domino's, how should I know? Are you hungry?"

"Starving," Jason said. "You know, if you want me to come over, all you have to do is ask."

"That's what I told him," Tim said. Then he ducked, a roll of paper towels narrowly missing his head.

Jason joined them at the table, eyes still on William, although he didn't seem upset by his presence. That was good. "So," he said, after taking a bite. "What have you been helping out with?"

"The studio!" Tim answered for him. "The new one. We've got the insulation in and half the drywall up. Before we do the rest, I want to wire—"

"Tim," Ben said gently, still on the other side of the kitchen. "Darling, would you help me in the other room? Please?"

"Oh! Right!" Tim grinned, picked up his plate, and left the room with Ben.

"Think they're going to do it?" William whispered.

Jason shook his head ruefully. "I don't know, and I don't want to."

"I thought I heard them the other night."

"First of all," Jason said, "I can't believe you're still into them like that. Second, you've been sleeping here?"

"Yup. In your old room. Now that you're gone, I figured I'd try to replace you. I'm even taking guitar lessons."

Jason shook his head. Then he laughed. "I always wanted a twin."

"Really?"

"No. And I like you just the way you are."

William wasn't sure what to make of that. They ate in silence, William finishing first and Jason pushing aside a half-empty plate. "It's really nice that you've been helping Tim."

William shrugged. "It's good for me too. Gives me something to do."

"So you've decided?"

"What?"

"To stay in Austin."

That depends on you, he wanted to say, but that kind of pressure wouldn't be fair. Instead he said, "I could imagine settling down here."

Jason seemed excited, but for a different reason than he hoped. "You really could move in! Ben was super sad before I left. I expected him to call a lot more than he has. Now I see why he hasn't."

"Only because I've kept him busy. You know how much I eat." William took a deep breath. "Besides, nobody could ever replace you. Not in his life, and definitely not in mine."

Jason was silent, but their eyes remained locked. Then he stood, carried their plates to the sink, and turned around. "I've gotta get to work."

"Okay."

"I have tomorrow off. We could hang out. If you want."

"Yes!" William said. He worried he sounded too enthusiastic, so he added a much cooler, "Sure."

Jason smiled. "Okay. My place? Around lunch time?"

"I'll be there."

He remained calm until he heard the front door close. Then he leapt to his feet, whooped, and went to find Ben. He hoped they weren't doing it, although it would be thrilling if they were. Either way, William was determined to share the news and reward Ben with a hug.

William's enthusiasm had waned by the time he arrived at Jason's apartment the next day. With Caesar in the picture, nothing had changed. He hoped their most recent kiss hadn't given Jason the wrong idea. He had meant what he said. No more cheating. What they had once done behind Kelly's back—that was the first and last time as far as William was concerned.

He knocked on the door, praying Steve… *Caesar* wouldn't answer. God was feeling generous with the miracles today, because not only did Jason answer the door, but they seemed to have the apartment to themselves. Unless the bedroom was occupied.

"You might want to be careful when eating these," he said, setting two Tupperware containers of cookies on the kitchen counter. "Mom kept giggling the whole time she packed them. I think she may have discovered hashish." Or maybe Errol had snuck some into her mixing bowl.

Jason opened the first container, eyes lighting up. He had an oatmeal cookie hanging out of his mouth when he opened the other, a whiff of peanut butter escaping into the air. William watched him chew and swallow, trying not to point out how freaking adorable he looked.

Jason moved the remaining piece of cookie away from his mouth long enough for a quick sentence. "Let's go for a picnic."

"Sure!" That brought back memories, except instead of Kelly being left behind… "Where's Caesar?"

"I don't think he'll mind," Jason said, already turning toward the fridge. "Let's see what we've got. They teach you how to cook in the Coast Guard?"

"Afraid not, but I'm no slouch."

Jason stepped aside so William could see into the refrigerator. "What can you do with this?"

They both studied the minimal contents, coming up with the answer at the same time.

"Sandwiches."

Soon they were standing side by side, working in unison. "I'll make yours," Jason said. "You make mine."

"Okay." William pointed to individually wrapped, flat, orange-colored squares. "Just don't use that stuff."

"Why not?"

"It's gross."

"It's *American* cheese."

William shrugged. "That doesn't mean it tastes good. Or like anything. I don't think it really qualifies as cheese. I prefer Swiss."

"I can't believe they let you into the Coast Guard," Jason said. "They should do a cheese test during recruitment, weed out the traitors. You like pickles?"

"I'm scared to answer. Are they American?"

"They might be Polish. No wait, it says 'kosher' on the label. I think that means they're kosher."

William grinned. Give him ninety more years of this. Please. Was that so much to ask? "You know where we should go?" William said, feeling daring.

Jason stopped what he was doing to look at him. "St. Edwards Park?"

"Yeah!"

"Never heard of it."

But of course he had. As they drove to the park, William began to regret his decision. Their first picnic together was a defining moment in their relationship, and as nice as the day had been, it had been wrought with frustration. They had made clear they wanted to be together, but were unable to act. These memories were on his mind as they sought out the original spot by a small creek, sat shoulder to shoulder, and ate their food.

"Ironic, isn't it?" William said.

"What?"

"Us being here. Last time you were single and I was in a bad relationship. Now I'm single and you're…"

"What are you trying to say?" Jason sounded offended. "That I'm in a bad relationship?"

"No! I'm sure he's really nice. I just meant it feels the same."

Jason snorted. "Oh, you mean you wish I was free to lean over, just like this, and kiss you."

William recoiled. "And then we had a discussion about not putting each other in awkward positions."

"Did we?" Jason grinned, his arm brushing against William's. "I don't remember that at all."

Was this an attempt at humor? Had Jason changed? Did he no longer care about promises or fidelity? "Don't tease me."

Jason became somber. "You're right, and you're wrong. I shouldn't tease you. You're totally right about that. But this picnic is nothing like the last one, because this time we're both free to do whatever we want."

"Meaning?" William asked, heart already thudding. "I don't want to have an affair. I don't want to share you."

"Caesar and I broke up," Jason said. "That's why I stormed out of the gallery the other night. I decided I couldn't handle it anymore, so I went home, and we agreed to end it."

William waited for the smile that always came after Jason had tricked him, but it didn't appear. "You're serious?"

"Scout's honor."

"You're not a Boy Scout."

"True, but I'm being honest with you. I swear."

"Wow." William's mind started to race. A second chance. They could be together! One nagging concern remained: Did this mean Caesar would no longer keep quiet about Boston? He supposed that depended on how amiable the breakup had been. "Is Caesar doing okay?"

Jason groaned. "You're so nice! Yes, the other guy is doing fine. He moved out already, and look." He pulled out his phone and held it up. The text message said something about a new job and a hot boss. Caesar certainly didn't sound bitter.

"Wow," William said, trying to consider the implications. They were both single!

"Yeah," Jason said, misunderstanding. "His parents should have named him Casanova instead."

He kept talking, but William didn't hear because he was still putting the pieces together. This was good news! Was it too soon to act? Did Jason need time to recover from the break-up? He didn't seem too distraught. From what Jason said, they had broken up over a week ago, which meant... That little shit! Jason had been playing him when visiting Ben and Tim's house yesterday, *and* at the apartment earlier, coyly not mentioning that they could be together. Time for a little revenge!

William made sure his tone was grim. "We need to talk."

Jason seemed confused. "We do?"

"Yeah. I contacted the Coast Guard. They have a position for me. I'd work as a technician. The pay is great, my room and board would be covered by them, and the benefits are amazing. I don't think I can turn it down."

Jason swallowed. "You're serious."

"Yeah."

"Where?"

William summoned up his best soap opera performance. "Alaska. I fly out tomorrow."

Maybe he should have been an actor, because Jason bought it so completely that he seemed on the verge of tears. William laughed to show he was only kidding and Jason's sad expression became indignant.

"You were kidding?" Jason said incredulously. "You seriously think that's funny?"

"About as funny as you keeping me in the dark all week," William retorted. "You have no idea how lovesick I've been. All I do is listen to The Cure and pace my old bedroom. It's pathetic."

"Geez."

"I know." William leaned closer. "I'm miserable without you."

"How come?"

"Because I love you." William moved in for a kiss.

Jason pulled back. "Say it again."

"I love you." He felt overjoyed that he was finally free to say it. William wanted the entire world to know! Why not? He leaned back, and as loud as he could, shouted, "Jason Grant, I love you!"

Then he was knocked backward, surprised to find Jason's full weight on him, but he recovered quickly. He stretched out on the grass, wrapping his arms around Jason, and reveling in the kiss that followed. They were together again. No need to discuss it or attempt to squeeze these emotions into mere words. They were back where they belonged. With each other.

Chapter Twenty-four

Paradise was full of simple pleasures, like tracing shapes on Jason's back in the early morning. Or hanging out with Ben and Tim in their yard, listening to their stories and telling the best of his own. Eating takeout Chinese food on the couch and enjoying horror movies together, or getting drunk with Jason and watching him sit shirtless on the floor as he strummed his guitar and crooned. Paradise was amazing orgasms, tender kisses, secret promises, and a hand in his when they went for late-night walks. Paradise was simple, but it was also fragile. Perhaps that's why it never seemed to last. Still, five months was a decent run.

"I ran into Caesar the other day."

They were in the car on the way to a movie. They didn't know which, having agreed to choose spontaneously once they arrived. Jason was driving, which allowed William to gauge his expression. It seemed fine. So far.

"At the grocery store," Jason continued. "It was so awkward."

"Really?" William remained tense, waiting for any of the dreaded keywords. Boston. Adam. Steve.

"Yeah. We both had nearly empty carts, so I couldn't pretend I was on my way out. We ended up shopping together."

Giving them plenty of time to talk. "Did he mention me?"

Jason laughed. "You're mean."

No, he was stupid for steering the conversation in that direction!

Jason shifted in his seat. "And yes, he did."

"Really?"

"He wants to go on a double date."

Now William felt a different sort of apprehension. "No thanks."

"I sort of agreed already."

"Oh."

"Sorry. Considering I dumped the guy, it would have been mean to turn him down. He's moved on. He's already seeing someone, so he won't be trying to get with me, I promise."

William wasn't worried about that. Jason had already made his choice. He just wanted Caesar to remain in the past. "Maybe he'll forget."

"We have plans with them on Wednesday."

"What?"

"You always liked double dates." Jason saw his expression and reached over to tickle his ear. "I suck, I know. At least I made it a weekday so we have an excuse not to stay out late."

Which in William's current situation, didn't really apply. He was working as a paramedic, a job that was familiar in many ways, including the long shifts—three sets of thirteen hours, waiting for anything to happen, responding to a variety of emergencies, and filling out paperwork—all similar to what rescue swimmers do. Racing to the scene of an emergency only to discover someone had cut himself while shaving, or had diarrhea from eating old leftovers—that was frustrating. People didn't call the Coast Guard for trivial reasons, or if they did, William wasn't dispatched to help. With the ambulance, he was required to respond no matter the situation, and a lot of people just wanted a ride to the hospital.

"Sorry," Jason said again.

"It's fine," William replied, returning to the present. "I always have fun when I'm with you. Let's just make it a short night, okay?"

"A short night with them," Jason said. "A long night for us."

William smiled. "Even better."

As the night of their double date approached, William felt increasingly nervous. He kept imagining Caesar accidentally calling him Adam, or he himself using the wrong name, and Jason seeing right through them both. Or maybe Caesar would get drunk and his bitterness would surface along with the truth. William's stomach was churning when they parked at the steakhouse and walked across the parking lot.

"That's them," Jason said.

He spotted Caesar right away, looking sharp in an untucked dress shirt and casual blazer. William felt underdressed in his light sweater and jeans. Caesar's date was nowhere in sight. Scratch that, his date was a woman!

"Uh…"

"He's bisexual," Jason murmured. Then he walked forward, extending a hand, but of course this turned into hugs. For all of them.

"So nice to meet you," said a petite woman by the name of Mia. She had short dark hair and expressive eyes, which were looking between them with genuine excitement. "You make such a handsome couple!"

"Thanks," he said. "You do too." Then it was his turn to hug Caesar. Refusing would seem weird, but he tried to keep his body angled away.

"Should we get a bottle of wine or something?" Jason asked when they were seated.

"Feel free," Caesar said, "but I'm driving, so none for me."

Jason looked over at him, questioning.

"I'll be designated driver," William said. He might not be comfortable behind the wheel, but at least he would keep his wits about him.

"More for us!" Jason said to Mia.

She laughed, still seeming thrilled by their presence.

They gave their drink orders to the waiter, pondered the menu, made their decisions, and settled into conversation.

"How's life in the Coast Guard treating you?" Caesar asked. "Is there a base down here?"

"No," William said. "I'm working as a paramedic these days."

"Really?" Caesar leaned forward, expression full of awe. "That's so cool! How do you like it?"

"Here we go," Jason said, sounding exasperated. When William looked at him for an explanation, he added, "Caesar has a thing for paramedics."

"I thought you liked veterinarians!" Mia said, swatting his arm playfully.

"Is that what you do?" Jason asked.

She nodded. "Just opened my own practice."

"Which one? I volunteer at—"

And so it went. Caesar wanted to hear anything William had to say about his occupation, while Jason and Mia had their own interests, complaining about negligent pet owners or discussing vaccinations. These separate conversations came together when the food arrived, but mostly the table remained divided. William relaxed, no longer worried that the topic would take an unexpected turn toward a drunken night in a hotel room.

"I need to use the restroom," Jason said when they were done eating.

"I'll go with you!" Mia said, rising to join him.

Caesar chuckled when they were gone. "Does this make Jason the girl in the relationship?"

William shook his head, not understanding. "Sorry?"

"You know how women like to go together to the restroom. It was a dumb joke. But seriously, what's the dynamic between you two?"

Was he asking who was on top? "You used to date Jason. Do you really need me to clarify?"

Caesar held up his hands. "Hey, I find it's different from couple to couple."

"True," he admitted grudgingly. He had been the top for Kelly, even though it wasn't his preference. "Still, it's really none of your business."

"Bottom," Caesar said, pointing a finger. "Tops always brag. Bottoms always avoid the question."

Amusement won over offense, William laughing. "Guilty as charged."

"If only I'd known that in Boston."

William glanced toward the restrooms in panic, worrying Jason was on his way back and had overheard. All he saw was overworked waiters. "It wouldn't have made a difference. I don't do that with just anyone."

Caesar studied him. "I take it you haven't told him yet?"

"No. I thought we agreed not to."

"I won't say a thing. I just figured since you guys are long-term now that it would have come up."

"No. Why would it?"

"I told Mia."

"What?" William scooted back in his chair, almost getting to his feet, but what would he then do? Burst into the restrooms and make sure Mia and Jason weren't having a shouted conversation through the wall? They weren't likely to talk much on the way back either. Still, this doubled the chances of the topic being brought up during this date. "Why would you tell her?"

Caesar smirked. "About us?"

"There is no *us*!"

"Easy. Mia is really into gay guys. Not just the sex, but all of it. Coming out, guys dating guys, forbidden love, pride… She likes my stories. Especially in the bedroom."

"Good for her," William said. "Just make sure it stays in the bedroom."

Caesar shrugged, even though he clearly found the situation funny. "Fine. No problem."

When the others returned, Jason didn't seem shaken. Everything was okay.

"Are we doing dessert?" William asked.

"Hell yeah!" Mia declared.

Jason seemed less convinced. "What have they got?"

Caesar picked up the small menu trapped between the salt and pepper shakers. "Let's see. Truffle fudge cheese cake, oven-warm cookie with ice cream… Oh! They have Boston cream pie!"

William stiffened.

Caesar wasn't finished. "Anyone want a cream pie?" He looked right at William. "In their mouth? No need to go all the way to Boston. They've got it right here!"

Mia laughed. Jason did too. William grabbed the menu from Caesar and glared at it. "I'll take the cookie." Then he passed it to Jason, who looked a little confused by his behavior.

"We'll share," he said.

"I'll take the cream pie," Mia said.

"We'll share," Caesar said, winking at her. He waved down the waiter and didn't make any more loaded references.

Conversation remained pleasant, but every muscle in William's body was tense until the meal came to an end and they had paid.

"What next?" Caesar asked. "Should we catch a movie?" He smiled at Jason. "A little putt-putt of the miniature variety?"

"I have a long day tomorrow," William said.

"Oh right," Caesar responded. "Those crazy long shifts. I understand."

"We should do it again sometime!" Mia said.

Jason nodded enthusiastically. "Definitely!"

They said goodbye in the parking lot, triggering another round of hugs.

"Sorry, man," Caesar whispered during theirs. "It was too good a joke to pass up."

"It's fine," William said, but it wasn't. He didn't like having a secret that someone could hold over him, and he especially didn't like that secret threatening his relationship with Jason. Only one solution. He would tell Jason himself. Better he find out that way than from a tasteless joke about pie, and if anything, William was pretty sure it hadn't been a creampie. More like a two-man bukkake. Ugh. That didn't make it sound better. At least one was cutely named after a dessert.

"That was fun!" Jason said on the ride back to his place. "I hope it wasn't weird for you."

"It was a little stressful," William admitted. He could expound, but he had learned long ago that a car was not the ideal place to have a potentially heated discussion.

"Caesar hasn't changed since we were teenagers," Jason said. "He still thinks of nothing but sex. Same sense of humor too. It's not for everyone."

William didn't mind him that much. Had Jason and Caesar never been together, he would have enjoyed the evening. Now he was scared of how it would end, but he wouldn't let that stop him. The truth needed to come out. Tonight.

Emma wasn't home when they arrived at the apartment. He decided to take advantage of the privacy. Jason had flopped on the couch, socked feet on the cushions. He suggested they watch a movie, but William remained standing.

"There's something I need to tell you."

Jason's happy expression faded. "People never follow that up with good news. If you'd gotten a raise, you would just say, 'Guess what, I got a raise!' Tell me you aren't leaving Austin."

"I'm not," William said. "It's about Caesar. I've met him before."

"At the housewarming party."

"Before that."

Jason's brow crinkled in confusion. "I don't understand."

"This was a couple of years ago. I was visiting Boston and went to a gay bar while I was there."

Jason's feet touched the ground as he sat up, his posture stiff. "Boston isn't so far from Yale, is it?"

"Is that where Caesar went to school?"

"Yeah."

"Oh. Well at the time, he was traveling for business, so I guess he had already graduated."

"He still lived up there until recently." Jason swallowed. "So is that it?"

"No."

"Okay. Ugh." Jason hid his face in his palms. "I don't know if I want to hear this," he mumbled through them. Then his hands dropped to his lap. "I guess my biggest question…"

He didn't seem to be able to finish, and William didn't make him. "We slept together."

Jason's head shook. "You're serious? This isn't some fucked-up joke?"

"I'm sorry."

Jason fidgeted, looking anywhere but directly at him. Then he stood and walked to the balcony door. Once he reached it, he turned around. "Why didn't you tell me?"

"I didn't know who he was," William said. "I didn't know his name."

Jason's expression became even more pained. "You slept with someone, and you didn't even know his name?"

Jesus that sounded terrible! "We used fake names. It was a game we played. We talked! We didn't just hook up right away. I never made the connection. I swear I had no idea who he was until the party, and then—"

"Is this something you did a lot? Did you get tested?"

"No! I mean… Yes, I got tested after I was with him and most other guys, but there weren't that many. Most were relationships and not just… you know."

Jason turned away. He opened the balcony door and stepped outside. William hesitated, not certain if he should follow. He waited a few minutes before he did. Jason was at the railing, starring into darkness, his thoughts no doubt equally bleak.

"Are you mad at me?" William said.

Jason exhaled. "I don't know. When this happened, were you and I still… I know we weren't together during any of that time, not officially. You didn't cheat. But were we still involved at all?"

"No!" William moved forward, wanting to touch him, but he wasn't sure if that was still allowed. Instead he stood beside Jason. "This was me trying to move on. The first two years I was gone, it was only you. When I decided I couldn't keep stringing you along, I figured I was the one who needed to move on."

"With Caesar," Jason spat.

"By having a one-night stand! Even before I found out who he really was, I regretted it."

"I doubt that," Jason said bitterly. "I've been with Caesar. I can't imagine anyone regretting it." He looked over, eyes suddenly vulnerable. "Did you two… How far did you go?"

"Blowjobs," William said. "Nothing more." Sure it had been a very crazy version of oral sex, but the details would only upset Jason. Hopefully he wouldn't ask for them.

"Once you realized who he was, why didn't you say something?"

That was the hardest question to answer, because the truth sounded like bullshit. *I didn't want to hurt you.* Really? Jason was definitely hurt now! If that was William's sole motivation, he would have kept the secret. "You were with Caesar at the time. If I told you then, it would have seemed like I was trying to sabotage your relationship. I didn't know that you weren't happy with him."

"And after I broke up with him?" Jason said, voice rising. "It sure would have been nice to know this before we got back together!"

William's throat constricted. "Would that have changed your mind?"

"Maybe!" Jason snarled. Then he grimaced. "I wish I hadn't shared that bottle of wine with Mia. Maybe we shouldn't talk about this now."

"Are you drunk?"

"Enough that I'm not sure I trust myself. I'm thinking some extreme thoughts right now."

"Like breaking up?"

Jason shrugged. The idea wasn't off the table.

"We weren't together," William stressed. "You said you had been with other people too."

"You think that's the same?" Jason said incredulously. "Fine! I guess now's a good time to tell you that I fucked Kelly. You know how we got closer after you left? I guess we got a little too close one night."

William didn't believe him, but it was an effective demonstration because just the idea made him feel hurt and conflicted.

"We didn't," Jason said, voice cracking. "Sorry. Like I said, maybe now's not the right time. I love you, but I think I need to be alone. To figure things out."

"Okay," William said. "Just please don't forget that I didn't know who he was. If I had, I never would have done what I did. Even if I thought you and I would never be together again, I still wouldn't have."

"I know," Jason said, attention on the shadowy trees again.

"Okay. I'm going now. I love you."

Jason didn't reply. William waited as long as he dared, then turned to walk away. He reached the front door before Jason grabbed his arm to stop him.

"Wait! This isn't fair. I don't… Ugh! I hate this!"

"I do too," William said, tears rising because he couldn't stand seeing Jason so torn up.

"You don't have to go," Jason said. "I know you didn't do anything wrong. Logically I get it, but emotionally, this is really messing with me."

"I'm sorry," William breathed. "I don't know what else to say."

"I'm done talking about it." Jason's hand took his. "Let's just watch a movie and try to forget about it."

"Okay."

They sat on the couch, Jason's hand still gripping his, but he didn't think either of them processed the images and sounds that emanating from the screen. Emma came home toward the end, providing a welcome distraction. She talked excitedly about her date, then told a story about someone throwing up in class. She made it funny, and for a little while their troubles seemed to be over, but at bedtime, the tension returned.

"I can take the couch," William offered. He could also leave, but he didn't want to.

"You're sleeping with me," Jason said. "Just sleep though. Okay? I'm tired."

And no doubt if they had sex, Jason would be wondering how it compared to what William and Caesar had done together. He made no attempt to touch Jason when they were beneath the sheets. William lay on his side, facing the wall. When an arm wrapped around him, followed by a body pressing against his, he felt hopeful that not all was lost. Not quite yet.

When he woke the next day, Jason was sitting up in bed, sheets around his waist. He was lost in thought, not noticing that

William watched him until he slid a hand across the mattress.

"Good morning," William tried.

"Morning," Jason said, ignoring the hand. He chewed his bottom lip. "I have a few questions."

"Okay." His throat was already dry, but now his mouth was too. He prayed that Jason didn't want details.

"I need to know why you didn't tell me. I know what you said last night, but once we were back together, or just before, I feel like you should have said something."

"I knew it would hurt you. And it did. I was hoping to avoid that, but when we were out with Caesar, I kept worrying he would say something, and I knew it would be worse coming from him."

"I don't like the idea of you keeping things from me," Jason said. "We shouldn't have secrets, unless it's dumb stuff like not telling me what I'm getting for my birthday."

"Not telling you every detail of my life isn't the same as keeping a secret. You haven't said who you slept with while we were apart, or how many guys there were."

Jason frowned. "Do you want to know?"

"Do you *want* to tell me?"

"Not really," Jason said. "I get what you mean, but this is different, because he's my ex." He shook his head, still conflicted. "It shouldn't matter. Why does this bother me so much?"

"I can't answer that for you. If it helps, I also feel weird about it."

"I think I need time to figure it all out. Alone." Jason finally took his hand. "I'm not doing this to punish you. I just know that, if we're together, I'll obsess over it and ask you things that are none of my business and that won't make me feel better. But if we're apart, I'll miss you and realize that you're more important than all of this. I know that already. I just need to experience it."

"Okay," William said. "I think it's a good idea. We'll let the air clear, set it behind us, and move on."

Jason nodded and released his hand. William slid out of bed, got dressed, and put on his shoes. He didn't want to leave without a kiss. Just a simple peck. Jason reciprocated, eyes apologetic when they didn't need to be.

"We're going to be okay," William said. "Call me when you're ready. I love you."

"I love you too," Jason said.

A small break. The idea scared William, but as he left, he tried to reassure himself by remembering they had survived four years of separation. However much time Jason needed, he was certain they could overcome this.

William stood in front of a door, holding a pie and unsure of the reception he was going to receive. After two weeks apart, a text message from Jason had appeared on his phone. He double-checked it now, just in case he had missed some crucial detail.

Ben and Tim are having a Thanksgiving dinner. 3pm their place. Want to get together then?

Well yeah! He wanted to get together whenever Jason was willing. William hoped he was forgiven. If he knocked, and Jason opened the door, would he be welcomed with open arms? Would they go somewhere private to continue discussing what he had done with Caesar? Or would they carry on as they had before, Jason trying to hide his resentment?

"Precisely what sort of pie is that?" a voice said. William turned to see a large man carrying one of his own. Marcello was glaring at the pie William held, as if threatened by it. "If it's pumpkin, I have no qualms about smashing it to the ground. I went to the trouble of hiring a bona fide grandmother to bake this one for me. You can't get more authentic than that."

"It's a pecan pie," William said, pocketing his phone so he could put a protective hand over the dessert. "Made by a bona fide mother. *My* mother."

"Wonderful!" Marcello declared, any trace of aggression disappearing from his face. "One of my favorites! I'm so glad our pies won't be competing against each other. Yours might be sweeter, but mine is softer and much more receptive to cream."

"This conversation is making me uncomfortable."

"I wouldn't have it any other way." Marcello peered at him. "Correct me if I'm wrong, but you seemed just as uneasy before all this talk of pie began."

"I'm just…" William glanced at the door, which was still closed. "I'm not sure what sort of reception to expect."

"From young Jason?"

"Exactly."

"A hug, a kiss, perhaps a little groping? At your age, physical affection takes precedence. Come to think of it, little changes when you get to be my age. You might as well start practicing now. Go ahead and knock."

William didn't budge. "I did something. When we were apart. I didn't cheat, but I was with someone he doesn't like. Or that he likes too much." He hesitated, but when Marcello nodded patiently, he continued voicing his concerns. "I'm a little confused, because Jason used to date this person, so he of all people should understand why I found his ex-boyfriend attractive. Right? Not that I knew who he was at the time. Sorry, I probably shouldn't bother you with all of this."

"There used to be this gorgeous little French place on the north side of town," Marcello said, as if participating in a completely different conversation. "A small Parisian café so authentic that I often wondered if it fell through some dimensional rift and ended up here. I first discovered it by chance when on a date with Tolga, a stoic but handsome man from Istanbul. My Turkish delight!" Marcello sighed. "He was elusive, not impressed by success or money. My wit didn't amuse him—perhaps due to a language barrier—and any physical advances were immediately rejected. I tried a concert, which gave him a headache, and a museum, which he yawned through. It was during one of these failed dates that we found ourselves hungry and in need of a quick solution, so by chance we popped into the little French café. Tolga perked up immediately. As soon as the first slice of baguette slathered with *tapenade noir à la figue* entered his mouth, he was a changed man. Tolga, as it turned out, had a passion for French culture, and for culinary adventures in general. I took him to Paris soon after. Then I took him in Paris. Ha ha!"

William shifted the pie to another hand, arm growing tired. As interesting as the story was, he didn't see what any of it had to do with him.

"Betrayal comes in many forms," Marcello continued. "The French café became a special place of ours. We returned often and even celebrated an anniversary there. Occasionally I would drop in to pick up some of the olive and fig spread that he loved so much. During one such foray, I was shocked to find Tolga seated at our usual table, a young woman across from him. I watched him hand-feed her a bite of the same spread I was there to pick up. Needless to say, I was hurt. I spoke words I now regret and left in a huff. Later I learned that she was his sister, but to my surprise, the hurt didn't go away. The café was *our* special place, a setting dedicated to our romance, each nibble of food an expression of love—at least in my mind. How could he invite anyone else there, even platonically, when it was meant for me and him alone?"

"That sucks," William said.

"No," Marcello said, shaking his head. "My own childish attitude is what sucked, as you put it. He wanted to share his passion for food with his sister. I wanted all of him, which isn't fair. What business was it of mine what he did when we were apart? Short of cheating on me, he deserved his independence. Unfortunately, I let my hurt feelings get in the way of something truly special."

William swallowed. "You broke up?"

"I'm afraid so."

"You aren't making me feel better."

"I'm telling you what you need to know," Marcello said. "Tolga wasn't good at expressing his feelings. That had nothing to do with his grip on English. Rather, he was a very guarded individual. Had he not been, I like to think he would have told me to get over it, that I needed to stop being petty and recognize that while misunderstandings happen, they are only ruinous when we allow them to be. From the sound of things, you and Jason had such a misunderstanding. Don't let it become more than it needs to be."

William exhaled. He needed to think it over, but it sounded like good advice. "Did you ever go back to that café?"

"Before it closed down?" Marcello asked. "Yes. Many times, but not to eat. Instead I would guzzle champagne and feel sorry for myself." His eyes went wide. "The champagne! I knew I forgot something. Here! My pie is in your capable hands. Promise to be gentle with it."

The pie tin was thrust into William's free hand. "I'll guard it with my life," he promised.

"I'll return soon," Marcello said, already turning to leave, but he relayed one more piece of advice as he went. "Shamelessness can be its own virtue," he called. "Most of my life has centered around that philosophy!"

William watched him go, then faced the house again, feeling

more determined. He knocked by kicking his foot against the door and was about to use his nose to ring the bell when the door swung open. Jason stood there, sheepishly at first. Then his expression softened and he moved forward for a hug. William stepped back.

"Pies!" he said in warning.

Jason noticed them and laughed. "Then you better stand still."

He did so and was rewarded with a kiss. Maybe he didn't need Marcello's advice after all. "I missed you," he admitted.

"Same here," Jason said, taking one of the pies from him. "Let's get these in the kitchen so our hands are free."

That sounded promising! He followed Jason into the house. They paused in the living room, where William said hello to everyone there. Allison waved and introduced her husband and son. Tim grinned at him in a way guaranteed to make William blush. Then they went to the kitchen, where Ben would no doubt hug him and say how glad he was that he was there. He always made William feel welcome, like an essential part of their lives. Right now Ben stood at the oven, concentrating on cooking.

"Hey!" William said to get his attention. "Happy Thanksgiving!"

"OUT!" Ben spun around, swinging a chef's knife through the air. Luckily they were too far away to be in any danger. "Both of you! Out! Now!"

"We're just dropping off pies!" Jason stammered. He turned to William. "Quick! Set them down!"

None of the nearby kitchen surfaces were clear. The kitchen resembled a warzone, the battlefield littered with half-chopped onions, crumpled boxes, empty cans, and pots and pans crusted with different sauces. They were forced to venture deeper into the room to set the pies on the table, Ben keeping a wary eye on them until they left.

"Jesus!" William breathed once safely in the living room. "What's going on in there?"

"He's been like that all day," Jason said, "since early in the morning, according to Tim. When I got here, he was hanging out in the garage just to steer clear."

"Maybe I can help," William said.

Jason raised his eyebrows. "Sure, go ahead and try, but this time you don't have a helicopter to lift you to safety."

"Maybe you're right," he murmured, eyeing their surroundings. Allison and Brian were cuddling on the couch. Tim was lifting up their infant son, Davis, and swinging him around, nearly taking out one of the lamps. The scene was inviting, but he wasn't sure if they were ready for it yet. "Do you want to go somewhere and talk?" William asked.

"About us?" Jason said, shrugging easily. "I'm good. Are you?"

"Yeah!"

The break had obviously worked wonders! Now he was glad Jason had insisted on taking it. He offered his hand, which was accepted and yanked toward the living room. Jason sat in one of the big side chairs, then pulled on him as if they would both fit. They laughed as he tried, William just managing to squeeze in. Davis watched with interest and reached out his arms. Tim noticed this and placed the baby on their combined laps.

"There you go," Allison said with a relieved sigh. "You've found new parents. Now Brian and I can return to a life of blissful solitude."

"Your loss!" William said with a grin, finger already trapped in a tiny fist. "You'll regret it eventually because we become a famous television family due to our new world record. Three people in one chair!"

Davis gurgled happily but Allison didn't look convinced. "I'm sure college kids have beaten you to that one," she said.

Tim puffed up his chest. "All right. It's up to me then. Let's break this record!"

He lifted Davis up so he could sit on their laps instead, Jason groaning in protest. William laughed and felt uncomfortable in the best way possible. Tim started bouncing Davis up and down, then decided to mess with them by bouncing up and down himself. It was getting painful when he stopped suddenly and sniffed.

"Man! Someone needs their diaper changed!"

Allison sniffed too. "That's not my baby! He might be a stinky little monster, but this smells more like... Oh."

In unison, they all looked to one side of the room. A stench was drifting in from the kitchen. William was reminded of the time he had attempted to fry pork chops at Christie's house, had gotten distracted, and burned the meat down to a charred gristle.

"That can't be good," he said.

"Have you never had Ben's cooking before?" Allison retorted. "This is pretty much standard."

"It's usually not this bad," Tim said, standing up. "He's just pushing himself too hard. If he'd let us help—"

They all turned when Ben entered the room, expression manic.

"Everything okay?" Allison asked.

"I forgot something?" Ben said, sounding unsure if that was true. "I need to run to the store."

Tim opened his mouth. "I can—"

"No!" Ben cut him off. "You'll get the wrong thing."

"What exactly do you need?" Allison said, seeming amused. "We could ask Marcello to pick it up on his way over. That giant house of his probably has its own grocery store."

Ben glared at her. "I need cranberry sauce. A very particular kind. Besides, I don't want to trouble him."

"Okay, okay!" she replied. "Just trying to prevent us all from starving to death."

"We can wait," William interjected, hoping to dispel tension, "but it won't be easy because it sure smells good!"

"I'll be right back," Ben said. "Nobody goes in the kitchen! You hear me? I mean it. Stay out!"

William looked at Jason, expecting him to be amused. Instead his brow was furrowed, his jaw clenching. "What's wrong?"

"Seriously?" Jason hissed. Then he shook his head. "This is exactly what led to you-know-what."

"Caesar?" William said in disbelief, trying to keep his voice down. "I thought we were past that?"

"Not when you keep making the same mistake!"

"I have no idea what you're talking about!" His voice was rising, but it didn't matter. The living room was clearing out. Ben had gone, Allison accompanying him, and the rest were using the opportunity to do exactly what they were forbidden: to go in the kitchen. Jason rose as if intending to join them, but William stood and grabbed his hand before he could walk away.

"I don't get what's going on!"

Jason spun around to face him. "You! That's the problem! You would rather lie than hurt anyone's feelings. It smells good in here? Really?"

William sighed. "I was being polite."

"You were avoiding the truth. Again. Remember what happened last time?"

William scowled. "You need to get over it."

Jason looked shocked. Then he glared and pointed to himself. "Now *I'm* the problem? That's how you're playing this?"

"Yes, because I didn't do anything wrong!"

Jason shook his head in disbelief. "It stinks in here. I need some fresh air."

He stomped toward the front door, William hurrying to keep up. He did his best to calm himself, treating this like an emergency situation. "You said yourself that I didn't do anything wrong. Before we took a break. We talked about it!"

Jason continued rushing for the front door.

"You need to see past your hurt feelings! Yes, I slept with Caesar. Yes, that's weird. No, I didn't mean to hurt you. Are you going to let that ruin our relationship? Is that really what you want?"

Jason stopped with his hand on the door knob, head bowed. "No. I don't want that."

William gently took his shoulder to turn him around. "I can't take back what I did. It's done. As far as I'm concerned, it's all in the past. The only one keeping it in the present is you."

"I'm trying," Jason said, studying the floor. "I thought I was over it, but then in there…" He gestured to the living room and made eye contact. "I need to be able to trust you."

"You really wanted me to tell Ben that it smells like he ruined dinner?"

"No, but you could have kept your mouth shut."

"That's exactly what I did when it came to Caesar. Look where that got me."

Jason's shoulders slumped. "This is so complicated."

"If I had slept with someone else, if that one-night stand had happened when and how it did, except with a stranger instead of Caesar, would you be mad at me right now?"

Jason frowned and thought about it. "No."

"To me he *was* a stranger. But I think I get it. You want me to tell you the big stuff instead of keeping quiet. I knew you would be upset about Caesar. If I did anything wrong, it was not telling you sooner."

"Yeah," Jason said, but not judgmentally. "That really is the only thing you did wrong. I get why you would want to sleep with him. I get why he would want to sleep with you."

"And once I figured out who he really was, I should have told you. Imagine how that would have looked though! Like I was trying to split you guys up!"

"And? I probably would have taken it out on Caesar and dumped him sooner."

"So we could be together?" William said, trying a smile.

Jason chuckled sheepishly. "Yeah."

William felt relieved, but he wasn't finished. Marcello was right. He wasn't ashamed of who he was, or what he had done. "I'm not going to stop being polite," William said. "Or nice. That's just me. If you want raw and confrontational, go date Kelly. But I can promise you that if something like this happens again, no matter how upset I think you're going to be, I'll tell you right away. Okay?"

Jason nodded. "Yeah. Okay. Sorry I snapped at you."

"Enough apologies," William said, pulling him close. "I'm more interested in the making up part."

They kissed, just a few shy pecks at first. Then Jason got serious, pushing him up against the wall, their lips and tongues tangling together.

"Maybe we should go up to your old room," William said, pulling away to catch his breath.

"Oh don't mind me," Marcello purred. "I was only watching to see if you needed any guidance."

They both spun around, only one of them not shrieking. Unfortunately, it was Jason instead of him. Marcello couldn't have been there long. He was shutting the door behind him, the necks of two champagne bottles in one hand. Jason went to take these from him, William trying to hide behind him until his erection subsided completely. They walked as a group to the living room, where they witnessed a funeral procession leaving the kitchen. Tim led this wearing oven mitts, an aluminum pan held before him. Resting in it was a charred and twisted beast. The others followed along.

Tim nodded in solemn greeting to Marcello. "I don't recommend anyone going in there until it airs out."

"Should I make a call?" Marcello asked with grave concern.

"No," Tim said. "I've got this one covered. All I need to figure out is what to do with this, uh… Turkey?"

A sound attracted their attention. Claws on glass. They looked to the sliding door. Chinchilla stood on the back patio, head cocked to one side.

"You're the paramedic," Tim said to William. "Think it'll kill her if she eats this?"

"You're better off asking my boyfriend. He's the animal guy."

"She should be okay," Jason said musingly. "Although I do recommend medical supervision."

"Good." Tim held out the pan. "You two take care of this. I'll deal with the rest."

Jason set the champagne on the coffee table and ran to the kitchen for an extra set of oven mitts. Once the turkey was in hand, William opened the door so they could go outside. Soon they were crouching over the turkey and tearing off dry pieces of meat to throw to the dog, Jason the most concerned.

"We need to make sure she doesn't get any small bones."

"I love you," William said, rising to his feet. When Jason looked up at him, he continued. "I'll probably hurt you again. I swear I'll try not to, but if and when that happens, please remember that I never wanted to, and that I love you with all my heart."

Jason stood and walked toward him. "I love you too. Don't ever let me push you away again. Okay?"

William took him into his arms, squeezing tight. "Okay, but right now I need to let you go."

Jason pulled back. "Why?"

"Because I think Chinchilla is planning on making a break for it. Or eloping."

They looked to where Chinchilla was walking backward, turkey trapped in her teeth and leaving a trail of charred skin where it dragged along the patio.

"Think we should stop her?" William asked.

"Who are we to stand in the way of love?" Jason said. "All we can do is chaperone."

"Together?" William asked, putting an arm around his waist.

Jason nodded. "Always."

Chapter Twenty-five

"Merry Christmas," Jason said, sliding a rectangular shape toward him.

William accepted the present, already perfectly content without it. They were sitting cross-legged on the floor beside a small artificial tree decorated with lights. Outside the day was fading to night. Favorite holiday songs were playing elsewhere in the apartment, which they had to themselves because Emma had gone to stay with her family in Houston. This was all the gift he needed—a long night off with just the two of them.

"Don't get too excited," Jason said. "I suck at gift-giving."

"You don't," William said, carefully unwrapping it. A book, which he had already guessed from the heft and size. He recognized it instantly. *The Finest Hours.*

"It's a true story about the Coast Guard," Jason said. "Do you have it already?"

His instinct was to say that he didn't and leave it at that, but he knew what Jason was asking. Had he read it? Yes, when Christie loaned him the book. "I loved it the first time I read it. I don't have my own copy though. Now I do!"

"Dang it!" Jason said, looking annoyed. "I told you, I'm not good at this."

"You did fine," William said, although he did feel proud that his two presents had gone over so well: a Blu-ray set of the *Nightmare on Elm Street* movies and concert tickets to see Spoon later in the year. "Maybe you could read it. That way we could talk about it. Like a book club."

Jason nodded. "Okay. But don't worry, I got you one more present."

The next box he handed over was small. William shook it, feeling something slide around inside. He was clueless about this one, and still a little puzzled after opening it. The Coast Guard theme continued with this gift: a round medallion engraved with the official seal and attached to a keychain. He liked that. What confused him was the attached key. "What's this go to?"

"My place," Jason said. "Or what I hope you'll start calling your place. I want you to move in. I know you're sick of living with your mom. I already talked to Emma about it, and she's fine with the idea."

William looked up, at a loss for words. Except for the two-week-long separation right before Thanksgiving, the previous six months with Jason were the happiest he'd ever known, at least when it came to his personal life. He still wasn't convinced he had chosen the right occupation, but he kept hoping he would get used to being a paramedic.

"No pressure," Jason said hurriedly, misinterpreting his silence. "At the very least, I want you to have a key so you can come by any time you want."

William smiled. "Thank you. I've never had my own place before. Unless you count the barracks, but they weren't exactly private."

"Is that a yes? I can make space for you. Half of the closet, half of the bedroom. We'll put a line down the middle like siblings who are forced to share."

"Don't bother," William said, leaning close. "I'd be on your half of the room every night." After they kissed, he reconsidered. "Well, maybe not *every* night. You know how crazy my work schedule is. Depending on my shift, we might not see much of each other."

"But we're more likely to when living together," Jason said.

"True."

"You still haven't answered. Remember what I said before about no pressure? I take it back. Say yes."

"Yes," William said with a chuckle, "but you have to be the one to break it to my mom."

After a few more kisses, they walked around the apartment to make plans. William was even more excited by the prospect when he remembered the apartment complex had its own pool. That would save him trips to the YMCA, assuming it met his needs. He didn't have a lot of possessions, so he wouldn't have much to move. Maybe a shelf for books, or more important things, like his Transformers. He liked the idea of sharing a home with Jason. This was a major step in their relationship, one he felt ready for.

"Is that your phone or mine?" Jason asked when they heard muted vibrating.

"Mine," William said after checking it. "Text message. It's Lily!"

Merry Xmas! I've got a present for you. Can you come by?

He grinned and texted back. *Sure! Is tomorrow good?*

I was hoping today. While my family is still out.

That gave him pause. *You know I'm with Jason, right? And you have a boyfriend!*

Oh. My. God. Someone is full of himself! I'm not trying to seduce you, asshole. I just can't stand the idea of seeing my family fawn over you. Again.

He laughed and looked up. "She wants me to swing by."

Jason made a face. "Does it have to be today?"

"She says it won't take long."

Jason grabbed the Blu-ray movie set, no doubt eyeing the extras again. "Fine. But tomorrow you're all mine."

"It's a deal. I promise." He kissed Jason and held up the key. "When I come back, I'll let myself in. Make sure to lock the door! I want to practice."

Jason laughed and swatted him on the butt to send him on his way. William grabbed a bottle of wine and his backpack before leaving, wanting to have something to give Lily in return. Despite all the dreaming, Austin rarely had a white Christmas. He was glad, since it meant he wouldn't have to navigate snow while on his bike. The house where Lily's parents lived wasn't too far anyway. He texted to say he'd be there soon and felt giddy on the ride over. He hadn't seen her since summer, but they had kept their promise and stayed in touch by texting or sending the occasional email. Catching up in person would be fun. So much had changed since they last saw each other. He was back with Jason, back in Austin, and back to waiting for the next emergency.

Her family had a nice house at the end of a cul-de-sac, the one-story home spread out over a fair amount of property. He remembered them as private people. William had only visited a few times for birthday parties or school projects. He and his friends usually convened at Holly's house instead. Once the girls had even snuck him in so he could take part in a slumber party.

He smiled at the memory as he walked up to the front door, the darkness of night chased away by festive Christmas lights lining the roof. He didn't envy whoever had the job of taking them down again! He rang the bell, putting on an exaggerated grin and holding the wine bottle at an angle like a waiter presenting it to a customer. When it came to making an appearance, Lily had him beat. In spades. The door swung open, revealing a beautiful woman with a white shirt stretched over a large belly. On it was a big red bow. Lily had either developed a passion for junk food, or she was pregnant.

"Surprise!" she said.

William nearly dropped the bottle. "Oh my gosh!" he said, staring at her belly. "You have *got* to start doing sit-ups!"

Lily pretended to glare, then stepped forward for a hug. William made sure to embrace her as gently as possible. Then he leaned back to look down. "I take it Dave was the one with a fertility problem?"

"Apparently so!" Lily ushered him inside. "You have no idea how much satisfaction it gave me to call him and tell him the news."

"This is amazing," William said as they sat on a couch. He set the wine on the coffee table. "I guess you're not going to be needing this."

"Enforced sobriety." Lily sighed. "It better be worth it!"

"Was your boyfriend excited?"

"No," Lily said. "Definitely not. In fact, he's out of the picture."

William's smile faded. "Are you serious?"

"Yup."

"What an asshole!"

Lily peered at him, as if trying to decide if he was kidding. Then she reached her conclusion. "Oh."

"What?" William said, not understanding what he'd missed. He looked her over again, stopping at the bow on her belly. She had promised him a Christmas present. The pieces clicked into place, except for two that he wasn't sure fit together yet. "How many months?"

"Six," she said, appearing vulnerable.

He didn't need to do the math. Lily had met her new boyfriend a month after they had been together. Maybe two. There was no way that… She had an active sex life though. He probably seemed like a jerk for asking, but he didn't want to react until he was certain. "Is it mine?"

"Yes," Lily said.

"You're sure?"

She nodded. "Dave and I hadn't slept together for months, and it was six weeks before I met—"

"It's really mine?" William said, voice cracking, but he didn't need any more reassurance. He wanted it to be true! Forget all the consequences and complications, he was going to be a father—something he had never thought possible—and the idea alone filled him with joy!

"Are those happy tears?" Lily asked, looking a little concerned, "or are you freaking out?"

William wiped at his cheeks. "Can I touch it? Please?"

Lily stared a second longer and then smiled, lifting up her shirt. William placed the palm of his hand on her belly. She took his wrist and moved it lower down. Then they locked eyes, and he held his breath, waiting for some sign of life. "I just ate," Lily said, "and it usually doesn't take long before—"

A kick! Or some other tiny movement, he didn't know. He smiled up at her. "I felt it!"

"I've been feeling her nonstop, especially in the last few weeks. She loves to kick. Maybe she'll be a swimmer, like you."

"She?" William said, another wave of emotion hitting him. "Are you sure?"

Lily laughed. "I can show you the sonogram. Want to see it?"

William pulled away. "Wait. I need… This is too much."

"I understand," she said. "Take a deep breath. There's no rush. I'm sure you have a lot of questions."

He did. "Why didn't you tell me sooner?"

Lily exhaled. "I wasn't sure if it would be fair. This was an accident, I promise. I had been careless a few times before Dave, and I never got pregnant then either. When he was a teenager, Dave got a girl pregnant. She had a miscarriage, so we both felt sure that I was the problem. Either that girl had been with someone else, or something happened to Dave since then. I don't know. Maybe it's just really hard for me to get pregnant and you have—" She snorted and covered her mouth. "I was going to say strong swimmers."

"I knew all that training would pay off," William said, matching her happy expression. Of course there was plenty to worry about too. A number of negative consequences were nibbling at the edge of his consciousness, but he ignored them, wanting to enjoy what still felt like a miracle. "You should have told me."

"I didn't know how you would react. When I explained to my boyfriend what had happened between us, he acted like he would be there. He said he wanted to be a father. I was pretty crazy about him, so I thought maybe it could work. My daughter would grow up believing that man was her father. I would have told you eventually, but you were starting your new life here. Then Rob broke up with me when I really started to show, and I decided I didn't need anyone to help me raise her. I still feel that way."

William frowned. "I want to be part of her life!"

"If that's what you want, then I'm open to the idea." Lily reached over to take his hand. "It's important you think all of this through. I know it's exciting now, but wait until reality sets in. We need to talk about how much of a role you'll play."

He swallowed. "I don't think I can be your husband."

Lily squeezed his hand and released it. "I wish all men were so sweet. I don't want to marry you, or be in a pretend relationship. We're friends, and I don't see that changing. But if you decide you want to be involved, most of your life will be different because of it."

Where he lived. The hours he worked. Jason. He tried to consider it all, but his mind was struggling to comprehend this twist of fate. As confused as his thoughts were, his heart felt certain of the answer. "I know I want to be involved somehow. There's no way I won't be. You're right that I don't understand it all yet, but I want to be a part of my daughter's—" He could barely get the words out, maybe because he had never expected to say them. "My daughter's life. Does she have a name?"

"Not yet." Lily placed both hands on her belly. "It's tradition in my family that the women all have flower names. My mother is Rose, and my grandmother is Petunia."

William made a face.

"I agree," Lily said. "My girl definitely won't be called Petunia. Or Primrose. Heather is nice. Or Poppy."

William thought about it. "Daisy?"

Lily cocked her head. "That's nice too."

"Maybe we should ask her," William said, leaning close to the belly to address it. "Do you want to be called Poppy? Heather?" He looked up. "Holly is a flower too!"

Lily grimaced. "As much as I loved our friend, I'm hoping our daughter turns out a little brighter than that."

"Okay then," William said, addressing the baby again. "How about Daisy?"

"Whoa!" Lily sucked in air. "She kicked hard that time!"

William grinned. "Then we've got a name!"

"Maybe. I can't believe how well you're taking this. I kept trying to imagine your reaction, but I never thought you'd be this enthusiastic."

"You're right that this is going to change everything, and I hope…" That he wouldn't lose Jason. "No matter what happens, I'll have a little girl in my life. That's what I'm focusing on now. The rest I'll figure out later."

"Your mother is going to be thrilled," Lily said. "Is she a grandmother yet?"

"Nope, and I bet she didn't expect me to ever make her one!"

"She'll want to see the sonogram."

"I do too! Actually, tell me everything from the very beginning."

They talked for nearly two hours. Lily told him how she had found out, how the doctor's appointments had gone so far, and how her family had reacted. When her parents came home again, their greeting was warm, although he could tell they shared the same questions that he and Lily did. How exactly was he going to be involved? How would this work? He and Lily agreed to discuss it again, once they both had more time to think. He said goodbye, got on his bike, and started the ride home. But home was no longer his mother's house. Jason wanted them to live together, which only complicated things further. Did they have room for a crib? Would he be okay with a baby there if William was allowed to take care of her sometimes? Lily was right. This would change everything.

When he reached the apartment complex, he saw a family get out of their car, arms full of opened presents as they returned home. It was Christmas. Not the ideal time to break life-changing news to Jason. Tomorrow would be better, but he had learned his lesson. No more hiding difficult truths. He needed to tell Jason. Right away.

William was pacing, unable to sit. He was too worried about Jason's reaction. His boyfriend was also nervous, standing up with his arms crossed over his chest, and he hadn't even heard the real news yet.

"So you and Lily slept together," Jason said.

William nodded. "Yeah. Before you and I got back together."

"Does that mean you're bisexual? Because I know a lot of gay guys who have slept with women. Usually when they're teenagers but… Has this happened before?"

"First and last time," William said. "I'm gay. Trust me."

Jason breathed out. "Okay. I appreciate you telling me, but you didn't need to. I like Lily. I'm not threatened by her. Wait, does she want more from you?"

"No. Not like that. She had feelings for me in high school, but she gets it."

"Cool," Jason said, heading for the kitchen. "Should we open a bottle of wine?"

Tempting. Maybe that would make the news easier to handle, or maybe it would make the reaction more volatile. "There's more," William said. "I need you to listen."

Jason turned back around, posture stiff. "What?"

"Lily and I weren't safe that night. She's pregnant."

Jason scoffed, like it was joke. When he saw it wasn't, his face went slack. "Is she going to keep it?"

"She's six months pregnant! It's a little late for that!"

"I don't know how these things work!" Jason said defensively.

"I wouldn't want her to have an abortion even if it is still possible!"

"Okay!" Jason held up his palms. "I'm just trying to make sense of this." He stood there in silence, eventually shaking his head. "Are you sure it's yours?"

Obviously he was still in denial. "It's my baby. A little girl. There's no doubt."

Now Jason looked hurt. "How many people have you slept with?"

"What's that supposed to mean?"

"Well, you keep dropping these bombshells, and they all involve who you've been with! What's next? I'm going to find out you had sex with Ben? Tim?"

William shook his head. "What's wrong with you?"

Jason didn't treat the question as rhetorical. "Having a kid with someone is up there with getting married."

"It's not the same thing."

"I know, but it's still serious, and I guess… I wish *we* were having a kid together. I know that's biologically impossible, but I pictured us doing that eventually. We could adopt. Now you're having a kid with someone else. Without me. You know what? Never mind. I'm sure I sound like a selfish asshole."

"You don't," William said, walking forward. He tried to hug Jason, but met resistance. "Maybe we can do this together. We can both be involved. And this doesn't mean we can't still adopt and share that experience."

"It won't be the same."

"Nothing will be," William said. "Except how I feel. I love you. That won't change. I hope you still love me too, even though I keep complicating everything."

Some of the tension left Jason's body. "This is nuts."

"I know. But it's also a good thing. A new life is coming into the world, and we get to be part of that."

Jason's jaw clenched. "You really think Lily will want me to be involved?"

"Sure," William said. "You can be the step-dad."

"Step-dad!" Jason repeated incredulously. "Okay, I'm definitely going to need that wine now."

William watched him go to the kitchen and open a bottle. He poured a glass for himself only, taking a few sips and getting lost in thought. When Jason noticed him staring, he grabbed another glass and filled it.

"I guess we should toast," he said, not smiling. "Congratulations."

William accepted the wine, but didn't raise it. "Are you mad at me?"

Jason was quiet before he answered. "No. Just confused. And I know it's going to make me look bad, but I'm worried this will be another Coast Guard."

"Meaning?"

"That it'll take you away from me."

William nearly smiled. "You are and will always be my baby. Now you've just got… I don't know, a little sister."

This was just ridiculous enough to make Jason laugh. "Seriously," he said, holding his glass up. "Congratulations. I'm glad there's going to be more of you in the world. That's definitely a good thing."

"So we're okay?"

Jason shook his head in exasperation, but his answer was positive. "We're okay."

Probably not the best time to propose, but as they clinked glasses, William felt like he wanted to pop the question right then and there. He was lucky, in more ways than he had ever dreamed possible.

William felt invigorated by the new year. After meeting with Lily, having discussions with his parents, and doing lots of online research, he developed a plan. The most important goal was to support Lily. He was disgusted to learn that FMLA, the Family and Medical Leave Act of 1993, promised women only twelve weeks of unpaid leave. Unpaid! Lily wasn't the only single mother, and that meant women were forced to choose between bonding with their children or providing financial support for them. Reprehensible. Especially since many other countries promised paid leave for *both* parents. Because of that, he decided his entire income for three months would go to Lily so she could stay at home with Daisy. The name was another decision they had made together. William couldn't stop saying it! Daisy, Daisy, Daisy… He yearned to help support her. This meant he wasn't moving in with Jason just yet. He didn't want to mooch off anyone, except his mother, who was being very supportive. William continued living with her so he didn't have rent and bills to pay, despite Jason insisting he was welcome regardless. The apartment key got plenty of use though, as did Jason's bed.

Daisy's imminent arrival hadn't ruined their relationship. At times Jason seemed enthusiastic, like on shopping trips for baby toys. At other times he grew quiet when the subject came up. William did his best to reassure him that the new baby wouldn't take his place. He had read in a parenting magazine that some fathers feel jealous of a new child. Maybe this was some weird equivalent. William tried not to overwhelm their time together with talk of Daisy, and clearly, Jason was trying to stay connected too.

"I finished reading your book," he said when they were taking a shower together one morning.

"Funny," William replied. "I don't remember writing one."

"*The Finest Hours*," Jason said, squirting him with the body wash. "It was amazing." He started rubbing the soap over his pecs. "You're amazing."

"Thanks," William said, "but don't confuse me with

the heroes in that book. Their situation was exceptional, and thankfully, like nothing I ever had to face."

"But you still saved lives," Jason said. "You're a hero too."

"If that's what you want to call me," William said, puffing up his chest, but Jason was ignoring it now, staring at him with watery eyes. "Are you all right?"

"Yeah. It's just that there aren't a lot of rescue swimmers."

"True," William said, turning around to rinse off. "We're an endangered species. That means you've gotta treat me nice."

Jason ignored this attempt at humor. "There are way more EMTs in the world. It's easier to become one than an AST."

"Look at you using the abbreviations!" William said. "I'm going to buy you more books like that. Soon you'll be talking like a coastie."

Jason still seemed solemn. That was easy enough to cure. They might be in the shower, but that didn't mean they couldn't get dirty. "Don't you ever miss it?"

"Sure," William said. "Wanna pretend to be a survivor in need of rescue? I'll let you ride in my basket."

That did it. Jason made a face before he started laughing. Then they worked on creating one of the finest hours imaginable.

Two in the morning. William looked at a bank clock as he rode past, vision blurred from exhaustion. He had worked a later shift than normal, having traded with someone who wanted Saint Patrick's Day off. The other paramedic had taken Christmas Day for him, so it was only fair. One holiday was bigger than the other, but today was notoriously bad for paramedics, due to how many people would be drinking themselves stupid. It had been a long night. He and Jason had breakfast together before his shift began, not expecting to see each other again until tomorrow. And yet, at the end of another hard day, the only thing that sounded more comforting than a warm bed was being close to his boyfriend.

William got off his bike, missing the satisfaction that had come with his work back in Cape Cod. Tonight he had responded to a teenager convinced he was overdosing on marijuana, a drunk woman who wanted to know if he could check her for STDs, two cases of elderly indigestion that were mistaken for heart attacks, and—the only real emergency—a domestic dispute where an intoxicated couple had beaten each other up. William longed for the thrill of a search and rescue, the physical exertion of being in the water, and especially the standards he and his other crewmen held themselves to. His partner tonight had been overweight and out of shape. While he normally didn't judge anyone on the state of their body, he was concerned that this person's condition would affect how they performed their duty, and sure enough, tonight William had been forced to ask a police offer to help him get a gurney down a flight of stairs. His regular partner wasn't much better, since Sharon chain-smoked. She always stepped out of the ambulance to do so, but the smell still followed her back.

He found himself drawn to Jason's apartment instead of his mother's place, seeking a sympathetic ear. Jason was a good listener, but William wouldn't put him through that tonight. Or in the morning when they were awake together. He trudged up the stairs to the third floor and let himself in, expecting the apartment to be dark, but the television was still on, the volume muted. Jason was stretched out on the couch, sleeping. He wore one of William's old Coast Guard T-shirts, which always hung baggy on him, and a pair of Transformer-themed pajama bottoms. This wasn't the first time William had seen him in such a getup. He supposed it was their equivalent of a woman wearing skimpy lingerie, since it made him feel just as amorous.

William put his things on the coffee table, took off his shoes, and crawled onto the couch. There wasn't really room for him to lay next to Jason, but he needed to be close to him anyway.

Jason stirred, looked up at him, and smiled. "I knew you'd be back."

"You were waiting for me?"

Jason nodded and stretched. "How was your day?"

"Fine," he lied. Feeling guilty, he amended his answer. "The usual."

"Wanna tell me about it?"

"I'd rather get in bed with you." William kissed him and stood. "Let's go."

"I'm too tired." Jason held out his arms, eyes moving over the uniform he still wore. "Rescue me."

At last! A chance to put his abilities to good use. William slid his arms beneath Jason and scooped him up. This caused them both to laugh. He was walking them to the bedroom when his phone vibrated on the table.

"Ignore it," Jason said, stifling a yawn. "It's still Saint Patrick's Day. I want to get lucky"

"Technically it's past midnight."

"I don't care."

Neither did William. They continued to the bedroom, William setting Jason down on the mattress. Then he started unbuttoning his shirt.

Jason spread his arms and legs wide, taking up most of the bed. On purpose. "Come snuggle."

William was pretty sure he had more in mind than innocent cuddling. Those Transformer pajamas were looking fuller than they had a few minutes ago. He stripped off his shirt, putting on a show, even swinging it in the air and flinging it away. Before hormones could take over completely, a worry elbowed its way to the forefront. What if that text had been from Lily? She wasn't due for two more weeks, but maybe there was some other emergency.

"Go check," Jason said, reading him perfectly.

"Two seconds," William said. "I promise."

He rushed to the living room and picked up his phone. Sure enough, it was from Lily. And something was wrong. Or maybe it was right. He couldn't decide! He reread the message just to make sure he wasn't mistaken.

My water broke!

He started walking back toward the bedroom to tell Jason, changed his mind, and went for the front door instead. Then he remembered how far away he was from Houston and texted back. *Call an ambulance!*

Relax, came the response. *My roommate drove me to the hospital before it happened. We're already there. I didn't want to text until I was certain.*

I'm on my way, he responded.

He turned in a circle, trying to decide what to do. The phone rumbled again. *Remember to breathe.*

William chuckled madly, then hurried to the bedroom. Jason was sitting up, wearing a naughty expression that turned to one of concern. "Everything okay?"

"The baby… It's happening!" William said. "I've gotta go! I need to borrow your car too. Thanks!" That's all the time he had. He grabbed his shirt and started putting it back on while returning to the living room.

Jason followed a second later. "You're driving to Houston?" he said. "At this hour?"

William looked up while pulling on his shoes. "Yeah! I don't want to miss Daisy being born!" He had taken a week off work at the end of the month just so he could be there. God, he hoped everything went okay! What if there were complications? He rose, noticing Jason still standing there. So much for their romantic night. He hadn't met her yet, but so far Daisy had terrible timing. "Sorry," he said. "I'll make it up to you."

Jason remained pensive. "Can I go with you?"

"Seriously?"

"Never mind. I get that this is private. Just be sure to send me a text and maybe a—"

"Yes, you can come along!" William smiled, near tears. "Are you kidding? I'm surprised that you want to!"

"Of course I want to. You're about to become a father!"

"Oh my god!" William said, head reeling. "We need to leave right away."

"Okay… Um." Jason went to the bedroom, reappearing wearing a pair of flip-flops.

"Let's go!" William said.

They made it to the door before Jason paused. "I forgot something."

"Hurry!"

He didn't understand the delay, nor did he wait. He was almost at the car when Jason caught up with him.

"Give me the keys."

"I can drive," William said.

"You're too emotional. And you drive ridiculously slow."

Sad but true, and right now all that mattered was getting to Houston in time. He tossed Jason the keys, got in the passenger seat, and felt frustrated by every stop sign and traffic light. Being on the highway helped, although he kept looking at the speedometer, feeling they weren't going fast enough. "A little more," he kept urging. "Just a little faster."

"I'm going ten over the limit," Jason said. "Any faster and we'll get pulled over. Besides, doesn't labor take a really long time?"

"Usually," William said, reaching for his phone. He sent a quick text. *Getting close to I-10. Are you dilated?*

The response was slow. *5 cm*

"Jesus," he breathed. *Slow down!*

Tell your daughter that!

"Everything okay?" Jason asked.

"I'm going to miss it," William said, feeling antsy. He considered the road ahead, and then checked behind them. Not many cars out at this hour. "Go faster. Please."

Jason's expression said he thought this was a bad idea, but he complied. They were still pushing ninety half an hour later when flashing lights invaded the rear window.

"Shit," Jason hissed.

"Think you can outrun him?" William said, only half-kidding.

They pulled over. A small eternity seemed to pass before an officer appeared at the window.

"Any reason you're driving so fast?" he asked.

"There's a baby on the way," Jason explained.

The officer hunched over, pointing his flashlight at William. Then he used it to search the backseat. "Unless she's in the trunk, you're pulling my leg."

"It's my girlfriend," William said, leaning over Jason's lap. "She lives in Houston. I'm in Austin. She's in labor right now." He held out the phone as evidence. He couldn't tell if the officer looked at it, but the flashlight did illuminate the paramedic patch on his arm. Would it be tasteless to point out the Coast Guard sticker on the back window?

"My wife was in labor for sixteen hours," the officer said. "You could probably drive back to Austin, take a nap, and still not have missed anything."

"Yes, sir," William said as politely as possible. "It's just that she's pretty far along already."

"License and registration," the officer replied. Damn it! Jason handed over his license, William passing him the rest of the paperwork. The officer hobbled back to his car and about five years later, returned again with a ticket. "Seventy-five is fast enough. Best of luck."

"Sorry," William said after they were on the way again. "I'll pay for everything."

"It's no big deal," Jason said, not even sounding annoyed.

"Sorry I called her my girlfriend. I thought—"

"I get it," Jason said. "It's easier than trying to explain it all."

"Yeah." Ten minutes later, leg bouncing with agitation, William checked the speedometer. "We can go eighty, right? Nobody drives the speed limit."

Jason pushed down on the accelerator until the GPS on his phone notified them of the upcoming exit. When they left the highway, they navigated deserted streets, finally reaching the hospital.

"Where should I go?" Jason asked when they pulled into the parking lot. "Emergency entrance?"

"Yeah," William said. As soon as they were close, his hand was on the door. "Can you let me out here?"

Jason nodded. William waited no more. He was out of the car and running to the entrance, only skidding to a halt when in front of the admissions desk.

"What can I help you with?" the nurse asked, confused by the uniform.

"Wife is in labor," he said. Great, now they were married! "Lily Cruise. I hope I'm not too late."

The nurse smiled and checked her computer. "I don't think you are."

Music to his ears! He was directed to the maternity ward, asked to put on scrubs, and allowed into a room. Lily was there, face contorted with pain, and when she saw him she reached out her hand. For a second he thought back to the girl he had once walked down halls with in high school, never imagining they would find themselves in this situation. Then he took her hand, and she damn near broke his fingers.

The rest was terrifying, exhausting, tedious, and more than anything else, magical. William had seen so many acts of bravery during his time in the Coast Guard, but none that compared to this. When he finally heard his daughter cry, he did too, because there she was. Daisy, his little miracle, squirming on her mother's stomach. He felt proud as he cut the umbilical cord, certain this was his greatest achievement, and felt envious when Daisy was placed in her mother's arms. He couldn't wait to hold her, shaken by the wonder of it all. He knew all too well that death was an inevitable part of this world. Sometimes it occurred spontaneously. How wonderful, then, that the same could be said of life. Lily seemed to have forgotten he was there, her sole priority the baby. He stepped back, content to watch them as

Daisy grew calm, closed her eyes, and fell asleep, not quite ready to face the world just yet.

"Six pounds, four ounces!" William announced when he found Jason in the waiting area. Then he laughed, because Jason was still dressed in his pajamas. "What are you wearing?"

"Shut up," Jason said. "I saw a guy come in wearing less than this. So everything is okay?"

"Not okay. Great! Come up to the maternity ward and see."

Jason rose, looking a little uncertain. "Are you sure I should be here at all?"

"I want you here!" He put an arm around his shoulders and guided him down the hall. "She's so beautiful. I can't wait for you to see her. Actually…" He stopped and pulled out his cell phone. "Lily made me promise not to show this to anyone because of how she looks. Like anyone is a super model after giving birth."

He passed the phone to Jason, who took it and stared at the screen.

"Isn't the little cap cute?" William said, craning to see. "God she's beautiful! She has Lily's skin, so hopefully no sunburns. The dark hair might still change. I'm hoping for blonde so she looks a little more like me. Not that Lily doesn't have great hair!" He looked up to see Jason's chin trembling. "You okay?"

"Yeah," he said, handing back the phone and wiping at his eyes. "I don't really want to talk about it."

The baby or the reason he was so emotional? "Okay."

"Here," Jason said, pushing a small brown bag into his free hand. "I didn't have time to wrap it. Sorry. Just don't expect much."

William had a blurry memory of Jason having the bag with him during the initial rush to the car. He'd been too worried and distracted to ask what it was. He opened it and took out two pink booties made of yarn. They didn't look store-bought. "Did you make these?"

Jason shrugged. "I figured if you could learn to sew, I could learn to knit. One of them is a little lopsided. I'll never tease you about sewing again, because this was hard. I'm pretty sure I'm done."

"They're perfect," William said. He looked up, noticing hair messier than usual and eyes tired from lack of sleep. Jason had been so cool about all of this and put up with too many sacrifices. William hadn't been around on many of his recent days off, just so he could visit Lily in Houston to check on her progress. Jason hadn't complained, even when driving to a far-away hospital in the middle of the night and getting a speeding ticket on the way. Now his boyfriend had a child with another person, and Jason's response to all this turmoil had been to learn to knit, just so he could make booties. Best boyfriend ever? "Thank you. For everything." He decided then that the rest could wait. Daisy was healthy, Lily was more than capable, and both of them were in safe hands. It was Jason he was worried about. "Let's get out of here. I'll take you to breakfast."

"Wearing this?"

"Then I'll take you shopping."

Jason managed a smile. "I texted Michelle. She said we could stay there, and that she would loan me some of Greg's clothes. Not that they'll fit."

Emma's parents. William didn't know them well. They lived in Houston, which was practical, and he knew that Jason had deep feelings for Michelle, who had been his caseworker when he was a teenager. "Think they'll be awake?"

"It's nine in the morning," Jason said. "I sure hope so!"

"Wow! I had no idea."

"Yeah. We could go there, eat some cereal."

"Sure!" William looked down the hallway toward the maternity ward, already wanting to see his daughter again.

"It's okay," Jason said. "You want to stay, right? I'll probably just crash anyway, so if you're not tired, no point in you coming along."

William looked him over, worried again. "I'll go with you."

"Seriously." Jason hugged him, kissed his neck, and started backing away. "You're needed here. Call me when you want to be picked up. Okay?"

"Okay," William said, still uneasy. "I love you."

Jason swallowed, expression strained. "I love you too." He turned and hurried down the hall. William looked down at the tiny booties in his hands, wishing more than anything that he could be two places at once.

Chapter Twenty-six

William found himself in one of Houston's more affluent neighborhoods. The houses here were impressive, bigger than those where Kelly's family or even Ben and Tim lived. They weren't sprawling mansions or multi-million dollar homes like celebrities own, but they were at the upper limit of practical square-footage. The taxi pulled up to such a house, prompting him to double-check the address that had been texted to him. William's eyes burned as he did so.

He was exhausted. Shortly after Jason left the hospital, Lily's family had shown up. Adrenaline kept William awake, as did a fevered excitement that he suspected felt a lot like drugs. This was pure though, without consequence. He shook hands, accepted hugs, relayed the same information over and over. Then he stood outside the nursery next to other beaming fathers and video-conferenced with his mother so she could see what his mind still struggled to comprehend. The delicate little life everyone was fawning over—he had helped create it!

Eventually both mother and child went to sleep, and he realized that he needed to do the same. That's when he called the taxi and had it bring him to this address. The afternoon was late, and he had run out of energy hours ago. He paid the driver and went up to the door. A tall woman with long brown hair answered his knock. Her expression was welcoming as she gestured for him to enter.

"You must be William. I've heard so much about you!"

"I've heard a lot about you too," he said. "You're Jason's hero."

Michelle smiled. "Funny, he says the same thing about you."

The inside of the house matched the outside. Vaulted ceilings, open rooms, and furnishings that appeared both comfortable and stylish.

"Are you hungry?" Michelle asked. "Jason is out grocery shopping with Greg and the boys, but I can whip you up a snack."

"I'm still too jittery to eat," William said, "but thank you."

"Congratulations on becoming a father!" Michelle said, leading him to the living room. He didn't see a television. Just two comfortable chairs that faced a couch, a glass coffee table between them. He waited for Michelle to choose where she wanted to sit—the couch—before he sat across from her.

"I still can't believe it's true!" he said

"I had no trouble believing it with any of my three kids." Michelle chuckled. "When you give birth, you *feel* just how real it is."

"I bet." William looked at the framed photos on the fireplace mantle. Most were of Michelle and a handsome man, or one of three kids—two boys and a girl he recognized as Emma. He was surprised by the family photo of Ben and Tim, Jason standing between them. Seeing his boyfriend made his stomach clench with concern. "Is Jason okay?"

Michelle's smile froze. "In what way?"

"I don't know," William said, struggling to articulate. "At the hospital, he seemed upset. Or maybe he was just emotional. God knows I was."

Michelle's expression became reserved. "This is a challenging situation for him."

"How so? I mean, I can think of a lot of reasons, but I'm not sure how he really feels about the baby. Or me."

"You can ask him."

"I will! I just wish I didn't have to. I've put him through so much lately. The last thing I want is for him to think I'm clueless about his feelings."

Michelle's brow crinkled. Then she exhaled. "Greg, my husband, works in real estate. He's very good at it too, enough that he was invited to speak at a conference in London. At the time, I had never really been out of the country, except Canada to visit my grandparents. Never across the ocean though. Once we could afford to travel that far, I had three little ones, and I wasn't brave enough to put them on an international flight. I wanted Greg to go without me, which he did. When he came back, London was all he could talk about. The pubs, fish and chips, the differences in the language. He even went to the Tate Gallery and shopped on Oxford Street. Do you have any idea how difficult it is getting him to go to a museum or shopping with me?" Michelle shook her head but laughed. "He had a great time, and before long I was sick of hearing about it."

"You felt like he was bragging?"

"Not at all! He was simply happy, and I was happy for him.

Mostly. I started resenting that he'd had this amazing experience without me. He's my partner. We do everything together. I don't need him with me every minute, but the big experiences, we go through those together. Usually."

William leaned forward. "Is that how Jason feels? Left out?"

Michelle shrugged as if she didn't know. "You'll have to ask him."

Fair enough. He needed to have this conversation with Jason, not his… aunt? His attention moved back to the photos on the mantle. "Are you related to Ben?"

Michelle smiled. "He's my brother-in-law. And before you wonder if Tim is my brother, ask yourself if there's any family resemblance."

William did so. "Ben was married before, wasn't he?"

"That's right. To my brother."

"Is that why he hasn't married Tim? It keeps bugging me, because they're crazy about each other, so what are they waiting for?"

"I don't think it has anything to do with Jace." Michelle pursed her lips. "I'm not sure why either. I've badgered Ben about it, but he keeps saying they're happy the way they are. Makes me feel old-fashioned."

"Me too," William said.

Michelle's eyebrows shot up. "So you're the marrying type?"

He chuckled nervously. "Maybe someday. But yes."

"Anyone in mind?"

His cheeks flushed. "Take a wild guess!"

"I'm flattered, but I'm already taken."

"That's not what I meant!" he said, feeling even more embarrassed, but then he saw she was kidding. They talked a little longer, and while it had nothing to do with the conversation, his eyelids kept shutting no matter how hard he fought against it.

"Why don't you take a nap?" Michelle suggested. "I've already got Jason set up in the guest room. I'm sure he'll wake you when he's back."

The offer sounded too appealing to refuse. Once she showed him to the room and gave him his privacy, he only had the strength to take off his shoes and shirt before he fell onto the bed and was instantly asleep.

* * * * *

When William opened his eyes again, the window was black, just enough of an ambient glow outside to see his surroundings. He was still on top of the bed, but half the comforter had been pulled over to cover him. He shoved it off and forced himself to get up, his body stiff and aching from being in the same position for too long.

But how long? He checked the alarm clock on one of the side tables. Nine at night! He groaned, always feeling disoriented when his sleep schedule got out of whack. He picked up his EMT shirt from the floor. It didn't smell very fresh. He probably didn't either. His stomach growled with hunger, and he felt fuzzy-headed when he walked down the hall. He located a guest bathroom and made use of it before continuing his search for signs of life. Voices led him to the kitchen. Michelle was lecturing a teenage boy about homework but stopped when she noticed him standing in the doorway. The teenage boy glowered at him, then stomped off.

"No more video games!" Michelle called after him. "I mean it!" The stern expression disappeared when she turned to William again. "I was wondering if we'd see you tonight. Jason tried waking you, but you wouldn't budge. He even put a mirror under your nose to see if you were still breathing."

William laughed, hoping that wasn't true. "I guess I needed sleep."

"What about food?"

"I'm starving," he admitted.

"We have leftover Mexican."

He would have eaten boiled raccoon if that's what she put on the plate. Instead he got four crispy tacos loaded with ground beef, tomatoes, lettuce, and cheese. He came very close to drooling as she prepared it. Only the distant sound of an electric guitar spared him. "Is that Jason playing?"

"Yes," Michelle said, adding a spoonful of salsa to each taco. "Greg insisted he wanted to learn how to play, so I gave the guitar to him as a birthday present. He's barely touched it. Soda okay?"

William nodded, accepting the plate and a cold bottle.

"Jason will be glad to see you. Why don't you go eat with him? He's in the rumpus room."

"The what?"

Michelle smiled. "That's what Greg likes to call it. Just follow the music."

He wandered toward the back of the house and found a large family room. A huge wall-mounted television was muted and displaying music videos, the entertainment center beneath it full of electronic decks. Two huge speakers sat in each corner. The remaining space was partially taken up by a U-shaped couch big enough to seat ten, a wet bar on one wall, and the sort of mess he expected in a house where teenagers lived. Jason was sitting cross-legged on the carpet, brow creased in concentration as he strummed the guitar, pausing to adjust the small amplifier next to him. When he noticed William enter, he started to set aside the instrument.

"Keep playing," William said, lifting the plate to show him. "I won't be good for conversation until I'm done stuffing my face."

Jason smiled, a reassuring sight, and kept playing. William sat on the couch facing his direction. Then he shamelessly devoured each taco like he was participating in an eating contest. Jason noticed, picking up the pace of the music as if to egg him on. When he recognized the song as *Wipe Out* by the Beach Boys, he nearly spit the food out in his need to laugh.

"I hadn't eaten since yesterday!" he said in his defense.

Jason stopped playing and tilted his head to one side. "How's Daisy? Is everything okay?"

William nodded and set down the empty plate to check his phone. No new texts or calls, which was a good sign. "How are you? Is it fun being back here?"

"In Houston?" Jason asked. "Austin is home now, if that's what you mean."

"I meant hanging out with Michelle and her family." William joined Jason on the carpet. "This is like visiting relatives, right?"

Jason thought about it while plucking at the guitar. Then he laughed. "I'm not sure. I never had many relatives. Maybe this is what it's like. Honestly, I've only been to this house a few times on holidays. July Fourth and once for Thanksgiving. I love this family, even though Michelle and Greg only eat organic. I couldn't find any chocolate either. What's up with that? And their sons act like I'm here to steal their stuff."

William nodded. "Sounds like relatives. A weird mixture of the familiar and the strange."

"Comfortable and yet awkward," Jason added. His eyes lit up. "Hey, now I know what it's like!"

God he was cute! William flopped onto his back, resting his head in Jason's lap. The guitar was set aside to better accommodate him. "Did you get any sleep?"

"A lunch nap."

"Wanna go back to bed with me?"

Jason laughed. Then sorrow crept into his expression, even though he tried to hide it. "Maybe later."

William studied him, refusing to let the mood remain somber. "I think I get it. I'm a dad now. There's nothing hot about being a dad. I've lost all my sex appeal. Admit it. You can barely stand to look at me."

"No way," Jason said, stroking his cheek. "You're a total DILF."

"DILF?" Then he got it and grinned. "I'll take that as a compliment."

"Good."

"You know I love you, right?"

Jason nodded, expression serious.

William pressed on. "I've been distracted lately, but I'm going to make sure we have a lot of time together. I swear."

Jason shook his head. "This is where you're needed."

"Right now, but when we're back in Austin—"

"I've been thinking about that," Jason said, his hand retreating. "You should move to Houston."

"What?" William sat upright, turned to face him, and waited for the punch line.

"They need you," Jason clarified, eyes guarded. "Daisy needs you."

"And I'll be there," William said. "I'll drive out on weekends and holidays or for emergencies. It's going to take a lot of patience from you, but I know where I belong. I don't need to move to Houston."

"You do," Jason said, getting to his feet. William did the same, wondering if they were going somewhere, but Jason only needed to pace. "I didn't have a father growing up and look what happened to me."

William's stomach sank. Now he understood. "If something happened to Lily, I would take Daisy. She also has two sets of grandparents, and her two uncles. My family is big enough that she'll never be put into foster care."

"It's more than that!" Jason said, turning to face him. "I saw what my mother went through trying to raise me on her own—the strain that caused her. Why do you think she started drinking? Or let that abusive asshole into our lives? Just think about that happening to Daisy. Imagine if Lily dates the wrong guy and he hurts your daughter."

The idea alone was enough to summon up anger. "Lily is too smart to… I'm not saying your mother wasn't, but they're different people and this is a different time. We have a better support network and—"

"If you're not here, you won't know what's going on. Maybe Lily will be at work when there's an accident or maybe one of the teachers at school will be a creep… You just can't know."

Jason was sweet for being so concerned, and considering his past, his feelings made sense. William understood he had seen a lot of dark times, but this situation was different. "You don't know Lily like I do," he said. "Trust me. Daisy couldn't be in safer hands."

"It's not just them," Jason said. "There's a Coast Guard station in Houston. You could go back to being a rescue swimmer."

William exhaled. "And what about us?"

Jason met his gaze. "What about the people only you can save? I can't stop thinking about that. You trained so hard to become an AST. If I wasn't in the picture, would you really have stopped after so few years? After all that work?"

"Jason—"

"Just answer the question truthfully. Please."

"No. I wouldn't have, but I wanted to come back to Austin because I *need* to be with you!" He stepped forward and took his hands. "I wasn't happy. Not completely. I never got over us being apart. I don't want that to happen again."

"I know," Jason said, voice hoarse. "I don't want that either. But we can't just think of ourselves. The situation has changed. You've changed."

"Meaning?"

"That you're going places I never will. The rescue work was amazing enough, but now you have a child."

"We can adopt. Together."

"A biological child," Jason stressed.

William dropped his hands. "You of all people are going to make that distinction?"

"I know how it sounds, but believe me, I've seen it firsthand. Parents were always different with their biological children. You might not want to hear it, but it's true."

"And you'll think I'll be like that?"

"I don't think you'll have a choice." Jason's expression was pleading with him to understand. "It's just how humans are built. Daisy is going to be your priority now. That's how it should be."

"I can have more than one priority." When Jason shook his head and started to turn away, William grabbed his arm. "I came back to Texas because I love you. Let me decide where I need to be and what I need to do. You're wrong that I don't have a choice. I'm staying with you. Understand? This is my decision, and I've made it. I *will* be there for Daisy. I won't fail her like your father failed you, I promise, but four years didn't stop the way I feel. Everything I went through to become an AST—and I was pushed to my absolute limit—didn't change how I feel about you, and neither will any of this.

Jason shook his head again, but he obviously wanted to believe William's words.

"I love you, Jason. Whether you like it or not."

William kissed him and felt tears that weren't his own on his cheek. Then Jason gave in, clung to him, and whispered the same promise back, but in a way that sounded like someone saying goodbye.

"I love you too. No matter what happens. I'll never stop."

"Tell me about Ben and Tim again."

Sheets rustled and a pillow was shoved aside, Jason's head revealed from beneath it. His hair was so tangled that he might never get a comb through it again, even once he finally got up and took a shower. William, as always, had risen with the sun and was already clean and dressed. Jason considered him with one eye, then the other when he decided to stay awake. "What about them?"

"You said they're engaged, right?" William raised the blinds and opened the window, letting light and fresh air into the apartment. "When did that happen?"

"Oh." Jason rolled over, but only so he could hug a pillow.

Sometimes William felt like setting the bed on fire, just to get him up and moving. "I dunno… A long time. Wait, what year is it?"

"Twenty fourteen," William said with a chuckle. "I'll get you some caffeine."

When he returned with a can of Mountain Dew, Jason was sitting up, sheets gathered around his waist as he scratched at his bare chest. He was smelly and half-awake, and yet William still found him irresistible.

"You know what?" Jason said, accepting the drink and taking a sip. "It's going on three years!"

"Three years!" William repeated incredulously.

"For real!"

He sat on the edge of the bed. "What's holding them back?"

"They don't want to jinx it." Jason noticed his eye roll and agreed. "I know. All that stuff with Ryan happened, but that feels like ancient history. You've seen them together. Every day is like their first date. They've got nothing to worry about."

"Maybe that's why they don't need to get married," William said. "Why bother when you're already living the honeymoon?"

"I shouldn't be surprised." Jason yawned before continuing. "It took forever for Tim to work up the nerve to propose. Another ten years and maybe he'll buy wedding invitations."

"We've gotta do something," William said. "Shotgun wedding?"

Jason shook his head. "I never want to see another gun in my life. Brooms might work. The wide kind used on shop floors. We'll sweep them together."

"What if we arranged things for them?"

"Like what?"

"Like all of it!" William enthused. "We'll book a venue, send out invitations, and handle the real work for them. All they have to do is show up."

Jason very carefully set down the can on the night stand, sank down into bed, and pulled the comforter over his head.

"Too much?" William asked, jostling him. "Hello?"

"Leave me alone!" Jason said. "I want to be lazy for just one day. You're exhausting."

"No I'm not." William pounced on him, pulling at the blanket, which Jason gripped desperately in return. "Come on. Don't you want to see them get married?"

"It's not legal in Texas," came the muffled reply.

"I don't care. Neither will they. I still want to see them take their vows."

Jason flung away the blankets and glared at William accusingly. "I get it now. This all about what *you* want. They're your favorite couple, and you're doing this just to see them make out after they're pronounced man and… man."

"Second-favorite couple," William said, leaning in for a kiss. Lucky for him, the over-sweet flavor of the soda helped conceal Jason's morning breath. "Please? Do it for me."

Jason mulled it over. "We'd have to pick a date. How do we do that?"

William rewarded him with another kiss before answering. "Spencer is always complaining about how he has two anniversaries these days. When he first met his wife, and when they actually got married."

"So we choose the day Ben and Tim first met?"

"Yes."

Jason shook his head. "I don't know when that is. I also don't remember them celebrating their anniversary."

William grinned. "Leave it to me." Then he reconsidered. "Actually, I need an excuse to talk to one of them."

"We can go see them today," Jason said. "We don't need a reason. They're always happy when either of us stop by."

"Who's most likely to know when they first met?"

"Ben," Jason said.

"Just make sure I get some alone time with him. Then we'll have our date!"

As it turned out, isolating Ben wasn't difficult because Tim was at work. They hung out in the living room, Jason eventually taking Chinchilla outside to play. That wasn't an excuse. Even though he spent most of his free time caring for animals at the shelter, Jason seemed compelled to do the same when around pets. Maybe that's why he still didn't have one of his own, since home was the only place he got a break. This reminded William of a similar situation that Ben, like everyone else, soon drew attention to.

"How's Daisy?"

"Fine," William answered. "She's a handful!" He had returned to Houston five times in the previous two months since her birth. While he was there, all Lily wanted to do was sleep, and all Daisy wanted to do was cry, poop, eat, and cry some more. She wore him down, but on each drive back to Austin, he fought against the urge to turn the car around to see her again.

"And is Jason doing okay?" Ben made the question sound innocent, despite how loaded it was. What he really wanted to know is if the baby remained an issue.

"He's doing good. You know how it is. Jason is always so patient with me, and this is no different."

Ben looked amused. "Patient? We're still talking about Jason?"

"Yup! He waited four years, didn't he?" William leaned forward, having found an opening. "Speaking of which, I was trying to figure out exactly how long Jason and I have been together. Do we count the years apart? I want to, but if I'm honest…"

Ben nodded in understanding. "I envy people who can give a straightforward answer to that question. Tim and I have argued about it a few times."

"That's right," William said, remembering a dinner from long ago. "You disagree."

"Kind of," Ben said. "He likes to count back to when we were teenagers. I tend to think of that as round one, which is separate from this relationship. This one started when we met at the gallery again."

"When was that?" William asked, trying to maintain his poker face.

"Gosh… Six years ago?"

"Yeah, but what day?"

Ben shrugged. "No idea. Why?"

"Just curious," he said lamely.

"Do you know your anniversary?"

"March sixth," he answered instantly. "Technically I was still with Kelly, but that's the first day I met Jason, and we both felt a connection."

"Your anniversary is the day you laid eyes on each other?" Ben smiled. "That's sweet."

"I'm serious about him," William said. "I'm not messing around. You need to adopt him. That way I can ask you for his hand in marriage."

Ben clearly found this sentiment charming, but William wasn't kidding. Not entirely. He was dedicated to Jason and couldn't imagine spending his life with anyone else. At the moment he was supposed to be planning someone else's wedding, not his own, so when he and Jason returned to the city, they stopped by the Eric Conroy Gallery.

Tim greeted them, flashing the smile that always made William feel like giggling.

"Got any new stuff?" Jason asked, glancing around at the art.

"Yeah," Tim replied, extending an arm toward the eastern wing. "Zombies, skeletons, and other dead things. You'll love it."

Jason wandered off in that direction.

William remained where he was. "How's it going?" he asked, mentally resisting a blush.

"A little slow," Tim said. "People come in here, like what they see, and try to take photos with their cell phones. Lately I feel more like a bouncer than a curator."

William laughed, wondering how he was going to steer the conversation in the right direction. Luckily, he had gotten Ben to talk a little more about that fateful night at the gallery. "I guess you didn't have that problem during your exhibition."

"Which exhibition?" Tim asked, seeming confused.

William tried again. "For your own art."

"Oh!" Tim laughed. "Yeah, that was a long time ago. We had cell phones then. People just weren't so crazy about using them."

"When was that exactly?" William asked, well aware it wasn't the most natural follow-up question.

Tim rolled with it anyway. "Five years ago, maybe."

"Yeah, but when?"

That earned him a funny look. "The actual day?"

William shrugged. "Sure. You didn't save a flyer?"

Tim scrutinized him, then became distracted by the question. "You know, I'm sure I did. Marcello had these cool posters made. I wonder if they're in the back?"

Soon he was in the back room with Tim, helping him open flat-file drawer after drawer in search of the past. Jason joined them just as they found a poster advertising the exhibition of a promising new artist.

"I like the butterfly," William said. "Was that a theme of your art?"

"Not really." Tim scratched the back of his head sheepishly. "I was hoping to attract the right sort of clientele with it."

William didn't really hear his answer. He was too busy eyeing the date and worried that, in his excitement, he wouldn't be able to remember it. "You're going to kill me for this, but…" He took out his phone and snapped a photo.

Tim found it funny, eyes shining as he looked over the poster. "That was a good night."

"Really?" William asked, hoping for more details, but Tim merely nodded and kept his answer short.

"Yeah. The best."

They hung out a little longer before they said goodbye and left.

"July thirteenth," William said once they were outside. "We've got our date."

Jason didn't appear so victorious. "Cool. Now we just need a place."

"That shouldn't be hard. We'll look online." William got a head start on the way home. While Jason drove, he searched on his phone. "I've found some beautiful options," he soon reported. "The prices are ridiculous though. This one is basically on the corner of a golf course. You can get married outside and have a party in the club house, but they want four thousand dollars."

Jason snorted. "They're crazy."

"I know. I also found a vineyard with a similar setup, and they want just as much."

"Do they provide the wine too?"

"I don't think either place gives you anything. You still have to worry about food, decorations, and everything else."

They exchanged worried glances.

"There's got to be somewhere cheaper," Jason said. "I'll help you look when we're back at the apartment."

Those results weren't much better. They found a bar and grill that wanted three thousand, but at least they would cater. That was fine for the reception, but where would the ceremony take place? Outside in the parking lot? They made call after call and kept writing down estimates, none of which were in their comfort zone. While technically they could afford some of them, the drain on their bank accounts would be devastating.

"We need to find somewhere free," William said. "What about St. Edwards Park? Nobody is out there. We'll set it up, have the ceremony, and remove the decorations before anyone notices."

Jason grinned. "I don't want to play lookout while Ben and Tim are taking their vows. What about your mom's house? We'll have the ceremony in the backyard, then—"

William tapped a rough guest list they had drawn up. "Fifty people or more crammed inside the living room if it starts to rain? I love my mom, but our house is already cluttered."

"Ugh." Jason rubbed his forehead wearily. "I think we've discovered the real reason Ben and Tim haven't done this yet."

"No kidding. I had no idea it was so expensive. You could ask Marcello."

"I don't like hitting him up for money."

"No, I mean his house. You know, the one with the ballroom?"

"True," Jason said, "but that's where Tim works. Not all the time, but he helps with most of the fundraisers. I want it to be somewhere romantic for them both."

"Their house," William said instantly. Every time he visited, the vibe was really positive. "They both seem happy there."

"They've got this thing about being alone," Jason said, eyeing him curiously. "I used to not get it. These days I think I do."

William smiled. "Oh yeah?"

"Yeah. That's why they live outside of town. They like the solitude." He nibbled a thumbnail, lost in thought. Then looked up. "It really would be the perfect place. I want this to be a surprise though."

"So we wait until a time they're usually not home, or make up some errand they both have to go on. Dentist appointments?"

"Not much of a wedding day memory. Besides, we'll need a lot of time to set up everything. More than a few hours. If only they had plans to go out of town."

William dragged the laptop toward him. "We can make that happen." He looked up a bed and breakfast. A couple of nights there was a lot cheaper than the cost of renting a wedding venue. He showed Jason, feeling excited. "We'll give them a trip as an anniversary present. I'm sure I made them suspicious by asking the things I did. They'll think this is the reason why, but when they come home…"

Jason peered at the website. "That could work."

"It really could! It'll be a lot of effort, but I'm willing."

Jason still seemed uncertain. "Think they'll be happy we did this?"

William shrugged. "You know them best. Do you think they should get married?"

Jason laughed. "If not them, then I don't know who!"

Sharon smoked one cigarette after another, standing outside the ambulance as a courtesy, not that it did much good. She was on the passenger side where William sat and monitored the radio in case they were dispatched. He was hoping for any assignment, no matter how trivial, just to air out the ambulance because smoke was drifting through his window like a ghost on the night air. He would roll up his window, but Sharon was talking about her reality TV shows, rambling on about who didn't sing well enough and had to be booted off the island, losing the chance to marry the bachelor. Or something like that. He could never keep up.

"I think he's sleeping with one of the judges." Sharon was saying, exhaling a plume of smoke in his direction. "He's got no talent. How else could he make it this far?"

William tried holding his breath until the smoke dissipated. When that didn't work, he decided to retreat. "Did we restock the saline we used yesterday?"

"I thought you did?"

"I don't remember. I better do an inventory. Monitor the radio?"

Sharon shrugged, tossed her cigarette butt to the ground, grinded it beneath her foot, and reached for her pack again. William moved to the back of the ambulance and opened a cabinet so he could hide his face behind the door. He sighed. Half an hour and this shift was done. Then he could go home, which meant Jason's place even though he still wasn't paying rent. Any lofty ideas William had about not staying there until he could contribute financially had given way to his emotional needs. Few shifts ended without him feeling like he needed a bottle of vodka. The alternative was a sympathetic ear and a pair of arms cuddling him in bed. That's what he always opted for, but tonight he was seriously considering that vodka.

"We've got a call!" Sharon said. He had to give her credit; despite the nasty habit, she was fast. She was already in the driver's seat, the ambulance's engine revving, when he made his way to the front. "Babysitter is in a tizzy. It's probably her first night and she's surprised by the amount of poop and puke. I bet her dollies never did that!"

"Infant?" William asked.

"Yup. Hold tight!"

Sharon always said that, and for good reason. Jason had once claimed, in a rare instance when William was driving, that he saw a tortoise overtake them. His coworker didn't share this problem. Sharon drove like the back of the ambulance was on fire and she wanted to outrace it. William tightened his grip on the handle above the window, eyes locked on the road.

"What else do we know?"

Sharon was uncharacteristically quiet. Even a few seconds of silence was rare. "She said the baby looked blue."

His stomach sank. "Is it breathing?"

"That wasn't clear." Sharon turned on the siren as they neared a busy intersection, maybe hoping the noise would drown out any further conversation. What else was there to say? Blue meant that baby wasn't getting enough oxygen. Every second was critical. William clamped down on his frustration and nerves, mentally going over potential scenarios and the best reactions to each. He went to the back of the van again and fetched a pediatric resuscitation system. When they arrived at a quiet neighborhood, he leapt out of the ambulance the second it started to slow.

William let himself in the house, the babysitter meeting him in the entryway. He was expecting a teenage girl, not an adult woman who was more likely to have experience and less likely to panic without need. She latched on to him, face streaked with tears as she tried yanking him toward the right direction.

"Show me where the baby is," he said, trying to make his voice sound both reassuring and authoritative. "You go ahead, I'll follow."

She finally stopped pulling on him and turned. They hustled to a nursery, the babysitter stopping next to the crib and howling. William looked into it and saw the baby on its back. If the lights hadn't illuminated the blue lips, the baby would have appeared to be sleeping peacefully. Sharon jostled him, arriving at his side. Then she sighed and shook her head, like they were too late.

That wasn't good enough for him! William had already collapsed one side of the crib. He fell to his knees to start resuscitation. He did so the old-fashioned way, trusting the seal of his lips more than the manual resuscitator. William was gentle with his breath, straining to see the chest rise, which it did. Good. He moved his mouth away, letting the lungs push the air out naturally before he bent over and tried again. Behind him the babysitter was shouting "I tried that, I tried that, I tried!" Her voice moved farther away, Sharon no doubt making sure he had the space needed to work. Another breath. And another. Nothing. William tried chest compressions, then returned to giving the child air. He wouldn't quit. Ever. If this was Daisy—

The thought hurt too much to complete. He just knew he couldn't stop. More oxygen, more compressions, a desperate scrabble at the pediatric kit he had brought, just in case there was something he had forgotten or hadn't yet tried. They could get the child to the ambulance. The oxygen tube maybe. Or the heart monitor.

"William," Sharon said, pulling at his shoulder.

He resisted, bending over the baby again, noticing a cartoon elephant on the mattress sheet, a football held in its trunk. A boy. He wouldn't let these parents lose their son. Not today.

"William," Sharon tried again.

Another breath. Then five more. As long as the brain was getting oxygen, everything else had time to kick in again.

"It's SIDS," Sharon said. "I've seen it before."

Another breath. Just one more would do the trick! He was wrong. *This* one though … If he just kept trying… He leaned back, the tiny face unresponsive and moist from his saliva, a white froth leaking from the nose. He could hear the babysitter's tormented cries. Sharon had a comforting hand on his shoulder or maybe it was to restrain him from trying again. William looked at the knitted blanket crumpled in one corner of the crib, then at the cheerful mobile hanging above, stars and moons and suns, all with faces and permanent plastic smiles. His eyes moved to the rest of the room, which was full of dreams and hopes. Never had the parents thought when decorating this space that it would be where their child would take his final breath. A sob broke from William's lips.

"It just happens," Sharon said. "It's nobody's fault. Even if we got here the second the call came in, it wouldn't have helped."

William looked up at her, understanding why she smoked so much, because he didn't see how he could face something like this again. Not without a crutch. He had always known a day would come when he wouldn't be on time, that the ship would have already sunk, the crew already drowned. He had just never expected that loss to involve a baby.

"I'll call it in," Sharon said, patting his shoulder. "Cover him up. Okay?"

William nodded numbly. He waited until she had left the room before he started crying. Then he forced himself to think of the parents. William stood. He wiped the baby's nose and cheeks clean. Once satisfied, he took the blanket and tucked the baby in, hoping the parents would get the same impression that he had—that their child had passed away peacefully while sleeping, an eternal slumber never to be disturbed.

Hollow. William opened the door to Jason's apartment, feeling like his insides had been scraped out and thrown away. His body was tired, his head ached, and emotionally… At times he felt nothing. Then a jolt of panic would hit him. He had already called Lily, who snapped at him due to the late hour. William didn't care. He had to make sure Daisy was okay, tempted to drive to Houston despite her reassurances, because SIDS could happen to anyone's baby, no matter how vigilant the parents. Daisy was still so young and at high risk until she got past her first six months.

"You're late," Jason said, appearing from the bedroom, but his voice was concerned, not accusatory.

Seeing him made William feel vulnerable, the floodgates opening again. Jason held him as he cried. The story poured out of him in small messy bursts as they sat on the couch, remaining in physical contact. Jason clutched his hand or held him while William wept. Eventually his head was lying in a warm lap, Jason stroking his hair, William's heart just as exhausted as the rest of him.

"You should go see Daisy tomorrow," Jason said. "That will make you feel better."

William rolled over to look up at him. "I promised Saturday would be just for you."

Jason set his jaw. "I don't care. This is important."

"I have to work on Sunday. We won't have a weekend together."

Jason's expression remained determined. He had made up his mind.

"Come with me," William said, touching his neck. "Please."

"Whenever you want me, I'll be there."

"I always want you." William rolled over again, closing his eyes. "I'd be lost without you."

"You'd be fine without me," Jason said, but his caresses resumed. "Tomorrow will be a better day. I promise."

William nestled in his lap, soft comfort easing him toward sleep. Before he could nod off entirely, Jason made him rise, led him to the bedroom, and as so often before, held him close, trying to keep the world's hardships at bay.

Chapter Twenty-seven

The next day was indeed better. They listened to music on the drive to Houston, Jason turning down the commercials to do parodies of them in a faux announcer voice. He invented all sorts of ridiculous products, the best being a special soap to help combat greasy goat balls. William laughed so hard at that one that Jason had the product make a few returns, even developing a jingle. He was clearly trying to keep William's spirits up.

The events of the previous day weighed heavily on William regardless. He kept seeking an impossible solution. He knew he couldn't bring the baby back, but he wanted to do something for the parents. What good would flowers or well-meaning words be against that sort of pain? He only hoped they had the sort of relationship he and Jason did, where they could depend on each other for support.

By lunchtime they had arrived at the two-bedroom apartment Lily shared with her roommate. Holding Daisy in his arms, seeing firsthand that she was healthy and thriving, worked wonders at chasing away his sorrow, but an edge of anxiety remained.

"I don't think it will ever go away," Lily confided when Jason left to pick up burgers. William had just finished changing Daisy's diaper, telling Lily a condensed version of what had happened the night before. They sat on her bed, the baby between them, as she continued. "A night hasn't gone by that I don't worry about SIDS or pneumonia or some health problem the doctors didn't detect. When she gets older and goes to school, I'll worry about other kids being mean, or someone trying to snatch her when I'm not looking. Don't even get me started on everything that can go wrong during the teen years. We'll never stop worrying. That's the price of loving her. All we can do is try our best to keep her safe."

William sighed. "You could have said all this *before* you seduced me."

Lily laughed. "Do you regret it?"

"The baby or the sex?" Then he answered seriously. "She's worth every ounce of anxiety and fear. I'd do anything for her."

"So would I. That gives her better odds. Right?"

"Yeah."

"It's nice to see Jason here."

William nodded. "He wants to be involved too."

"That's sweet." Lily looked mischievous. "I've noticed though, that he never holds Daisy."

"No?" William thought about it. "You're right! He always refuses."

"I think he's scared."

"Of babies?"

"Only one way to find out."

They both agreed on the same goal. William tried first. After they had eaten, he asked Jason if he would mind holding Daisy. The response was a mumbled excuse. Lily was cleverer in her approach, waiting until William was washing bottles. "I need to run out and check the mail," she said, holding out the baby. "Could you take her?"

"I'll get your mail," Jason said.

"Not with the neighbors on alert," she replied. "Someone has been stealing mail. If the neighbors see someone they don't recognize out there, they'll call the police. Assuming they don't start shooting first."

Jason turned to William, who held up two sudsy hands and shrugged helplessly.

"Just real quick," Lily pressed. "Five minutes."

Left without a choice, Jason complied. He insisted first on sitting. Lily sat next to him, showing him how to arrange himself and support the baby's head. Soon Daisy was cradled in his arms. Lily didn't go outside for the mail. William stopped the washing-up, drying his hands hurriedly so he could get out his phone and take a photo. Jason looked up from the squirming bundle in his arms and noticed them both.

"You guys suck," he said, catching on at last, but he smiled and looked down at Daisy with the same wonder that William often felt. "Young lady, you have the same eyes as your father. The same smile too! Just not as many teeth." Then he started talking in a silly voice. "Where'd all your teethies go? Huh? Who stole your little teethies?"

He was hooked. From the way Daisy gurgled in response, she was too. When Lily offered to take her from him, Jason shook his head. He rocked Daisy, cooed at her when she started crying, and fed her the milk that Lily had pumped earlier. Only when Daisy spit up a little on his shoulder did Jason hand her back to her mother. Lucky for him, Lily had placed a towel over his shoulder before he had started burping the baby.

That evening they went to Michelle and Greg's place for dinner. When they had learned Jason was in town, they suggested that he and William stay with them. The dinner invitation was extended to Lily and the baby too. With the couple's two teenage boys joining them, it was a full and lively table. Lily and Daisy returned home afterwards, and the boys wandered off to play video games, leaving the rest of them in the rumpus room. Greg and Jason were drinking beer. William joined Michelle in a bottle of wine, conversation coming easier with each glass.

"Can I tell them?" Jason asked at one point.

"About what?" William asked.

"The wedding."

Michelle nearly leapt to her feet. "You're getting married?"

"No," Jason said, laughing as he toyed with the electric guitar in his lap. "Someone else is."

"Ben and Tim?" Greg asked, voice a little terse.

"That's the idea," William said. "We're tired of waiting, so we're going to surprise them. We have a date picked out. The place too! The ceremony will be at their house."

Michelle seemed confused. "Without them knowing?"

They explained their scheme, feeling proud until Michelle started poking holes in it. "When were you planning on sending out invitations? You need to let people know in advance, especially if they'll need to travel. You also need to make accommodations. What about the suits? And the cake?"

William and Jason exchanged glances.

Michelle wasn't finished. "Who's going to preside over the wedding?"

"I want to be best man," Greg said. "To both of them. Unless you picked someone already."

"I hadn't even thought of that," Jason admitted. "Um… Could I get another beer?"

Greg laughed, and by the time he returned with two more bottles, Michelle was dictating a list to them. They still had a lot of work, and only about six weeks to do it, but at least they now had help. Michelle and Greg both insisted.

Once their hosts had gone to bed, William and Jason exchanged glances, then started laughing.

"We would have ruined their wedding," Jason said.

"Yeah. It would have been a disaster."

"Maybe we should get more people involved. Um. You know."

William was pretty sure who he meant. They had started thinking of him as the easy way out. "Marcello?"

"Yup." Jason considered the list again. "All the catering stuff, he'll make it go away."

"Except the cake!" William said. "I have an idea about that." His mother had been taking culinary classes and was considering a new career. "I think my mom would do a good job. I know she would welcome the challenge."

Jason yawned. "Okay. Wanna call it a night?"

"Sure." His shift didn't begin until the next afternoon, so they wouldn't have to wake up too early. They could have a nice breakfast, see Daisy again, and then drive home. William took longer in the bathroom, wanting to make sure he was clean. The wine had awakened his libido, and the hour wasn't so late. He had planned for this, bringing a travel-sized bottle of lube with him. He took enough time that, when he returned to the bedroom, he worried Jason had dozed off already. Instead his boyfriend was sitting upright and staring at his phone, thumb swiping occasionally.

"Reading anything good?"

Jason looked up, eyes watery, expression awed. That answered his question!

"Another Coast Guard book?" William asked with a chuckle.

Jason nodded. "Every time I read stories like these, I picture you out there. It's incredible what you did."

William's heart fluttered with pride, but barely managed to take flight since all of that was in the past. "Are you rereading, or is this a new one?"

"A new one," Jason said, tapping a few times and then turning the phone to show him the cover. "You should read it."

And be reminded of what he was missing? This was the third such book Jason had read, and if it was anything like the previous two, the resulting conversations would be bittersweet. Wanting to avoid this, William stripped off his shirt, casually flexing a muscle or two.

Jason didn't even notice. "I have an idea."

"I'm tired of talking about the wedding."

"Not that. An idea for us."

"A kinky idea?" William set the small bottle of lube on the dresser.

Jason peered at it and laughed. "Looks like you already thought of one, but first…" He put down the phone and patted the mattress. "Come here." He scooted over so William could sit on the bed, then took his hand. "What if we moved to Houston?"

"What?"

"You would be closer to Daisy, and also—" He started to reach for his phone, then thought otherwise. "How many Coast Guard air stations are there in Texas?"

William didn't have to think long. "Two. One in Galveston, and one—"

"Here," Jason said. "In Houston. Is that perfect or what? You'd be close to your daughter, and you can go back to doing what you really want. I know you're not happy being a paramedic."

"It's a good job," William said. "I'm helping people."

"Right, but are you happy?"

"No," he admitted. "It's hard work. So is being an AST, but that's what I trained for."

"It was your dream," Jason said, still smiling. "Moving to Houston is the perfect solution."

"For me. What about you?"

The smile faltered. "I've been thinking about that too. You would work two or three day shifts, right? You wouldn't be home at all on those days?"

"Most likely."

"Okay, well during those, I would drive back to Austin. I'd get my time with Ben and Tim, and I could put in my hours at the shelter. I'd have to find a day job here—"

"And during hurricane season, when I'm on call and gone even more than usual? Or what if I get dispatched? It happens. That could mean weeks of you being alone."

Jason gestured to their surroundings. "I've got friends here. I won't be alone."

True. He had support networks in both Houston and Austin. William would be a lot less worried knowing that Michelle wasn't far away, or even Lily, because they got along great. This could work!

Jason wasn't done. "I can ask work about transferring out here. There are a few locations in the same chain. I don't know if I'd still be a manager, but that's okay. The only problem is Emma."

William winced. "That's right. Didn't she move to Austin just to be with you?"

"Mostly because she likes the scene, but yeah, also because we're besties. I'm pretty sure she'd forgive me eventually. I would keep paying rent until she finds a new roommate. Maybe she would even transfer back here before the next semester. So what do you think?"

William scooted closer. "You'd really be willing to do all that for me? I know how much you love Austin."

"And now you know how much I love you."

That deserved a kiss. Before it became too heated, he pulled away. "You don't get to choose what base you're assigned to. Even if I was still active duty, all I could do is put in a transfer request and hope that something opens up."

"But it's worth a shot," Jason persisted. "You could ask about Galveston too. That wouldn't be as good, but it's only an hour away."

"From Houston. Four hours from Austin."

"I could drive it."

"You wouldn't be as close to Michelle and her family."

"I'll make new friends. It's worth looking into. Right?"

William thought about it. Christie had a lot of connections through her family, and she still pestered him all the time to return to active duty. "I'll see what I can do."

Jason grinned. "Thanks."

"Don't thank me!" William spluttered. "You're the one willing to uproot your entire life just to make me a little happier."

"Didn't think I had it in me, did you?"

"No," William conceded. "I'm not trying to make you feel bad, but I always wondered why you didn't come visit me in Cape Cod. I understand why you wouldn't want to live there, but a short trip would have been nice."

Jason grew somber. "I didn't want to distract you. That's why we broke up, remember? You needed to focus. And later, when you came home for visits and it felt like we were still together, I guess I was intimidated. I didn't understand half the things you were talking about. I thought about it though. Not visiting, but moving there."

"Seriously?"

Jason nodded. "I loved you." He laughed at the past tense. "I still do, but back then, I knew a weekend wouldn't be enough, that when the trip came to an end, I would go back to missing you and feeling lonely. So I started looking at job listings and pricing apartments."

"What stopped you?"

Jason exhaled. "I've moved around my entire life. I was always in Houston, but never in the same house or with the same people. Austin was the first time I felt like I was settling down. Don't take this the wrong way… I'm not saying I love them more than you because it's a different sort of love but—"

"Ben and Tim," William said, understanding immediately. "They're your family."

"They're not," Jason said, averting his gaze. "Not technically, but they sure feel like it to me. I didn't want to give that up. I still don't. Maybe I'm selfish."

"Then I am too," William said, "because I always fantasized about you moving to Massachusetts. I wanted you there, don't think I didn't! It just wouldn't have worked with the base situation, or me having to stay in the closet. By the time that was no longer an issue, I had already pushed you away." He swallowed, thinking about how close he had come to losing the greatest love of his life. "I won't make that same mistake again."

"No?" Jason asked.

"No. I promise."

"Then where are you running off to?"

William had hopped out of bed and was working on his jeans. "I thought I'd prove my dedication to you."

Jason grinned, looking him over. "That won't be easy. I'm hard to convince."

The jeans tumbled down to his ankles. "And I'm already hard."

After undressing completely, William slipped beneath the sheets, thrilled to discover that Jason was naked. He climbed on top, pressing their bodies together. They kissed, and usually they would do a lot more, working their way up to the most intimate act, but William felt too much. He kept thinking of the sacrifices Jason was willing to make, could see the happy future he had envisioned for them both. Helicopters, waves, swimming, rescues, and at the end of those long shifts, returning *home*, which was so much more than just a place. Jason would be there waiting for him. Daisy wouldn't be so far away. William would have it all, thanks to Jason's willingness. In return, he would give everything that he could.

"You sure?" Jason whispered.

William had already reached back to position the cock between his cheeks. They were rushing into it, not having played around first. "Just go slow," he said.

Jason reached up, cupping William's cheek in his hand. "I've got all night."

"Speak for yourself," he replied, lowering himself with a gasp. "Something tells me I'm not going to last that long." He did pretty well, all things considered. The pain he had braced for never arrived. Sometimes it all worked out that way—in life and in the bedroom—all the pieces fitting together just right and feeling like a dream come true.

A large green field, illuminated by lights and surrounded by stadium seating. In the middle of it, a dirt path traced the rough shape of diamond. Several men in uniforms were spread out over this unlikely environment, each obsessed with chasing a small ball just so they could fling it away again. William watched all of this, not understanding the appeal. He had nothing against baseball, or sports in general, but he'd never found it entertaining. His brother Spencer should be sitting here instead, and would be if he hadn't gotten food poisoning the day before. Still, the excuse to spend time with his father made the game more bearable. Especially since he needed advice.

"I have a question," William said, "and I want you to know in advance that I don't mean to be offensive."

The stadium erupted in cheers.

"Dad?"

His father looked at him like he was crazy. "That was a home run."

"Oh," William said, clapping a little.

"Sanders hit the ball out of the field with bases loaded. Did you not see that?"

"Sorry."

His father shook his head, then patted his arm. "Tell you what, next time I'll tell you when to get excited. Just so you blend in. Deal?"

"Sure!" William said, not faking his enthusiasm. That way he wouldn't have to pay attention at all.

His father sighed and shook his head. "What did you want to ask me?"

William considered the right way to phrase the question. "When did you know that Mom was the one, and why didn't you realize sooner that she wasn't? You know what I mean?"

"No." Lewis thought about it. "Wait, you want to know why your mother and I got together in the first place?"

"No, I get that. You guys found each other attractive and other stuff I don't want to think about. But you also decided to get married, even though it wouldn't work out in the long run. Was it because she was pregnant with Spencer?"

Lewis laughed. "I'd like to see you ask her that! And no, she wasn't pregnant when I asked her to marry me. I popped the question because she was the one."

William shook his head. "Obviously she wasn't."

"She was," his father insisted. "At the time. People change. That can't be helped, but back then, we were in love. We were happy. If I could go back and do it all over again, I'd *still* ask her to marry me."

"Because you wouldn't have had us otherwise."

"Even if you boys never existed. I mean it! I loved her. I still do. We just weren't meant to spend the rest of our lives together."

"But that's what marriage is."

"Not according to all the people who have gotten divorces." Lewis tried signaling the roving hotdog vendor and failed to get his attention. "Listen, when two people get married, they're agreeing to a commitment more serious than dating. You don't just call it quits after an argument, or because you get bored. But in the long term, if the situation changes and neither of you are happy, you aren't required to suffer until your dying day. That would be stupid. Your mother and I had many wonderful years together. I don't know if she feels the same, but I don't regret marrying her one bit."

"Okay," William said, still not satisfied.

His father nudged him. "This is about Jason, isn't it?"

"Maybe."

"I can tell from your face that it is. I don't think you should rush into anything, but you boys have known each other a long time, am I right? And you've been living together?"

"Yeah."

"Do you argue much?"

"Not really."

"Then if you want to ask him, ask him."

William laughed. "You make it sound so simple."

"Because it is. You want to spend the rest of your life with him, and his answer will tell you if he feels the same way. If he says yes, give it your best shot. Life might have other plans in store for you, but there's no predicting what that might be, so for now, just follow your heart and hope for the best."

William tittered, pulse racing. "I just hope he says yes."

"He will," his father said, nodding in certainty. "I love all three of you boys, but you're special. Spencer is too much like me, and Errol lives on another planet, but you... You're the one thing your mother and I got right."

"Thanks," William said, his voice a croak. "I love you too."

"Good. Now go get your old man a hotdog. I'm starving!"

William hopped up, already deciding his dad deserved a beer as well. Better make it two. William needed something to help calm his nerves, because he was going to do it. He would ask Jason to marry him!

"Can we talk?"

Never good words to hear. William looked up at Lily with concern. She was in Austin visiting her family and had reserved the last day of her trip for him. They were in the living room of his mother's house, Lily about to drive back to Houston. William only needed to finish changing Daisy's diaper before they left.

"Is everything okay?" he asked, resuming his task.

"I'm fine," Lily said. "We both are. It's good news."

"Oh! Great!"

"I didn't see this coming," Lily continued. "I'm flattered honestly, but I was headhunted."

"Sounds painful," he joked, even though his stomach sank. He finished his work and tried to comfort himself by smiling down at his daughter, who had one of his fingers trapped in her tiny hand and was gnawing and slobbering all over it.

"It's a really good job. Better pay and less management over my head. They have on-site daycare too. You have to understand, the finance industry is usually a sausage-fest. They don't worry about childcare. This company is different. I won't be the only woman working there, and it'll be good for Daisy—for us both—to be that close all day."

William steeled himself. "Where is it?"

"Portland. The one in Oregon."

He nodded, having guessed the east coast instead of west, but he had already known the job wouldn't be in Texas. Regardless, the idea of them moving so far away still hurt, so he did his best to argue against it. "I can pay for daycare," he said. "I'm sure there's somewhere close to your current office, so it wouldn't be so different."

"It's more than that." Lily's tone was patient. "When I say better pay, I mean a *lot* more. I'll be able to get my own place. My roommate didn't sign the lease expecting to live with a screaming baby, or to help with her so much. With this new job, I can rent a house, and before long, put a down payment on one of my own."

"We can get a house together," William said. "I didn't want to ruin the surprise, but Jason and I are talking about moving to Houston. There's a Coast Guard air station there."

"You've reenlisted?"

"No, I'm still on reserve. I was waiting on a friend of mine to see if I get stationed there."

"So nothing has been put in motion yet?"

"Right."

Lily exhaled as if relieved, and he knew then that she had made up her mind. Telling him was only a courtesy. "I know this is hard for you, but I'll be able to provide a better life for her."

"If it's money—"

"It's not just money!" Lily said, sounding exasperated. "I don't want to rely on you or my parents or anyone else. I care about my career. I've worked hard to get where I am, but I'm not getting paid what I deserve. We just hired a new guy, and he let slip how much he earns. It's more than I make, and I've been there for three years! We have the same damn position!"

William swallowed. "That sucks, and I'm sorry. But what about me?"

"I'll fly you up there as much as you want. We just have to plan ahead to get reasonable fares, but I looked into it, and it's possible. I still want you to be a part of Daisy's life. I'm sure she does too." Lily put her hand over his, the same one Daisy still held, and they were all connected. He just hoped it wasn't for the last time. "I'm not pushing you out. I swear. I would never do that to you. But I'm thinking of her future as well as mine."

On a logical level, he knew she was right. He also wanted his daughter to grow up in a house, to live somewhere that allowed pets, to have a yard to play in, a mother who was always near… All of it sounded good, but emotionally, he had looked forward to being part of that life. He had thought those dreams could come true in Houston. "When do you start?"

"Six weeks." Lily looked pained. "I hope you're not angry. Or hurt."

"It hurts to think about losing you both, but angry? Of course not. I'm proud of you." And he was. He hadn't intended to become a father, but if he had, he couldn't imagine a better mother for his child than Lily. "Just send me photos every day. And videos. Actually, how far do those baby monitors broadcast? Maybe you could put one in each room so I can still see and hear everything."

"You're really okay with this?"

"The adult in me is. The rest is kicking and screaming."

Lily smiled. "Thank you. You'll be a part of our lives every single day. I promise."

"Someone's got mail!"

William had just returned from another late-night shift. No serious emergencies tonight, just a head wound that would require stitches and a bite from a dog that had all of its shots. He and Sharon ferried these people to the hospital and treated the others on site. William was glad not to deal with anything life-threatening. He just hadn't expected to return home to such a chipper boyfriend.

"Who's it from?" he asked, setting down his things.

"Christie Patel," Jason said. "That's the woman from your unit, right? The one who can get you transferred to Houston?"

"I never said that." William accepted the envelope, feeling guilty. He hadn't told Jason about Lily's new job, needing the previous two days to let it sink in. Part of him still hoped she might call to say she had changed her mind.

Jason was still beaming at him. "Open it!"

He did so, first scanning the letter she had written before moving on to the next page. Christie had sent a list of every current and upcoming vacancy. He skipped down to the eighth district, relieved when he didn't see Houston or Galveston listed there, because that meant the idea of reenlisting wouldn't have worked out regardless. Even if Lily chose to stay in Texas, the local air stations didn't have an opening for him. He looked up and shook his head. "Sorry."

Jason's face fell. "Really? What about Galveston?"

"Nope." He put the letter back in the envelope. "Lily's moving to Portland anyway."

"What?"

"I just found out when she was here. She got headhunted by a firm up there."

Jason struggled with disappointment, but managed to get past it. "I'm sorry."

"It's okay. I guess it wasn't meant to be."

"What about Daisy?"

"I'll still see her. I'll take trips up, or Lily will come back to Austin to see her family.

"And the Coast Guard?" Jason said, looking like a kid who had heard that Christmas had been canceled. In other words, adorable.

William chuckled. "They'll have to manage without me. Come here. If you're going to feel sorry for me, I at least want some snuggles."

Jason gave him a hug, which felt good. People often said it was the thought that counts, and in this case it was trite but very true. Jason had been willing to turn his life upside down just to make William happier than he already was. Not many people were so generous, and now he intended to return the favor. William would dedicate himself to Jason's happiness. "It's just you and me again," he murmured. "You've had to share me with the Coast Guard, with Lily, with a baby…"

"It hasn't been easy," Jason said, playing it up. "Does this mean I get to be selfish now?"

"Yeah." William nuzzled their noses together. "I'm all yours."

Chapter Twenty-eight

William was getting cold feet, and it wasn't even his wedding! The big day was upon them, and in retrospect, they had been crazy to think they could handle this on their own. Despite the temptation to do so, they hadn't allowed Marcello or anyone else to take over completely. The wedding was their gift to Ben and Tim, and they wanted to be responsible for its realization. That meant pinching every penny and calling in favors. At this point, half the guests were involved in setting up the ceremony. Greg was in charge of the decorations, having experience in staging a house to make it presentable for sale. Michelle was helping him, which was good because before she intervened, there had been talk of a mechanical bull. Kelly would be their photographer. William's mother took the cake—literally—and even Caesar was involved, although at this point, William didn't remember how. Wedding planner had once seemed like a joke profession. Now he respected anyone who could do this for a living without losing their sanity.

While all this activity was going on at Ben and Tim's house, William was still at the apartment, reviewing a to-do list and making sure they hadn't forgotten anything.

"I'm heading over there now," Emma said, entering the living room of the apartment she still shared with Jason.

He looked up from the couch to see that she was wearing a tuxedo, her hair cut short and slicked back. He whistled appreciatively.

"This old thing?" Emma said, attempting a twirl and nearly falling over. "Pretend that looked cool."

"You've got style!" William said. "Something tells me it's not just the wedding you're dressing up for. Who's the lucky lady?"

"You'll find out later. I'm on the way to the house. Need a ride?"

He shook his head. "I still have to get ready. I'll see you there. Oh! Say hello to Jason for me."

She shook her head. "You've been apart for what… one whole night?"

"That's one night too many," William replied.

After she had left, he continued working his way through the list, crossing out one item after another. Everything was done. All he needed to do was get dressed, pick up the cake, and head over to Ben and Tim's house. He took a quick shower, trying to not get nervous about what else the day entailed. The life-changing event that had nothing to do with the wedding. When he was ready, he went to the dresser in Jason's room. The left side was his. Inside the underwear drawer was a box, the very one he had once stolen. Black and velvety, it opened on a hinge. Jason had mentioned it recently, wondering where it had gone to. William asked a few casual questions, learning that the ring Tim had proposed to Ben with had once been in that box. The inside was currently empty, awaiting another promise, and another answer.

William took it and got ready to leave. Usually he would get on his bike, but he still needed to go by his mother's house. Unless he intended to balance the cake on his handlebars, he would need a ride. Jason had the car, so he was stuck. William wanted to kick himself. He should have asked Emma to wait! He still could call her. Or someone else who might not have left already.

He grabbed his phone, sending a quick text. *Are you there yet?*

I won't be late, came Kelly's response. *Don't worry.*

Think you can pick me up? I need to run a few errands.

After today, you're going to be so indebted to me. I love it!

That was as good as a yes. William sent him the address, then paced, occasionally taking out the ring box and staring at it, hoping for inspiration. He still didn't know what he was going to say. Or what Jason's response would be.

He met his ride downstairs, providing another address before remembering it wasn't necessary.

"Won't your mother be surprised to see me!" Kelly said with a smirk. "Especially since both of us are dressed up like we're going on a date."

"She has plans," William said, brushing at the white dress shirt he wore. The pink paisley tie was supposed to make up for how plain it was. "How do I look?"

"Handsome as always," Kelly said, but he didn't seem to be flirting.

That was good, because William needed a favor, but first he wanted to feel out the situation. "You look good too. No date? The invitation said you could bring one."

A smile tugged at Kelly's lips. "He'll be there."

"Really?" William asked, a little confused. "He's meeting you at the wedding?"

Kelly nodded. "He's part of Marcello's entourage." He reached for his phone.

William tensed and kept an eye on the road. Then he looked at Kelly's phone when it was handed to him. The guy on the screen was handsome, if a little gruff in appearance. "He's not going to beat me up, is he?"

"Nathaniel? I'll try to keep him in line."

"Are you two serious?"

"I love him more than anyone else in this world." Kelly glanced over. "That wasn't meant to hurt you."

"No, I get it," William said. "I'm glad you found someone. That's what I wanted to talk to you about. I haven't told anyone this, but I'm going to pop the question."

"Just to be clear, you're going to ask for Jason's hand in marriage?"

"Yeah."

Kelly pursed his lips. "Couldn't you have let me imagine, just for one minute, that you were distraught about me having moved on?"

William chuckled. "Sorry."

"You're not, and neither am I. I'm glad you two made it. This makes a better story. In the future, I'll tell people that you left me for the man you would marry, not some floozy."

William laughed out loud. "Is that what you've been telling people?"

"Maybe. This is exciting news! When are you going to ask him?"

"Today. After the ceremony. I'm not sure when, exactly, but I was hoping you would be there."

Kelly made a face. "My presence won't be a mood killer?"

"Not like that," William said. "I was hoping you could capture the moment on film. Assuming he says yes, I would like to have a photo to look back on."

Kelly was quiet. "Do you want to hear something strange? Remember the charity ball? The shut-in?"

"Way back when? Yeah!"

"While you and Jason were…" Kelly shook his head. "While I was accepting that you and I couldn't be together any longer,

I had a brief conversation with someone I thought I'd never see again, but eventually, I did. That's how I met Nathaniel."

"Really?" William said, picking up the phone, but the lock screen had him blocked.

"I still use the same pin number," Kelly said, eyes searching.

If this was a test, William hadn't forgotten. He entered it, missing a time when they had been so close. Then he considered the photo again. "He does look sort of familiar."

"He was your boss for the night."

"No!"

"Really. He's probably making one of the wedding waiters cry as we speak. Strange, isn't it? You were falling in love with the man you'll no doubt marry. I was doing my best to stop you, and in the process meeting the man… Well, we'll see."

"Would you marry him?" William pressed. "Pretend he asked you right now."

Kelly's leg started to bounce nervously. Then he nodded. "In a heartbeat."

William laughed happily, eyes misting up. "Funny how life works out. Isn't it?"

"Yes." Kelly shot him a smile. "Yes it is."

"Happy endings all around."

"That's the plan! You really don't drive after all this time?"

"I do when I have to. Mostly I try to bum rides off of ex-boyfriends. Or take my bike."

"You and that damn bike!" Kelly said with a chuckle. "Is it still the same one?"

William nodded. "Same one."

His driver grew quiet when they reached their destination.

"Memory lane?" William asked.

Kelly nodded, then checked his watch. "We better hurry."

They hustled inside, going first to the kitchen. Most of the refrigerator had been cleared out to accommodate the cake. His mother had done a wonderful job—three tiers, each decorated with blue and silver roses. She had even managed to find two grooms for the top, one wearing a white tuxedo, the other in black.

"You're going to have to sit in the backseat with that thing," Kelly said. "That way it doesn't topple over if I hit an unexpected red light."

"No problem."

"Ready?"

"No. Just one more thing. I'll be right back!" Without an explanation, William ran up the stairs to his room. There, in the same dresser drawer where he had kept his high school athletic awards, was one much more special to him. He opened a long blue case, revealing a yellow ribbon with red fringes. Attached to it via an ornate clasp was a golden disc. It depicted a survivor being pulled from choppy waters into the safety of a small boat. His lifesaving medal. William had felt extraordinarily proud to receive the award, and it remained his most treasured souvenir of his service. With Jason's recent interest in the Coast Guard, and considering all that it symbolized—the four-year sacrifice of their time apart—he hoped it would make an adequate gesture.

Doubt stirred. Most hopeful suitors went to the mall and bought a ring. Maybe he should have done that too. But this would mean the same thing. When Jason saw the little black box, he would understand that this was a proposal. Hopefully. William opened the lid, having to remove the inlay to make room for the medal. Then he snapped it closed again, tried to calm his nerves, and went back downstairs.

Kelly was waiting for him. "Ready?"

William breathed out. "That's a very loaded question."

"Because of Jason?" Kelly's smile was reserved. "If I were in his shoes, I know what my answer would be. You've got nothing to worry about. Except for getting the cake there in one piece."

Crying at weddings. What a silly stereotype. He thought of all the wedding scenes in cartoons he had seen when growing up, and how without fail an anthropomorphic animal of some type would start howling, rivers pouring from its eyes. Now he was on the verge of doing the same thing. The setting was beautiful, the backyard barely recognizable after its magical transformation. Freshly planted white flowers created a natural pathway to steps—just three—that led to a small stage, an arch of twisted branches before it. An older man with graying temples waited there, ready to preside over the wedding, arranging papers on a small desk that would make this marriage as close to a legal union as possible, despite the law still excluding same-sex couples. The guests were all seated and waiting, anticipation growing. William was among them. The signal had been given! The grooms were going to appear at any time. As music started flowing from Jason's guitar, all heads turned to look toward the house. Ben and Tim had always been a beautiful couple, but now they were stunning. And evidently not at all surprised, because they both wore tuxedos, Ben in white, Tim in black. Their walk down the aisle was slow, each of them distracted by family and friends gathered there, grasping hands or waving at people farther away. When Ben looked right at him, tears in his eyes, William couldn't take it anymore. He started crying.

Funny how joy could overwhelm the body just as much as sorrow, but this felt much better. Having led them to the altar with his music, Jason took a seat in front of him, joining Michelle's family. William reached out to touch him, massaging his shoulders, certain they had done a good thing. Jason placed his hand over one of his, squeezing it tight, no doubt overwhelmed by emotion himself. William tried to get himself under control as Ben and Tim spoke their vows, reading to each other the letters they had prepared. He hoped someone had the foresight to record a video of all this, because most of the words were lost on him. Those he heard only set him off again, especially when they exchanged rings.

Thank goodness boring paperwork followed next or he'd be completely overcome. While this took place, William looked around to see plenty of cheeks just as wet as his own. Jason had done a better job of holding it together, and was having a quiet conversation with Michelle. William waited for them to finish because he wanted to wrap his arms around him from behind and give him a great big hug.

"I guess we were in a letter-writing mood," Tim announced from the small stage. They were facing the guests again. Tim handed a piece of paper to Ben. "Do you want to read this one?"

Ben nodded, accepting it. He consulted it briefly, then his eyes rose, seeking out someone in the audience. Jason. "To our future son…"

William covered his mouth with his hands. Two things had been long overdue, and it looked as though both would be resolved today. Ben and Tim were married, and now they would have a son. They'd had one for many years, or so it always appeared to William. Jason already had a family who loved and cared for him. Now, in the presence of a lawyer, they were making it official. Ben asked Jason to join him on stage, but he didn't move. Not until Michelle said something to get him going.

Then Jason walked stiff-legged up the aisle, as if in a dream. Ben and Tim embraced him. The audience burst into applause. William needed all of his willpower not to leap over the chairs and join them in a group hug. Before this could happen, they led Jason to the desk where more papers would be signed.

"This is all your doing," William said, leaning forward to address Michelle. "Isn't it?"

"I like to think it would have happened without me," she responded, eyes wet. "Just like Ben and Tim getting married, sometimes people need a gentle push. I'm determined to make a family of them. Of all of you."

William grinned. "Just leave the rest to me."

She looked surprised, then pleased when he nodded in confirmation. The day had been full of happy occurrences. Why not go whole hog? Their attention was drawn to the front again, Ben and Tim standing to either side of Jason, holding his hands in the air.

"Ladies and gentlemen," Tim said, addressing them all. "May I present to you, our son, Jason Grant!"

William leapt to his feet. He wasn't the only one. Tim's grandmother was already rushing forward. She was surprisingly spry for her age. Others had risen as well, moving forward to offer their congratulations, to hug Jason or each other or just to blow their noses. So much love was in the air that it was ridiculous. William called on all of his patience because getting to Jason took a long time. When they reached each other, Jason's chin trembled. "I've got parents," he managed to say. Then he started crying.

William took him in his arms, the tears flowing again. "You're so loved," he murmured. "By everyone here. You deserve all of this."

Jason squeezed him back, not letting go as the crowd slowly dispersed. Except for two figures. William felt a strong hand on his shoulder. He looked over to see Tim smiling at him. Ben was rubbing Jason's back and trying to calm him.

"You okay?" he asked.

Jason mumbled a response into William's chest that none of them understood.

"I think he wants a group hug," William suggested as casually as possible.

Tim laughed. "We thought you'd never ask."

A second later there was plenty of squeezing, more laughter, and a lot more tears.

Choosing the right time to propose wasn't easy. Today was about Ben and Tim. William didn't want to steal the limelight, and he felt they all needed time to take a deep breath. Eating helped, as did dancing. Ben seemed to enjoy that more than his new husband did, shaking his hips or twirling, lost in the music. Tim could only try to keep up. William was out there as well, the grass an unlikely dance floor, although he didn't have a partner. Jason was busy playing his guitar, accompanying the music, head bobbing to the rhythm. William watched him while dancing, occasionally turning his attention to the happy couple.

Tim noticed him looking, his panicked expression becoming one of hope. "Mind if I cut in?" he said. "That's your line, not mine."

William shook his head, not understanding. "Huh?"

"Say it!"

"Oh! Mind if I cut in?"

Tim stopped moving and gestured for William to take his place. Then he fled. Ben laughed, not missing a beat as his feet kept moving. William joined him. Could this day get any better? Seriously. He needed some random tragedy to balance things out, because this was one dream come true after another.

"You've got some moves!" Ben said appreciatively.

"All part of rescue swimmer training," William joked. "Helps calm survivors when they see you dancing on the deck of a ship."

"Please tell me that's true!" Ben turned his head, seeking out Jason. Or — considering what he said next — making sure that he was outside of hearing range. "I'm told there might be another big announcement soon."

William rolled his eyes. "Michelle is *terrible* at keeping secrets."

Ben grinned. "She's got her own agenda. I'm with her on this one. I've got a son. Now I want a son-in-law."

William lost the rhythm for a second, then caught up, more energy in each step. "I was thinking of asking today, but I don't want to take away from—"

"Do it!" Ben said. "I'll consider it a wedding present. The best one I could ask for!"

The song came to an end, replaced by a ballad. Was he seriously about to slow dance with Ben? For real? Ben shrugged, as if not averse to the idea, and opened his arms. Then a black tuxedo came between them.

"Mind if I cut in?" Tim said.

"Actually, I do," William tried, but he was already ancient history. Ben and Tim were in each other's arms. All he could do was enjoy an up-close view for as long as he dared—without seeming too creepy—before he retreated to the sidelines. He wasn't alone. Almost everyone there had stopped to witness a slowly spinning embrace of tender perfection.

The sun grew orange and heavy as the day wore on, many of the guests leaving. That was fine. He and Jason had spent most of the time mingling with other people, but now they could be together. They picked at the food, drank a glass of champagne, and went inside to escape the heat and enjoy the quiet.

"I still can't believe it," Jason said, leaning against the kitchen counter and shaking his head. "Who adopts a twenty-four-year-old?"

"Awesome people, that's who. You've been their son longer than that. Don't you think?"

Jason nodded. "I had hoped. And there were times when they said as much, but… This is for real. I know it sounds cheesy, but now I feel safe."

William shook his head. "What do you mean?"

"Like the future is secure. I never had that growing up. I didn't know where I would be the next month, or with who. Maybe nobody does."

William thought about the way his parents' divorce had turned his world upside down, how upset he had been, even though his family remained the same despite being divided. "It's not normal what you went through," William said. "I'm glad you don't have to feel that way anymore."

Speaking of the future… now might be the time, but this wasn't the place. William was determined to do this right. He looked around for inspiration, wanting better than a mundane environment like the kitchen. He noticed the window and how dark it had grown outside, the stage where Ben and Tim had married now illuminated.

"Come look at the lights with me," William said. "Please."

They left the house and entered into a serene environment. The DJ had gone home, a playlist of soft music streaming from Jason's phone. Marcello was slow dancing with Tim's grandmother. As for the two grooms, they had pulled up chairs to the buffet and were sitting in front of the spread like kings, goofing around with each other. Off to the side, Kelly was taking photos of Allison with her baby. William nodded at him as they passed, hoping it was enough of a signal. Kelly nodded back, but then gave new directions to Allison. Had he not understood? It was about to happen! Wasn't it?

They reached the stage, his boyfriend sitting on the top step and holding out his hand. William took it, sitting next to him. Jason seemed lost in their surroundings. He became William's sole focus as he searched his heart for infallible words.

Jason sighed wistfully. "I hate when a party is over."

"Really?" William asked, slipping his free hand into his pocket. "Why?"

"Because endings are sad. They always make me cry."

"Even when they're happy?" His fingers touched the ring box. As casually as possible, he slowly slid it free and placed it next to him.

"Especially when they're happy because then I don't want it to be over."

There were some things he didn't want to end either. Ever. William removed his hand from Jason's and pulled him closer. "I don't think of it that way. To me it's more like when a war is over. The chaos has finally ceased." They had been through so much. The struggle at the beginning when Kelly was still there, the years apart, and all that had happened since they had gotten back together. For once, their future seemed clear of obstacles. "Everything is calm and peaceful again."

"And kind of sad," Jason said.

"Hm." Sounded like he needed cheering up. "Hey, remember when I asked you for four years?"

Jason's eyes darted to meet his. "Now I'm getting sadder."

"I know, I know. What if I asked you for four more?"

Jason's brow furrowed. "That's not funny."

"I'm dead serious," William replied. "Except this time, I want you to come with me. On a journey. Of sorts."

He looked down at the black box beside him, his hand shaking a little as he reached for it. Then he held it up so Jason could see. Except he wasn't looking. Jason's attention was somewhere across the yard. William cleared his throat. No luck. "Uh, I sort of need you to look at me."

That got Jason's attention. He turned his head toward him, noticing the box right away. Instead of elation or surprise, he seemed confused, peering at the box as if trying to see the contents.

"Okay," William said with a chuckle. "Not the reaction I was hoping for."

Jason blinked and shook his head. "Sorry, but is that from my old room?"

"I needed a box," he said hurriedly.

"Yeah, but it was in my underwear drawer."

William's nerves were frazzled. "Just take it, okay?"

Jason still seemed apprehensive, so William his arm free and opened the box for him. The puzzlement only increased when the contents were revealed. William reached in, took hold of the ribbon, and held up the medal. He hoped Jason would recognize it. Then again, those books he was reading didn't have many photos in them. At least his eyes had lit up, fixated now on the gold disc. William was tempted to start swinging it back and forth and hypnotize his way into a successful proposal.

When Jason looked to him for clarification, William explained. "It's a Lifesaving Medal. This is the life you helped me save. I figured it's a nice symbol for what I'm asking for. A life. Together. Just give me four years. We can stay right here in Austin, if you want. And at the end of that time, when I've done my best to prove myself, I'd like to be standing right here with you."

"And what?" Jason asked, a smile appearing.

It matched his own. "And then we'll give Ben and Tim some serious competition."

Jason's eyes were searching as he reached out, fingers warm on the back of William's neck. Jason pulled him close, their lips meeting. Somewhere in the distance, he was vaguely aware of clapping, but the rest of him was lost in that kiss, which felt like a promise of its own. Then he pulled away to hear the answer to his question.

"What do you say? Is that a yes? It didn't feel like a no."

Jason seemed to weigh his response carefully before he spoke, tone warm when he did. "Four years."

"I'm supposed to wait four years to get your answer?" William said, not sure if he understood. "Is this some sort of punishment?"

Jason shrugged enigmatically. "Take it or leave it."

"Okay," William said. They would take it slow, but judging from the way Jason's hand gripped his own, the outcome was hopeful. "I suppose that's only fair. It's my turn to wait, and when the four years are up, I'll stand on this stage with you and ask my question again. I'll say 'Jason Grant, will you spend the rest of your life with me?' And you'll say… Come on! Give me a hint! What will you say?"

Jason grinned. Finished with words, he kissed William again. Contained within it was all the reassurance he needed. They felt the same way. Of course they would be together!

"I love you," Jason murmured against his lips.

"I love you too," William said, pulling back to consider him.

"I hate to interrupt," a voice said. Tim was there, holding two champagne glasses.

"He loves to interrupt," Ben said, standing at his side. "I begged him not to."

"I wanted to be the first to congratulate them," Tim whined. Then he winked, leaned forward, and offered the glasses. "Congratulations. Unless he said no. Either way, I figured booze was called for."

Jason laughed happily, taking a glass and passing it to William before accepting one of his own. Ben had two flutes too. Handing one to Tim, he came up with the perfect toast. "Here's to our ever-growing family."

"We might have to buy a bigger house," Tim joked.

They clinked glasses and drank.

"Thank you both," Ben said. "I'm not sure this day would have happened if not for you."

"We would have gotten around to it *eventually*," Tim said. "Seriously though, thanks for forcing us to do this while we're still photogenic. You forgot one tiny detail though."

"What?" Jason asked, sounding concerned.

"The honeymoon. No one has told us where we're going."

William locked eyes with Jason. Then they groaned in unison.

"The bed and breakfast you came from," Jason said, improvising. "That was your honeymoon. You just did it in reverse order."

Tim glowered. "Doesn't count."

"We could drive you somewhere tomorrow," William tried. "San Antonio? There's stuff to do there. Um…"

Ben shook his head ruefully. "Stop being mean and tell them."

"We planned our own honeymoon," Tim said. "And we want you guys to come along."

"That's not how it's supposed to work," Jason said. "Don't you want to be alone?"

William felt like clamping his mouth shut! "But if you've already booked the flights…"

Ben laughed. "Jason, you're our son now. I'd say a family vacation is long overdue. Wouldn't you?"

"You're not sharing a hotel room with us," Tim said. "We need privacy. Gotta consummate this sucker a bunch or it doesn't count."

William was pretty sure his cheeks were glowing red. If he brought the glass close to his face for a drink, the champagne would probably start boiling. "Where are we going?"

"Acapulco," Tim said, "mostly because Ben giggles every time I say it, or anything else, in Spanish. *No es así, mi mariposa?*"

Ben shrugged, not understanding but giggling shamelessly.

William beamed at them, feeling twice as lucky as he did before. Not only was he going to marry the man of his dreams, but he was getting the coolest possible in-laws as part of the deal!

William awoke in Jason's arms. They had spent the entire night that way, which was unusual. The only time he remembered that happening was their final night together before he left for the Coast Guard. Except it hadn't been final. Thank goodness for that. He remained where he was, content to let his eyes wander around the apartment bedroom. When Jason stirred, William sat upright, letting his chest be used as a pillow.

"Ready to get up?" he asked.

"Just a couple more hours," Jason murmured. "Go back to sleep."

"I'm too excited," William said. "I feel like it's our honeymoon!"

"We don't leave until tomorrow."

"I know. But still…" He thought of the previous night, how he and Jason had been the last ones to leave the reception, nearly forgotten as Ben and Tim focused more and more on each other. They were so in love. From the way they acted around each other, anyone would think they had just met. "Do you think they're still doing it?"

"Huh? Who?"

"Ben and Tim. Do you think they slept at all, or do you think they've been going at it all night?"

Jason looked up at him with an incredulous expression. "Those are my parents you're talking about."

"Oh! Right. I'll have to get used to that. I didn't mean it in a pervy way."

Jason slid his hand beneath the covers. "You're rock hard."

"Okay, so maybe I did mean it that way."

"Just keep your fantasies to yourself."

"No promises," William said, gasping as Jason pumped his hand up and down. Eventually he moved his hand away again.

"You'll have to finish on your own. I'm too tired."

"I'll wait until you're not," William said, pulling him closer. He was content to caress his back, thoughts drifting in a more innocent direction. "My mom sent me a text last night."

"Yeah?"

"Mm-hm. She wanted to know if I have a fiancé."

"Do you?"

"I hope so," William said tentatively. "I'm not totally sure I understood your answer."

Jason pushed himself upright. "We're getting married."

"But you want to wait four years?"

Jason sat up the rest of the way, suddenly much more awake. "I had an idea. When you were asking me for four years… You know how you made it sound like you were leaving again?" He held up his hand to stop any response. "I get it now. Your proposal was romantic, but I asked myself in that moment what I would do. I have everything I ever wanted here, but if you needed to leave, this time I decided I would go with you."

"Wow. So when you said four years—"

"Hold that thought," Jason said, scrambling out of bed.

He went to the dresser and opened a drawer. William didn't pay attention to what he brought back, namely because Jason was nude and he was enjoying the view. It was soon obscured. Jason sat cross-legged in bed, pulling blankets over his lap. He worked on freeing stapled pages from an envelope, then turned them, studying one.

"Is that the letter from Christie?" William asked.

"Yeah!" Jason looked up. "Guess what?"

He turned it so William could see and pointed at one of the lines.

"Astoria?" William said, reading it.

"There's an opening coming up at the end of summer." Jason leaned over and grabbed his phone, tongue sticking out one corner of his mouth as he tapped the screen. "I hope I'm right because…"

"It's not far from Portland," William said, realizing what he was getting at.

"Two hours," Jason said "That's not bad. You'd be close to Daisy, even closer than Houston is to Austin, and you could go back to being a rescue swimmer. It's just like our original plan!"

William's elation was short-lived. "It's not, because in that plan, you were a short drive from Houston. And you would come back here when I'm on duty for days at a time."

"I still could sometimes," Jason said, not sounding so certain himself.

"What about your work at the shelter?"

"I'm sure there's plenty of needy animals for me in Oregon. That's what I meant with my answer. I'll give you another four years, except this time, I'd go with you. I do want to move back here eventually, but think of the people you could help." Jason rose and went for the dresser again, this time grabbing the medal and holding it up. "This is just one life. You've saved more than that, right? Think how many more you could save if you had more time. Twice as many? More?"

"I want to," William said, throat feeling tight. "Believe me, I dream about it all the time. I loved that work, but we're finally together, and I hate the idea of you being lonely, even for a few days. Or my work getting in the way of our relationship."

"I'll keep myself busy, and if I ever start to resent you for being gone so much, I'll have this to remind me that it's worth it." Jason trapped the golden disc with his free hand, squeezing it tight. "I'd want to come home eventually. To my family. But think of it; Four years for you to save lives, and to be there during some of the most important years of your daughter's childhood."

"Our daughter," William said. "If we're getting married, she's yours too."

Jason's mouth dropped open. "I hadn't even considered that. I don't know if I'm ready to be a parent."

William laughed. "That makes two of us." He leaned forward. "Give me four more years, and I swear, the rest belongs to you. But if you think you can't handle it… I know how much you would be giving up. Are you sure?"

Jason grew solemn and thought about it again. In the end he shook his head. "The only thing I'm sure about is wanting to be with you. I don't think it matters where we are."

"Okay," William said, slowly smiling as he considered the implications. "Four years?"

Jason nodded. "Four years."

The honeymoon was over. But not in a bad way. The trip to Acapulco had been a wonderful adventure and a much-needed vacation, but now they had to go back to work. William helped Lily make the move to Portland. While there, he stopped by the air station in Astoria. He had already put in his request to return to active duty and to be stationed there, but he figured making a personal appearance couldn't hurt. Just being around the helicopters again and speaking the jargon lifted his spirits. Jason was right. William wasn't happy being a paramedic. He wanted to use the skills he had trained so hard to acquire while he was still young enough to do so. Astoria itself was a little secluded, and he didn't find an apartment he was satisfied with, but one of his potential crewmen offered him a couch to sleep on until he figured it all out.

That was the plan. William would go first, get settled, and then send for Jason. The good news came a few weeks later: He was back in the Coast Guard! Soon he'd be diving into freezing cold water and asking himself what the hell he'd been thinking by returning to this life. At least he would have someone waiting at home, willing to warm him up again. Jason cried when they parted. William did not. This separation would be short. A month apart, two at the most, and they would be together again.

That was how it was supposed to be. That was the promise. He hadn't expected it to be broken.

The letter arrived at the end of William's first week in Astoria. He didn't open it right away. He waited until he was off duty, on a day dedicated to apartment-hunting. He began the morning that way, telling each leasing agent that no, he wouldn't be living on his own. His fiancé would be joining him soon. Only when he went to a diner for lunch did he open the letter, wanting to pretend that Jason was sitting across from him and that the messy handwriting was their shared conversation. The first two words made his stomach sink. The letter didn't begin with *Dear William* or *Hey Baby*. Instead it said…

I'm sorry.

Please don't think I lied, or that I wanted to trick you. I thought I could do this. I really did. I know the reason will sound like an excuse. I'm afraid to even tell you. Maybe it would be better to never contact you again, or to come crawling back after enough years have gone by, but I love you, and I know that you love me, so please try to understand. The only home I had ever known was taken from me when I was seven. Even before then, because once my mother invited that abusive man into my life, I no longer felt secure. I no longer had a home. Think for a minute about how much you remember from your early life. I bet kindergarten is a blur. You might have some memories from first grade, but how many? That's how old I was when Child Protective Services took me away. When I got older, sometimes I looked back on the life I missed and wondered how much of it I had made up. All those memories of feeling loved and safe, maybe they were all a fairy tale. Eventually I decided they must be. I grew up and put away childish things. More than ten years went by, me without parents, unconditional love, or anything like a home. I tried to make my own, but I guess I don't get how they work, because I failed. I was in trouble, falling flat on my face again. Michelle caught me. She sent me to Austin and the impossible happened. I found my family. Even before Ben and Tim adopted me, I felt safe. They made sure of that. I feel like I belong here.

I can't walk away from that. Not even for a few years. I can only imagine how stupid that must sound to you, because your family is here too. But they've <u>always</u> been there for you. Mine hasn't, and I'm scared that if I'm gone, Ben and Tim won't love me as much. Or that without a biological bond, the connection will fade and disappear. They've told me that will never happen, but it's hard to undo a lifetime of damage. Like I said, I know it's not a good enough excuse. I don't expect you to forgive me. I just want you to understand.

Please don't come back. Don't turn away from all the people out there who need you. Someone once rescued me and it made all the difference. It made it possible for us to meet. I believe in our love. I don't know why you're different, but I don't think you'll stop loving me. But I am worried that you'll no longer like me. If I'm wrong, there's one promise that I really will keep. Four years. I can give that to you again. I can give you eight or even twelve. If you come back to me wrinkled and gray, I'll still love you just as much and want to be your husband. For now, I'll keep your medal close to me at night. I'm going to dream of you, and if you'll have me, I'll try to visit. No matter what happens, you'll be in my heart. I'm proud of you, and I'm sorry you can't feel the same way about me.

Yours,

Jason

William reread the letter, thinking of countless responses and all the arguments he could make to coax Jason into sticking with their plan. They were meant to be together. Logic had nothing to do with it. After everything they had been through, this was supposed to be their victory—the time when they were finally allowed to explore their potential. He could picture them taking road trips to Portland to discover the city together. They would stand on the beach, holding hands and gazing out across the Pacific Ocean. They would picnic in forests that made St. Edwards Park look like a patch of grass, buy an old house on the edge of town and fix it up, cuddle on the couch and get drunk when winter snowed them in… Their lives were meant to be lived side by side!

The waitress brought him a refill of Coke, taking away a mostly empty plastic glass and replacing it with another filled to the brim. Easy come, easy go. William exhaled. Then he read the letter a third time, trying to understand how Jason felt—what it meant to grow up without a family. He struggled to imagine his own life without the security of home, or the comforting guidance of parents. Jason must have been so relieved to find that again after so many years. Decades. He had still been willing to give it up too, even though he ultimately failed to do so. Maybe it was for the best. William could imagine Jason bravely making his way to Astoria and sitting in a lonely apartment for days at a time, wondering if he would still have a home when they finally returned to Austin and fearing that the love his adopted parents had for him was slowly dying.

Ben and Tim. He could remember once, when visiting their home with Jason, how he had trailed behind. William had watched as Ben ushered Jason into the house, eyes shining with pride. Then Ben had fussed over him, worrying if Jason had eaten enough and was taking care of himself. He also remembered the way Ben's eyes closed when they hugged goodbye, like he was determined to savor the moment. As for Tim, he always acted like his best friend had shown up, eager to show Jason changes he'd made to the house, or tell him funny stories about gallery patrons. Occasionally he would look at Ben, grinning broadly with an expression that said, *"Isn't this the best thing in the world? Our son is here! Isn't it great?"*

Jason would be okay in Austin.

At least he didn't doubt William's love for him, believing it would survive separation again. Maybe he was right. It wouldn't be easy though. William took out his phone. For a long time he considered what he would say, his food growing cold. He thought of disorderly hair and piercing eyes, a guy willing to do just about anything to win his heart, loving him shamelessly and insisting William do the same. Brave in all aspects except one. He supposed everyone was allowed a fault or two. William laughed at memories they had made together and clenched his jaw against tears at others. Then he sent his response. Two words. One promise.

Four years.

Epilogue

The helicopter zoomed above the treetops, the gust from the rotor blades sending snow flying, making visibility difficult. Leafless branches reached for the sky like dead fingers. Naked trees were easier to see beyond than the green pines that could provide shelter. That was where their survivor was likely to be, when really, he should be in a clearing. If he was still conscious after being missing for more than a day, and if he heard the helicopter coming, William prayed the survivor would go to where he would be visible. Astoria definitely wasn't short on trees, or undeveloped land. He understood why people came here to hike. He just didn't get why they didn't wait until spring. It was January! Stay at home and pig out on leftover Christmas candy!

"There!" The AMT pointed, William following the finger to another clearing. He saw gloved hands waving in the air and breathed out a sigh of relief. The sun was already going down and they had been talking about returning to base. They would still do so, but not empty-handed. William was lowered down. He checked the survivor's condition, hooked the man to himself, and they were carried up again. All a matter of routine.

The reporter waiting at the base when they returned, camera crew and all—*that* made him nervous. Astoria provided a nice quiet existence, meaning news crews didn't have much to report on. This, combined with reality television shows that followed a few different bases—one close by—meant heightened public interest in what the Coast Guard did. He knew Jason was a fan of those shows and once asked casually if William might appear in an episode. Not likely. He and Jason stayed in touch, texting or video conferencing whenever possible, but so far he hadn't visited.

William ignored the news crew, talking instead to the paramedics who were waiting to whisk the survivor to the hospital. He had new respect for what they did, having been in the trenches himself. The survivor was being rolled on a gurney toward the ambulance when he reached out with red frigid fingers to grab William's hand and spoke. "I want to know the name of the man who saved my life!"

William smiled in response. "Jason Grant."

The man frowned. "But your uniform… It says Townson."

"That might be my name, but trust me, Jason made this possible."

The survivor appeared confused as he was rolled into the ambulance, but he smiled and waved just before the doors shut. People tended to forgive any odd behavior when you had just rescued them. Once the vehicle was on its way, William gave a quick statement to the news crew, taking note of the station and asking if the footage would be streamed online. That way Jason could see. It might not be reality television, but it was close.

His heroic actions were rewarded with paperwork. Once that was done, William checked the clock, relieved to see his shift had ended hours ago. Time to go home. He didn't live on the base. Housing there was scarce, and he hoped that someday he might not be living alone. For now, he still was, and so he had chosen humble accommodations. The apartment complex—if it could be called that—had once been a motel. Some units were large, the walls between rooms having been torn down. His was still what a traveler would have stayed in overnight: a large space for a bedroom, a small kitchenette in one corner, and a separate bathroom. He walked up the concrete stairs, traced his finger along the frosted rail, and opened the door to his home.

The interior was dark and silent. Maybe he should get a dog. Or even just an alarm system to shut off. Anything that demanded his attention. William ditched his clothes, showered, and got dressed again, still coursing with too much adrenaline to sleep. What to do with himself? Get a burger? Watch a game show? Jack off for the umpteenth time this month? He looked around the room, reminded of his quarters back in Cape Cod. The silence was deafening, but it didn't have to be. People who loved him lived nearby. Two hours to Portland. Daisy would be asleep by the time he got there, but Lily never minded him showing up. He could crash there and enjoy the morning with his little girl. Or he could sit around feeling sorry for himself.

William hopped to his feet, grabbed the keys, and went to the door. He paused before opening it, hand on the knob. He sometimes dreamed of opening the door to find Jason standing there, smiling sheepishly with a backpack over one shoulder. William would shake his head ruefully, invite him in, and then… everything. He wanted it all.

William grasped the knob and turned. The door opened. Concrete and a railing, beyond it a parking lot. Exhaling, he locked the door behind him and was halfway down the stairs when he felt his phone rumble. A text message.

Just making sure you haven't forgotten about me.

William fought down a smile and texted back. *Who is this?*

Jason.

Doesn't ring a bell.

It will. Eventually. I'm your husband in the future.

Oh yeah?

Yup. We live in a small house, spend Sunday mornings in bed, and eat all our meals together. We even start a family of our own.

William grinned. *And then what?*

Forever.

Jason sent the word and William felt it in his heart. They had been struggling since the day they first met. Falling in love hadn't been hard. Finding a place for them alone, or time enough for two—that had been the only true challenge. William wasn't giving up, and he knew Jason wouldn't either. Their love for each other was constant, too strong to be weakened by separation or distance. In that way they were eternal. Forever had begun when they first laid eyes on each other. With any luck, someday they would spend the rest of it together.

Hear the story in their own words!

All of the *Something Like…* books are available on audio too.*
Listen to Tim's tale while you jog with him, or ignore your fellow
airline passengers while experiencing Jace's story again. Find
out which books are available and listen to free chapters at the
link below:

http://www.jaybellbooks.com/audiobooks/
(*Something Like Rain* forthcoming, due out Fall of 2016)

Benjamin Bentley and many other beloved characters from the *Something Like…* series make their triumphant return in this collection of short stories and bonus material. *Something Like Yesterday* travels to the past where Eric Conroy attempts to find love against a backdrop of intolerance and political upheaval. In *Something Like Fall*, Ben meets Jace's family and tries to cope with many changes in the years that follow. Allison Cross finally gets her dues in *Something Like Tonight*, examining the relationships in her life during a girls night out. *Something Like Eternity* takes the series where it has never gone before as Victor Hemingway seeks out his ultimate destiny. Also included is a character guide and a timeline of key events thus far. Laughter and tears await you in this very special anthology!

For more information, please see:
www.somethinglikeseries.com